Who Speaks for the Negro?

BOOKS BY ROBERT PENN WARREN

WHO SPEAKS FOR THE NEGRO?

Robert Penn Warren

Random House   New York

FOURTH PRINTING

© *Copyright, 1965, by Robert Penn Warren*

All rights reserved under International and Pan-American Copyright Conventions. Published in New York by Random House, Inc., and simultaneously in Toronto, Canada, by Random House of Canada Limited.

Library of Congress Catalog Card Number: 65-16759

The author and publisher wish to thank the following for permission to use material quoted:

DIAL PRESS, INC. *Nobody Knows My Name* by James Baldwin, Copyright © 1961 by James Baldwin; and "Down at the Cross: Letter from a Region in My Mind" from *The Fire Next Time* by James Baldwin, which appeared in *The New Yorker,* November 17, 1962.
FIDES PUBLISHERS, INC. *The New Negro,* edited by M. H. Ahmann.
GROVE PRESS, INC. *The Subterraneans* by Jack Kerouac. Copyright © 1958 by Jack Kerouac.
OXFORD UNIVERSITY PRESS LTD. *Race and Colour in the Carribean* by G. R. Coulthard.
STUDENT NONVIOLENT COORDINATING COMMITTEE The Graham letter, originally published in the Student Voice publication.
THE CONDÉ NAST PUBLICATIONS INC. "Disturbers of the Peace: James Baldwin" by Eve Auchincloss and Nancy Lynch Handy (*Mademoiselle,* May '63). Copyright © 1963 by The Condé Nast Publications, Inc.
THE VILLAGE VOICE "View of the Back of the Bus" by Marlene Nadle. Copyright 1963 by The Village Voice, Inc.
WORLD PUBLISHING COMPANY *The Mark of Oppression* by Abram Kardiner and Lionel Ovesey. A Meridian Book.

MANUFACTURED IN THE UNITED STATES OF AMERICA

Design by Tere LoPrete

With thanks to all those who speak here

I believe that the future will be merciful to us all. Revolutionist and reactionary, victim and executioner, betrayer and betrayed, they shall all be pitied together when the light breaks . . .

A character in *Under Western Eyes,*
by JOSEPH CONRAD

Foreword

I have written this book because I wanted to find out something, first hand, about the people, some of them anyway, who are making the Negro Revolution what it is—one of the dramatic events of the American story.

This book is not a history, a sociological analysis, an anthropological study, or a *Who's Who* of the Negro Revolution. It is a record of my attempt to find out what I could find out. It is primarily a transcript of conversations, with settings and commentaries. That is, I want to make my reader see, hear, and feel as immediately as possible what I saw, heard, and felt.

No doubt the reader, were he more than the silent spectator which he must here be, would put more probing questions than mine, and would have other, and more significant reactions. But my questions may provide some continuity from interview to interview, and my reactions may give the sense of an involved audience.

Along the way Dr. Anna Hedgeman said to me: "What makes you think that Negroes will tell you the truth?"

I replied: "Even a lie is a kind of truth."

But that is not the only kind that we have here.

The interviews were recorded on tape. In almost all instances the person interviewed checked the transcript for errors. Many of the interviews were long, sometimes several hours, and in a few cases there was more than one conversation. It would have been impossible, and undesirable, to publish all the transcripts. I have chosen the sections which seem to me most significant and exciting, and within these sections have sometimes omitted repetitions and irrelevancies. I have not indicated such omissions. But except for a rare conjunction, transition, or explanatory phrase, I have made no verbal changes.

Robert Penn Warren
February, 1965.

Contents

Who Speaks for the Negro?

1 ❧ The Cleft Stick

West Feliciana Parish is some twenty-five miles north of Baton Rouge, Louisiana. Before the Civil War it was a region of great plantations and beautiful houses. Even now some of the houses yet stand, and you can pay a dollar and enter to inspect the dusty or tarnished or mellowed grandeur.

The Reverend Joe Carter lives in West Feliciana Parish. He is the first Negro there to be registered to vote:

> Well, I met the CORE—Ruby Livermore, that's his name. And Ronnie Moore. And I met them on a Thursday in August. They explained to me concernen the red-ishen and I told them that I had tried and that I couldn't get none of my neighbors to go with me.
>
> I knew that I was a citizen of the United States and not only our own little parish, because I was fifty-five years old and I had never done anything to go to jail, to be disenfranchised, but the state or the parish laws, and through these I did not get to red-ish, and I could hear over the air and on the television they wanted ever citizen to vote. Well, after they explained to me concernen of the vote, you know, which I wanted to do it anyway, and I was glad to lead the people here out of their ig-rance and enlighten them about how to go about it. So I made an agreemint with them how I would go down and ask the Redg-strar, but I tell them that I didn't just want to go by myself. I would like to have somebody to go with me. Well, at that time there was only just me—one— from the West Feliciana Parish. He [Ronnie Moore] said, "Well, Reverend Davis, he wants to red-ish."

So we made an appointmint with him to see Reverend Davis that day, and Reverend Davis sent me word that we would go to Harmon and ask to red-ish, which we did, he made arrangemints for nine o'clock. He was there. Well, a few minutes after because they had a flat, but it wasn't far enough behind the appointmint for me to get disgusted and ignore him. So we went down to the Redg-strar's office, which Ruby and Ronnie wanted to go with us. I told them, no. I would rather to go by myself, you know, go before my people without haven the strangers with us. And they says, "Well, if you-all go down and have any trouble, let us know." Well, they told us where the car would be, which we didn't see the car as they had turned. They were walken. But they told us what type of car they would drive, which was a white car.

When we went in the courthouse we didn't see nobody, we didn't hear nobody. Well, they didn't have any signs you know—"Right," "Left," "Redg-strar's office." Well, we seen the Sher'ff's office, we seen the jury room, and we seen the Circuit office. We had to inquire where was the office, which was with no name on it. We walked around a little and we couldn't find the place and it was some laborers, which were from Boyd, Kirby and from some parish town, and they did some little somethen there and had them in the parish jail and had them worken, on the courthouse there. And Reverend Davis asked the boys, "We looken for the Redg-strar's office." And one of the boys said, "Over yonder." Well, we had already been over there, so that was surely false, and where do our people red-ish to vote—so they couldn't say no more.

Well, there was a white man there. We said, "White folks, can you tell us where the Redg-strar is, please?" He said, "In there." Well, it was two doors, but he just say, "In there" —he didn't tell us no special door. So we turned round and Reverend Davis went back to the Assessor's office and asked him, so he just say, "Up there."

Well, we went on up and I said, "It must be in this hall." The Reverend Davis say to me, he said, "Well, we both can't talk at the same time. And now you just listen and let me talk." Well, we agreed on the outside to do so.

Well, we still didn't see nobody, so when we went down in the little hall to see the Redg-strar's office, I imagine from about here to that wall there—from the main hall—by time we got to the door, just before we got to the door, the Redg-strar, he walked out the door and pulled it behind him and stood in front of the door. Said, "Good mornen, boys, what can I do for you-all?" Well, we spoke to him, "Mornen." So Reverend Davis said, "Well, we come to see if we could red-ish to vote." He said, "Well, I can't appear you now, but you got to bring somethen. You got to show somethen. You got to carry somethen."

Well, Reverend Davis turns, he says, "I really don't know what you mean—by that. You tell me what you mean, prob-ably I can produce what it takes." He said, "Well, you got to go back home and get your two redg-stered voters out of the ward where you live."

Well, at that time the High Sher'ff had come down the hall and standen facen this small hall, that one right there. So Reverend Davis said, "Well, the High Sher'ff knows me, and not only that—all of you knows me here." He says, "Yes, I know they call you Rudolph Davis, but I couldn't swear to it. I couldn't tell it was you upstairs." As I turned, he said then, "Here boy, here boy, you boy." Well, I was looken at the Redg-strar, you see, and I turned around and I said, "You speaken to me?" He said, "Yeah, you come here." So, I turned round and went on back out to him, and when I got out to just about to where he was he walked off down the hall, like he was goen back to the Sher'ff's office, and he had a pencil and a card in his hand. He said, "What's your name?" I said, "Reverend Joe Carter." He attempted to write, but he made one mark. He said, "What's the matter with you fel-lows? You not satisfied?" I said, "Not exactly." He said, "Well, if you ain't, from now on you will be—you hear?" I said, "Yes sir." He said, "Go back where you come." I turned to go back.

He said, "I ought to lock you up." Well, I didn't say any-then. I just kept walken. Just before I got to the hall, anyway, he said, "I really ought to lock you up." I didn't make him any answer. Then he hollered to the Deppity, "Grab him, Dan, don't you hear him raisen his voice at me? Consider you're under arrest."

Well, I turned my face to him, you know. And then he searched me—started at my heels and come on up, searchen me. Said, "Take him out there and put handcuffs on him. Lock him up." Then he put my arm down and put it behind me. He said, "Go on out, you." Well, I went on out—take me on out to this car, facen my face across the top of the car, and he reach in with his hands, got his handcuffs—but he still held this left arm behind, and he shook it out of his shackle—and he locked the hand. Well, when I heard the handcuff lock, I just laid the other one back there. They locked me and put me in—told me, "Git in there."

Well, I had pulled my hat off and laid it up on the car. He took my hat and thowed it in the back of the car, where I was, and there was another white man, which the other white young man, when he told [the Deputy] to grab me—they both grabbed me.

Well, I had never been to the jail. I didn't know where the jail-house door was, but I saw a hall and they said, "Go on in there." So I went on up in there and [the Deputy] asked me —he says, "Who's been talken to you?" I said, "Nobody." He said, "You've been over in Clinton, and that damned nigger—" I said, "I ain't been to no Clinton." "Who been talken to you?" I said, "Nobody been talken to me. Don't you know we got radios and television and I read the papers." I said to him, "The *Journal* says it wants all citizens to red-ish and vote."

So, we're goen on into the jail, and they unlock me, put me in the cell. So they went on back down the hall. They come back about ten minutes later, this young white man, he —I didn't know him—he come back and unlocked the jail cell and told me to come out. So, I come on out and they told me to go on down the hall, so I went on down the hall where there was the little office they had in the jail. When I got in there the Deppity had set up his fixen what he had—so he took my fingerprints first and then he—after he took my fingerprints, then he stood me over side the wall and he take my picture, and after he'd taken my picture, then put me on the scales, took my weight, took my height, and asked me how old I was. So I told him I was fifty-five, three months and five days old today; so after that, he asked me did I have any sisters. I told him yes. I told them I had two daughters—they both live in Scotland, here. And, I had to give my oldest daughter's house number, as far as street and 1740. My baby girl had just moved and I hadn't been there to the new house and I couldn't give them their number, but I told them she's in Scotland.

They take me on back, but when they was unlocken the cell—see, I had my clothes, my hat. Then the High Sher'ff, Mr. Percy, he come in the hall. He said, "Take his hat from him. He don't need nothen." So they took my hat. So he said, "Search him agin." So they searched me over—said, "Take all his clothes. He don't need nothen, nohow." So they went back there and got a uniform and then they made me pull all my clothes off. They given me the uniform. "Put him," he says to the Deppity, "put him under that shower." Says, "Get him a shower—he's musty—stinks." So, I didn't say anything. I didn't say anything to him. He says, "Who been talken to you?" I said, "Nobody." He said, "You ain't goen to tell me, huh?" I said, "Well, I ain't got nothen to tell you."

I put that coverall on and they went on in.

They sent me my dinner down, and no spoon to eat with. They had a spoon up in the grates up there. I don't know how long it had been up there. The man brought me my dinner, he said, "Get that spoon up yonder and eat, you." So I say, "I don't need it because I don't eat this." But I just expect they don't own a garbage can. Well, I stayed in that jail from about nine thirty till two thirty without water. Their faucet was broke and you could get water out of it, but I didn't know—you see, I had to put all my weight up on it to get the water on—and then when I get it on I had to do the same thing to get it off, but I thought it was broke all the time because the threads were stripped on it. So anyway, the wardman, he told me how to get the water on and how to get it off.

About nine thirty or a quarter to ten that night, they came back—somebody has got money from somewhere. I don't know where they got it from, but they come in that night and call me to get up, come on and get out of there. Well, I got up and they give me my clothes and I pulled the coveralls off and come back in the office—and had to sign a bond—and had to sign that I had gotten my car back, with all my papers, which I didn't get them all because I had a test paper there that Ruby and Ronnie had give me, you see, before I went in there to red-ish, I let them know that I did understand how to fill out the redg-stration blank. Well, I had that up over my sun glare—of my car—but I had signed a paper that I had my car back in good standen, but I was still in jail. I didn't know whether wheels was on my car, but I had to sign it because they had me in jail and I couldn't get out to see the car.

Well, when I did get out I reached over there, before I got in my car, and my paper was gone. So, I didn't say anything. Well, Ruby, he got in the car with me and he asked me if I got harmed. He said, "Well, check the car and see if you got the paper." Well, I said, "No, I don't have my redg-stration papers." But, you see, by being a minister, I always carry my Bible, my Psalm Book, and my Pastor's Guide. I keeps that in the car. Any time you see the car, you see that—with a coat. Care how hot it is—I always carry the coat, because lots of times I be caught up the road for—have to bury some baby or somethen, and I keep those books with me.

Well, I went in the car and they didn't take nothen but them test papers. That's all they took from me. So, after I got home, well, I had a bunch of people there, waiten for me. When I got home, my wife said, "Joe, you oughtn't have went down there." She said, "Now, if you go back down, I'm going to leave you." I said, "Well, you can get your clothes and start now, because I'm going back." So I say, "I'm on my way back tomorrow."

Well, we heard from the neighbors—they said, "Don't go back, don't go back tomorrow. You let us study these things and send somebody that's rich."

That did not settle it for good and all. A school was organized, and when all was ready, in October, twenty-three Negroes went down to the courthouse. As they waited outside, their instructor came out.

"Well, he come out and tole us, so I was the first man who made the attempt to red-ish, so I tole them I was goen to be the first man to go back."

He was.

This narrative was spoken to me one afternoon in the office of Mr. Lolis Elie, the legal representative for CORE in New Orleans. The Reverend Joe Carter had been brought to New Orleans by Ronnie Moore, who had been, not long before, a student at Southern University, the Negro university in Baton Rouge, but was now a worker in voter registration, in West Feliciana Parish, where he had explained to Joe Carter "concernen the red-ishen," and more recently in the town of Plaquemine.

Plaquemine was a dangerous place to be, with violence never far below the surface, and at first glance, Mr. Moore seems a most improbable "activist." He is quite young, rather tall but slightly built, shoulders rather narrow, skull tall and narrow with a touch of the Watusi elegance. The structure of his face from the eye sockets down to the mouth, is somewhat concave, coming forward again at the lips and set of the mouth. He wears horn-rimmed glasses, looks sober and withdrawn, perhaps humorless; and that slight concavity of face somehow accentuates the expression of studious withdrawnness. But the jaws are strong.

The hands, I notice, are long and thin—elegant, again—and as he sits listening to the narrative of Reverend Carter, with his face still and masklike, the eyes focused at a downward angle behind the horn-rimmed lenses, the fingers, for a time, keep moving ever so slightly, then suddenly stop and lie close together, immobile, looking carved. His color is medium brown.

The Reverend Carter is a black man, with something of a faint dusty bloom on his blackness. He seems older than his fifty-five years and is, according to my notebook:

rather short or just at medium height, looking shorter because of breadth of shoulders, strong and looks muscle-bound, large, slow work-hands, dry and rough to the handshake, palms preternaturally pale and pink when you get a glimpse, nails carefully cleaned, blue suit clean and well-pressed, white oxford shirt, button-down collar

*like a Madison Avenue type, blue knit tie a little bedraggled, a craggy
face, suggestive of the face of a black Robert Frost, same hewed-out,
weathered quality.*

His speech is careful and slow. He is anxious to say things just as
they had been, now and then pausing to let the word come right in
his head. And there is always that careful use of detail or circumstance, that attention to things that the unlettered man achieves by
his very unletteredness, by his need to hang on to the specificity of
things; for the image in his head, not any written word or abstraction, is his fundamental contact with reality. With Reverend Carter
this habit of mind gives an impression of slow, groping, undistract-
able earnestness.

As he talks there is no self-consciousness. He is too involved in
trying to say what there is to say. Ronnie Moore has shepherded
him here to the city, but he shows no trace of being in the role of
an exhibit. Out of his massive slow-boned dignity that has survived
the years, he is kindly to Ronnie, if anything; with a sad, knowing,
fatherly kindness.

Reverend Carter went through the fifth grade—the fifth grade in
a Negro school in Louisiana, nearly half a century ago, and that
would have been even worse than the fifth grade of a white school
there. But he reads his Bible. He lives with his Bible. As for his idea
of "voten and rights," he says he got it "off the TV screen." He adds,
". . . for the gov'mint say for us to vote."

Later I think that I have seen this old man somewhere before. Of
course, I had seen aging Negro men like him, back in my boyhood
in Kentucky and Tennessee. And I had seen them in Louisiana, up in
West Feliciana, long ago, when I used to go there to stand in the
silence of the moss-draped oaks of the old graveyard at Saint Francis-
ville. That palpable silence, the never-violated shadow of the spreading live oaks and the windless gray garlands of moss, had seemed
to absorb everything into a Platonic certainty—even human pain.

: 2 :

Back in the winter of 1929–30, when I was living in England, I had
written an essay on the Negro in the South. I never read that essay
after it was published, and the reason was, I presume, that reading

it would, I dimly sensed, make me uncomfortable. In fact, while writing it, I had experienced some vague discomfort, like the discomfort you feel when your poem doesn't quite come off, when you've had to fake, or twist, or pad it, when you haven't really explored the impulse.

The essay was a cogent and humane defense of segregation—segregation conceived of with full legal protection for the Negro, equal educational facilities, equal economic opportunities, equal pay for equal work. The essay envisaged segregation in what I presumed to be its most human dimension. That was what I had been raised to believe in. My maternal grandfather, who had ridden with Forrest, had not "believed in slavery." My father would say that "if you treat a Negro right, he'll treat you right," and at least on one occasion, when the Depression was coming on and he needed every dollar he could get, his attitude meant that he could not evict a Negro renter, because, as he said, "You can't do that to a man who has no place to go." And, too, if one of the children in our house had used the word *nigger,* the roof would have fallen. Yes, the essay was very humane, self-consciously humane; and that self-consciousness indicated an awareness that in the real world I was trying to write about, there existed a segregation that was not humane.

In the little town in Kentucky where I was born and raised, there was an oak tree that stood by the decrepit, shoe-box-size jail, the jail and the oak being set on the edge of an empty field. The tree may have long since disappeared, I don't know. But that scene is very vivid in my memory, for when I was a child I scarcely ever passed down that street—which was only a piece of country road that had somehow got mislaid in town—without some peculiar, cold flicker of feeling. The image of that tree which I still carry in my head has a rotten and raveled length of rope hanging from a bare bough, bare because the image in my head is always of a tree set in a winter scene. In actuality it is most improbable that I ever saw a length of rope hanging from that tree, for the lynching had taken place long before my birth. It may not, even, have been that tree. It may, even, have been out in the country.

I don't remember how I first heard about the lynching, certainly when I was a very small child, for I do remember how it had to be explained to me, probably by an older boy. I remember, too, that I got the idea that this was something men might do, might mysteriously have to do, put a rope around a man's neck and pull him up and watch him struggle; and I knew, in shame and inferiority, that I wouldn't ever be man enough to do that.

But to return to my essay, the humaneness was self-conscious because even then, thirty-five years ago, I uncomfortably suspected, despite the then prevailing attitude of the Supreme Court and of the overwhelming majority of the population of the United States, that no segregation was, in the end, humane. But it never crossed my mind that anybody could do anything about it. When I wrote the essay, I was a student in England, and had been out of the South for almost five years; and the image of the South I carried in my head was one of massive immobility in all ways, in both its virtues and vices—it was an image of the unchangeable human condition, beautiful, sad, tragic.

When I actually got back to the South, the "unchangeable human condition" had changed. The Depression was there, and conversation always turned on the question of what could be done to claw out of that desperation; but that meant to "change" things, even if for some people the change desired was to change things back to their old unchangeableness. But that would be a kind of change, too. So there was no way to avoid the notion of change: you had to take a bite of the apple from the mysterious tree that had sprung up in the Confederate—no, the old American—garden. The apple might, incidentally, have given some knowledge of good and evil; but it certainly gave a knowledge of more profound consequence, the knowledge of the inevitability of change.

For me, during that decade, one change was the slowly growing realization that I could never again write the essay.

So, one night, in Baton Rouge, in the spring of 1939, I was sitting in a car on a side street that borders the north side of the campus of LSU, waiting to meet somebody who was to come out of the last show of a moving-picture theater. The street was deserted. Suddenly a Negro boy, about fourteen years old, slipped out of an alley beside the theater, and gave a quick look both ways. But he was not quick enough, for a husky, youngish man emerged that instant from the theater entrance, collared the boy, yanked off his own belt, and expertly, with one hand, folded it into a double strap, and began to lay on the boy's bum. The work was not very vigorous, for the man was using a considerable amount of breath in a monologue: "I told you if you ever again—I told you I'd sure God—" etc. Between dramatic howls, the boy was protesting innocence and making promises—about something that was not clear to me.

What was clear, in the speed-shutter instant, was my own complex reaction. I had felt some surge of anger, I had put my hand on the latch of the door, and then had, in that very motion, stopped. Let us not discount what simple cowardice there may have been in the hesitation. But what I actually felt was not fear—it was something worse, a sudden, appalling sense of aloneness. I had never had that feeling before, that paralyzing sense of being totally outside my own community. I have had it since, not a few times: sitting in the living room of a friend, even in Vermont, talking with a gas-station attendant or with a chance companion in a train or plane, listening to a taxi driver. But most recently I have had it in Clarksdale, Mississippi, sitting in the house of a Negro, in the middle of the night, with the curtains drawn to make a blackout as tight as in wartime London, and with the young Negro guard sitting somber and silent, his .32 handy on a little table.

But at the time of that scene in front of the theater in Baton Rouge, in a sudden access of shame, I overcame my paralysis. I pushed the door open, set foot to ground. Then, mercifully, I was saved. A bulky, blunt-headed, blunt-faced youth—say, 215 pounds, and wearing the purple-and-gold of an LSU football sweater—appeared out of nowhere. "Hey," he demanded of the man with the belt, "what you doen to that nigger?"

The man's hand with the belt dropped.

"Git on away, nigger," the youth commanded, in seignorial confidence.

With that, the hero sauntered down the shadowy, empty street toward the corner drugstore for, one presumes, a double chocolate malted milk to settle his stomach before bedtime.

I had been saved. I had not had to get "involved."

: *3* :

A short time ago, after an absence of many years, I went back to Baton Rouge. Now, for the first time in my life, I visited Southern

University there, the largest Negro university in the world. It lies upriver from Baton Rouge, beyond the vast tank farms and refineries of Esso, which glitter in a complicated silver geometry, like a vision of the great new perfected world to come, with the constant flame jetting up, day and night, from a pillar or pylon, like the altar of some crew of gigantic robot vestals. After this splendor of futurity comes the campus of Southern University. It too has something to do with the future.

South of town, downriver, lies the great campus of LSU, where grandeur has long since flowered beyond Huey P. Long's wildest dreams. There is something else there beyond Huey's wildest dreams: some fifty Negroes in the Graduate School.*

The office of Dr. Felton Gradison Clark of Southern University is like the office of many other university presidents—the atmosphere, *mutatis mutandis,* of "betterness," of wealth and power, of broader perspectives and more serious issues, of, in short, worldliness. Worldliness, for this is the point where the real world makes its sharp and sometimes anguishing contact with the make-believe world of the academy. The contact was made here in 1960, when students from Southern University began the sit-ins at Baton Rouge, and the State Board of Education laid down its ultimatum that demonstrators withdraw from action or be expelled. Dr. Clark appealed to his student body to help him save Southern. He said: "Like Lincoln, who sought to preserve the Union, my dominant concern is to save Southern University." And the student body, perhaps remembering another quotation from Lincoln about "half slave and half free," promptly voted to continue the demonstrations. The University was closed briefly.† When it reopened, there was a boycott of classes. But the University, and Dr. Clark, survived.

Dr. Clark is, in a sense, Southern University. His father, Joseph

* In 1935 Long said to Roy Wilkins: "I'm for the poor man—all poor men. Black and white, they all gotta have a chance. They gotta have a home, a job and a decent education for their children. 'Every Man a King'—that's my slogan. That means every man. Niggers along with the rest, but not especially for niggers." Long, according to T. Harry Williams, was willing to carry the Negro as far as he safely could at the moment. ("Trends in Southern Politics," in *The Idea of the South,* ed. Frank E. Vandiver.)

† For several weeks, according to Louis Lomax. (*The Negro Revolt.*) Officials of the University say for "about seven days"—only between terms.

Samuel Clark, founded it. The father is buried on the campus, near the President's House. That spot is the shrine of Southern University, and until lately, after the exercises of Founders' Day, there was a student pilgrimage to the grave, to sing the Alma Mater and place wreathes—a ritual of continuity.

I stand in the handsome, worldly office and stare at the photograph of what must be the founder. The son enters.

Dr. Clark is tall and carries himself well, is extremely well-groomed—with small touches of elegance like the discreetly turned-back cuffs of the sleeves of his gray suit—speaks in a voice of fine natural modulation, has poise and self-command, and is charming. In fact, I have yet to meet the president of a Negro college or university who is not charming—and almost always the charm seems as natural as breath. There are, of course, some—white and black—who scrutinize such charm as merely professional equipment for use on philanthropists, philanthropoids, politicians, and members of boards of supervisors. But how could a man, year in and year out, charmingly endure the indignity of certain contexts if the charm were not natural? At the worst, let us say that such charm is a beautiful by-product of an ugly situation. Why should Negroes be ashamed—as some now are ashamed—of charm, of courtesy, of humor? Isn't their being ashamed derived from some frighteningly gross-minded and uncharacteristic reductiveness that mechanically equates a thing with its origins? Anyway, aren't charm and courtesy and humor so rare in the world that we should be grateful to have any we can get? Does anyone, Negro or white, have to regard charm and courtesy and humor as a black-face turn borrowed from a minstrel show, and therefore to be repudiated?

Dr. Clark, as I am setting up the tape recorder, reads my mind, anticipates me, refers to the sit-ins and his ambiguous position, saying, "Your friend Vann Woodward didn't think too highly of me in that business, in his article in *Harper's,* did he?"

"No," I say, remembering what Vann had written:

> In President Felton G. Clark of Southern University, Louisiana found a disciplinarian who needed little prompting. . . . Upon re-opening the University, the president required all students re-admitted to register anew. . . . Among those who did not return, according to well-informed faculty members, were many of the best students and campus leaders.

"We at Southern," declared President Clark, "are interested in education, and nothing else."

Dr. Clark does not become defensive. He merely says, with a shrug and smile, neither shrug nor smile more than a delicate hint, that there are some situations more complex than they seem. Then, with calmness: "If I had things to do over, I would do them a little differently."

As we begin the tape Dr. Clark says that integration is inevitable, "and not only in education."

WARREN: But what will be the function of the now Negro universities in that period, after the transition has been made?

CLARK: You know, I wish I'd known you were going to ask me that, because I wrote an article in the *Journal of Negro Education,* about three or four years ago. . . . And I said essentially this—the function of the Negro college is to become a good institution, like any other. Now, since our recent upheavals, the social intensification as it were, I think there's another role, to emphasize a degree of thoroughness and aggressiveness, so that it can prepare itself to be the kind of quality institution that other institutions are. In other words, we've got to admit that we're playing *catch-up.*

WARREN: Do you envisage the registration of white students in Negro colleges?

CLARK: As a matter of fact, the Baton Rouge paper yesterday carried the story of a white girl in New Orleans who has filed suit to enter our branch of Southern University there. I think, though, the process is going to be slower in Louisiana because of social factors, than in a border state like West Virginia or Maryland, where in what was once a predominantly Negro college a third to a half, or sometimes more, of the student body is now white. In Louisiana, as good as Southern University might be, there will be people who won't want the stigma of going to a Negro college. But the proof of the pudding will be in the eating—and that young lady filed suit yesterday. She's practical-minded, she doesn't see why she should travel five or six miles to Tulane or Loyola.

WARREN: Let's turn to another topic. Why should the Negro Revolution occur now—and not, say, thirty years ago?

CLARK: It's part of a world movement for freedom, for a sense of identity—

I seize the word *identity*. It is a key word. You hear it over and over again. On this word will focus, around this word will coagulate, a dozen issues, shifting, shading into each other. Alienated from the world to which he is born and from the country of which he is a citizen, yet surrounded by the successful values of that world, and country, how can the Negro define himself? There is the extreme act of withdrawing as completely as possible from that white world. There is the other extreme of "self-hatred," of repudiating the self— and one's own group. Clearly, neither extreme offers a happy solution. Yet there is no simple solution of half-and-half, for the soul doesn't operate with that arithmetical tidiness.

But Dr. Clark is continuing:

CLARK: . . . and we see that there are other people who feel as we do. These desires have always been in us, but this world movement has intensified our consciousness, has given us courage in thinking that we are part of the whole thing.
WARREN: You think that the key is in the reaction of the American Negro to the rise of Africa and Asia?
CLARK: Plus the fact that even in America we now talk about making democracy work. When I was studying about democracy, I was pretty much using symbols, I was merely committing words to memory. But now we have Americans saying that democracy must be a real thing.
WARREN: How much do you attribute to the rise of a new generation—the result of a long process of education and preparation?
CLARK: Oh, I think a very significant portion. However, I would say this, I think we have always had it—

I do not ask what the *it* is. For Dr. Clark is not the first to insist that the urge to break out of slavery, out of segregation, out of deprivation, was always there; to insist, by implication, that there had never been happy strumming of the banjo by the little cabin door; that there had never been the well-adjusted Sambo.

As he talks, I am remembering a minister in Bridgeport, a very intelligent and well-educated young man of force and conscience, leaning at me in his little study, beside the bookcase in which, behind glass doors, were exhibited his framed diplomas; the young man insists, with sudden passion, that "it could have happened any time, any time—say thirty years ago—why back then Dr. Mays, Dr. Benjamin Mays, he could have been our Martin Luther King—it could have happened!"

But it didn't happen, despite all the resentment and will which must be passionately insisted upon; it didn't, after all, happen. We shall again encounter this resistance to the notion that time is significant, that an evolution has been necessary.

But Dr. Clark, though he insists on the long-rooted resentment, does not resist the notion of time, of history, of social process, as the matrix in which moral issues evolve. He is sixty years old, even if a vigorous sixty; he has seen much happen and much *not* happen. But in regard to that resentment, the Negro, he says, always had it:

CLARK: The old Negroes, the new Negroes, the newer Negroes. But what has happened now is that the methodology is different. In other words, whereas I might hesitate a bit, or you might hesitate a bit, this younger Negro now just steps right into the middle of the thing, you see. His fears are being overcome. But always the Negro has had a longing to be a human being. Listen to the Negro melodies, listen to their content, read the history of somebody like Harriet Tubman, and you'll find there's always been this desire, to be a person, this quest for identity.

We are back to the continuity of will, back to the notion of identity. But I raise the question again of why now—now and not then, whenever *then* was—we should find the high degree of ability among Negroes, the confidence, the complicated structure of leadership. I mentioned the old March on Washington movement. The program A. Philip Randolph evolved, back in 1941, on the eve of World War II.

I am driving at the notion that the gains made by Negroes—at least the crucial and sensational gains—have come only when the Negro's aspirations could intermesh with some more general social crisis. I want to know how Dr. Clark responds to that notion.

CLARK: I think the Negro had seen parallels. He'd seen for example, labor. There was a time when labor, as such, occupied almost the same position that the Negro had to occupy. But the Negro has seen what organization has done, what intelligence has done. In fact, there was a time when capital and labor were in conversation, and capital was on one side of the table, a well-dressed man, Yale lawyer, Harvard lawyer, and four laboring men on the other side, in overalls, afraid to open their mouths. But now when labor and capital meet, there are two Harvard lawyers to speak to each other, two Yale lawyers to speak to each other.

WARREN: To pick up the question of identity for the Negro, long ago in reading Du Bois' *The Souls of Black Folk,* I first ran across the notion of the cultural split, the psychic split, in the American Negro. I have a quotation here:

> It is a peculiar sensation, this double consciousness, this sense of always looking at one's self through the eyes of others, of measuring one's soul by the tape of a world that looks on in amused contempt and pity. One ever feels the two-ness—an American, a Negro; two souls, two thoughts, two unreconciled strivings, two warring ideals in one dark body, whose dogged strength alone keeps it from being torn asunder.

CLARK: I don't think that is as valid a point of view now as it might have been in the earlier days. And I think that all human beings want first, last, and always, to be human beings. I don't think that they want to be—at least, I don't look at myself as wanting to be—an African. Or even, necessarily, an American. I hope that doesn't sound like heresy. I think that I have more in common with human beings than I have with Negroes, than I have with Africans, than I have with Frenchmen, than I have with anybody else. And I think if Du Bois wrote that then, which he did, he wrote it when we didn't have the same world perspective that we have now. You see, Du Bois was one of those persons who are way out in front. If you read his *Souls of Black Folk,* you can see.

And there's a little bitterness in him too, which anybody can understand. Here was Du Bois, a man who, had he not been a Negro, could have really blossomed out into true greatness.
WARREN: He's a man who got trapped, not in his race, but in the race problem?
CLARK: Exactly. Also Du Bois did feel strongly about the African ties. I know what I am talking about. I almost married his daughter. In fact, except for my wife, she is the only girl I ever gave an engagement ring to. He felt very strongly about the African heritage, but he felt just as much, just as strongly, about being a person. And I think that now, even more than then, the Negro, like anybody else, is driven more by human drives than he is by all these other things. By the wish to be a human being, whatever the attributes of a human being are.

But here I am thinking again of my friend the minister in Bridgeport. "There's something in blackness," he had said. "If I see a black person going down the street, somebody I never saw before, my heart goes out to him in a special way." I asked him if he feels the same way toward a stranger who was merely colored—Chinese or Hindu, but not black. "No," he had said, and sitting beneath the wall shelves on which are arranged the books a well-educated young minister would have, books ranging from the New Testament (in Greek) to Karl Barth and Pearl Buck, had added: "There's something in the idea of blackness and of Africa. I have never been to Africa, but I can always tell the African strain in music, I can feel it."

But his friend, another minister, young, dark, sitting there to one side of the desk, in that little study, had said: "Africa—it means nothing to me. I am an American. That's all I know."

It is a dialogue that goes on and on, day after day, in many voices; and even as I am listening to Dr. Clark, I am remembering an afternoon at the Conference on Nonviolence, at Howard University, the previous fall. The auditorium had been packed—mostly Negroes, but with a scattering of white people. A young girl with pale skin, dressed like any coed anywhere, in the clothes for a public occasion, is on the rostrum. She is leaning forward a little on her high heels, speaking with a peculiar vibrance in a strange irregular rhythm, out of some inner excitement, some furious, taut élan, saying: "—and I tell you I have discovered a great truth. I have discovered a great joy. I have discovered that I am black. I am black! You out there—oh, yes, you may have black faces, but your hearts are white, your minds are white, you have been whitewashed!"

The audience stirs, is caught up, breaks out in wild excitement.

Later that afternoon, a white woman who had been there, who had taught for some years in a Negro university, was to say to me: "I never felt like this before. I thought I knew these people. I work with these people, and I like them, and I thought they were my friends. Now I don't know what to feel!" She shivered. Her good-looking, still young, clean-modeled, sensitive face looked drawn and, at the base of the nostrils, streaked with white. For a moment she looked sick. She would have to go back to a classroom and look at the faces before her, some of them white as her own, and wonder. She would have to wonder if all that those young people looking up at her wanted was to be human beings, just like her, human together. At this moment, as she sickened at the prospect of what they might want and feel, would the words which Dr. Felton Clark was later to speak to me have been a comfort to her—how we are all human, how we all want to be human together?

But if, at that moment, she heard any words in her head they were more likely the echo of the words of Malcolm X: "White devils!" And if she saw any face it must have been the long face of Malcolm X grinning with sardonic certitude.

She is a "white devil"—no more, no less. And she writhes and struggles and is sick at being caught in that stereotype, in the embrace of that merciless, crushing Iron Maiden; for that is what the excitement that had vibrated in the young girl's words and had run through the audience like wind, means—that, despite all her good feelings and good works, she is to be crushed in that stereotype, no matter whether it is called "white devil" or "ofay" or what.

Now in the quiet, handsomely furnished office of Dr. Clark, a thousand miles away and three months later, I have just asked Dr. Clark, who knows, no doubt, a great deal about the white man's stereotype of the Negro, if the Negro's new sense of identity, to which he had earlier referred, is a prideful reinterpretation, even inversion, of that very stereotype—if, in other words, the new sense of identity is not the insistence on individual identification, but the acceptance of a group identification, *nigger* becoming pridefully *Negro,* but either way by reference to a group, not to the individual.

> CLARK: Well, I see two or three things here. I think that the self-image doesn't stop at the stage when I say, "I'm proud I'm a Negro." That's just one stage. You see, maybe there are three. Maybe the first stage was, "I'm ashamed I am a Negro." Then, next, "I'm proud that I am a Negro." Then, last, "I am glad to be a human being." I know that's my thinking, I don't apologize, nor am I necessarily proud. I just want to be a human being. Because evolutionarily—in an evolutionary way—I don't know who I was maybe ten million years ago.
>
> WARREN: Who knows?
>
> CLARK: Or what I will be. In fact, Robert Embree of the Rosenwald Fund wrote a book entitled *Brown America.* He predicted that in the next few years there wouldn't be a Negro race, in terms of the color factor. I think I heard Margaret Mead say once—or was it Myrdal or Boaz—that there is not a pure Negro in America.
>
> WARREN: Maybe some African exchange student arrived last week.

Making my little joke, I suddenly wonder how grim the little joke is. I remember the statement of Norman Podhoretz, the editor of *Commentary,* that the "Negro problem can be solved in this country in no other way" than by assimilation; and I remember some of the sardonic reactions that view has occasioned—especially from Negroes. Is this a way of saying to the Negro that he must be a non-Negro before he is "acceptable"? That he must, in the words of Elijah Muhammad, head of the Black Muslims, "wake up, clean up, and stand up"—then bleach up? Is this a way of saying to the Negro that we cannot accept him unless we put him into our melting pot and build a fire under it and do a tribal dance around the pot while he boils in the pot, and then eat him in a tribal feast—like the old cartoons of black cannibals "accepting" the white missionary?

But meanwhile some Negroes don't seem quite as anxious as they used to be to be boiled and eaten in our ritual feast. Malcolm X cries out: "We worshipped the false beauty of the slave-master's leprous-looking woman." And, as a matter of fact, at least according to *Time* (January 3, 1964), there has been a substantial decline in the sale of bleaching creams and hair straighteners.

I switch the topic:

WARREN: Some time back I read an article by Dr. Kenneth Clark, the psychologist, on Martin Luther King. I'll quote a passage:

> On the surface, King's philosophy appears to reflect health and stability, while the black nationalists betray pathology and instability. A deeper analysis, however, might reveal that there is also an unrealistic, if not pathological, basis in King's doctrine. . . . The natural reactions to injustice, oppression and humiliation are bitterness and resentment. The forms which such bitterness takes need not be overtly violent, but the corrosion of the human spirit which is involved seems inevitable. It would seem, then, that any demand that the victims of oppression be required to love those who oppress them places an additional and probably intolerable psychological burden upon those victims.*

CLARK: I think you've got to remember that Kenneth Clark is writing as a psychologist, and he's looking at the question in a very raw sense. But Gandhi had the same point of view [as Dr. King]. Jesus Christ had the same point of view. I think that if Martin Luther King's attitude is to love your enemy and attain your objective through nonviolent means, he's entitled to that point of view. Now, who knows whether it will work or not? I think that what Kenneth Clark says is true. James Harvey Robinson, in *The Mind in the Making,* refers to the fact that one of the struggles of mankind is to overcome his animal ancestry. And the natural impulse is to strike back, in the same way, if anything with a little more of the same. But again, we try to be civilized beings. But Jesus Christ said, "I am the Prince of Peace."

WARREN: Does Kenneth Clark call that pathology?

* "The New Negro in the North," in *The New Negro,* ed. M. H. Ahmann.

CLARK: Yes. And again, if it's pathology, I guess Christianity is pathology.

Has President Clark settled this whole question in his own mind? I don't know. So I turn to Dr. Kenneth Clark's notion that though nonviolence might have had some effect in the South, it will not work in the North, and from that to the racial turmoil in Northern cities:

CLARK: I think that the race trouble in the North is bringing to light something that a number of us suspected. And it is making many Southern white people sort of lick their chops, as it were—to say, "We're not the only vulnerable ones, not the only guilty ones." Simultaneously it's making many Northern white people search their consciences, to determine whether or not they really have been thinking straight on this issue. I sensed this [the Northern prejudice against Negroes] when I first went to New York, for example. I lived on 122nd Street, and whenever I'd go to the movies I'd go to the one on 115th Street—which in those days was the dividing line of Harlem—and I got a kind of preferential treatment, I was always put on the front row. Or I would go to the one place we could eat on 125th Street, and there were always two highly desirable tables reserved for Negro people. Racial prejudice was there, but just more subtly done, and in some instances, as in the movie or restaurant, it was a kind of preferential thing.

It [racial trouble in the North] is going to make the South want to take pride and say, "Well, now we're going to prove to you we are the friend of the Negro by doing things that a friend would do"—something different now from what we would expect, for the South has always said, "We are the best friends of the Negroes." That's the kind of credit that I call a canine credit—"I like my dog, there's nothing I wouldn't do for my dog"—but, "Don't forget, you're a dog." But I think that now the South is just going to say, "We're going to prove to the North that we are the Negro's friend"—but by doing things a man would do for a human friend, rather than things that a friend would do for a sub-human friend.

I should have asked President Clark how many Southerners would admit guilt, even in the backhand way of rejoicing in Northern complicity in guilt. And how many—even as a slap to Yankeedom—would take it that the old notion of noblesse oblige and "best friend of the Negro" called for a settlement truly friendly and not of the sort that President Clark defines as "canine credit." I should have asked him how many Southerners see in the troubles in the North merely another justification, both practical and moral, for segregation and the hard line—and find in the Northern troubles the hope of allies.

But I did not. Perhaps because some hope in me responded to the hope of President Clark. I was at that moment remembering something said to me by a young lady in the Law School at Howard University. She hoped for a decent settlement in the South, because the Negro and the white man have a common history on the land, and there is, even in the midst of violence, still some basis for a human recognition—a recognition which, she said, she found less basis for in the great Northern cities, she being born and reared in Virginia. I ask President Clark if her notion makes sense to him.

It makes sense to him, he says, and he leads the conversation to the common ground for action the Negro and the poor white in the South should have—the old Populist argument. So we talk about history a little, about Lincoln's views on race, and what view the Negro may reasonably take of Lincoln. President Clark says he would judge him on "the manifest intention of his entire life," his desire for "decency and goodness for everybody." And this, by a strange comparison with Lincoln, who, though a white supremacist, signed the Emancipation Proclamation, leads us to Earl Long's relation to the Negro in Louisiana—and to Southern University:

CLARK: When Earl Long was running for governor, he said, "Now listen, all of us believe in segregation, ain't no point in talking about that." But on the other hand, we never asked Earl Long for any help that he didn't make the effort to give it to us. But again, what person running for office in Louisiana would say, "I'm for integration." I have had some politicians —if I called their names you would know them—tell me, "Dr. Clark, I know what we *ought* to do on that, but you people don't have the vote. Now when you get a half-million votes, I'll do that. I'm a professional politician, I go where the votes are."

WARREN: That's honest.

CLARK: Well, that's the reason I believe very strongly in the vote.

*   *   *

Ronnie Moore, too, believes in the "vote." As a student at Southern, he had not believed in letting committees sit around and discuss "my rights." He is a realist, too, and is set for the long haul; he says that success is to be measured, not in immediate objective results, but in "motivating" people, that much has been done "when you change one heart or one mind." But he is willing to take risks for specific gains, for "one lousy cup of coffee" or one voter registered.

He had been involved in the sit-ins in Baton Rouge and was suspended. He is now working for voter registration in Louisiana, where few Negroes vote—certainly not in the town of Plaquemine, south of Baton Rouge, where Ronnie Moore at the risk of his life has been organizing registration, and certainly not in Plaquemines Parish, downriver from New Orleans, where Judge Leander Perez reigns. Judge Perez, back in 1960, exhorted a Citizens Council meeting: "Don't wait until the burr-heads are forced into your schools. Do something about it now." For demonstrators in Plaquemine there waits the monstrous ruin of Fort St. Philip, where mosquitoes big as kildees are said to eat cattle alive, and where, no doubt, they were eating Confederates on the night of April 23, 1862, when Admiral Farragut ran the defenses and, by dawn light, proceeded upriver to lay New Orleans under his guns.

So now, as I read the transcript of the tape in which Dr. Clark says that he believes very strongly in voting, I think of Ronnie Moore. And I think of Reverend Joe Carter, all alone, going to register in West Feliciana Parish. There is some irony in this juxtaposition in my recollection—Dr. Clark in his office with me, Reverend Joe Carter standing naked in his jail cell.

But how much irony? What is the quality of this irony?

Would it have been self-indulgent heroics for Dr. Clark to defy his

Board?* Should Dr. Clark have supported the demonstrators and had the University closed down? What obligation did he owe his students to keep their education in process? Or how neatly did self-indulgence coincide with an obligation to keep the University open?

We have no answers to these questions. Dr. Clark is caught in the cleft stick of history, in the tragic dilemma of opposing goods, and opposing evils. And only Dr. Clark—and God—can assess the purity of his heart. Meanwhile, he is, to some, a classic example of the Uncle Tom. But he continues:

CLARK: I believe in a multiplicity of approaches, to any problem—I mean social problem. The vote is important. And I've heard people say, "Oh, education will solve things." Well, I know so many people who have all kinds of degrees and honors identified with the academic process, but they are still narrow in their point of view, so maybe they need some help—

Who are "they"? Are they Negroes? Are they whites? Who needs the "help"? And what kind of "help"? Then I wonder if he is being deliberately vague, deliberately making me work it out for myself.

CLARK: Maybe they need some nonviolence, maybe they need some violence, maybe they need some everything else. Some fifty per cent of our national budget now is for armament. We don't expect to go to war, but if we have to go to war, we're going to go to war. We're hoping to settle this thing peacefully—around the conference table. But if we have to have a war, we're going to have a war, and we're going to say it's a righteous war, it's a just war.

As he talks I wonder, first, how he got off on this topic—the United States vis-à-vis Russia. But is he talking about that

---

* Once in conversation I asked an eminent historian (not Southern) what he thought of the fact that Senator Fulbright had signed the round-robin among Southern members of Congress back in 1954. In substance, he replied: "He had no choice. It was his duty to sign. He cannot be spared from the Senate. It would be self-indulgence for him to make the gesture of refusing to sign—even for principle."

"war"? What is "this thing" that we hope will be settled around a conference table? Who is the "we"? Is this all a kind of parallel —a parable—a riddle? If he is speaking in riddles, then the "we" is not the United States. The "we" is the Negroes, who, according to his riddle, are ready, if necessary, for their "just war."

Is this the Uncle Tom?

But I remember that he has said he wishes he had "done things a little differently."

How differently?

: 4 :

". . . and when I finished high school," the man is saying to me, "my father—he was a truck driver—all he wanted was to get me a job driving a truck. He thought that would be just great. That was the most and highest he could think about. For me." Then added, with the twisting of an old bitter blade: "Or for him."

The man is smallish, strong, compact, with a dark, rather flattened face, the mouth wide, the nose wide at the base, the hair rather nappy and close to the skull like a knitted cap. There is a streak of premature gray in the hair, to the right of the not-high brow. He wears dark-rimmed horn glasses, and when he is excited, the eyes, with glints of yellow in the iris, stare straight and unblinkingly at you from behind the lenses, as though the lenses were not there. The glasses seem like a poorly chosen disguise. His name is Lolis Elie, and he is a lawyer, practicing in New Orleans.

As he tells about his father's ambition for him, he jerks in his chair, behind the desk, and the chair squeaks. One of his two partners, Nils Douglas by name, a tall, lanky, basketball-player type of young man, a yellow man, is sitting there, too, and he says, with a trace of satiric humor: "So your father didn't want you to be a lawyer?"

"No," Lolis Elie says, shortly, not looking up. He has big hands, hands that don't seem to go with his stature, much less with those horn-rimmed glasses, and when he falls into himself, he stares down at his big, dark right hand, which grips a pencil and, with unnecessary pressure, draws some squarish design, or writes some key word, not once, but two or three times, on the yellow legal pad on the desk before him. His hand is doing that now, and he stares down at it.

"But you made it," Douglas says.

He has made it. This is clearly the office of a lawyer—not grand, but a lawyer's office—on Dryades Street, in one of the many widely dispersed Negro sections in New Orleans. Above the entrance to the building there is a sign saying CORE. The sign is slightly askew. The stairs leading up to the suite of offices are dark. I look out the window. It is drizzling, with that gray, spiritless, windless, endless dissolution of sky which is February rain in New Orleans. It will not be good for Mardi Gras. But the biggest crowd in history, a cab driver has happily told me, is in town. The cab driver was white. The Negroes do not feel that they have much to celebrate.

I look up at the framed diplomas on the wall. The diplomas prove that Lolis Elie, whose father had wanted him to be a truck driver, has made it.

"My father didn't want me to try, either," Douglas says. "He didn't think I could make it."

Being a lawyer is a white man's job.

The Korean War, it seems, is what let Lolis Elie cross to a white man's job. It was GI money that got him to Howard University. Then, when he heard that Loyola University, at New Orleans, was to desegregate the Law School, he came back home to New Orleans to Dillard University, which is Negro, to finish his pre-law studies.

But the war meant more than GI money. It meant, he says, some change of feeling toward the Negro: "The desegregation of the armed services is possibly one of the most significant things that has happened in this country. We slept with guys, sat up with guys, ate together, and they were guys who admitted frankly and freely that they had certain misconceptions—you know, they'd find themselves preferring a conversation with me, than with a guy next to me, if for no other reason than we were both raised in a city. Or maybe they liked the way I played poker."

And when Lolis Elie talks in this strain, you feel that the war meant something more than a change in feeling toward the Negro. It meant, perhaps, the change in the feeling of at least one Negro toward white men.

But something else that is casual in his statement, almost irrelevant, whirls off to a tangential significance. Some guys have talked with him maybe for no better reason than that he, like them, came from a *city*. The Negro Revolt—or Revolution, or Movement—is primarily a city business, and in it is often implicit something of the city man's contempt for the hick, the rube, the yokel. Among the young Negroes from Northern cities who come to work in voter registration in Mississippi or Louisiana, there is sometimes a hint, or more than a hint, of condescension. Even in a romantic admiration for the courage and fortitude of a Reverend Joe Carter there may lurk this condescension. Joe Carter is a hero, but a hick hero.

And why should it be otherwise? Why should not the Negro take on the attitude and tone of the TV and ad-man culture? And why should he not turn the values of that culture against the black brother stuck in the black mire of Mississippi or the red clay of Alabama?

It would seem, in fact, that something as innocent as showing off before the country cousins was what got poor little Emmett Till into trouble. He was just showing how you did things in Chicago.

WARREN: I have here a statement from *Nobody Knows My Name,* by James Baldwin:

> . . . the most trenchant observers of the scenes in the South, those who are embattled there, feel that the Southern mobs are not an expression of the Southern majority will. Their impression is that these mobs fill, so to speak, a moral vacuum, and that the people who form these mobs would be very happy to be released from their pain, their ignorance, if somebody would show them the way.

ELIE: Considering the fact that, in gubernatorial elections, the most extreme candidate on the race issue usually wins, we might take him to be the representative of the mob and of the Southern majority. And looking at the Beckwith* trial, we find Ross Barnett, the ex-governor of the State of Mississippi, walking in to shake that man's hand in the courtroom

---

* Byron de la Beckwith, then on trial in Jackson, Mississippi, under indictment for the murder of Medgar Evers, Field Secretary of the NAACP. The first trial resulted in a hung jury. More of this later.

while the trial was going on, and there was no hue and cry
on the part of any white element in Mississippi about his
action. So this is why, in my mind, there are serious doubts
as to whether it's not fair to say that the mob does represent
the majority of the South.

WARREN: So it—the mob—does represent the majority in
the South?

ELIE: If we say that the demagogues do not represent the
majority of the Southern people, then we have to say that
the majority of the Southern people are silent.

WARREN: Yes, you would have to say that. Silent and without leadership. For instance, I have here a quotation from
the report of the Louisiana Advisory Committee to the Commission on Civil Rights, and it says that during the long
controversy in New Orleans "the vast majority of the 'top'
leadership . . . made no statements in regard to this all
important issue." The report maintains, in fact, that the top
leadership actually resisted pressure from other citizens,
responsible citizens, to make them speak out.

ELIE: That's not altogether true. I've had personal experience
with some white leaders.

WARREN: Who showed themselves?

ELIE: Well, it depends on what we mean by—by "show
themselves." I'm talking about men who went on television,
after the first school crisis [in New Orleans], to make appeals
for order. They bought a four-page ad in the newspaper.
And from the day they made their appeal on TV there were
no further disorders. Which means that the people with the
real power—the power structure—can do anything they
want, even though they may be in the minority. When they
put the word on the Mayor, then the Mayor tells the Chief
of Police, and it ends just like that. So I don't think it's fair
to say they haven't showed their faces at all.

How much irony is there here in this defense of the "top leaders"
of New Orleans? There is always something edging the words that
Mr. Elie utters, quivering and licking along the edges like new
flame along the edge of a piece of newspaper in sunlight, too pale

yet to be seen. But the irony is clear enough in his next sentence: "Well, they're moderates, but they haven't made as much noise as even moderates would be expected to make."

Mr. Elie knows his moderates, has served on many committees, has now and then reached agreements. Like getting the agreement for a plumber's license changed to the signatures of two responsible citizens—instead of two master plumbers—for it had been impossible for a Negro ever to become a plumber; white plumbers would not sign the application.

But, he says, when agreements won't stick, when the Mayor goes back on his word, they—the "power structure," one of the clichés of the Movement, you hear it everywhere, on the lips of college freshmen and field hands and cab drivers—they, the power structure, will not join in forcing the issue.

ELIE: For example, the Mayor put this in writing—I wish I I had a copy of it here, I was present—the Mayor stated that the signs [of race designation] would be removed from all the public toilets, and this was three or four months ago. For the most part they are still up. So when we went back, then the Mayor just hedged, and we threatened him with demonstrations.

And as a result of the Mayor's position, we have not been able to get any more fruitful negotiations going, which means that before summer, or not later than summer, you will have major demonstrations in New Orleans. As a matter of fact, New Orleans will be the main focal point for demonstrations in the South, in the summer of 1964.*

WARREN: Unless a change takes place?

ELIE: Now it would have to be a radical change. At this point grievances are so high until there's no doubt—no, I don't want to negotiate any more! If I'm called I tell them

* Later (*Time,* April 24, 1964) Mr. Elie emphasized the possibility of violence in the summer if the Civil Rights Bill was not passed: "It is frightening to think of what will happen. There may be armed rebellion—and I wouldn't say one word to discourage it." As a matter of fact, there were no disorders in New Orleans in the summer of 1964—as there were, despite the passage of the Civil Rights Bill, in New York and several other cities. One is bound to wonder how far Mr. Elie's gloomy predictions reflect a state of his own mind and a trait of his character.

I'm no longer working at that—I'm devoting my time to court fights, to voter registration, plus giving demonstrations what support I can.

We talk about the orderly desegregation of the schools in Baton Rouge, about the bi-racial committee there, about the agreement to admit Negro doctors to the hospitals, about the composition of the committee, about what one prominent white businessman in Baton Rouge, not a member of the committee, had said—how "we must recognize that the Negroes have just grievances, how basically their demands are just." And I ask Mr. Elie if such progress, so long as it is steady, would modify his fatalistic view, earlier expressed though not on the tape, that there can be no solution merely in terms of social progress and "good will." But he is sick of negotiation, of "social progress."

ELIE: I dislike having to have the attitude I have, but I'd be less than honest if I said I didn't possess it. Changes of the kind you mention do nothing to change the basic problem. Such changes do help our side, but frankly, such changes just harm the white man's side—what I mean is, such changes give the Negroes a little taste of freedom, so to speak, and it just makes them push that much harder.
WARREN: That's always the case, isn't it? Gain means acceleration of desire?
ELIE: Right.
WARREN: And gains mean increased power of organization?
ELIE: That's right, that's exactly what I'm saying. Which means that my fatalistic attitude toward this thing certainly isn't changed. What I am asking is plain and simple. At what point, when will it be possible for white people to look at black people as human beings?

He has, at last, said it. It is not signs on toilets. It is not plumbers' licenses. It is not the evasiveness of a mayor. It is not the evasiveness or heel-dragging of a bi-racial committee. It is a look in the eye. It is that look in the eye that denies human recognition.

How little—or how much—is he asking for?

So I ask him a question: I ask him if he can't accept the process of practical amelioration, through working arrangements—jobs, training, education, the vote—as leading toward the human recognition?

> ELIE: I don't deny that for one minute, and this is why I'm still a member of CORE and not a member of the Black Muslims. Because I believe that if you do all these things with the hope that—well, if I accomplish this, then these people are going to realize that I'm human.

He pauses, he looks down at his big hand clutching the pencil. Then he suddenly stares at me, and the lenses do not seem to be over the eyes. The eyes are naked and outraged.

> ELIE: You know this is the twentieth century we are talking about and our people have been on this continent for near four hundred years, and there hasn't been any recognition to date. You know that!

*   *   *

Mr. Elie's other partner, Robert Collins, has come in to join us. He is unlike either of the others, unlike Elie's compact, taut, suppressed angriness and blackness, unlike Douglas's athletic height, his thin but muscle-packed forearms showing below the rolled-up sleeves, the tall but smallish skull, the calm, careful and reflective speech. For Mr. Collins, at ease in his comfortable fleshiness, with the smoothness and blandness of his light-brown face and recessive features, in his careful grooming decorously this side of sharpness, is the very picture of the young American professional man, the young executive who is on his way. His tone is bland, too. You feel that in disputes he will play the moderator, he will aim at the "practical solution."

For you soon guess that the conversation going on now in your presence is but the continuation of a conversation, an amiable wrangle, that goes on day after day among these men, on many topics.

They are talking about religion.

Douglas is a Catholic, of a sort: "was baptized," went to Catholic grammar school and high school, and law school at Loyola, "but it's not satisfying."

Elie is a Methodist, but among the churches he doesn't "see any difference." His father was a Catholic, his mother was a Baptist, and his wife is a Methodist. He "didn't use to go to church," but in the end he said, "Well, the hell with it," and goes. But this does not seem to be quite a full account of his feelings. The topic seems to turn him broodingly inward. Does he want something that he cannot find—some absolute? Does the tone of his phrase "Well, the hell with it" express some unsatisfied desire?

I ask him if Christianity will no longer serve the Negro in America.

ELIE: The Christian religion won't serve. The Muslims—they may think they are fighting the white American, or white people in an international sense, but they are really fighting this Christianity, and they are right. The church supported slavery, the church supports segregation. When this segregationist—this woman—when she said to the Archbishop, "Well, Archbishop, you are telling me now that segregation is sinful, but where has the Church been? Look, when did it become sinful? Is it something that was always sinful, Father, or is it something that just got sinful, since 1954?"

These people, the segregationists, have the right to ask that question. The biggest hypocrites in the world have been the Christians. I agree with the Muslims insofar as they say the Negro should reject Christianity—all it means is turning the other cheek. The preacher in the white church tells the white kids to slap the Negroes, and the preacher in the colored church tells the Negroes to turn the other cheek. Oh, I could show where Christianity has failed me as a Negro!

We turn to politics, rather to the possibility of political power for Negroes in New Orleans, and here Mr. Douglas, who has been calm and detached on the matter of religion, brightens. He has given me copies of some of his articles attributing the political powerlessness of the Negro in New Orleans to the fact that there is no solid Negro community, geographically speaking.

> WARREN: You say that this dispersal of the Negro population in New Orleans is a liability. But would it not seem that this dispersal might actually make for integration, rather than work against it—with relation to the problem of school attendance, with relation to the ghetto problem?
> DOUGLAS: I don't think that, no. But built into my position, of necessity, is the theory of contradictions. The dispersal of the Negroes does have a deleterious effect on anything we try to do—we don't have a community to work with, we have only a population. But more than that, there's another kind of dispersal, a kind Myrdal makes reference to —the fact that we've had a matriarchal family set-up and this makes the dispersal go even further than geographically. If the family isn't a cohesive unit, we can't learn to work with other people, to make a community, because this is the starting point—brothers and sisters, fathers and mothers, working together.

Here, with the mention of the matriarchal set-up of many Negro families, Douglas has touched on a point that many people, white and black, take to be the key of the Negro problem—the key, at least, of the "Negro's Negro problem." The matriarchy is, of course, a heritage of slavery, the result of the fact that the Negro was not regarded as a person. The father was merely a biological father; he had no rights, dignity, or authority, and therefore had no role in the family. In many cases he was not even present, and if he was present he might be sold off, or the family broken, at the whim of the owner. But even now, since the Negro woman, generally speaking, has a less precarious economic value than the man, his role may be unstable. He may be in the family, ultimately, on sufferance. To this fact, as Douglas points out, something of the lack of cohesiveness, of training in cooperative work, may stem. But other things, as psychologists tell us, may stem from it too—apathy, a confused or weak sense of identity, sexual disorders, juvenile delinquency.*

* See pp. 52–59, 292–295.

Douglas, however, stresses the need for cohesiveness. If the Negro learns this, he can help himself, and he says that "you can't expect other people to assist you unless they feel that you are, first of all, making an attempt to help yourself."

The notion is very important to Douglas—the notion that all the Negro needs—or should want—is an equal chance to help himself, an equal chance to compete. But Elie will have none of this, breaking in bitterly, pointing at Collins, at Douglas.

ELIE: You're a lawyer, you're a lawyer, you have an equal chance, you can do all right. But you are talking about a group of people who are illiterate, you are saying that you want to give them a chance to compete? With the people who are running the country? What the hell good is an equal chance!

DOUGLAS: I don't want anybody to give me anything, and I think this is part of the civil rights movement. Our chief complaint about the administration of justice, and about the legislative set-up, is that the entire panoply of state government, city government, and whatever other kinds of government you have, is thrown into the balance against the Negro, and I think a substantial step forward will be made when we get some semblance of fairness, not only in your civil cases, but in your criminal cases, and also in your civil cases. The system is so invidious that it permeates unconsciously the mind of a judge when he decides what is the money value of a Negro child who has been killed in an automobile accident.

WARREN: Have you ever found yourself discriminated against from the bench?

ELIE: I think I can best answer that by telling you we try civil rights cases, we represent CORE, and we've been going to Clinton, Louisiana, for many months now, and the judge before whom we try these cases is a director of the Louisiana Citizens Council. I don't think it takes much imagination to realize that we've experienced discrimination from the bench. No—let me put it this way, the judges don't discriminate because I'm a Negro. If they're going to discriminate, they discriminate against my client—who is a Negro. And even if he's represented by a white lawyer, it isn't going to do him very much good.

COLLINS: I think we have experienced discrimination in both ways. I can think of one very good case in which there were Negroes on both sides, as clients. But I think we had a judge who was prejudiced against us as Negro lawyers. Yes, it's something you don't like to admit, because really it puts you out of competition in the market, for we have less to sell if we can't get for our clients the same thing as anybody else. As Negro lawyers we don't have the practice among Negroes that we should have. We would like to think that Negroes would discriminate in our favor, perhaps a false notion of race pride but also because of the fact that we can do just as much for them as any other lawyer.

DOUGLAS: There's another kind of discrimination from the bench, too. We have had occasion to discuss with judges and district attorneys certain civil rights cases, and on more than one occasion we have been blatantly told by some judge —and I'm sure he was sincere when he said it—"I lean over backwards to help the Negro. When he should get three years I give him one. When he should get a year I give him a suspended sentence."

And this is exactly what I meant when I said earlier that I don't want anybody to do any favors for me. If I'm wrong, then say I'm wrong! And when I'm right, I want to be right! Don't you see that this judge strikes at the essence of justice —that he strikes at the very core of everything a man lives by? Right and wrong become intermingled and mixed up.

How stubborn and proud Douglas is in his will to be given nothing but a chance, nothing not earned by right. And how fixed he is in his idea that civil rights, enforcing the rules, will solve everything in the end. All a man needs is a chance. Segregation is more insidious than slavery ever was, he says, "because segregation robs a man of the only thing he can use, and that's the feeling that he can stand foursquare and meet whatever there is to challenge." And you feel that Douglas, in his grim refusal of more than his "right," can stand up.

. . .

Our conversation drifts to other topics—anti-Semitism among Negroes, the proposal to solve segregation in New York City by busing children, the matriarchal structure of the Negro family, the notion that each gain made by Negroes has been a kind of by-product of a general social situation. The most striking quality in this little group is independence of mind. If there is an official "Negro line" they do not seem to have heard of it.

Elie on Anti-Semitism:

I hate to think that Negroes can be anti-Semitic, but on the other hand, they would have to—some of them would have to be—for this is part of America. You have to hate something, you know, and if you don't, then you can't be American.

Elie on Busing Pupils into Harlem:

Well, I was discussing this with [a friend] last week, and I said to him that I'm not at all certain that I would want to send my kid to school in Harlem, and I think it's unrealistic to believe that any segment of the people in New York City would let theirs go. For Harlem has the worst schools, the worst every damned thing—and these people are going to send their kids to Harlem! And my friend said he doesn't know a single middle-class Negro who would be willing to send a child to Harlem schools. He says you'd get more resistance to an enforced sending to Harlem from middle-class Negroes than you would from whites—because the middle-class Negroes are on the up, and they send their children to private schools.

Elie on the Negro Matriarchy:

It's been unfortunate that the Negro male has been willing to take as much as he has taken [of the white man's oppression], and to have his women and children subjected to this. Of course, one reason for this is the matriarchal system.

Douglas on Negro Gains as a By-product of a General Social Situation:

The civil rights movement is the complete example of this. It is the result of the lack of decisive balance between the United States and Russia. With the competition between the United States and Russia, we'll have government officials and corporation officials coming to the college door and sifting out the better brains of the Negro students, and apparently this is already happening on a small scale. But I don't think there's been a change in the moral climate.

Collins on Right and Law:

We're working to see victories not only because a thing is the law but because a thing is right—is thought to be right.

Elie on Change in the Moral Climate:

There's no possible question in my mind that there is more public opinion now to enforce race justice than there was.

It was toward the end of the long interview that Lolis Elie, rather strangely, said this about the improvement in the moral climate, and then thought back to his old days in the Korean War, the night talks with some guy who preferred him maybe only because the guy liked the way he played poker. These recollections of a discovered rapport, a new sympathy, undergird, it would seem, his notion that the moral climate has improved. But there is that other side to him, the angry fatalism that denies all social progress, and makes him cry out and demand when—when!—will white men recognize him as a man. It is this angry fatalism that had made him tell me, the day before, that he was about ready to become a Black Muslim, that he was about convinced that the white man is a white devil and "there's nothing in his history to disprove it."

Lolis Elie, like Dr. Felton Clark, is caught in a cleft stick. But not of history. Of himself.

: 5 :

There is also in New Orleans a man named Israel Augustine, a lawyer, with a prosperous-looking office at 1470 North Claiborne Street. He is very tall, very well built (his coat not cut to de-emphasize his fine shoulders), with a brown face, the face large, with large eyes and a large mouth that is ready to give a good honest smile. He is not yet crowding middle age, but the carefully brushed hair is growing gray. Today he is wearing a very dark silk suit, or a synthetic that looks like silk, for the weather is warm and humid. His tie is discreet. His father (whom I have met, a dark man, not negroid in feature, now old but erect and dignified) was a school superintendent in New Orleans, and this middle-class life had protected the young Israel from "hard knocks on account of race."

Later, however, he had an inclination to, or at least an understanding of, violence. This impulse had been absorbed in the bitter struggle to get started as a lawyer, for he, like Nils Douglas, reports that many Negroes do not trust a Negro lawyer, there's a "stereotype of Negro lawyers among Negroes." Negroes want to go to the white lawyer who has "influence." But things are getting easier now. In 1952 there were only two Negro lawyers in New Orleans and now there are twenty-five, so Negroes have more and more "exposure" to lawyers of their own race.

Augustine is with the Southern Christian Leadership Conference, the organization founded by Martin Luther King, Jr. He believes that you can't win against the white man by "out-hating him," that "the mind is a powerful weapon," that Dr. King "has far from finished his growth." But he is a practical man, and his chief interests now are in voter registration and the founding of a bi-racial federal savings and loan company. He says that the charter for the company has been granted in spite of efforts to prevent it by the lobby of white loan companies of New Orleans that fought it all the way to the Home Loan Board in Washington.

He and his partner take me to lunch at an elegant Negro restaurant, with walls of burgundy-colored tapestry and white moulding, and give me a splendid New Orleans meal. It is a new restaurant, one of the symbols of the progress being made in New Orleans. But the taste in music here, Mr. Augustine says, is poor: no judgment about "dinner music," too much jazz. He says that such a restaurant has competition from a place like the newly desegregated Hilton, where Negro banquets and parties are given. The desegregation of the Hilton has hurt Negro caterers, too, he says. Integration is a complicated thing, but you've got to be prepared to compete. Otherwise, what? When he says this he lifts his head just as Nils Douglas does when he says it. He is a very reasonable and studious man: he knows that change takes place in time, that there are no solutions without cost.

So I ask him what he understands by the slogan "Freedom Now" and he says: "I have a five-year-old daughter, and on TV she sees the advertisements for the Lake Ponchartrain Beach—it's an amusement park—all the games and rides and things that children love. It's like a fairyland to her, and she talks about going there. I can't tell her why she can't go. I can't burden her. Not now. I want her to be able to go when she's big enough. She'll be big enough soon."

: 6 :

Some time back in Vermont, I was talking with a young man. He was a clean-cut, intelligent, vigorous young man, just graduated from the University of Vermont, idealistic, wanting to do something, he said, to be of use to society, not just to make money. He asked me what I was working at, and I told him. He thought it was fine, he thought Negroes ought to get a break.

Then he begins to tell me about a little trouble they had last year at the University. He asks me if I ever heard of "Walken fer de Cake."

I say no. So, he tells me.

"Walken fer de Cake" is the name of an annual festival at the University of Vermont, the big event of the year. There is, I gather, a big dance, preceded by a dance competition. Each fraternity enters a team of two dancers, dressed up in flamboyant tail-coats of bright silk and satin and wearing top hats—in blackface. Each pair does a furious and complicated buck-and-wing, in unison. The victory in this is glory for the sponsoring fraternity.

Last year, one of the few Negro students at the University wrote a letter of protest to the school paper. Then the NAACP threatened pickets. The fraternity council knuckled under.

"It made the alumni all over the state awful sore," the young man says. "Why, up at UVM, that's the big thing of the year, there's a lot of sentiment gets built up around it. It hurts people to have a thing like that—a real tradition—tampered with. Hell, it's not race prejudice—not in Vermont—it's just a tradition—you might say a sentiment."

Then he adds that they don't have any Negro problem in Vermont.

Brattleboro, Vermont, has won the award of an "All American City," given by the National Municipal League and *Look* magazine, an award also received by such better publicized, but no more deserving, communities as Westport, Connecticut, and Berkeley, California. The local newspaper is called *The Brattleboro Daily Reformer*.

One of the reforms undertaken by the editors was the reform of Senator Russell of Georgia, whose proposal to redistribute the Negro population of the United States the paper called "short-sighted, impractical and cynical." In documenting these charges—which would seem to require little documentation—the editors express considerable solicitude for the Negro: "Thus Vermont, for instance, would stand to accept 40,000 Negroes most of whom would come here without the least idea of what the climate is like and most of whom would be miserable."

Vermont has no Negro problem. Furthermore, Vermont does not intend to have any.

2 ❧ A Mississippi Journal

It is morning, and the before-breakfast plane from New Orleans to Jackson, Mississippi, glides through the brilliant air. The plane is not high now, and the farms and roads and trees and houses and the numberless little glittering ponds—stock ponds—look like the toy landscape, with tiny bits of mirror to simulate water, set around the track of my eight-year-old son's electric train, far off in Connecticut.

Even the airport at Jackson, as I find when I enter, does not look real. It has the unreality of an airport anywhere—in Topeka or Istanbul or Tokyo—the gleaming, dehumanized, blank promise that every place is any place, and no place is anywhere, and everywhere is no place. It is very comforting, that promise. That promise is the truth that will make you free.

But I do not want to be free. I want to know what it feels like to be in Jackson. So I go to the news stand, there in the glittering airport, and buy the Sunday edition of the Jackson *Clarion-Ledger*.

In the cab I find out what it is like to be in Jackson. The driver is a youngish, burly man—seeming fat at first glance, but with that hard, smooth-faced, small-nosed fleshiness that you often find in the deep South. The belly of such a man bulges, but bulges with muscle. This man lolls back in his seat, drives the cab with only two fingers of the left hand on the wheel, and lays his right arm along the back of the front seat. I look at the hand. The flesh bulges on the hand, and the fingers, in repose, do not lie together, side by side, because the flesh bulges up to the first knuckle joint, forcing the fingers apart. The hand looks, somehow, babyish, awkward, indolent, but you know that it can move fast. The back of the hand and the back of the chubby, powerful baby-fingers are sprigged with coarse black hair. He is from the country, he says, but since Korea has been driving a cab in Jackson. He has done right good, he says.

He is talking about the Byron de la Beckwith trial, which, just two days before, had ended in a hung jury. The driver is surprised that Byron—he calls him Byron—didn't get off. He bases his view on logic and justice. "Now Byron couldn't done it, he was too smart to leave a gun layen round to be picked up [the presumptive weapon had been found and fresh prints on it identified by the Jackson police as Beckwith's] and besides he was seen in Greenwood thirty minutes after the killen by a sheriff and two police and they wouldn't of lied.

"But them two taxi drivers in Jackson what swore Beckwith ast 'em where Evers lived sure swore to a damn lie. No real taxi driver is ever gonna git the habit of tellen about folks. Take me, I picked up a lady last week and she said please not tell her husband where, and I said, 'Lady, if you pay me the fare I ain't sayen nuthen to nobody.' So them taxi drivers lied, tryen to make some money out of it. Or somethen.

"But the boss kicked their asses out. Said, 'Git yore asses out and don't ever set them asses back in no Yellow, even if you're payen fer it.' But don't git me wrong now, I am in favor of punishen a guilty party, if'n he is proved guilty. I am always in favor of doen the right thing, but I ain't in favor of lyen."

He is in favor of doing the right thing. That is something we all have to believe about ourselves. He sinks into himself, brooding.

"Taxi business is fallen off," he says then. "I always made a good liven, eleven, twelve years. But last week I didn't make no liven. It is this-here Beckwith trial. White folks don't want to do downtown shoppen and git caught. When them black sons-of-bitches start out-ragen out, and doen things."

Two days before, on Friday, February 7, there had, in fact, been a riot—or near-riot—on Lynch Street, which separates the halves of the campus at Jackson College, a Negro institution supported by the state. The police had committed a good deal of armament, including their new tank.*

---

* The tank is like an oversize Brink's armored car, with 1½-inch plate, 2-inch bulletproof glass for the windshield and gun ports, a steel-enclosed engine. The crew is composed of ten men, with driver and auxiliary driver. The armament includes a submachine gun, ten .12-gauge shotguns, tear-gas

I had seen the report of the Jackson College riot in the *Jackson Daily News*. It had a big photograph, front page, center, top, of police in serried rank, holding riot guns at the ready and wearing helmets and expressions of the utmost dedication and heroism, with the caption:

JACKSON POLICE READY
Lt. C. R. Wilson, right, lines up a group of Jackson policemen to quell racial demonstrations at Jackson State College Monday night. Police were forced to use tear gas and blasts from shotguns to break up a protest involving about 1000 Negroes.

The photograph has a dramatic chiaroscuro that would make Rembrandt's *Night Watch* seem like a Renoir picnic.

To the left of the picture is the riot story. To the right is the current report on the Beckwith trial. To the lower left is a story of the Senate debate on the Civil Rights Bill (then pending), headed *Right of Dead Men to Vote Upheld* (an excerpt: "Rep. George Andrews, an Alabama Democrat, said the Civil Rights Bill would bring federal 'control' of elections, anyway, 'so why not outlaw vote frauds, too?' "). To the lower right is a story on Alabama resistance, with the headline: *Wallace May Test LBJ with Force*. This is the whole wide world, as pictured by Jackson journalism.

That evening I see an eyewitness account of the Jackson College riot* in the Sunday edition of the *Atlanta Constitution*, signed by Harold Martin, a distinguished journalist, who had been in town to cover the Beckwith trial.

I've seen a Marine outfit storm a fortified hill in Korea with fewer men and less fire power than the mayor sent out to prevent this anticipated riot. Some 300 policemen blocked off roads leading to the campus and took up stations along the campus fence . . . the crowd was orderly enough as the students started toward their

---

launchers, and tear-gas cannisters. The underbody of the vehicle has a jagged, knife-sharp steel strip running around, edge downward, to prevent hand-grip for turning it over. The tires remain vulnerable, and to date the ingenuity of the police department has been incompetent to meet this challenge. It is reported that at the time of the riot, the crew had not yet got the hang of things and managed to release a cannister of gas inside the tank.

* There were, in fact, two separate disturbances. The first mass of students was dispersed earlier, largely by the efforts of Charles Evers. More trouble was anticipated after a basketball game.

dormitories. But the sight of the cops, with shotguns, carbines, tear gas and searchlights at the ready, seemed to enrage them. They started yelling "hey, boy," and other insulting things at the cops and a few rocks began to fly, and the cops, who were tense and jumpy, started shooting into the air. And this set off another barrage of bricks, rocks and bottles and the cops started shooting in earnest, at running figures on the campus, into the shadows and toward the rooftops of the buildings.

They said there were snipers up there, but I didn't hear the "zing" of any incoming rifle fire, nor did any police get shot . . . But three Negroes did get shot . . .

And to me it seemed a pretty foolish performance all around. Two or three of Jackson's six Negro policemen, it seems to me, could have handled any disturbance that came up . . ."

Besides the students who had been shot, not fatally, several other persons were clubbed with the butts of riot guns. Charles Evers, the brother of the murdered Medgar, helped disperse the crowd of students—going among them, begging them to get back on campus.

But now my driver is taking me to my hotel, in the center of Jackson. It is the "best hotel" in a thousand little American cities. The desk is cordial, in a splendid Mississippi accent. At breakfast I read my new *Clarion-Ledger*. After the local news, I turn to the magazine section. I find a long article on Lincoln. He is praised for his "humanity," and "his respect for the dignity of every man."

This is Jackson, Mississippi. This is two days after the hung jury for Byron de la Beckwith. This is two days after the Jackson College riot. I wonder what people here all over Jackson are thinking as they turn to the magazine section of their home paper and read about Lincoln. Then I realize that the magazine section is canned somewhere far away, a kind of K-ration for the Sunday-morning mind of America, North and South. It is like the gleaming and anonymous airport; it is a nexus with that great world beyond, where every place is any place and no place is anywhere.

But this complication should not trouble the minds and hearts of the citizens who live and vote in Jackson, Mississippi. Even Mississippians slip, now and then, into that rarefied atmosphere of that fourth dimension called America. Especially when federal money is involved. They slip, fiscally at least, into that fourth dimension.

They slip over to collect the handout: for every $218 paid in taxes to the Federal Government by Mississippi, Washington returns $327.

: 2 :

Number 1075 Lynch Street, some half a mile nearer the heart of the city than Jackson College, is a very large gray cement structure. On the ground floor is a Negro-owned and directed savings and loan company, two quite well-appointed and well-furnished shops, one a shoe store, the other a clothing store, both Negro-owned, and a large entrance and lobby admitting to offices on the second floor and to the large Masonic auditorium on the first floor, to the rear.

By eleven thirty on the morning of my arrival, I am in the auditorium, sitting down near the front a little to the left. A group of some one hundred and fifty people are present, the group looking small and huddled, down toward the front in the big high-ceilinged room. Far in the back three or four white men—if they are white men—are sitting at a little table. One has a piece of paper in his hand. I take them to be reporters.

This is a meeting of COFO—Council of Federated Organizations —and the question under discussion is voter registration. Many of the people present are delegates who have come to report on progress in their home counties. Though most of the delegates are middle-aged or even old, a young man is presiding at a small lectern down in front of the chairs. He is of medium height, of good build, with a rather large well-shaped head, a preternaturally serious expression on his light brown, almost yellow face, the seriousness emphasized by horn-rimmed glasses. He is wearing overalls and a dark sweater—overalls, or levis with a denim jacket, being the uniform pridefully sported by members of the Student Nonviolent Coordinating Committee (SNCC—"Snick"). For overalls, as one young man once said to me, "make it easier for them to drag you when dragging-time comes. You want to make it nice and easy for them."

The young man now presiding is a member of Snick. His name is Robert Moses, and he is a field worker for voter registration. He is presiding until Dr. Aaron Henry,* the state president of the NAACP, arrives.

* Later a delegate of the Freedom Democratic Party of Mississippi to the convention in Atlantic City.

Robert Moses speaks very calmly, in a voice that is rather soft and slow but with enunciation almost pedagogically careful, as though he were teaching a foreign language. There is a touch of the pedagogical, too, in the way he handles a question from the floor. He rephrases everything into a kind of basic English, with meticulous but not obtrusive indications of the logical stages involved. But in his extraordinary calmness, there is nothing of the condescension of the pedagogue.

He is an academic type. Not long ago he was a student at Harvard, doing graduate work in philosophy.

"I liked philosophy," he was to say to me later, "so I wanted to study. I wasn't sure I would teach—but there wasn't anything else at that time I wanted to do." Now, standing there in his calmness, he is teaching. And now he does not know what he wants to do. He is doing it.

Now the representative from Holmes County, an aging black man who reminds me of the Reverend Joe Carter, is saying: "In foretimes we had a hard way to go, a man go to the office [to register] and Sher'ff, he made him git out. But Bob Moses first to come and give a inklen of how to git together." For about six months now, he says, they have been meeting twice a week, and Bob Moses "teach us the things we should know. About ballots, and things." He continues: "The most trouble is in ourselves, to go up. Not so much afraid—just negligent. We just don't flock in."

"It's not apathy," somebody else gets up to insist. "It's fear—of brutality and economic revenge."

But this whole question of apathy, just touched on in the meeting, is not easily settled. There are those who deny the very existence of apathy. For instance, Lawrence Guyot, who has been deeply and courageously engaged in voter registration, testified, under oath, in a hearing on Mississippi and civil rights, on June 8, 1964: "Apathy, to my knowledge, in Mississippi, as far as voting is concerned, does not exist." But Ronnie Moore, back in New Orleans, has told me that the problem is "motivation," the changing of "one mind or heart." And according to a worker for CORE at North Carolina State College in Raleigh, in the fall of 1964, just before the Presidential election, even with the registrar accompanying the CORE worker to the very door of the home of the prospective voter, it was difficult to persuade many Negroes to register; and she added that there was no fear of reprisal, not there, just "apathy."

It is hard to sort out motives—fear or apathy. And the question is, in a sense, a false question, if taken in the perspective of time. Fear and frustration make for apathy; hope and desire are deadened, and numbness sets in. And now, in that meeting, that Sunday morning in Jackson, another speaker rises, a woman of education and experience of the world, and says: "People are set in their ways, you won't get them to change overnight. It's slow to make them understand the importance of their own vote when for three hundred years they didn't even count as individuals."

As this woman says, why shouldn't there be apathy, or all the dead weight of dead hopes and desires which we can assemble under that word? Apathy is common among white citizens, why shouldn't it be common among Negroes? As put to me by a man in Lexington, Virginia, who had been trying in the fall of 1964 to get white votes for Johnson back in the coves off the Shenandoah: a hill man would say, "We jest ain't that kind of folks, to go down and be registeren and voten."*

But some Negroes hate to admit that there may be apathy among Negroes. They flinch from the word. And, obviously, for a man dedicated to the task of voter registration to admit apathy is to undercut his own courage and will. People tend to believe what they need to believe.

Fear of brutality, of reprisal—that is easier to deal with. And its stirs your own anger, gives a target for anger. Also it makes better propaganda. But there is an even deeper reason to deny the force of apathy: if once you grant apathy, you have half granted the truth of the old stereotype of Sambo: "Hell, our niggers don't want to

---

* Many foreign commentators on America, including Myrdal, have remarked on "the relative inertia and inarticulateness of the masses," and on political apathy. There are, of course, some sound historical reasons for this, including the two-party system in which issues tend to get blurred and absorbed. On this general point David Riesman, in "Observations on Intellectual Freedom," in *Individualism Reconsidered,* says: "This very apathy has its positive side as a safeguard against the overpoliticalization of the country: the apathetic ones, often not so much fearful or faithless as bored, may be as immunized against political appeals, good or bad, as against commercial advertising." It would seem that, after the Supreme Court decision of 1954, there was, in general, an "apathetic" tendency in the South to accept the new order; then the "politicalization" was accomplished by the hard-core segregationists—and the opportunists. In other words, as Yeats puts it,
      The best lack all conviction, while the worst
      Are full of passionate intensity.

vote, they're happy the ways things are, all our niggers want is to be left alone."

It may be true that all Negroes want is to be left alone. But what, exactly, does "to be left alone" mean?

Mrs. Harvey—for that is the name of the last speaker, a tall, very handsome, fashionably dressed gold-skinned woman of some forty-three or -four—goes on from her remarks on apathy to speak of letters she has received from Connecticut and Vermont, offering assistance in the big registration drive projected for the summer of 1964. One, from a woman of Westport, Connecticut—a Quaker, it appears —offers to bring fifty to one hundred women trained in nonviolence techniques and in methods of registration.

Dr. Aaron Henry has now taken charge of the meeting. "The question," he says, "is whether we'll accept outside help." And he repeats the word *accept*. And adds, firmly: "Not *asking,* but *accepting.*"

For one of the most important aspects of the Movement is the jealously guarded notion that Negroes shall be in control, shall be independent, may "accept," but will not "ask." Not ask for a damned thing. There is an old habit to break, for some people in this room may still have, deep down, that habit of "asking." A psychiatrist in Connecticut has told me that among his Negro patients, even among those of whom it would seem most improbable, he sometimes finds, if he goes below the surface, the archetypal figure of Sambo, supplicating. Dr. Henry is not going to miss a chance to strike at that old figure.

But a man rises to say, "We need that help. We've got a long way to go."

After the vote, Dr. Henry announces that the ayes have it. "So, Mrs. Harvey," he says, "you wire your friend. You wire her *yesterday.*"

There is general laughter. There are realists in the room. Dr. Henry is a realist. He is grinning.

Then discussion turns to the chief business of the meeting—the launching of a project called Freedom Registration. There are 425,-000 Negroes in Mississippi eligible to vote, Robert Moses says. "Let us register them ourselves," he says, "on our own books, each county with its own board of registration, with requirements in line with the Constitution. We can show the people of Mississippi and the Justice Department of the United States that the people *will* register."*

Then, in the middle of the discussion, a tall, dark man rises with an air of angry authority and demands that the doors be guarded. The crowd now has grown by another hundred. "Check everybody in at the door!" the tall, dark, angry-sounding man commands. "Don't let anybody in not identified. No newspapermen!"

This tall, dark, angry-sounding man is, I learn, Charles Evers.

Robert Moses, in his calm way, orders two men to the door to keep out any unauthorized persons. Then, even more calmly, with a tone of sweet sadness, he says: "Be gentle with them." It is the only trace of humor I am to see from him. The audience thinks it is very funny.

I leave the meeting shortly afterwards. I am going to have dinner at Mrs. Harvey's house and then interview her. On the way out I notice that the table in the back where the white men had been sitting when I came in—the men I took to be reporters— is gone. The men are gone, too.

As I walked out the door of the auditorium, my first thought was that I had been witnessing the funeral service for Sambo. "Not asking," Aaron Henry had said, "but accepting." For a central fact of the whole Negro Movement is the will to independence of action, to power, to respect.

But who was the Sambo who is being buried?

He was the supine, grateful, humble, irresponsible, unmanly, banjo-picking, servile, grinning, slack-jawed, docile, dependent, slow-witted, humorous, child-loving, childlike, watermelon-stealing, spiritual-singing, blamelessly fornicating, happy-go-lucky, hedonistic, faithful black servitor who sometimes might step out of character long enough to utter folk wisdom or bury the family silver to save it from the Yankees. Sambo was the comforting stereotype the South-

---

* In the hearing on June 8, 1964, already referred to, Lawrence Guyot states that, according to the 1961 Civil Rights Commission report, there were twelve registered Negroes in Forrest County, Mississippi. After some five months of demonstrations there were one thousand applicants for registration. He uses this impressive fact, of course, as an argument against the idea that there is apathy among Negroes. Apathy is, of course, a relative and fluctuating thing.

ern white man had of the Negro—that is, when he wasn't worrying about a slave insurrection or advertising for a runaway. But the stereotype was not confined to the South. Sambo was in the North, too—in minstrel shows, for instance, or in the song that, with humorous condescension, defended the not widely popular idea of using Negro troops in the Union armies, "Sambo's Right to be Kilt." Later, North and South, Sambo lived on—in white eyes—as Pullman porter, bootblack, yard boy, sharecropper, waiter, barber, elevator operator, the Three Black Crows, and Step-and-Fetchit. Sambo, it was said, was "just the way niggers are." He was eternal and immutable.

But historians and psychologists now regard him as neither eternal nor immutable. He had not lived in Africa. And insofar as he came to exist at all (for some people would deny his existence), he was a social product, particularly a product of the slave system of the United States. In the Catholic countries that practiced slavery, the position of the slave, despite all brutalities and discriminations, we are told, was different. The Church insisting on the sacraments, defined the slave as a person. If he was baptized, for instance, he had an identity; if he was married, he was, in the eyes of the Church, the responsible head of a family with dignities and obligations. The state, like the church, might, in theory at least, interpose between the owner and the slave; and according to Gilberto Freyre, in *The Mansions and the Shanties,* slaves, more than once, took up arms in support of the monarchy, remembering that they "had received positive protection from kings and popes." Furthermore, the tradition of Roman law, with the echo of the Roman slave system under which the slave was merely an unfortunate person who, before capture, might have been a scholar or prince, gave no weight to the idea of innate inferiority. On the point of inferiority, the Spanish and the Portuguese, especially the latter, had had a long contact with colored peoples of various degrees of civilized accomplishment; the relatively small number of white women in Brazil for a considerable period tended to confer status on the imported Africans; and even much later it was not uncommon for the sons of concubinage to be educated in the Big House or Mansion side by side with the legitimate children, and then to be manumitted into the professional class. In many cases, the African slaves, especially Sudanese Muslims, brought to Brazil a higher level of literacy and civilization than that possessed by their masters. Another, and perhaps the most significant, difference between, say, Brazilian slavery and that of the United States, lay in the continuity of his own African culture which the slave might enjoy and which supported his sense of identity. There were, according to Freyre, "schools and houses of prayer," and a "true Mâli elite," with the interpenetration of Mohammedan practices into the local Catholicism; and the slaves in Brazil often did not lose contact with Africa, for a regular trade was maintained, sometimes in bottoms owned by freedmen in Brazil, and until the end of the last century there was frequent repatriation of Negroes from Bahia, a whole city, in fact, being founded by them in Ardra.

This is the basic line of argument that in Latin American countries, particularly Brazil, the slave tended to maintain an attitude toward himself and the world that, by and large, was lacking in the United States. The point is not, of course, that there were no horrors in the slave system (or rather, systems) of Latin America, or that there were not great variations from place to place, and from time to time in the same place, as economic and other conditions changed, or that race prejudice never existed. The point is simply that the slave's effective reaction to his situation was often different. The history of Brazil, for instance, is a history of insurrections, rather than abortive servile revolts, the most famous being that of Palmares, a Negro "nation" of considerable civilization which was founded in 1631 and endured for seventy-six years before being overwhelmed. But we do not need to go back into history. There is modern Brazil to look at.

The system in North America, however, worked more or less consciously to unman the slave and rob him of any sense of identity. As with the African imported elsewhere, there was, for the slave brought to North America, the traumatic experience of capture and the horrors of the long voyage.* But the difference was that in North

* As a kind of parallel for the shock of the capture and voyage we may take the description by Erik Erikson of the condition of certain discharged American veterans of World War II suffering from "loss of ego synthesis: Obviously the men are worn out by too many changes (gradual or sudden) in too many respects at once; somatic tension, social panic, and ego anxiety are always present. Above all, the men 'do not know any more who they are': there is a distinct loss of ego identity. The sense of sameness and of continuity and the belief in one's social role are gone." (See "Identity and the Life Cycle," in *Psychological Issues,* vol. I, no. I, 1959.)

America the stunned slave was dropped into a society that did not recognize him, in even the most minimal sense, as a person. He was defined as a chattel, a thing, and his inferiority (by which Protestant Puritanism could rationalize slavery) was the basic assumption of the system. Furthermore, any sense of cultural continuity was destroyed. To him now appeared the master, who was not only the embodiment of oppressive and irresistible power, but the source of all benefits. So deprived of any support, from either his own past or the present system, the Negro tended to do what all persecuted peoples tend to do—accept the values of the dominant group and internalize them. And the most destructive value that can be internalized is the certainty which the dominant group holds of its own total superiority.

It is not maintained by this argument that there is anything special in such a tendency on the part of the Negro. The drift in that direction is always there, it seems, in any oppressed group. We know something, for instance, about self-hate and anti-Semitism among Jews, and no doubt a study of self-hate among Southerners would develop some interesting data. For one extreme example we have the accounts of how Jews in Nazi concentration camps sometimes accepted the values of their oppressors; some, for instance, carried bits of the clothing of their guards as fetishes. For another example, we may turn to the technique and results of brain-washing by the Chinese Communists as practiced on foreigners and, especially, native Chinese.*

Even if the values of the dominant white man are, to a greater or lesser degree, accepted by the slave, he will, almost certainly, remain ambivalent—like the child who internalizes the values of

* In *Slavery*, by Stanley Elkins, is the most systematic presentation of the psychological effect of slavery on the Negro in the United States. There have been various criticisms of the book, but it would seem that they involve supporting material and overstatements rather than the central thesis. For instance, if it is established that Samboism did not emerge until the nineteenth century, this means that the significance of the voyage, etc., is reduced, and that one must look more closely into the context of slavery in the later period. For instance, would there be a correlation between such a late development of Samboism and the hardening and expansion of the system? For supporting material, see Kardiner and Ovesey, *The Mark of Oppression*. For Jewish prisoners in Nazi camps, see Gordon Allport, *The Nature of Prejudice*, and Bruno Bettelheim, "Individual and Mass Behavior in Extreme Situations," in *Journal of Abnormal and Social Psychology*, 1943. For Chinese brain-washing, see Robert Jay Lifton, *Thought Reform and the Psychology of Totalism*.

parents because he is dependent upon them but at the same time resents the dependency. The natural rage and protest of the slave, which constitute one pole of this ambivalence, can take many forms, the most ordinary form being the substitution of another attitude. The bowing and scraping of a Sambo or the forelock-pulling of a European peasant may be, then, the index of an old hatred. The old hatred, the old rage, may contribute to the creation of servility. It may come about unconsciously, with the servility an expression of the ambivalence—concomitant acceptance and rage at acceptance. Or it may come about consciously, with the servility assumed as a matter of tactics; and as a parody may be an act of deliberate, though secret and ironical, aggression. But even so, servility as aggression may shade over, under long pressure, into real Sambo-ism.*

By this general line of argument, insofar as Samboism existed, it existed in a system which constantly compounded the effects. Since the slave was not regarded as a person, he could have no responsible family life. The child born to a slave woman followed the condition of the woman, and the father had no right in the child. So the system struck at his masculine role and personal dignity. And at the same time there was no masculine model for a child. Even if the father remained present, he was not standing in a position of power, he was devalued before his own son.

According to this line of thought, the whole question of identity for the Negro would take on a new dimension. It may be seen to involve not merely the tension between Negro-ness, or an African heritage or the *mystique noire,* as against the values of white America, but also a struggle between the will to maintain identity at all and the forces that make for the creation of Sambo. Or as Thomas F. Pettigrew puts it in *A Profile of the Negro American,* when he describes the situation of the modern Negro, the Negro is torn between the "personal self" and the "role" demanded by society. Just as there are some white people who see all Negroes, past and present, as Sambo, there are some people, Negro and white, who deny that Sambo ever existed. They stare into history, or about them now, and see millions of Nat Turners and Frederick Douglasses.

---

* Dancing and clowning, two more attributes of Sambo, may also be interpreted as a result of the inhibited affective life of the slave. Here feelings ordinarily throttled, including the impulses to aggression, bleed off.

There were, indeed, suicides of Africans on the Middle Passage, and the famous mutinies. Even after Africans had long since forgotten Africa, even after generations of the pressures of the slave system had presumably converted them into "niggers," there were insurrections. And there were runaways—enough, it is clear, to make a burning issue of the Fugitive Slave Law. But real insurrections were few, and involved few slaves, and none came to anything (except to keep fresh in the Southern mind and conscience the nightmare of Haiti); and betrayals by nonparticipating slaves—i.e., by Sambo—of plans for insurrection were not unknown. In any case, common sense might repudiate either extreme view of the question; there were, no doubt, some Sambos and some Nat Turners, with many shadings along the psychological spectrum in between, and sometimes both Nat Turner and Sambo might inhabit the same man.

As an aside, we might ask if craven submissiveness is necessarily the only explanation of the fact that there were relatively few insurrections. Is it too hard to believe that sometimes, even across the bar of race and oppression, human recognition might, however, timidly, extend back and forth? And would it necessarily be a mark of degradation for a slave to shrink from the blood bath? When it came to striking the blow with his own hands, Nat Turner shrank. But, then, would human recognition and a shrinking from the blood bath be a mark of Samboism? Du Bois has called Negroes not only the "strongest," but the "gentlest of the races of men."

Many Negroes have recognized an emotional maiming caused by the slave system. Du Bois describes Sambo, and understands how such a thing as Samboism might come to exist: "The long system of repression and degradation of the Negro tended to emphasize the elements in his character which made him a valuable chattel: courtesy became humility, moral strength degenerated into submission, and the exquisite native appreciation of the beautiful became an infinite capacity for dumb suffering" (*The Souls of Black Folk*). Or again, he says that the white man tampered with "the moral fiber of a naturally honest and straightforward people." In *Why We Can't Wait* Martin Luther King, though he says that the Negro had never been "really patient" under slavery and had developed the germ of nonviolence as a protest against that oppression, remarks on the "almost scientific precision" of the slave system "for keeping the Negro defenseless, emotionally and physically"—

and the word *emotionally* implies the thesis of Elkins that damage had been done to the very psyche of the slave. Dr. Stuart Nelson, vice president of Howard University, in commenting on the Southern system of segregation in the time of his boyhood in Kentucky, said to me that the Negro tended to accept the white evaluation of him in some deep way, and that the result was "to rob the Negro of the power to resent, either externally or internally." Diane Nash, a student at Fisk and secretary of the Nashville Nonviolent Movement during the period of the freedom rides, in wondering why so many Negro faculty members of Negro colleges do not defend expelled students or associate themselves with the Movement, comes up with the answer that "Jim Crow does something to the Negro . . . stymies his ability to be free."* And James Baldwin, again and again, refers to the "castration" of the Negro by the social system. Furthermore, it is clear that the very fact of the strenuous insistence in the Negro Movement on independence of action is some indication of the special need for independence—the violence and the indiscriminateness of the attacks on Uncle Tom-ism would seem to imply that there must be an Uncle Tom lurking somewhere—perhaps, even, in the depth of the person making the attack.

The Reverend Milton Galamison, tacitly accepting the Elkins thesis, bitterly summed up the matter to me: "You see, the difference between other institutions of slavery and the American institution of slavery is that in no other instance, to my best knowledge, was a slave actually dehumanized and deprived of the image of being human, so that in other instances in history when slaves were freed they became people like everyone else. In America this was not true. Apparently in order to justify slavery the early Americans found it necessary to dehumanize and completely emasculate the Negro."

It is hard to to guess how many Sambos there were, or how much Samboism. But there is one thing we do not have to guess about: slavery was not wildly popular among slaves, And with the deep ambiguity in the origins or expressions of Samboism, there could be no certain way for the white observer to distinguish the true from

---

* "Inside the Sit-ins and Freedom Rides," in *The New Negro,* ed. M. H. Ahmann.

the tactical Sambo. It would be only human, in fact, that sometimes a Negro might have some difficulty in distinguishing the two in himself. Samboism would be best regarded as one psychological pole of the slave's experience, with the other, shall we say, Nat Turnerism. But we must remember that the experience was always that of an individual with all the complications and shadings of his individuality. Though we must have generalizations, we do well to remember, too, that they are hazardous, for in the human being there may always hide the secret antithesis of what seems most obvious waiting for a change of weather for it to have its day. For one example, if Negroes internalized white values, they were also in a strategic position to remark the white foible and white filth. For another example, we can remember that, though not many years back, E. Franklin Frazier, in *Black Bourgeoisie,* bitterly deplored the frivolous aimlessness of middle-class students in Negro colleges, it was from among such students that the sit-ins and the militant Student Nonviolent Coordinating Committee developed. And Ralph Ellison points out that "some of the older sharecroppers who are sheltering and advising the young Northern crusaders [in the South] would seem to look, talk and, when the occasion requires it, *act* like this alleged 'Sambo.' "

How many Sambos? How much Samboism?

The questions are not really important. The real point is that Sambo's day is over.

: 3 :

Mrs. Martin Harvey—Clarie Harvey—is an able and energetic woman, active in church and civil rights work; the founder of Woman Power Unlimited; and with her mother, who is now aging, the manager of complicated business concerns in Jackson inherited from her father—a large undertaking establishment and an insurance agency being the main enterprises. Her husband, one-time president of the New York Youth Council and the first Negro president of the United Christian Youth Movement, is a dean of Southern University, in Baton Rouge, and they have, as she puts it, a "commuting marriage."

She comes naturally by her energy and intelligence. Her paternal grandfather and his brothers were plantation slaves but were never whipped, for if the master was angry they hid in the woods, knowing that, when his temper cooled, he would never give out more than a minor punishment to such good workers. The plantation, at Hazelhurst, in Copiah County, is now owned by the descendants of that slave grandfather—it is, Mrs. Harvey says, "kept in the family." On the maternal side, the great-grandfather was a man of furious ambition. "My mother," Mrs. Harvey says, "tells of him working so that when he would come in from the fields, you could hear the sweat sloshing in his boots." He wound up with a plantation in Lauderdale County, with "many people working for him and living there as sharecroppers and tenant farmers." Then the family branched out into the grocery business, and later into other interests.

Mrs. Harvey is proud of this inheritance of energy and ambition and self-discipline. And she is proud, too, of the fact that, back in the 1920's, her father, with two friends, founded the NAACP in Jackson, Mississippi. For several years those three men were the only members, but they hung on.

Mrs. Harvey's father founded, too, the first Youth Council in Jackson, and was a nationally prominent lay minister in the Methodist Church; and this inheritance of religious conviction and an ideal of social service is also something that has shaped her life, from her days at Spelman College in Atlanta, to the present. When she attended the World Conference of Christian Youth in Amsterdam, Holland, in 1939, she was confirmed in what she calls a "concern for the larger community."

Mrs. Harvey's attitude toward the Movement is in the context of these concerns. For instance, she sees the solution of the "Negro problem" and that of the "poor-white problem" as essentially linked together: "I think that the two have to go hand in hand, and I don't think you can help one without helping the other, and I don't think you should help one without helping the other." Her basic assumptions come out even in our talk about Myrdal's outline of what would have been an ideal plan for a Reconstruction policy—especially on the matter of compensation to Confederate slaveholders for the slaves emancipated, and payment to Confederate planters for land which would be redistributed to the freedmen. I asked her if this policy, even with those stipulations, would make sense to her.

MRS. HARVEY: Very good sense.

WARREN: You find no emotional resistance?

MRS. HARVEY: No.

WARREN: Sometimes a Negro or a white Northerner will say: "Why pay a slaveholder for slaves he had no right to hold? Why subsidize his immorality?" Or: "Why compensate rebels for their land?"

MRS. HARVEY: Well, when you start thinking that way you're not thinking of people. You're thinking of a label—"rebel" —you're thinking of rebels, slaves, you see, and if you talk in those terms, and you think that way, you build up your prejudices and your resistances. But they were all people, dispossessed people—whites and Negroes. How do you treat human beings who have gone through a serious, traumatic experience, like a civil war?

But Mrs. Harvey does not confuse her own religious and social convictions with the Movement as such.

MRS. HARVEY: Religion per se has not been active in the Movement, as I know the Movement, but many of the people who have been involved have been involved because of their religious orientation. I don't think it has been the initiative of the church itself. Religiously orientated people have taken leadership, like Martin Luther King, but I don't know how many people in his church would even follow him in the Movement, you see.

WARREN: You find a great deal of bitterness from responsible Negro leaders, who say, "I'm sick of Christianity. It's been a trap!"

MRS. HARVEY: I think this is because they don't differentiate between what Christianity has become, the way it has been institutionalized, and what Christianity really is—as Jesus lived it, as we have it in His teachings and His practices.

So I ask Mrs. Harvey what she thinks of Kenneth Clark's view of Martin Luther King.*

* See page 23.

MRS. HARVEY: The matter of nonviolent action, I think, toward the dominant groups in American life has been the pattern of the Negroes generally throughout the years. He took the razor to himself to get his frustrations off—i.e., within his own racial group on Saturday nights. Or he'd beat his wife, but he never would take—I wouldn't say he never would, but very rarely—this overt aggressive action against the dominant group. Negroes have a sense of humor about them [the whites], laughing at them—their weaknesses and foibles and also a sort of trying to outsmart them. I think that the Negro pattern of reaction in American life has been toward this nonviolence, rather than away from it—a continuous pattern in the life of the Negro.

WARREN: Dr. Clark's idea would deny the Christian premise?

MRS. HARVEY: That's true. The other thing I think is that Dr. Clark doesn't reckon with the three kinds of love that Dr. King is talking about, you know. You don't love a person as a brother, you don't love him sexually—and you don't love him because of any of the things that he does to you, or against himself. But you love him because he's a child of God, just as you are a child of God. And this is the type of love he is talking about.

WARREN: Dr. Clark says that Dr. King is applauded by whites because he comforts them—he continues to stereotype the Negro as, you know, passive, unresisting.

MRS. HARVEY: Some whites who applaud him do so out of genuine appreciation of his efforts to change the image of America. Others may erroneously think his nonviolence means acceptance of the status quo when really it is an aggressive force which speaks to the conscience of the wrongdoer.

WARREN: What about Negroes and Dr. King? Do they think he flatters the white man's preconceptions?

MRS. HARVEY: I've heard what the Black Muslims say about him. But I've never run into any individual who says that. But I have run into individual Negroes who feel that he is agitating too much. And some feel that he is in it for personal gain, or merit.

WARREN: How widespread do you think such notions are?

MRS. HARVEY: Not very widespread. But there is another thought that I want to get into the hopper, while you are talking about nonviolence on the part of Negroes. There is a feeling, and the COFO people will verify it perhaps. There are many Negroes that feel they have been patient too long, and that the Justice Department is not doing anything about their grievances, and therefore they feel that they must take things into their own hands, and here you have the possibility of violence erupting from the Negro against the white group.

WARREN: What would that mean—literally?

MRS. HARVEY: Well—it would mean a fight—it would mean mob violence, it would mean physical action with guns and knives. Now this would solve nothing, it would compound the problem, is the way I personally feel about it, but they— this stuff is so built up in them and all these frustrations—the things you heard about today at the meeting, about going down to register and the Registrar disappears. And so they stay all day, and somebody comes and says, "Well, we've got to close up now, come back tomorrow." You see, all these harassments and frustrations are just at the explosion point for a lot of people.

WARREN: Would there be selected targets for this violence —say a particular person or persons?

MRS. HARVEY: No—indiscriminate, uncontrolled.

WARREN: Any white man—any white child—anyone gets it if he is passing?

MRS. HARVEY: Yes. Uncontrolled.

*   *   *

This is nine years after the murder of George W. Lee, in Belzoni, and of Lamar D. Smith, in Brookhaven, workers for voter registration. This is seven years after the murder of Clinton Melton, in Glendora. This is five years after the lynching of Mack Charles Parker, in Poplarville. This is three years after the shooting of Herbert Lee. This is two years after the shooting of Corporal Roman Duckworth. This is one year after the machine-gunning near Greenwood of James Triss, a worker for Snick. This is eight months after the murder of Medgar Evers. This is nine days after the murder of Louis Allen, who had signed a statement that he had seen a member of the State Legislature kill Herbert Lee, without provocation, and had offered to testify if given protection by the Justice Department. This is two days after the trial of Byron de la Beckwith has ended in a hung jury.

There have been no convictions. In some cases there have not even been indictments.*

This is, also, two days after the riot at Jackson College. As I rode across Mississippi with three workers in the Movement, we talked about the riot and one said, "If it has to come, that maybe was the time to let her rip. It was about ready to blow. They would have run wild, right through the yards and over the lawns and fences and flower beds of the white section, with rocks and bottles through the plate glass. That would have been it. Nothing could have stopped it. Then troops. Then the showdown."

Mrs. Harvey does not want it to end that way. But she is afraid that it may.

*   *   *

She has, in fact, some hope for a settlement. With the founding of her organization, Woman Power Unlimited, which came into existence to take care of the needs of the imprisoned freedom riders in 1961, there grew a new notion of what might be done.

MRS. HARVEY: We began to take a look at ourselves and say, well, maybe there is another way of life that's possible even right here. Maybe we don't have to send our children to Los Angeles and New York and Chicago for jobs when they get educated. Maybe they can get their jobs right here if we do certain things ourselves within our community—why not stay here and do something about it?

WARREN: Is it a problem of organization?

MRS. HARVEY: A lot of the problem is the lack of creative

* A member of the Advisory Committee of the Civil Rights Commission told me that, in the first five months of 1964, there were five unsolved murders around Natchez; and since then the number of unsolved crimes has mounted.

leadership. The lack of leadership has been great in the white group as well as the Negro group, because so many of our best people have been siphoned off, some of the best minds.

They go, she says, for jobs. And as she says this I am thinking of James Silver, whom I do not know, and of his presidential address before the Southern Historical Association, at Asheville, North Carolina, on November 7, 1963. He says that they go for jobs and opportunities. But he says something else, too: He says that they go because they can't stand the world of "double-think" and "double-talk," and the brutal and brutalizing pressure to conform to the values of the "closed society." But some, he says, go for the simplest reason of all: they are driven out.

But who drives them? So I ask Mrs. Harvey the same question I had asked Mr. Elie, in New Orleans.

WARREN: James Baldwin says that the Southern mob does not represent the will of the Southern majority.

MRS. HARVEY: I think that makes sense. But the mob, of course, gets the publicity. The real tragedy in the South is the people of good will who remain silent—who let the mob take over.

But she clings to the idea that a reconciliation is possible—even saying that "the poor whites and the poor Negroes" can have a rapport and a working relationship.

MRS. HARVEY: I can't tell you how, but I don't really feel that they have a great antipathy for each other. I think they have been used by the power structure—pitted against each other—and that they could work together, given an opportunity to do so. I had an experience the other day, sitting in the bus station in Hammond, Louisiana. I was sitting in what was formerly the white side of the station, and I was the only Negro there. All the other Negroes were sitting where they had been accustomed to sit before the law was changed. I had eaten breakfast and taken a seat one seat away from a white lady. She leaned over to me and said: "Are you an insurance lady?" I had one of my business brief

cases with Collins Insurance Company stamped on it. She
began to talk. She was definitely "poor white," but she
didn't have any resentment because I was there—she didn't
mind other people staring because we were talking. She was
talking about her personal problems. I think this is pretty
typical. Now if she could get a job where Negroes were
working, and they were all together, being benefited by it,
I think it would work out.

WARREN: Do you think—as do some people, Baldwin among
them—that the South cannot change until the North changes?

MRS. HARVEY: That would not be my feeling. My reason for
remaining in the South and working and struggling is because
I am hoping the South will point the way—because the problem is so serious and intense here. I hope we can point the
way for the whole nation.

* * *

I recall what, in the spring, one eminent journalist, who had
lately worked in Mississippi, told me was on order by the Jackson
Police Department: two searchlight trucks with protected lights,
two hundred new tear-gas masks, two hundred new shotguns, twenty-
nine new motorcycles with shotgun scabbards, three convoy trucks
(military surplus) with orange covers to designate anti-riot squadron.
I remember the special "nigger truck"—a tractor trailer, with steel
cages. I remember the two buildings at the Fair Grounds with hog-
wire on the windows. Of the expected army of voter-registration
workers, Mayor Allen Thompson said: "I think we can take care
of twenty-five thousand."

They were getting ready for summer.

Were they getting ready to "point the way for the whole nation?"

: 4 :

The next morning I am sitting in the private office of Charles
Evers, upstairs at 1072 Lynch Street, the same building where the
meeting had taken place the day before. He arrives, forty minutes
late—a tall dark man in his early forties, athletic looking, with

large hands, a smallish, tall-skulled, well-formed head, a baritone voice. He is the man who, with that air of angry authority, yesterday had ordered guards put on the doors of the meeting. But now he is not angry, he is harried and apologetic. He can't stay, he just wants to apologize, for he has to rush off to the office of the Chief of Police, on a "brutality case."

I wait, and study the office. Under the glass on the desk are several items—a poll-tax receipt, two newspaper clippings, a white card with the words written, in ink: "No man is ruined until he has lost his courage." On the desk is a name block: MR. C. EVERS. On the ledge of the long set of windows overlooking the street, placid among books and photographs, is another name block: MR. EVERS. It is, clearly, the name block of the dead brother.

On the end wall of the longish, rectangular room, facing the desk, are several photographs. One of Medgar Evers is in the center. To the left is a picture of President Kennedy, with Charles Evers and the widow and children of Medgar Evers—a picture taken in the White House, after the hero's funeral of Medgar Evers in Arlington Cemetery. To the right of the picture of the dead man is one of Charles Evers in a radio broadcasting room; he was a disc jockey in Decatur, Mississippi.

On the door to the outer office hangs a large chart of the Judicial System of the United States.

The gas heater hums. Now and then a car passes in the street below. Outside a typewriter clicks. There are muted voices, once or twice laughter, muted but with the timbre of Negro laughter. I notice another name block on the ledge under the row of windows: BURT LANCASTER.

President Kennedy in the White House, the chart of the Judicial System of the United States and Burt Lancaster: the world outside, beyond Mississippi.

A young man, white, comes into the inner office, where I am waiting. He is big, husky (though running a little toward fat), handsome, sloppily dressed (college sloppy) in rather tight dark trousers, and a T-shirt, light brown. His name, I learn, is Neil Goldschmidt, a graduate of the University of Oregon; he has put in a hitch in Washington working for Senator Neuberger of Oregon, and is now with the NAACP. But, he says, he doesn't feel tied to any organization—will "follow principle," his own, if he finds it in conflict with organizational policy. He is going back to school next year, to study law. He allows that if I want to see some interesting people, I have come to the right place.

My notes on the conversation with Goldschmidt put down a half-hour later run:

Not sure Atlanta crisis justified—not planned and not coordinated—situation in Mississippi is that you can't afford any division of opinion [among members of Movement], certainly not in public, but things far enough along in Atlanta to permit that luxury—but the militants wanted a victory, a show, at any cost—Mayor of Atlanta probably acts in reasonably good faith—Chapel Hill same mistake— 80% integrated and it might have been better to proceed by negotiation—in one restaurant of sit-in, owner poured ammonia in mouth of demonstrator and wife urinated on man on floor—why want to integrate such a vile place?

Different organizations always want to know "who gets credit?" NAACP had really given up Mississippi, but CORE and Snick are committed and this has pressured NAACP back in.

It develops that Mr. Evers cannot see me today.

: 5 :

Besides Robert Moses, whom I have seen at the COFO meeting on Sunday, there is another Moses in town—Gilbert Moses, no relation. I find him in the decrepit second-floor office of the *Mississippi Free Press,* an eight-page weekly, with the motto: "The Truth Shall Make You Free."

He is young, vigorous-looking, personable, of a rather pale color. He had left Oberlin because he wanted to be either an actor or playwright and had gone to New York with the hope of working in the off-Broadway theater. He supported himself there as a copy boy for the New York *Post.* In New York he got involved with picketing—the White Castle picketing in the Bronx. He doesn't know, he says, that he can "talk about the motive." But he was— and is—"working on some sort of philosophy, something that has to do with the individual being of the utmost importance, that the individual himself could make a great deal of difference in any system

—an outsider, a new element." So finally, he said to himself: "Not only why me, but why not me, and this catapulted me, sort of, into the demonstrations." He is anti-religious, anti-theological, thinks that religion has been a "great stumbling block," for it prevents thought: "even nonviolence, when it's organized from that basis, is harmful, and Black Muslim religion also." But, he adds: "I am much more in sympathy with the Black Muslim creed than I am with King's philosophy." He admires the "piercing clarity with which Snick approaches the problem—the positive, radical approach." But he belongs to no organization. Perhaps, like Neil Goldschmidt, he does not want to feel committed to an organization, perhaps it violates his philosophy of the individual.

Gilbert Moses keenly feels, he says, the "split of the psyche" of the American Negro. "Negroes have certain unique experiences that a white person is unable to share. I think that it [color] is more of an intangible thing made tangible, an imposed tangibility. This uniqueness means more than other things we actually pride ourselves on, even though we reject the stereotypes—the rhythms, the morality bit, and the sports. There's a certain pride in this *negritude,* which, in fact, encompasses the stereotype that we fought against."

This he connects with his hope of being an artist: "The only way I, as an artist, am able to use my unique experience, is by turning back to the people whence I came, to help them to seek solutions, honor, in a level that would involve Negroes themselves. I think we will have an honest, positive *negritude* only when Negroes go back and work within their own culture to produce their culture."

He is referring, he says, not to African culture, which is not available, but to the American Negro's need to start over again.

I ask him if it is possible that a "Southerner," a man down here on the streets of Jackson, in his blind, blundering way—not a thoughtful man, say—is partly, among other motives, trying to defend his own sense of cultural identity against the pressures of an outside world, and that he has somehow fixed on his relations to the Negro as a necessary aspect to his cultural identity.

And he says: "That's a baited question."

And I: "It's baited—yes. But that doesn't mean I'm trying to dictate an answer."

And he: "Certainly not."

And I: "Any good question is baited."

He begins to answer by saying that "the conservative Southerner tends to be more fundamentally American than perhaps Americans in any other region," but somehow we wander off the point and never get back. Along the way, however, it emerges that he does not intend this "Americanism" as an unmixed compliment: some of the old American attitudes "are almost used as blankets to conceal any further thought."

And certainly, he is much more optimistic about a settlement in his home town of Cleveland, Ohio, than in Mississippi.

Why is he in Mississippi? Not merely to work directly for the cause. He has a very special, personal cause. He is establishing a repertory theater. Already it has such sponsors as James Baldwin and Harry Belafonte. He is already working with a group, including students from Jackson College and Tougaloo, learning techniques for use in traveling. He wants to play in the country, where the "real communities" are, to have "a collective religious phenomenon in the South," "a ritual in favor of thought for farm workers and cotton pickers." To give "propaganda in favor of thinking," and "any good play would be educational and propagandistic at the same time."

I suggest, *Hedda Gabler,* for instance?

And he: "Not with this audience because of the level." Then he adds: "I could direct Mr. Albee."

I am not certain that I see how *Who's Afraid of Virginia Woolf?* is more relevant to the world of the cotton picker than is *Hedda Gabler.* But the plays actually planned are, he says, *Purlie Victorious, Mountain of Stars,* and one of his own which he describes as "a documentary of Jackson, 1963."*

He talks of the attempt of white sympathizers, or workers, to identify with "Negro-ness." The white man adopts their slang, and "whatever dance craze the Negroes are avid about at the moment, he assimilates." But some Negroes approach with distrust any white who does that, he says; and he relates this to the Negro's attitude to those "whites who are so eager to know you because you are a

---

* The Free Southern Theater was in operation in the summer of 1964. In the winter of 1964-65 it did a ten-week tour, mostly in Mississippi, followed by the presentation, at the New School and the American Place Theatre, in New York City, of two plays from its repertory, *Waiting for Godot* and *Purlie Victorious.*

Negro." And that leads to the white liberals in general: "The Negroes have found out that these white liberals with whom they plotted in dark rooms at night really don't want to take the final step, which somehow means to them some sort of amalgamation of the races."

I ask him if he is implying that the Northern liberal is fine as long as he's doing it in Mississippi, and he replies: "We find a lot of absolution of guilt."

I ask what about the notion expressed by many Southern whites and some Negroes, that many of the workers from outside are emotionally unstable. He says that that is not his impression —nor, for what my limited experience is worth, is it mine. But he goes on to add: "There are different ways of looking at it. There are Negroes who join the Movement who are askew, emotionally disturbed. We find hoodlums joining the freedom riders. When I first came down to meet them, I was surprised to find how many would ordinarily have been hanging out in the streets of Cleveland and were now involved in fighting for freedom. I was surprised and disappointed. But you can look at this in two ways—a person trying to find himself through some sort of commitment. And if it's backed by an honest attempt at self-evaluation, if you find things here that you can do, then this would seem to be the path of struggle that everybody should finally go through."

But in general, he says, "the Negroes who come here are, in fact, the most determined and intelligent."

Sitting with us is a young man, recently out of Oberlin, who also works on the *Free Press*—a poet, by the name of Richard Murphy —a very tall, thin, bespectacled young man, slightly awkward in motion, as though fearful that his bones might break, and with an expression marked by a slightly pained, but sometimes beautiful, spirituality. He is white. His voice sometimes sinks to a wisp of sound, as he turns inward. He prefers to have Moses talk.

But once you get accustomed to the voice—the rather charming diffidence—and leave off watching those delicate pale filaments of sound that float across the air like spiderweb in sunlight, Murphy is rewarding. For example, when we talk about time in social change and how this relates to the slogan "Freedom Now," he says: "I wonder if a leader responsible for social change can ever be asked to understand the due process in time."

And I: "Perhaps the leaders do, but know something else, that it's never politic to state it that way."

Murphy: "No, I think then they cease to be leaders."

: 6 :

That evening I rent a car to drive up from Jackson into the Delta —that region of black cotton land, so rich it makes the soles of your feet greasy. With me are three young men, workers in the Movement. One of them is driving my car.

The sun is setting big and red, far away across the flat land, which is sprigged, here and there, by dark groves of trees. The whole western sky is stained like blood. It begins to fade, and now the new dark gathers over the land. Later in the dark, far north of Jackson, we see a glow, then a brilliance of lights, like a city. It is the enormous power plant of the Mississippi Light and Power. Ablaze with lights, glittering like silver, a fantasy, totally unreal, it heaves up out of the darkness of the land.

This, too, like Charles Evers' office, stands for the *outside*, for the world beyond, the world of science, technology, industry, modernity—and the Supreme Court.

We whirl on past. The land flows evenly away from the eye, on all sides, with a heavy, somnolent peace, into darkness. Now and then, up the flat, straight road, a tiny point of light pricks the dark. It hangs there a long time. Then it begins to grow. It is a car coming. The light grows slowly, is suddenly big, blazing at you, the car is hurtling at you, never slackening, ninety miles an hour, and then it snatches past you, ripping the two inches of air between you, with a nasty, nerve-searing sound like ripped tin, and the high-pitched snarl of the motor descends to a thin whine behind you; is suddenly gone.

Along the highways in Mississippi, they used to put up little black skull-and-crossbones signs to mark auto deaths. Sometimes you would find a whole cluster. People would make jokes about such a spot. Then laugh, and slam down the accelerator to the floor. That used to be Mississippi. It still is.

I look down at the speedometer. It is over ninety. I wish the boy who is driving would slow down, and I say so. He does, for a minute.

. . .

Some months later, an anecdote told me by James Farmer, of
CORE, happened to make clear to me why the Snick boy would not
stay slowed down. Medgar Evers had been driving Farmer up this
same road, on the same errand I now had, to make a night call on
Dr. Aaron Henry, the president of the NAACP up at Clarksdale, in
the Delta, and Farmer had shown some apprehension at the speed.
Medgar had said that if you are a black man in Mississippi, you never
let anybody pass you at night, you never let anybody have a chance
to stop you or ditch you. Too many people have been stopped or
ditched.

*   *   *

It is late when we find the Fourth Street Drug Store, which Dr.
Henry owns and operates. Fourth Street is poorly lit, deserted now,
but the store is open. Inside, the store is like a thousand other drug-
stores in small towns, all over the continent—all the odds and ends
that constitute the stock of a drugstore, the truss ads and the aspirin
ads and the nasal-spray ads and pictures of pretty girls brushing
their teeth, the bright ads fading a little, some lost in the shadowy
corners of the store, for the full lights are not on. The evening wears
on, the last customer goes out, nobody passes in the street, the
owner pushes two or three things back into place—the habitual
gesture of the owner shutting up, getting ready to knock off, another
day another dollar. The last light gets switched off. He locks the door,
drops the keys into his pocket, looks up the familiar street into the
familiar shadows. Tomorrow he'll come down the street in daylight
and open the door and it will be another day. In the Fourth Street
Drug Store.

If, during the night, they haven't bombed it again. Or knocked out
the glass.

*   *   *

In the living room of Dr. Henry's house, the guard is waiting. I see
a revolver lying on a little table, a couple of shotgun shells. The
curtains of the windows are drawn tight. The guard is a man of about
thirty, rather tall and limber, lolling back in an easy chair. He has

taken his shoes off and moves silently when he goes to peer through a slit between the curtains. I am not introduced to him, but I do meet the daughter of the family. She seems distrustful and strained. The young men who have come with me stay in the living room with her and the guard.

Dr. Henry takes me back to the bedroom that belongs to him and his wife. The closet door stands ajar. I see a gold slipper lying on its side just inside the closet door. I see the folds of a robe or a dress hanging in that shadow. It is a room like a thousand rooms, the bedroom in the house of a moderately prosperous businessman in a small town.

The house is set near the street, parallel to it, and this bedroom is on the street side. I hear a car pass. I think of the guard peeking through the slit in the curtain. The walls are clapboard, thin. These walls have been raked before with fire from a high-powered rifle.

I ask Dr. Henry how he first got involved in the Movement.

HENRY: I believe it goes back to a point before I could even remember. I remember the traumatic experience of being separated from a lad that I had known since birth, when it came time to go to school. And we were living in the rural. I was born in this county, and his parents and my parents were the best of friends and, of course, Randolph and I became inseparable. And to have to go to one school and he to another at the age of six or seven was one of the early crises of my life, and I just never forgot it.

WARREN: This was a white boy?

HENRY: Yes, Randolph was a white boy, and I understand from my mother that as children, as babies, they would leave him with my mother at times, and me with his mother at times, and we both nursed each other's mother's breast. When it came time to go to school we looked forward to it, and here the great experience we anticipated was so negated by the question of racial prejudice that separated two kids who loved each other dearly.

James Baldwin, in "Fifth Avenue Uptown," has remarked: "The Southerner remembers, historically and in his own psyche, a kind of Eden in which he loved the black people and they loved him."

Is Aaron Henry remembering his own Eden? In any case, the memory is crucial for him.

HENRY: Since that time, I can't remember a time when I was not concerned about the race question.

WARREN: But that's different from actually moving into an organization.

HENRY: I became a member of the NAACP as a high school student, when the senior class of '41, in Coahoma County, were encouraged to take out membership. And in the service there was an immediate need for NAACP philosophy, with the instances of racial bigotry we ran into; and coming out of the service and into college—on the campus of Xavier University, I was—there was a strong civil rights movement.

WARREN: This is after the war?

HENRY: Yes, sir. And upon coming home from college in '50 we did not have an organized NAACP in the community, and in '52 we organized the NAACP here and I became its president and have remained president of the local branch.

WARREN: I know you have been prominent in it—so prominent that, I'm told, you might, on a toss-up, have had the bullet that Medgar Evers got.

HENRY: I've heard that too, we get it from what we consider reliable sources within the news media. I'm not anxious to die, but I'm not afraid of it. One thing that the death of Medgar accomplished for me, it freed me from the fear of it.

I am looking at him out of the side of my eye. He is not looking at me. He is hunched forward in his chair, humping his strong heaviness of shoulders, hands on knees, staring at a spot on the wall, rather low, beyond the dresser. He is not talking to me. He seems to be talking to himself—to be going over some old ground with himself.

I ask if there had not been a deep friendship with Medgar Evers.

HENRY: Yes, sir. It goes back to about '50. We began working in the freedom movement together.

WARREN: There have been acts of violence against you?

HENRY: Well, yes. Our house was bombed and set afire, shot into, the store's been bombed.

WARREN: The store windows have been knocked out, haven't they?

HENRY: Yes, sir. The windows were knocked out pretty frequently. You see what happens—these things usually happen late at night, and some wild, careening cars come through and they shoot at random. Perhaps not aiming, just shooting.

WARREN: Bombing isn't quite that casual, is it?

HENRY: No, the time they bombed the house we were all asleep. The concussion woke us up and, of course, the incendiary set the house afire, and we were able to get the fire out before any serious damage was done to any of the people —any of the family, or any of the visitors who happened to be here at the time.

WARREN: Do you think the bomb was meant to intimidate you, or destroy you?

HENRY: I think it was meant to destroy us.

Dr. Henry has, clearly, made a commitment to the NAACP. I ask him what about criticisms of it from other Negroes. He says that most of the criticisms are "expressions that do not come from the heart, but from the lips, in some passion, and are not really aimed at casting a derogatory picture of the NAACP, but more to cast a pleasant picture of an organization for which the man might have a persuasion, other than the NAACP." He says, too, there is some jealousy, because of the old history, and some criticism for the "moving slower than others would have us move." This leads to the question of dependence on legal action.

HENRY: The NAACP has served as an apparatus to determine actually what the law is—without which there would be no direct action, knowing previously what the final legal outcome is going to be. Now, I don't mind violating many of the Mississippi statutes, but those that I violate I know are in contrast with what is the law on the federal level. I think that the NAACP has clarified this course of direct action. The good old NAACP has established this right in our minds. Were it that the official, legal position had not been established, I doubt very seriously if the protest that we are now waging, of a nonviolent nature, would be continued to be waged in this restrained, dignified manner—because without that hope, the knowing that the United States sanctions what we are doing—then we would be in open rebellion against the country.

This leads to Dr. King and the philosophy of nonviolence. I read him the quotation from Dr. Kenneth Clark.*

HENRY: Well, Dr. King's philosophy is built on the understanding of Christianity. I agree with Dr. Clark that the adoption of the ethic of Christianity is not, shall we say, common sense.

WARREN: It's not *common* human nature either.

HENRY: Christianity is not common human nature.

WARREN: What is it—redeemed human nature?

HENRY: It's redeemed human nature. And only in this context can we understand Dr. King's philosophy, which is the philosophy of many others of us, that Jesus Christ forgave His oppressors and that we must be able to forgive those who oppress us. But King is very careful in identifying what he means by love—love of the oppressor.

WARREN: Some of Dr. King's admirers say that his philosophy is the only basis for a future society in this country.

HENRY: In Ghana and Nigeria and other countries where the Negro has emerged to freedom, he has *driven* out the white oppressor. The land has been left to the blacks. But here in America, our white brother and our black brother are going to be still right here. Therefore, it has to be this symbiotic kind of response and respect, one for the other.

WARREN: How does this relate to the question of the split in the Negro psyche—the sort of thing Du Bois talked about, and others more recently?

HENRY: The desire of the Negro to retain Negro-ness and the assimilation into American culture? My position is, I don't care which develops. I would like to be considered on par with any other man in America, because I was born in my

* See page 23.

father's house. If it's a Negro's desire that he perpetuate as best he can the culture of Africa, of the Negro, well and good. On the other hand, if he wants to be part of the mainstream of American life, and accept his friends because he likes them, rather than because of race—who perhaps develop in time to become tea-colored—I don't think it would cause me to have strong feelings either way.

The Negro's vision of himself in a white man's country: this reminds me of the "rumor test" which, according to a psychiatrist friend of mine, has been given in New Haven in connection with the "human redevelopment" program, and I describe it to Dr. Henry.

WARREN: We start with a picture of several people, some Negroes, some whites. A white man standing in the foreground holds a knife or a razor. The picture is shown to one member of a group of Negroes. He's supposed to tell Number Two what's in the picture. Then Number Two tells Number Three. So on through ten or fifteen people. Invariably—they—

HENRY: Get it wrong!

WARREN: Get it wrong. The person now reported to hold the knife is a Negro. What does this mean?

HENRY: I think that the stereotype here is perhaps answered in jest by Dick Gregory. Dick said that the fact that Negroes are usually depicted as carrying a knife is because the white people won't sell us guns. It's a sort of get-even weapon—you can buy a butcher knife and take it home to the kitchen. But I see as many white fellows with knives as Negroes.

WARREN: Certainly, that's true.

HENRY: But a Negro would come nearer getting arrested for it, and so we get more publicity for it.

WARREN: Well, in any case, in New Haven, far away, a significant number of Negroes, it seems, accept this white man's stereotype and put the knife in the Negro's hand.

HENRY: Mississippi is a mutation of America. The bigotry in Mississippi is perhaps more overt than in New Haven, but wherever you have Western culture, why I don't know, there is always with it the existence of white supremacy. I haven't seen *Pravda* espousing the Negro cause to the point you see Negroes in the Presidium, either.

We come back to his personal situation, his relation to the local police, a long complicated story, the harassing of his family—the telephone calls at any hour of day or night.

HENRY: The calls are about some kind of violence or vulgarities or obscenities, which no man would want his wife to put up with. But she's able to ask back with a question like, "Certainly you mustn't be a Christian, or you wouldn't do this?" When Rebecca, our daughter, answers the phone and a man says, "I just shot your daddy," she just looks at the phone and says, "Aw, fellow, are you kidding?"

WARREN: Your guards are armed?

HENRY: They are armed, yes, sir!

WARREN: With guards here you've had no further trouble?

HENRY: No, and I suppose it's due to the fact that after Medgar was killed I went to the Chief of Police and revealed to him the source of information I had about threats to my life. He told me he had heard threats too. You see, he and I have been involved in libel difficulty. At one time I was arrested on a morals charge.

WARREN: Here?

HENRY: No—in an adjoining county, where the Chief of Police of my city and the prosecuting attorney of my county were the only interrogators. In fact, they later brought a libel suit against me because I had told them that I felt they had had a part in concocting this fabrication. So now I asked about the City Police Department supplying me protection, and he told me he didn't have the men to spare, so we hired a guard, and the next couple of nights he came down to the house and arrested my guard and took my gun and—

WARREN: The Chief of Police—of Clarksdale?

HENRY: Of Clarksdale, yes. But that set off a furor in the community and many people donated us now more guns than we had before, and of course, there have been no more confiscations.

. . .

When a car passes in the street, Dr. Henry does not break a sentence, does not change the rhythm, does not turn. But you can sense a sharpening, a focusing, of his being.

I read Dr. Henry the quotation from James Baldwin that says the Southern mob does not represent the will of the majority.

HENRY: Yes, I think that's true—and I think that many people in the South are not permitted, because of real or imagined fears, to espouse the goodness that they really feel in their hearts, and—

Some weeks before, in conversation, Vann Woodward had said: "The big trouble down here is fear—and it's the fear the white folks have of each other."

Dr. Henry goes on to say that often political opportunism prompts the fanning of racial bigotry. Expediency, he says, and not hatred or revulsion.

HENRY: For when you study the history of men like Vardaman and Bilbo, you will find that in many instances these men sired Negro children, by Negro women, which gives you to understand that they really didn't hate the Negro.

Political exediency, he says. But the Negro is going to get the vote and—

HENRY: —and once the Negro acquires the right to vote, you are going to have a whole lot of white people talking about how good they used to be to Negroes even back then, and how they felt about Negroes even then, but were afraid to say it. I think it is sort of unbelievable to the white majority, too, that the Negro really holds no vengeance about what happened yesterday, and if they, the white people, will really begin right now, they'd be surprised how fast and how easily we forgive. But the white man is afraid his deeds are going to follow him, and he feels that once the Negro gets in power, the Negro is going to remember all of the dirty deals that he

has gotten from the white community. But if we get the right
to vote, it is our determination to really show America how
democracy can really work, how the freedom we seek for
ourselves will be definitely shared by everybody else—because we realize that freedom is a peculiar kind of com-
modity. You can only keep it by giving it away. None of us
have the vengeance and the hatred to carry.

WARREN: This feeling is fairly general, you say?

HENRY: Yes, sir.

If what Dr. Henry says is true—that the Negro does not harbor
the desire for vengeance—then the Southern whites are all the more
stupid in not following the classic pattern by which a ruling class
absorbs and channels the thrust from below. Such a class, understanding the logic of a historical moment, can make concessions
gracefully, can even, with an honest idealism, initiate programs,
and thus can maintain political influence and social guidance on the
form and operation of the new system. But, with what seems an
insane disregard of the future, the segregationists drive toward a
stark polarization. Whom the gods would destroy—

WARREN: I have a quotation from a Negro social scientist
saying that the Negro's plight in the South will be lightened
only when the plight of the poor white is. What about that?

HENRY: I think it is pretty much a true statement. The power
structure for too long has manipulated the Negro against the
poor white and the poor white against the Negro. Every time
there's a crime committed against a Negro, they say, "Oh, it
wasn't us—the big white people—that did it, we don't do
that, it's the rednecks." And they have told the white illiterates
that every crime, particularly a sex crime, is committed by a
Negro upon a white woman. And of course they do this because sex is the thing that the most limited mind can com-
prehend, that's the scarecrow they use. Now, to me, that's a
serious indictment by the white male of his white woman—to
feel that the only thing that keeps her from embracing every
Negro she sees is because the white man keeps his foot on
the Negro's neck. And this thing about Negro men seeking in-
satiably the association of white women—now most Negro

men I know wish to God our white brothers were satisfied with their own women, as we are with ours. You can hardly come to any Negro neighborhood at night without seeing some car with a white man circling, trying to find some Negro lady to have pleasure with. Well, now, my position is this— if she wants him and he wants her, that's two people's business.

WARREN: A private matter?

HENRY: A private matter. And if they want to get married— that's a private matter, too. I take a dim view on the legality of my state that negates the possibility of holy matrimony between the races, but there is nothing about adultery and fornication. Now I think the best thing that could happen to Mississippi would be an alliance between the Negroes and the poor whites—a Populist movement that would break the stranglehold that the power structure now holds on both the Negro and the poor white.

We wander over several other topics. I ask why Negroes are slow to try to register—is it fear? Not of reprisal, so much, he says, but fear of being embarrassed, of failing the test, of showing ignorance. I ask about the split between the Negro middle class and the mass, and he says that white pressure has done much for Negro unity, that this is because of the involvement of the children of the "black bourgeois," that "once Momma's fair-haired boy is in jail and has been slapped around by the police," she is ready for the "civil rights struggle." On the question of the Negro's vested interest in segregation, Dr. Henry, like Nils Douglas, back in New Orleans, says that "in any sociological change, there are going to be casualties, and the Negro people have got to be prepared to take their chances in the open market, and not rely upon any advantage that race might give." As for the hung jury in the Beckwith trial, he calls it "the second act of a well-written drama."

Is it? That had seemed—and still, in sober judgment, seems— absurd. Absurd—even though in the second trial the jury is again hung, the judge has allowed Beckwith out on $10,000 bail (quickly raised by admirers in his home town of Greenwood), and the prosecutor, Waller, says that the defense has been stronger this time; it may be of no use to push for a third trial.

I am sure that the trial was not a well-written drama. But I am sure now that Aaron Henry is surer than ever that it was.
We pass on to anti-Semitism among Negroes.

HENRY: If this is anti-Semitism, I'd like to have it defined as such. In the fight for human dignity we have never under-estimated our opposition, but we have overestimated our support. We thought that naturally we would have the Jewish people on our side. We thought that naturally we would have labor on our side. Because the enemies of all three are usually found in the same group. But we don't have the Jews sup-porting us.*

WARREN: In Mississippi?

HENRY: No.

WARREN: But you do elsewhere?

HENRY: Yes, elsewhere. And it is this image of the Jew on a national level that caused us to feel that we could count on Jews here. But frankly, some of our oppressors are found in the Jewish community, which is a statement I am sorry to have to make.

WARREN: Is this because Mississippi Jews, for instance, are more vulnerable even than Gentiles to social pressure?

HENRY: I think so. But I would think they would know that once the white man clubs or clobbers the Negro into submis-mission, the Jew probably is next.

*   *   *

But meanwhile there has been irony in the morning paper—in the headlines of *The New York Times* of April 22, 1964.

* Anti-Semitism among urban Negroes is sometimes said to be a form of displaced aggression, the rent-collector and the storekeeper being his obvious targets. But in *Black Boy,* Richard Wright, raised in back-country Mississippi, says that "an attitude of antagonism or distrust toward Jews was bred in us from childhood." And Du Bois, in *The Souls of Black Folk,* makes constant reference to "the Jew," "the Jew fell heir," "owned now by a Russian Jew," "only a Jew could squeeze more blood from debt-cursed tenants," "the Jews have seized it." It is summed up: "thrifty and avaricious Yankees, shrewd and unscrupulous Jews. Into the hands of these men the Southern laborers, white and black, have fallen; and this to their sorrow." I do not know how much, if at all, Du Bois can be said to mirror the general feeling in the South among non-Jewish whites.

NEGROES ATTACK JEWISH STUDENTS

15 Boys and 2 Rabbis Hurt
in Melee in Brooklyn

The injured students range in age, according to the *Times,* from 9 to 12 years old. The attackers, "some armed with bottles, sticks, garbage-can covers and tire chains," were heard to yell anti-Semitic epithets and shout "you don't belong in this country."

*   *   *

I ask if the younger generation of whites in Mississippi is changing its attitude on the race question.

HENRY: This is a thing I would like to believe, but when I observed the riots at the University of Mississippi, and observed boys with fuzz on their chins—and girls who still wore too much lipstick, not knowing really how to be well-groomed. And realizing that these kids from the day they were born had heard only that the Supreme Court was not the law of the land—and this had been drummed into the minds and hearts of these kids in their formative years. I would like to say that we can count on the younger ones to be more tolerant—but when you realize that the greater amount of violence, the bricks that were thrown, the people who were knocked off stools in sit-ins, the kids who bombed our house, they were nineteen and twenty-two.

WARREN: You identified them?

HENRY: They were captured the same night, and we understand that each one had about five hundred dollars in his pocket.

WARREN: Paid to do it?

HENRY: We think so. But still that is an image of youth expressing racial intolerance.

WARREN: I've heard it said that the riots at Oxford set back progress ten years—the effect on the young.

HENRY: I think it was that riot that has really hurled us into what can become a new era. I say this because prior to the riot, our contact with the campus, the University, was next to nothing. Since the riot, almost weekly, sometimes daily, there are students and faculty persons who come by here just to exchange ideas and views. These students and faculty would not have dared to be seen in the company of the president of the NAACP prior to the riot. The riot actually freed them.

WARREN: Well, that would seem to prove that there's something to be said for the younger generation.

HENRY: Some young and some old, yes.

He tells me, too, that a number of the white Methodist ministers (Dr. Henry is a Methodist) in Mississippi are working to get rid of the jurisdictional system of church organization which supports segregation—to "get a church doctrine, a legality to preach the brotherhood of man." I ask him about people like Ira Harkey, the editor of the Pascagoula *Chronicle,* and the editorial, edged in mourning black, on the front page of the Clarksdale paper, when in 1956, a jury failed to convict a man named Kimbell, accused of the cold-blooded killing of a young Negro.

HENRY: It was a courageous act. It reflects the thinking of a man named Guy Clark, who actually served as the advertising manager, but was a liberal force in the Clarksdale *Press Register.* I don't think you'd find an editorial of that nature today.

WARREN: What became of him?

HENRY: He died of a heart attack. Guy was an heir of the founders of the city—almost a real liberal, a very good man.

WARREN: A man who, because of his social position, felt free to express his views?

HENRY: He'd been expressing them all along, so that editorial was nothing unusual.

WARREN: Do you find that kind of maverick very often? The man of privileged position who uses his privilege for independence?

HENRY: Not very often. The fear of social ostracism, the fear of being called a nigger-lover, and mostly the fear of the children being tagged—"Your daddy is a nigger-lover"—

that pressure keeps many people from being the kind of good men at heart they are.

*   *   *

Dr. Henry believes in that goodness of heart. He believes that this is what must be liberated to fulfill itself. Somewhere back in his mind is the image of the little Randolph, the friend whom the world snatched from him. The world must be changed.

He knows what he wants of the changed world. It is reported that at an inter-racial meeting some time back—yes, strangely enough, there are still such events in Mississippi, ignored, unrecognized, denied—an old lady, white, asked Dr. Henry what the Negro wants. And he replied: "What you got."

No more, no less.

And now to me he says: "I think that my white brother owes me a deep debt of gratitude when I permit him to give me my rights piecemeal. They're mine now—he's lucky I don't grab them all right now."

*   *   *

Here is one more passage of our dialogue:

WARREN: Myrdal gives what he would consider to have been a rational program for the reconstruction of the South in 1865.

HENRY: Is this from *An American Dilemma*?

WARREN: Yes. He says, among other provisions, that there should have been compensation for the slaves emancipated, that an adequate amount of land should have been expropriated to accommodate the freedmen, but with compensation to the Southern owners. Does this make sense?

HENRY: I'd like to answer it my way.

WARREN: Please do.

HENRY: I take the position that if the white community had accorded my grandma and my grandpa, at the time they were freed, recognition for labor they had given free, that they could have lived like millionaires forever. The big thing wrong with the way the slaves were freed was none of us possessed the land. And from land come all things that are conducive to life. Even after the Negro began to work and acquire land, it was not too long before the white man who owned the land in the first place had connived and somehow secured all the land back, and the Negro reverted to a share-cropper. So it doesn't disturb my morality at all to advocate that we now become serious considerators of a land-reform program.

WARREN: On a program with compensation or without?

HENRY: With compensation, yes.

WARREN: Would you have been for compensation in '65?

HENRY: I don't really know.

WARREN: That's Myrdal's big point, of course.

HENRY: I don't really know. When I understand the human labor for free that these plantation owners used, I don't really know whether they were entitled.

WARREN: Myrdal's point is that there was a bankrupt economy and the fact that it was left bankrupt is a contributing factor in our present situation.

HENRY: I think the big mistake was removing the federal troops too soon. I think—

He has veered away.

I think we can understand why. It is very human that he should. But forgetting 1865, I believe that he is telling the truth when he says that for 1965 he does not "have the vengeance and the hatred to carry."

: 7 :

Number 1017 Lynch Street, the headquarters of Snick, is a clean, white, rather new store front, a big glass window, as for display, on each side, door in middle. Inside there is an empty space, then a third of the way down the length, an office has been boxed off, leaving a wide passage to the right. Toward the back is a much larger space, with another office boxed off at the rear.

I have come to keep a nine A.M. appointment with Robert Moses. He is not here.

NOTEBOOK:

Cement floor, big battered picnic table, with empty Coke bottles and piles of papers, desk across from it, totally cluttered—floor with cigarette butts and trash—and brisk young woman (white, lanky, spinsterish, sharp nose) sweeping floor (charwoman-secretary), young colored man, student type, who walks about muttering histrionically (for my benefit?), "Oh, America, land of the free," then sighs—now and then an appreciative sound from the lanky girl.

He: "I'd help out if things weren't so chaotic. I don't know what to do." Does begin to help, collecting her sweepings in big cardboard box.

Girl turns to me: "Mr. Moses used to be on time, but not since he got married." I sit on a folding metal chair, that has been mashed forward by violence or a too heavy load, and it slowly spills me forward if I don't brace my feet as I write. A large dog, rather like an Irish setter, comes out of rear office, retires. Sound of crunching bone in office. Negro boy goes into rear office, softly picks guitar in that privacy.

Along the wall are stacks of cartons of books (many half burst open), contributions to library for Negro children (not permitted to use Public Library). On walls two large tacked-up maps, one USA, other Miss., posters for registration, one a picture of two children sitting forlornly on steps of shack, and words: GIVE THEM A FUTURE IN MISSISSIPPI—other poster full of upward-stretched arms, and the big word: NOW.

Girl on phone calls out to boy: "You know where Doug is?"

Boy from office: "He's off sleeping in my sleeping bag." Picks guitar back there.

Telephone rings in office. Boy picks up phone: "Listen, we need a five-hundred-dollar bond—two situations—can put up property for one but need peace bond—yes, you sent a sixteen-hundred-dollar bond but that's not enough."

Now 9:20. Two very young boys—16?—come in, wander about, as on a stage—one pats the dog that is now out of back office, they go out.

One of the young boys re-enters blankly, picks up a book, reads. I see another copy, pick up, Living in Our Democracy, *by Deveroux and Aker, about fifth- or sixth-grade level, a gift from California. Boy pores over it, sucking cigarette.*

*   *   *

Moses comes, preoccupied, unsmiling behind his big glasses, blue denim trousers, white shirt, open collar, dark denim jacket; greets me, offers aimless abstract handshake.

Moses decides the office is too confused for an interview, and we go up the street to Number 1072, back into the now empty auditorium, where the meeting had been on Sunday. We set up the recorder on a small table in the rear.

WARREN: This is Robert Parris Moses.

MOSES: I am with the Student Nonviolent Coordinating Committee.

WARREN: In Jackson, Mississippi. Where were you born, Mr. Moses?

MOSES: In Harlem, raised in upper Harlem, went to school in Harlem until high school, and then I went to Stuyvesant High School, downtown. We took an exam, a city-wide exam to get in.

WARREN: What was the ratio of Negroes?

MOSES: Out of a graduating class of a few thousand, not more than a handful were Negroes.

WARREN: Did Negroes try for it?

MOSES: Over a city-wide basis my impression would be that there was usually no effort, really, in the Negro junior high schools to prepare people for the tests and encourage them to take it.

WARREN: Was there apathy among the students—the kids?

MOSES: They'd have the feeling it was something out of their range.

WARREN: I hear it said that part of the problem of voter registration is the fear of not passing.

MOSES: The fear of being embarrassed.

WARREN: Let's cut back to your career.

MOSES: I graduated from Stuyvesant in '52, then I went to Hamilton College. I graduated in '56, and went to graduate school, at Harvard, in philosophy, and stayed a year and a half. I picked up an M.A. at the end of my first year, then we had family trouble—my mother died the next year, my father was hospitalized, and I dropped out. Then I got a job teaching at Horace Mann—that was '58—and stayed there three years. Then came down here.

WARREN: Were you ambitious for an academic career when you went to Harvard?

MOSES: Well, I wanted to get the doctorate. I liked philosophy, I wanted to study. I wasn't sure I would teach—but there wasn't anything else at that time I wanted to do.

WARREN: How did you make the shift to active participation in the Movement?

MOSES: It was really a big break. I wasn't active at all until 1960, when the sit-ins broke out. It seemed to me something different, something new—and if—I had had a feeling for a long time—

WARREN: Before this you had a feeling?

MOSES: Yes. There was a continual build-up and frustration—back I guess as early as high school. And then in the teaching—confronting at every point the fact that as a Negro—I mean, first that you had to be treated as a Negro and you couldn't really be accepted as an individual yet—even at any level of the society you happened to penetrate.

WARREN: You wouldn't have felt it, you think, if you had taken your doctorate, then gone to a good college to teach?

MOSES: I don't know. But the fact was I gradually got the feeling that no matter what I did it would always be there, even though things were better and different than, say, my father's time.

WARREN: Had your father had ambitions like your own?

MOSES: Probably yes. But he was caught in the Depression, with two families to support. He had finished high school but he hadn't gone to college—there was no money—then he got a job in the armory and decided to keep that—I don't know, we had long talks about it, talks which I can now see were really about the question of opportunity, about whether he was satisfied or not—you know, his whole purpose in life. Anyway, he had decided to put his energies into his personal family. There were three of us and he wanted to see us all through school and college.

WARREN: It sounds as though you were very close to him.

MOSES: Yes.

WARREN: How do you respond to Dr. King's philosophy?

MOSES: We don't agree with it, in a sense. The majority of the students are not sympathetic to the idea that they have to love the white people that they are struggling against. But there are a few who have a very religious orientation. And there's a constant dialogue at meetings about non-violence and the meaning of nonviolence.

WARREN: Nonviolence for Snick is tactical, is that it?

MOSES: For most of the members it is tactical, it's a question of being able to have a method of attack rather than to be always on the defensive.

WARREN: What about the effect King had at moments of crisis in Birmingham?

MOSES: There's no question that he had a great deal of influence with the masses. But I don't think it's in the direction of love. It's in a practical direction—that is, whatever you believe, you simply can't afford to have a general breakdown of law and order. And in the end everybody has to live together. Negroes understand this very well, but they put it in terms of "When they're all gone we'll still be here, and we have to live with the people here."

WARREN: "They all" being the workers who come in and then go away next week?

MOSES: Yes—but we try to send workers to communities where they can stay and live.

WARREN: The objection of the local Negro might have either of two meanings—a positive one, a vision of a society of men living together under law—and a negative one, a fear of reprisal after the outside workers have left.

MOSES: Exactly. They mean it largely in the negative sense. But in the end there can be an appeal they understand—that is, in the end the Negroes and the whites are going to have to share the land, and the less overlay of bitterness, the more possible to work out a reconciliation.

WARREN: Some Negroes say that such a reconciliation may come more easily in the South, because of a common background and a shared history, than in the great anonymous Northern cities.

MOSES: Well—I really don't know. The country has such tremendous problems—I mean, every time you try and get a break-through in, say, the Negro problem, you run into a deeper, tremendous problem that the whole country has to face. Jobs, the question of education—these things are tied so deeply into problems that run deep into the major institutions of the country. And the whole question of automation, and armament. I get lost. I don't see ahead to what the shape of this country will look like in ten years. The fantastic changes—as deep, say, as the Industrial Revolution.

We talk a little about more specific issues. I ask him about busing to balance schools racially in great cities like New York and Washington. He has been far removed from the issue, he says, down here in Mississippi—and if you go to a little town like Glendora or Liberty or Greenwood it is another world. But he thinks that the whole school system, everywhere, aside from the question of race, is failing to meet the needs of the times, that the level of education is the immediate key, not integration as such. But both education and integration are tied together with housing and employment in a vicious circle, with only some ten or fifteen per cent—the rising Negro middle class—able to break out, and with the lag of the Negro's earning, on the national percentage, becoming more and more marked. But the poor white man, the unskilled man, is caught, too, in the same process: "They're the people who don't have a real voice in Congress"—who are outside the umbrella of organized labor, with the Negro.

WARREN: Have you suffered violence?

MOSES: Once I was attacked on the way to the courthouse—two Negro farmers and myself. Going to register, and walking down the main street three young fellows came up and began to pick an argument—they singled me out and began to beat on me. I had about eight stitches on the top of my head.*

WARREN: With their fists?

MOSES: Well, apparently—but it turned out after, he had a knife which was closed. We went to trial, and a couple of days later he was acquitted. We came back to town—this little town—Liberty—a town of maybe a thousand people. It has a long and vicious history. Just last week one of the farmers down there was killed and—

WARREN: He had consented to be a witness in a murder trial, hadn't he?

MOSES: Lewis told the truth to the FBI, but the local authorities, he had told them what they wanted to hear.

WARREN: Then told the FBI the truth and was willing to testify if given protection?

MOSES: Yes, and we believe that the FBI leaked this to the local authorities, and the Sheriff, and the Deputy Sheriff came out, you know, and told them—Lewis—what they had learned.† And they had been picking on him ever since— that was in September '61. At one point a deputy sheriff broke his jaw—and then they killed him. With a shotgun.

WARREN: Have there been any arrests on that?

---

* The assailant was Billy Jack Caston, a cousin of the local sheriff and the son-in-law of a State Representative, F. H. Hurst. Howard Zinn, *The New Abolitionists.*

† The charge that in the South the FBI is packed with Southern-born agents and is racist is not uncommonly made by Negroes. It is alleged, for example, that Dr. King advised civil rights workers not to report to the FBI acts of violence in Albany, Georgia, because the agents were Southern. To this, Hoover replied that King is "the most notorious liar in the country," and asserted that four out of the five agents in Albany were Northern and "that seventy per cent of the agents in the South were born in the North." (*The New York Times,* November 19, 1964.)

Since that time Dr. King and Mr. Hoover have met for an "amicable discussion" of their differences. "I sincerely hope," King said, "we can forget the confusions of the past and get on with the job . . . of providing freedom and justice for all citizens of this nation." The issue, of course, is not really the percentage of Southern-born agents of the FBI working in the South. Negroes have not been alone in protesting against what the American Civil Liberties Union has called "the absence of a psychology of commitment [in the FBI] to enforcing laws which guarantee Negroes equal rights." The ACLU has suggested a separate unit in the FBI to investigate civil rights violations. (*The New York Times,* December 2, 1964.)

MOSES: I doubt that there will be.

WARREN: Do you believe that the leak was intentional?

MOSES: I believe that, and we said as much to the Justice Department.

WARREN: Back to you, have you had other attacks?

MOSES: Last year in Greenwood we were driving along.* Some white people had been circling the town—about three or four carloads. One followed us out of town—there were three of us in the car—and they opened up about seven miles out of town—just bullets rained all through the car—the driver had a bullet in his neck, and he was slumped over in my lap, and we went off the road. We had to grab the wheel and stop the car. He had a forty-five lodged about an inch from his spine. None of the rest of us were hit—just shattered with glass. This is all interesting because Beckwith—the fellow who was tried for killing Medgar—well, the people who shot us that the police arrested—there were some arrests on that—they answered to the same general description as Beckwith—middle-aged, middle-class people. They've never been brought to trial.

WARREN: The same type as Beckwith?

MOSES: I think there was a conspiracy up there—and we wrote letters and sent telegrams to the Civil Rights Commission asking for an investigation. Of course, they say there're no grounds justifying—no grounds.

WARREN: You are just married, aren't you?

MOSES: Yes.

WARREN: What view does your wife take of your hazardous occupation?

MOSES: Well—that's hard to say because she doesn't—I mean you don't really confront her. I mean, you just go on living.

WARREN: You take it day by day?

MOSES: Otherwise, there's no real way to confront that except to—within yourself, try to—you have to overcome the fear.

---

* The companions were Randolph Blackwell, of the Voters Education Project in Atlanta, and Jimmy Travis, twenty years old, ex-freedom rider, now member of the Snick staff. Travis was operated on and survived. The episode is one of a long series of acts of violence.

And that took me quite a while, you know—quite a while.
WARREN: Can you put your philosophy to work on that?
MOSES: Not the Harvard seminar. It goes back when I was
in college and I had a French professor who did a lot of work
in twentieth century literature, and I read a lot of Camus. And
I've picked it up again. When I was in jail this last time I
read through *The Rebel* and *The Plague* again. The main
essence of what he says is what I feel real close to—closest
to.
WARREN: Will you state that?
MOSES: It's the importance to struggle, importance to recognize in the struggle certain humanitarian values, and to
recognize that you have to struggle for people, in that sense,
and at the same time, if it's possible, you try to eke out some
corner of love or some glimpse of happiness within. And
that's what I think more than anything else conquers the
bitterness, let's say. But there's something else.
WARREN: What?
MOSES: Camus talks a lot about the Russian terrorists—
around 1905. What he finds in them—is that they accepted
that if they took a life they offered their own in exchange.
He moves from there into the whole question of violence
and nonviolence and comes out with something which I think
is relevant in this struggle. It's not a question that you just
subjugate yourself to the conditions that are and don't try
to change them. The problem is to go on from there, into
something which is active, and yet the dichotomy is whether
you can cease to be a victim any more and also not be what
he calls an executioner. The ideal lies between these two
extremes—victim and executioner. For when people rise up
and change their status, usually somewhere along the line
they become executioners and they get involved in subjugat-
ing, you know, other people. Of course, this doesn't apply for
us Negroes on any grand scale in the sense that we're going
to have a political overthrow in which we are going to
become political executioners.
WARREN: But it does apply in terms of inside attitudes?
MOSES: It applies very much, I think. We're going through
a big thing right now even in terms of attitudes of the Negro

staff towards the white staff, and it's very hard for some of the students who have been brought up in Mississippi and are the victims of this kind of race hatred not to begin to let all of that out on the white staff. And we just had a tirade—one staff person a few days ago just, you know, for about fifteen minutes, just getting—letting out what really was a whole series of really racial statements of hatred. And we sort of all just sat there. The white students were, in this case, now made the victims. You know it's a process mainly of cleansing, but the problem is whether you can move from one to the other—that is, whether you can move Negro people from the place where they are now the victims of this kind of hatred, to a place where they don't in turn perpetuate this hatred.

WARREN: What are the actual criticisms—I don't mean necessarily valid criticisms—of the white participants in this movement?

MOSES: Well, first, the white people come down and have better skills and have better training. The tendency always is for them to gravitate to command posts. But Negro students, you know, actually feel this is their own movement. This is the strongest feeling among the Negro students— that this is the one thing that belongs to them in the whole country; and I think this causes the emotional reaction toward the white people coming in and participating.

WARREN: What about the resentment against young white persons who come into such an environment as this, and then try to enter romantically into Negro taste in music, Negro taste in this, that and the other—who want to enter, to join, to become more Negro than Negroes.

MOSES: Well, it depends. The distinction that the students themselves use is where a person is white—that is, they make the distinction between white people who somehow carry their whiteness with them, and some white people who somehow don't.

WARREN: But this difference remains?

MOSES: Yes, well, the Negroes say that they're not really *white* white people. Some people transcend that distinction and move on a plane that people are human beings.

WARREN: I was referring to the sense of amusement, and

perhaps even resentment, at the white man who tries to go Negro—

MOSES: The white person who carries his whiteness and who, in addition, may be trying to move into this area—that person becomes an object of amusement.

WARREN: Speaking of splits in identity, what of that split Du Bois speaks of—the tension between the impulse to Negro-ness, the *mystique noire,* and the impulse to be absorbed into the white West European-American culture—and perhaps blood stream?

MOSES: For myself I don't think the problem has been this kind of identity. It's not a problem of identifying with "Negro-ness." But neither do you want to integrate into the middle-class white culture, since that seems to be at this point in vital need of some kind of renewal. But in the struggle you find a broader identification, identification with individuals that are going through the same kind of struggle, so that the struggle doesn't remain just a question of racial struggle. Then you get a picture of yourself as a person, caught up historically in these circumstances, and that whole problem of identifying yourself in Negro culture—or of integrating into the white society—that disappears.

Here I think of how Dr. William Stuart Nelson, of Howard University, in answering the same question about Du Bois, described to me his similar effort to understand and appreciate his heritage and yet transcend any chauvinism: "I would want to defend everything of good that I could possibly find in my past. I think every man has a right to do that. He has a right to search for everything good—I mean in his group past. Not to try to build up an ego. The group past. And I'm on the search for it. In Africa I'm looking for it, and in the South I'm looking for it, and in my parents I'm looking for it. Having discovered it and made use of it, in increasing my own feeling of personal possibility, I'm willing to say, 'This is for any group that wants to use it, any other man to use, any other society.' It becomes part of mankind. It belongs to mankind. I think that is the way society ought to work."

WARREN: What relation, if any, do you see between your students and the Beats?

MOSES: One thing, the Beats were left without a people—without anybody they might identify with.

WARREN: Anti-social?

MOSES: Yes. Reacting against everything, they closed in on themselves—for their own values and things like that. What happens with students in our movement is that they are identifying with these people—people who come off the land—they're unsophisticated, and they simply voice, time and time again, the simple truths you can't ignore because they speak from their own lives. It's this the students are rooted in, and this is what keeps them from going off at some tangent. It's this that is put into opposition to what life is now. We had this meeting last Sunday—

WARREN: Yes, I was there.

MOSES: There are some in leadership who are against that kind of meeting.

WARREN: Why?

MOSES: They're for the kind of meeting where you get well-dressed, cleaned-up Negroes. They don't want the other people. They're embarrassed. Those people don't speak English well. They grope for words.

WARREN: "Red-ish" for "register."

MOSES: Right—they can't say that word. But it's that embarrassment the students are really battling against. For society needs to hear them, and as long as the students are tied in with these, their revolt is well-based. Not like the Beatnik revolt.

WARREN: Has there been a change in the climate of opinion—the white attitude toward the Negro, or toward the Negro problem?

MOSES: When I was at Hamilton the white attitude was: "Well, we have to do our part—the society has the overall problem, and our part as an educational institution is to try and open a door for two or three Negroes, and let's see what happens." The difference from the period before is simply that earlier they weren't interested in even opening a door. Well, while I was there I was glad to have the opportunity, but still I was deeply bitter about some of the realities of the campus and of the white attitude. You're getting another change now.

WARREN: Has the white man's picture of the Negro changed here?

MOSES: I'm sure it has. The Sheriff in Canton told some of our fellows, he told them, "Well, you all are fighting for what you believe is right, and we're fighting for what we believe is right." Now that seems to me to be a tremendous change.

WARREN: It surprises me, to tell the truth.

MOSES: That is the recognition of an equal status—that is, you're a person. Now these guys at Canton, they're not well-educated or anything like that. Just from the South—Negroes born right here—but here the Sheriff is saying to them, "You have something you believe in. So we both have sides—two sides of the same fence." That's a tremendous change.

WARREN: How do you give flesh in history to the concept "Freedom Now"?

MOSES: I don't know that that's a concept. It's an emotional expression, an attempt to communicate—we have a poster in our office and all it says is "Now!"

WARREN: I saw it.

MOSES: That's to say how we feel. This is the urgency.

WARREN: It's a poetic statement?

MOSES: Right.

* * *

I come out of Number 1072 Lynch Street and go toward town. I have an engagement for lunch, miles away at Tougaloo College. As I go down Lynch Street I am thinking of the conversation long ago between Robert Moses and his father.

And I am thinking of my own father. He was born in 1869, son of a Confederate veteran, and raised in the Reconstruction South. His mother died when he was quite young, and his father when he was in his teens, leaving several younger children, three of them by a second wife who was not much older than my father himself. He buckled down to run the family, postponing his own ambitions, studying at night, later taking courses at a little college at night—

or rather, being tutored by an instructor at the college. I have his old Greek and German grammars, faded, yellow, falling apart. I have lost the old copy of Dante's *Inferno* with the illustrations by Doré, which had belonged, I think, to his father. I have the poems he wrote; I had an anthology in which one or two were printed, more than sixty-five years ago, but it is lost. He studied law by himself, the copies of Blackstone and Montesquieu were in the house for years. Meanwhile, he did his duty to the family left in his charge. He got married fairly late.

I am remembering what the father of Robert Moses said to him "about whether he was satisfied or not—you know, his whole purpose in life," and how "he had decided to put his energies into his personal family," and I hear in my head, clear as can be, my own father's voice—an old man's voice—saying to me that he had had to choose, had had to realize that certain things were not for him, but he was happy.

I think, then, that I understand something about Robert Moses.

*　　*　　*

I go on down Lynch, then swing left off Lynch, opposite the white store front of 1017, which houses Snick. Opposite 1017 is a vacant lot, and on the lot a very big billboard with the picture of the Statue of Liberty, lifting high the torch. The bold letters read:

Think　　Speak　　Register　　Vote
PROTECT YOUR FREEDOM
Contact Your Civitan Club

It does not say to contact Snick.

*　　*　　*

: 8 :

The next morning I am again waiting in Mr. Evers' office. He arrives, a little late, a little harassed, but clear-eyed and cordial. He is wearing black trousers, and a lightweight, bright-red sweater, with a thin black line along the edges. He begins to tell me how the Citizens Council had been calling on the phone all yesterday.

"It's a form of intimidation," he says, "so we've decided to give them a taste of their own medicine, have a committee call them all day—so their phone is tied up."

We turn to personal matters, to his early life. He and Medgar had "worked as a team" from boyhood, organizing chapters of the NAACP in counties in the middle part of the state and then up in the Delta. Then he, Charles Evers, was president of the Negroes' Voters League. By that time he was in the "funeral business," and vulnerable to economic pressure: "They broke me. I had a couple of lawsuits. I was fined, I was sued for personal damages—I was parked at an intersection and a white lady, in a parking lot, she got in her car and tore into my car—and they sued me for five-thousand-dollar claim and they said I injured her back, and—that was confirmed in the courts."

I ask if that had been appealed.

He says he couldn't get an attorney to represent him. "Later I got to be the first Negro disc jockey in Mississippi, but they got me fired from the radio station in Decatur, Mississippi." When he had a restaurant they revoked his license. Then they asked the casket companies not to sell him caskets and embalming fluid.

"I had to give up business and seek employment. I couldn't find it anywhere in the state, so I told Medgar—I said, 'Look, Medgar, I'm going away, and I'll send money, but you stay here and keep carrying the fight on, and I'll go and send money back and try to buy some property and get enough income, and we'll have enough money so we can continue the fight and set our people free—and free ourselves.' But I said, 'Any time you need me I'll be back, whether it's day or night.' And I told him, 'Remember the pact we made when we were boys—that whatever happened to one of us, the other would carry on until the same thing happened to him, until he couldn't—until physically he was prevented or until something else we couldn't help.' "

I am a little disturbed by his rhetoric. He is not talking to me, across the desk, in the room above Lynch Street. He is talking to a hall full of people, to a meeting under the blazing sky, to a crowd. Or talking to himself. I wish he could really remember what he and

Medgar had really said, word for word. It is not a question of there being no truth behind the rhetoric. But I feel that the truth—and the emotion of that truth—have become officialized.

By a question I try to bring him to some recollection of what actually happened, what was actually said: "This was your agreement as boys?"

> EVERS: Yes. We must have been about—oh, I must have been about fifteen, I guess, and Medgar twelve. Why we said this—there was one day we were sitting at a Bilbo speech—the late Senator Bilbo was campaigning for re-election. He would stomp and he would lambaste the Negroes and tell everybody he was going to send them back to Africa and—
>
> WARREN: Which town was this?
>
> EVERS: Decatur, Mississippi—the county seat of Newton. We'd always go and listen. We were about the only Negroes who would go up and listen, and we'd always go and sit right in front of him. My dad had always told us we were as good as anybody, and God loved us all, and we had the rights of anyone else. It was brought up in us.
>
> We were sitting down in front—and I remember it very clearly—he [Bilbo] said, "You see these two Negroes down here—if you don't keep them in their place, some day they'll be in Washington trying to represent you."
>
> And I sort of looked up at him and smiled, and he said, "He's even got the nerve to grin at me."
>
> And then, that day, Medgar and I said, "Well, some day, he may be telling the truth." And Medgar said, "You're right, Charlie—some day we may be in Washington representing all the people of Mississippi." And from that day on we decided that that was something we could do.

That was, he says, the day of commitment. But the commitment was backed by many things. By a big thing like the lynching of a friend of the family who "was accused of insulting a white lady," and who was hung up in a pasture nearby and shot in two by shotguns, and "his clothes laid there in the pasture for weeks and weeks, and we used to go by and see them." By a small thing like the fact that white people would call your father and mother by their first names, and wouldn't say "sir," or "ma'am." Then there was the day when their father stood up to the storekeeper who had a "great reputation of beating Negroes if they didn't pay the bill he said they owed"—grabbed a bottle and stood up to him and dared him to reach in the drawer for his pistol. "So I knew then," Mr. Evers says, "that white men are cowards, and they are easy to become excited if you show any type of nerve or any courage at all they will quickly turn and run."

When I ask him if he would generalize this—that all white men are cowards—he thinks a second and says, "No, not all, those who live violently." Then adds: "I noticed as we grew up, we'd watch cowboy pictures, and we'd notice how all the bad white men would always try and sneak and shoot the other brave men in the back. These are the type of things that helped us understand that Negroes and whites—to a certain extent—are the same, that a coward is a coward."

After the war (both brothers saw active service) they came back and, while students at Alcorn College, began to organize NAACP chapters and work in voter registration, with the predictable consequences, including threats to the father. "So when we came home my dad told me, and so I said, 'Well, Dad, I was involved in New Guinea and I fought in the Philippines, and I want to fight here in Mississippi and have the things we fought for there.' And Medgar felt the same way, and Medgar said, 'We're going to register.' "

So the next day they went to register.

"Mr. Brand, who at that time was Circuit Clerk, he said, 'Come here, Charles, and you Medgar,' and he carried us into a room and he talked to us. He said, 'Now, look, son, now I don't have no right to tell you not to register and not to vote, but if I were you I'd just go back and wait. The time will come when you can register.' And I told him, I said, 'Mr. Brand, we've waited too long already.' He said, "You're going to cause trouble.' I said, 'I don't care what the trouble is, I want to register.' So he carried me in and we registered."

But they did not vote. There was a crowd—"I won't say hoodlums —with shotguns and overall pants on and rifles"—that blocked access to the ballot. But Mr. Brand saw that they got ballots. It was all predictable: the shotgun muzzle stuck in the side—"You damned Evers niggers, you're nothing but trouble!" The white man they had raked leaves for as boys, begging them to go away. The white lady begging them to go away and not get killed. "And I told her, 'Look, you've beaten us but you haven't defeated us. We'll be back.' And I told Medgar, 'Don't turn around, Medgar, just back out the door.' And we backed out the door. And somebody yelled, 'You damned Evers niggers are going to get all the niggers in Decatur killed.' "

They walk down the street. A car, shotgun muzzles sticking over the side, escorts them at a walking pace. They are armed too—"We'd always be well armed." The talk back and forth is drearily predictable, scarcely worth putting down, like a quarrel among children:

"Nobody's going to take a whipping from any of you white people."

"We're going to kill you niggers."

"One thing, I'm going to get one of you first."

But they keep on walking and the car turns off.

That afternoon they don't go on back to Alcorn. They wait for the predictable mob to burn their father's house: "So we planned. I said to Medgar, 'You stay in the barn, I'll get in the garage.' I said, 'We'll have 'em, we'll put 'em in a cross fire.' For by now we had learned the best way is to get people in a cross fire and you can't miss."

Medgar had been in Normandy, in the landing. Charles had been in New Guinea and in the Philippines. They had had their lesson at the public expense. But nobody came that night to find out how well they had learned their lesson.

I ask Mr. Evers what kind of a man this Mr. Brand had been.

"A fairly decent man. He never showed any resentment for us— he never showed he was for us, either. I feel he was a fair man. There were many who were fair."

He goes on to say that many whites do not approve of this type of thing, but the white men who differ from these extremists are in much more danger than the Negro, "because reprisals will come much severer than would come to us, and that's why so many good people in Mississippi are afraid to speak out—and there are many."

But he cannot estimate them in the majority.

Then he goes back into the rhetoric: "We took a chance in France, we took a chance in New Guinea, we took a chance in Manila, to fight for democracy, to fight for the things we believe in, the things this country was established for. I say, if I have got to come back to Mississippi—the two of us felt this way—and be denied these things, then my fighting and my sacrifices, all the years have been in vain. I say, if I have the nerve and the courage—"

*   *   *

On Exposure and Change:

Fifteen years ago there were few Negroes in Mississippi who were willing to stand by us. Before the World War II, we thought the whole world was just like Mississippi.

On Nonviolence:

The only way we have is through nonviolence, there's no other way. Because bloodshed has never solved any problems. I think a good example of violence is Birmingham. Birmingham was the worst disaster—the worst thing that could ever happen in America. I don't believe in violence, but I believe in protecting myself. I wouldn't ask any Negro any more to be driving along in his car and let a bunch of white hoodlums ride beside him and stop him and start beating him.

On the Cause of the Riot at Jackson College:

EVERS: I personally had been asking the City of Jackson to place a light or some protection there for the kids, and they had told me it was being studied by the engineering department.

WARREN: Were you on the committee that went to the Mayor?

EVERS: No, he didn't want to see me—the Mayor won't even talk to me.

WARREN: Reverend Horton went, didn't he?

EVERS: I believe so. Reverend Horton, Reverend Smith—they went.

WARREN: Did the Mayor later say that nobody had come to him?

EVERS: Well, the Mayor has even said that no one at all had ever been there, and even the Board of Education said they had asked—they had requested and money had been set aside for an overpass. But the Mayor said he didn't know anything about it at all.

WARREN: Yet there had been a committee calling on him?

EVERS: Oh, yes, there had been a committee calling on him.

On the Beckwith Trial:

Of the verdict I feel—and I guess maybe I'm a little liberal in my thinking—that there was someone on this jury who wanted justice done. And I feel that the prosecutor did everything in his power, and the Jackson Police Department, to bring about justice. I feel somewhere there's been a change of heart in Mississippi. If it was rigged, it was the first time in the history of Mississippi that they even thought enough of a Negro to even rig a trial. Even to try and impress the outside world.

On the Funeral of Medgar Evers in Washington:

I had a lot of calls and quite a few friendly letters, stating they thought it was a very dramatic thing. Although they remained anonymous. I often get calls from many whites, telling us to keep on, to keep it up, because victory will be ours.

On Senator Bilbo and Race Prejudice:

Senator Bilbo knew that in order to stay in Washington and get that fat salary and live on a flower bed of ease, he had to lambaste and discredit Negroes. Senator Bilbo, as an individual, did more for individual Negroes than any governor we ever had. He began to contribute buildings to the state institutions—new buildings at Alcorn. He wasn't as vicious, actually, within, as he pretended he was, because there are so many incidents where it's been proven that he was not only a friend to certain Negroes, but he was even intimate with Negroes. It has been rumored that he even had children down in Poplarville by a Negro woman.

On the Mississippi White Man:

It's a funny thing about this Mississippi white man. He admires any man who stands up for what he believes. They admired Medgar. They didn't particularly love him, but they admired him. That's why, when I go all over the country, people criticize me when I say that in Mississippi we are freer than Negroes in Chicago and New York. Because we know where this man stands. In Chicago and New York you wonder. They rub you down and they grin in your face and they stab you in the back.

But once you convert this Mississippi man, it is like when Christ converted Peter. Once we can prove to the Mississippi whites that what we are fighting for is right and just, then Mississippi will be the best place in the world to live.

It's one thing about the Southern white man, in most cases once he says he'll do something, if you can get him to stand up, once he commits himself, you can just about trust what he says. Not in all cases, but in most cases. You can just about trust him because he's fought so hard. And I found out one thing about them, that if they give you their word, they hate to be made out a liar.

On Senator Bilbo and the Funeral of Medgar Evers:

When Medgar's body was carried to Washington, after he was assassinated, it didn't bother me too much. I had never broken down until we got to Washington and I sat in the limousine waiting for them to bring his body out of the church. They rolled him out of the church and put him in the hearse, and as we began to pursue to the cemetery, it all came back so clear, that many years ago Bilbo had predicted this, and now here we are, representing all the people, in Washington. And that was the time I broke down.

* * *

When Mr. Evers, in the first part of the interview, told me of the episode at Bilbo's speech, I felt something contrived, arranged, about the narrative, something too pat about the oath taken, something false in the language. In the same way there seemed, at first hearing, something stereotyped in the narrative of their going to register, and in the words of Mr. Brand, in the account of their trying to vote, I felt the predictability, in the scene of the crowd, in the conversation as the car followed down the street, the night-long wait to lay a cross fire on the mob. It all ran like a piece of fiction tediously conventional, a tissue of echoes.

Memory and rhetoric and unconscious contriving—the freezing of facts in public repetition that can only become less and less true as language hardens—have, undoubtedly, played some odd, sad tricks here. Charles Evers, age fifteen, and Medgar, age twelve, never talked as they are reported to have talked.

But does this scene correspond to something that did happen? For they did come back and work in voter registration, they could have prospered and "lived in richness," they did accept persecution, Medgar Evers was indeed shot down in the dark, Charles Evers does walk, day and night, knowing that an eye stares through a telescopic sight, at his back.

Somewhere in the fable, there is fact. Or do facts, always, strain to flower into fable? And the dreary clichés, do they give us, after all, the fresh, appalling vision of truth?

The car moves slowly down the street, shotgun muzzles sticking over the side.

* * *

There is a sort of footnote to the interview with Charles Evers. On the evening of Saturday, February 15, 1964, at the Andrew Jackson Hotel, in Nashville, the NAACP sponsored a Freedom

Fund dinner and dance, the profits from the occasion, at ten dollars a plate, were to go to the National NAACP Legal Defense and Educational Fund. The speaker was Charles Evers. On the afternoon of February 17, the *Nashville Banner* carried a story across the top of the front page, headed:

EVERS REJECTS NON-VIOLENT TECHNIQUE
If White Man Shoots at Negro,
We Will Shoot Back

The armature of the story lay in the following paragraphs:

"I have the greatest respect for Dr. Martin Luther King, but non-violence won't work in Mississippi. You get on your knees down there praying for justice and those white hoodlums will stomp your brains out," Evers said.

"We have made up our minds," he said, "that if a white man shoots at a Negro in Mississippi, we will shoot back."

"If they bomb a Negro church and kill our children, we are going to bomb a white church and kill some of their children."

In other words, according to the report, Mr. Evers, in abandoning nonviolence, had advocated not merely action in self-defense, and not merely selective reprisal, but totally nonselective reprisal—"some of their children"—the *lex talionis,* an eye for an eye. Since such an attitude would clearly be in contradiction to that expressed to me only a week earlier, I wrote to Mr. Evers.

He replied that his views had not changed; and charged that the "*Nashville Banner,* as well as many other Southern newspapers, deliberately misquoted" him.* He added, "Specifically, I did not advocate killing *any* children or bombing churches; I said there are Negroes who are willing and will shoot back."

Meanwhile, the *Mississippi Free Press,* on February 29, in a lead story, reported Evers' claim that he had been misrepresented, that "he had not meant that he advocated violence, but that there were extremists on both sides."—the same language about "extremists" that is used by white people in Mississippi.

---

* The reporter whose by-line was on the story is Robert Churchwell, a Negro and a graduate of Fisk University, who has been with the *Banner* some fifteen years. The *Banner* maintains that Churchwell has an unimpeachable record for accuracy, and that there was no local protest about this particular story.

It is all very shadowy. The distinction between prediction and prescription is always shadowy, but here we have shadow upon shadow. A great deal hinges upon those words allegedly uttered in Nashville: "*We* have made up *our* minds . . ." or "*we* are going to bomb a . . ." *We* is not some "extremists." Were those words ever uttered? And if they were uttered, what is the real significance of the fact?

Take a man whose own brother has been shot in the back, who lives with the rifle pointed at his own back—is it hard to imagine that such words, in a moment of excitement, with the lights and faces before him, might slip out, unwittingly? For would not the potential of those words be there for any Negro living in that world of white violence? But if they did slip out, would the fact, however unfortunate, mean more than that this feeling is potential in the situation, for any Negro? We may remember what Mrs. Harvey regretfully said, that many Negroes in Mississippi have reached the point where they are ready for violence, "uncontrolled, indiscriminate." But remembering that, we may remember, too, that immediately after the killing of Medgar Evers, his widow, when she stood in the mass meeting at Jackson and any violence might have broken out, did not speak in the language of the *lex talionis*.

: 9 :

NOTEBOOK:

Overheard as I wait to pay meal check in hotel—Dining-room Hostess to Cashier:

HOSTESS: *You see in the paper about that new Kennedy half-dollar?*

CASHIER: *Yes, I did.*

HOSTESS: *Well, Mr —— said he ain't going to have any of them in his restaurant.*

CASHIER: *Well, I don't blame him.*

HOSTESS: *I don't want any, either.*

CASHIER: *What would he do if somebody tried to pay him with one of them?*

HOSTESS: *He won't take it.*

. . .

Since then, as a gesture of contempt, Kennedy half-dollars have been offered for sale, in one store window, at the bargain price of twenty-five cents. But the case to hold the souvenir costs seventy-five cents.

So patriotism and business acumen intersect.

*   *   *

I have in my hand a copy of the *Press-Scimitar* of Memphis, Tennessee, February 11, 1964, featuring an editorial that urges the Senate to pass the Civil Rights Bill immediately. It ends:

> It is simply that an overwhelming majority of Americans, speaking thru their elected representatives, believe it is high time that constitutional guarantees of life, liberty, pursuit of happiness and equal treatment for all citizens be put into practice.
>
> This temper of the times can be ignored by the Senate only at the expense of the national welfare.

Memphis is often said to be the capital of the Delta. But it is, clearly, not.

: 10 :

In the afternoon I go to Jackson College, where I ask questions of two groups of students, some eight or nine in each group. Three members of the faculty are present, courteous and helpful, including Dr. Jacqueline Clarke, who teaches sociology, and is the author of *These Rights They Seek.* Some of the students are very bright, with an air of intellectual independence, but at least one of the faculty present takes the tone of a kindergarten teacher. "Is this exposure an educational experience?" he asks. And they all reply, dutifully, in chorus: "Yes, it is."

I go for a conference with the president, another tall, fine-looking man, with great natural charm and a heavy sadness of face. He is smoking a cigar while we talk, but clearly without pleasure. It is late afternoon, in winter, dusk just coming on, with the sound of young voices calling across the campus, muffled beyond the windows.

The president merely suffers the conversation, the meaningless words we interchange, holding the cigar in his hand and staring at it during the benumbed ritual. The riot, he says, wasn't caused by anybody on his campus. It was "outsiders." His students don't want trouble, they just want an education. He says this two or three times.

As I walk across the campus to get a cab, the professor who guides me says that I must believe that all the president wants is to save the college. To save it for the kids.

Then he changes the subject. He begins to tell me that Bilbo did not really "hate Negroes." He begins to tell me that he was, in fact, "intimate" with some. He says the same thing about two other well known Mississippi politicians. This theme appears again and again.

Why?

*   *   *

NOTEBOOK:

Check out at hotel—cashier rude, lately there has been, in fact, a general coolness, no "good mornings" at desk—reason: my "mission" or Negro cabs to door two or three times? Now limousine to airport, over in Rankin County, past the glittering new outlying supermarkets and shopping centers, just like Fairfield, Connecticut, the same signs, the same development houses, the same hiss of tires on the same concrete—USA, willy-nilly—sunset slow, blood-red, magisterial over the flat land, lights coming on in the dusk. Here and there, in the thickening dark, are abandoned shacks, where Negro tenants once lived. Then the airport.

*   *   *

Note on the Beckwith Trial and the "Secret Voice"

From *The New York Times* of April 12, 1964:

District Attorney William L. Waller told a reporter at the beginning of the [second] Beckwith trial that he had received much encouragement since his all-out effort for a conviction in the first trial.

This support apparently comes from civic and business groups who feel the time has come to break what is known in the Mississippi Delta as "the unwritten law"—the right of a white man to discipline, with violence if necessary, the Negro who violates the code of conduct established for him.

The jury, however, was again hung. There has been no third trial.

*   *   *

Note on a Voice Not Secret

James W. Silver has, for twenty-years, been Professor of History at the University of Mississippi, at Oxford. On November 7, 1963, at Asheville, North Carolina, he gave his presidential address before the Southern Historical Association. It was entitled: "Mississippi: The Closed Society."*

In the course of the address, he said: "The social order that refuses to conform to national standards insists upon strict conformity at home. While complaining of its own persecuted minority station in the United States, it rarely considers the Negro minority as having rights in Mississippi."

For some years Dr. Silver took his chances on being shot in the back—by some hero, from the dark, of course. But now he is not at Ole Miss. After twenty-eight years, he has gone North.

NOTE ON THE SUMMER PROJECT

Though the Summer Project of 1964 in Mississippi is long since over, it is too early for a full and clear assessment of its results. But certain things can be discerned.

There had been a considerable faction in the civil rights organizations that wished to by-pass Mississippi and let it stew in its own

* Subsequently absorbed into his book of the same title.

juices until gains had been made and consolidated all around the borders of the state. But by May, 1961, when the first freedom ride in the Deep South, sponsored by CORE, initiated what amounted to a special movement, the direct attack on segregation in Mississippi had obviously begun. With less immediate public effort the work of Snick for voter registration was under way; and by the summer of 1963 the assassination of Medgar Evers, of the NAACP, had hardened the will to see the campaign through to the end.

Medgar Evers' death and his burial in Arlington Cemetery drew new forces into the campaign in Mississippi. To the youthful impatience of many of the Negro workers in Mississippi was added the impulse of such groups as the Yale and Stanford students who, in the fall of 1963, helped stage a mock election to dramatize the political situation in the state; and as a matter of fact, to set the stage for the Summer Project of 1964. It is true that, in the winter of 1963-64, a strong faction in Snick (and outside of it, too) opposed the entry of white students—certainly of whites in any significant proportion—into the picture in Mississippi. But this possessiveness in regard to the Movement, and the will to independence, with doubtless some tinge of race chauvinism, did not survive the hard logic of advantages that would accrue from massive white participation.

By the summer of 1964, the operation was in full swing, and under the auspices of COFO—the Council of Federated Organizations—there were, in addition to Snick, CORE, and the continuing and deep-rooted NAACP, a number of other groups: the Southern Christian Leadership Conference, the National Council of Churches, the Lawyers Constitutional Defense Committee, and the National Lawyers Guild. Besides the workers regularly affiliated with these organizations, there were over six hundred young volunteers, mostly students.

Given the nature of the participating organizations, there would be, obviously, a considerable division of function. Snick, with some one hundred paid field workers, CORE, with forty, and the NAACP, with its regular staff and the network of chapters, were in a position to carry, as it were, the main burden of the direct assault. Snick, with its effective dramatizing of the role of youth, the powerful appeal of the personality of Robert Moses, and the reputation for a romantic but scarcely defined radicalism—what Gilbert Moses has called the "piercing clarity" of its approach—managed to define itself, in much of the public press and in the minds of many people, as the dominant organization, the very spirit of the Summer Project. This is the more remarkable for two reasons. First, the NAACP has old and peculiar loyalties in Mississippi; it has courageous local leadership, Charles Evers and Aaron Henry, for example; and it has the great symbolic force of its martyr, Medgar Evers. Second, two of the victims at Philadelphia, Schwerner and Chaney, were paid field workers of CORE; and it was Negro workers of CORE who disappeared into the Negro community of Philadelphia, won the confidence of the local people, and gradually assembled evidence, including, Mr. Farmer says, an eye-witness account of the death of Chaney, which it turned over to the FBI.

The registration of voters was a declared purpose of the Summer Project. The results here are not impressive. The most optimistic figure I have encountered is some twelve hundred new registrations, but some eight hundred of these were in Panola County, where a favorable federal court ruling on a voter-registration suit had struck out eighteen sections on the test form, including the constitutional interpretation, to leave something equivalent to a literacy requirement. In other words, the new registrations for all Mississippi, outside of Panola County, were only some four hundred. Even the most sanguine guess shows no improvement in the rate of registration since the Voter Education Project, sponsored by the Southern Regional Council, threw in the sponge with 3,871 new names on the books to show for two years of effort. At that rate, according to a speech by Martin Luther King in Mississippi that summer, it would take one hundred and thirty-five years to register half the potential Negro vote in the state.

This small showing for the summer seems, at first glance, disappointing. But we must ask, "Disappointing to whom?" Certainly, despite some whistling in the dark and some prophecies concocted for public consumption, there could have been no starry-eyed expectations among Negro leaders on the spot who had had experience with the ruthless system of repression that surrounds the registrar's office in every county courthouse in the state—a system which, outside of Panola County, allowed only four hundred registrations to filter through out of, according to Aaron Henry, thirty-nine thousand applications. What, presumably, the leaders expected was, for one thing, to dramatize this very system of repression, and by the dramatization involve the Federal Government and national (perhaps even some local) public opinion. They have done that, handsomely; and with their thirty-nine thousand applicants for registration, they have dramatized the fact that at least some Negroes would, after all, like to vote.

Conversation with people like Robert Moses, Stokely Carmichael, James Forman, and Aaron Henry, though they do not underestimate the long-range importance of the ballot, does not leave one with the impression that they attach mystic significance to it, or fail to see it in a tissue of interrelated concerns; and in that tissue the ballot is both a means and an end. It is not only a means to be achieved; the actual process of achieving it is, in itself, a means for something beyond the ballot. For one thing, as I saw so clearly that morning in the Masonic auditorium in Jackson when Robert Moses was conducting the meeting, the work for voter registration is, in itself, an elaborate educational process, a process involving, as I saw it that morning, the rudiments of English syntax, of the syllogism, of American history, of political organization, and of the simple business of planning and working with other people—this last a capacity which some analysts claim the Negro American has sadly lacked. There are, too, the actual Freedom Schools and community projects. But the work in voter registration involves, most importantly, the development of the will to stand up and act. All of these things are basic for the long-range growth of political power, but they are equally important for the growth of other kinds of power—and for the fulfillment of a person.

As James Forman has said to me, the "primary focus" of Snick was not to build a particular organization but to give a sense of the unifying issue and to develop leadership in the local communities. Now, after the summer, Negroes point with pride to Mrs. Fannie Lou Hamer, who, after being thrown off the plantation where for eighteen years she had been a sharecropper, learned to take jailings and harassments and beatings, and wound up as a candidate for Congress on the Freedom Democratic ticket, in the Second Congressional District, and as a delegate of the same party to the Democratic National Convention at Atlantic City. The development of Mrs. Hamer goes back to the day she crossed the threshold of the registrar's office and got thrown off the plantation.

Not every Negro who tried to register in the summer of 1964 will wind up as a Fannie Lou Hamer or Aaron Henry, but none will ever be quite the same again; and this awareness is what makes it possible for a person to respond to leadership. The spreading of such awareness was a fundamental intention of the Summer Project, for if the Negro Movement is, in its higher echelons, largely a middle-class manifestation, it has been aiming for a long time now to create a mass base. And the men who ran the Summer Project were good enough psychologists to understand that a mass base is not created by preaching abstractions; it is created by involvement, by acting out. The idea of registration would, in itself, give a meaningful focus for organization and a target for acting out. Even if the actual registration was too small to make an immediate political impact, the organization of the Freedom Democratic Party, which had originated as an educational and propaganda device, a mere acting out, became a practical weapon.

At the Convention in Atlantic City the Freedom Democratic Party provided the only real issue and the only sporting interest: Would the delegation, headed by Aaron Henry, be seated? Until the Wednesday morning before the seating of the delegations there were the requisite eleven votes in the credentials committee to force a fight on the floor of the Convention. But this was the last thing in the world the political professionals wanted, and at this point the compromise was offered that the Freedom Democratic delegation should have two seats at large, to be taken by Aaron Henry and the Reverend Edward King (white) of Tougaloo College, with the status of "honored guests" for the other delegates. What the Freedom Democratic delegation was holding out for was either the floor fight (with a good prospect of victory) or the plan offered by Mrs. Edith Green of Oregon that all members of both delegations who would take the loyalty oath be seated (with the good prospect that a substantial number of the regular Democrats from Mississippi would refuse the oath). Against the advice of older heads (including Martin Luther King, and, it is rumored, Aaron Henry himself*), the compromise was rejected. As several Snick workers have told me, a crucial element in the decision was the fact that the Democratic Party tried to dictate the persons who would be delegates-at-large—

---

* James Farmer pointed out that he thought the rejection of the compromise would be "morally right but politically wrong."

a piece of tactlessness that corroborates Anna Arnold Hedgeman's statement that "Negroes are seldom supported [by whites] when they select their own leadership." In this general connection, Stokley Carmichael, who was actively involved in the operations at Atlantic City, said to me: "I do not think the word *compromise* is the correct one. The delegates of the FDP felt that it was not a compromise, but rather a decision which was handed down to them. If it was a compromise then the FDP would have had a chance to save something. They were not consulted. The Democratic Party said, 'Here, take this, it's all we will give you.' "

The situation was, to the Negro at least, a paradigm of the behavior of the white liberal, who long ago, in *The Rescue,* was described by Conrad, in the person of Captain Lingard: "He prided himself upon having no color prejudice and no racial antipathies . . . only he knew what was good for them." As for the Negroes' resentment, at the Convention, at those who "knew what was good for them," it is reported that Carmichael, when he heard the news of the proposal, burst out, "This proves that the liberal Democrats are just as racist as Goldwater!"*

Whatever the motive for the rejection of the compromise, what the leaders of the Freedom Democrats did not at that moment know, as I am told by a Snick worker, was that the effort for a block of signatures for a minority report in the credentials committee had now dissolved. So the chance for a floor fight was gone, and with it, now, the chance for a second-best victory—the seating of two delegates-at-large. Even the second-best victory would have been big, for the Freedom Democratic Party had parlayed this real threat out of a piece of play-acting.

But the issues raised by the existence of the Freedom Democratic Party were not closed at the Convention. In January, 1965, the party challenged the seating of all the putative members of Congress elected in Mississippi in the fall of 1964, emphasizing the situation in the Second and Fourth Congressional Districts, where the number of

* There is some speculation, how well-grounded I do not know, that politicians as astute as Johnson and Humphrey could not have been ignorant of the reaction of Negroes to the handpicking of the FDP delegates by whites; this, if substantiated, would mean that Johnson and Humphrey wanted the compromise to be rejected, as the easiest way to get themselves off the hook.

disenfranchised Negroes exceeds the total registration of both Negroes and whites, and where there is prima-facie evidence that the Fourteenth Amendment has been violated by a deliberate exclusion of voters.*

Even if this attack should fail—and even if the courts should finally rule that the word *Democrat* may not be used in the name of the party—the story will not be over.†

As Aaron Henry puts it, the Freedom Democratic Party has "established a liaison" with the National Democratic Party. Furthermore, the near miss at Atlantic City was enough to loosen rivets in the bottom of the regular Democratic organization in Mississippi, and next time it may well not be a miss. Robert Moses and his friends have a sense of strategy, a sense of timing, and a capacity for organization, and it may develop that, in the long view, they were wise to sacrifice the advantage of an immediate victory. In any case, attempts to register Negroes in the South are bound to have substantial support from Johnson Democrats. Every Negro registered in the South is a vote for Johnson, and the Democrats, in the ironical turn of the time, now find themselves in the position of the Republicans in the Reconstruction; liberalism and political savvy merrily mate, and Democrats are building up a backlog of dependable black votes.

* Mrs. Fannie Lou Hamer, Mrs. Annie Devine, and Mrs. Victoria Gray, named in an election run by the Freedom Democratic Party, challenged the seats of Congressmen James L. Whitten, William M. Colmer, and Prentiss Walker. But the seating of Congressmen Thomas G. Abernathy and John Bell Williams was also challenged. The Freedom Democratic Party and certain Negro organizations, notably Snick and CORE, planned to maintain a vigil at the Capitol, pressed for the seating of the winners in the Freedom Democratic Party elections as well as the rejection of Messrs. Whitten, Colmer, Walker, Abernathy and Williams. But one segment of liberal opinion held that the two issues are entirely separate. For instance, the Commission on Religion and Race of the National Council of Churches stated that the attempt to seat the Freedom Democratic candidates "clouds the clear issue of the legality of the present election system" in Mississippi. (*The New York Times,* December 29, 1964.)

† On November 17, 1964, a chancery judge ruled that it is a violation of statute to register or attempt to register the name or part of the name of a party already registered. (*The New York Times,* November 18, 1964.) In reply to this ruling, Fannie Lou Hamer said: "I want the name Freedom Democratic Party inscribed on my tombstone."

. . .

If a purpose of Snick and of the Negro Movement in general was to create a dynamic Negro community capable of initiating action, the Summer Project apparently contributed to that by bringing into cooperative contact young Mississippi Negroes and a number of outsiders. Undoubtedly, as Robert Moses had said to me of such contacts, some friction would be involved; there is bound to be, he had said, the natural fear that the outsiders, especially white outsiders, with their better education and greater self-certainty, would "gravitate to command posts," and since "Negro students feel this is their own movement," there is the "emotional reaction toward the white people coming in and participating." Some of the fears expressed by Robert Moses were, in fact, realized. James Farmer, on this point, tells me: "A result of the Summer Project—and this was somewhat unfortunate, I think—was that the Project did not involve [enough] local people. In many cases, local people who had been involved in the Movement pulled out when they saw these skilled youngsters from the North. Now we find that after the students left, some of the local people are coming around again and saying, 'Well, maybe you need me again.' " But the cooperation that did exist was for the segregated Negro a fundamental step in education. The Negro could have contact, in the only meaningful way, with the world beyond Mississippi, and he might feel himself, for the first time, a part of American society. As one young man on the Summer Project —a college teacher—said to me, perhaps the most significant result may be in the higher horizon it brought to the young Negro. But the same notion might be applied to the white worker: he might have found out that a Negro is not an abstraction which he may decorate with certain self-indulgent theories, feelings, and fantasies, like a Christmas tree.

There are, however, some other results of the summer which import contradictory implications into the picture. Though a fundamental intention of the Summer Project, and of the Mississippi operation in general, was to create a mass base, there had occurred, by the fall of 1964, according to some workers, a widening breach between some of the intellectual theoreticians of the high command and the ordinary Negro citizen of the state. Some of the theoreticians have not only seen the Movement as directed toward a reordering of society in general, but have preached the doctrine that the Mississippi operation is only an aspect of a world-wide peasant revolution for land reform. However, according to James Farmer, the ordinary Negro in Mississippi is concerned with making a living, getting an education for his children, getting a vote, and not being pushed around, and is "not much interested in the internal problems of Vietnam." Or as Roy Wilkins put it in another connection: "I think he [the Negro] is a conservative economically, I think he wants to hold on to gains in property and protection. I don't see him as a bold experimenter in political science or social reform."

Further, though another important intention in Mississippi was, by pressing for registration and by organizing the Freedom Democratic Party, to educate Negroes in the principles and practices of political democracy, there are reports—again from workers in Mississippi—of a tendency among certain leaders to by-pass, in the actual operations of the party, democratic procedure and to take the attitude that "father knows best." In deploring this "manipulation from the top" (which, we may remember, is not unknown in the major parties), James Farmer says that the "decision-making procedures have not been clearly enough drawn up to allow for grass-roots participation." In any social movement, of course, from the American Prohibition Party to the Russian Revolution, problems of the role of authority are bound to arise; and in a society like that of Mississippi, the temptation to paternalism, if not to dictatorship, must be vivid, even to the most high-minded. This temptation is the reverse of the coin which, on the obverse, is the romantic worship of the purity of experience of the simple man.

Another contradiction develops in the relation of leadership to the white world. The Summer Project was undertaken as an extremely ambitious experiment in bi-racial cooperation, the most ambitious thing of the sort to date. But with the failure at Atlantic City to achieve an immediate practical victory in the National Democratic Party, and with the development, it may be surmised, of differences of policy with some of the white collaborators (for instance, with the National Council of Churches on the matter of screening and on the attempt to seat Mrs. Hamer, Mrs. Devine, and Mrs. Gray), and with the original failure to get an indictment against the twenty-one persons arrested by the FBI in connection with the Philadelphia murders, and perhaps as the result of the kind of friction predicted by Robert Moses, there is now the inclination on the part of at least some members of the high command in Mississippi to pull back from the white association, to distrust white attitudes and motives, to assume, as Farmer interprets the feeling of many of the younger people, that "there are no real friends [among whites] who will stand up when the chips are down," to "go it alone" at whatever cost.

This increasing alienation affects not only relations with the white world but with certain Negro elements with whom, even in COFO, the cooperation had been uneasy, notably the NAACP. The aggravation of the split is indicated by a memorandum circulated in the upper echelons of the NAACP, in January, 1965, urging that the organization withdraw from COFO rather than lend its prestige to "an organization which is attacking us at the base and spreading false information." The memorandum continues: "We must also consider whether we want to support a gimmick approach to registration and voting, and the creation of a third party, which has never been effective in this country, and certainly has little hope of success in Mississippi except to become a frontgroup for an all-Negro party." The crucial nature of the split appears in the fact that Aaron Henry, elected in January, 1965, as a member of the board of directors of the NAACP, was pushed to choose between that organization and COFO—and by implication the Freedom Democratic Party. The retort of COFO was that if the NAACP wished to avoid destruction it might work harder in Mississippi—and, presumably, on the terms laid down by COFO.

The real danger in the split in Negro leadership in Mississippi (and elsewhere) is that a fundamental polarization of the Negro group would thicken the atmosphere of violence. There are people like one summer volunteer who, back at his home college, walked into a professor's office, picked up a knife lying on a desk (used as a letter opener) and said: "This sort of thing isn't much good unless you really know how to use it. We've taken to firearms." Then he added that firearms are very educational and said: "Next summer we're going to do a lot of educating down there." If the leadership is really fractured, we could, conceivably, see the development, at one extreme, of a terrorist program which, in idealistic form, would mean deliberately "giving one's own life in exchange" for one taken as an act of justice, but would more likely mean the blind, unselective violence of a Stern Gang or an Algerian bomb-squad.* For moral justification, the terrorists would say, with a disturbing logic, that the white supremacy is maintained by violence now, and that violence is the only thing the white man understands. To retort that such a program would be suicidal for the Negro Movement means nothing to a person who has accepted a certain attitude toward the world and himself—the attitude of Samson in the temple, an attitude that, in fact, implies "suicide" as a value. As Tom Kahn, in *Dissent* (Summer, 1964), puts it: "A segment of the Negro leadership and perhaps among the rank-and-file almost want the movement to have a tragic ending which would somehow illuminate the human condition in all its frailty." And the dramatist Le Roi Jones is quoted in *Commentary* (February 1965): "Guerilla warfare is inevitable in the North and South." And he goes on to add: ". . . you can't use nuclear weapons against us when we kill a few cops . . . there is no way of saving America."

This is not to say that such an extreme wing will necessarily develop in Mississippi. Those who are capable of "philosophizing" terror are men of experience, impressive intellectual power, and humane sentiments. But the wild impulse to destruction, and self-destruction, lurks in even the wisest and best of men, and circumstances of protracted tension invite it forth from the dark oubliettes of human nature. Let a white man, for instance, suppose himself in the shoes of a Negro standing outside the courthouse on the day when—after, let us assume, the presentation of persuasive evidence of guilt—the men accused of the Philadelphia killings come forth into the sunshine, grinning and slapping one another on the back and passing around the famous supply of Red Man tobacco.

For some time before the summer, there had been, by all accounts, little hope among Negroes in Mississippi of any settlement without a fundamental confrontation. A confrontation, in general, would not necessarily imply violence; the technique of Martin Luther King is to create a confrontation, to bring into the open and to crisis elements which have been concealed and subacute. But

* See pp. 108–110. At the Conference on Nonviolence at Howard University one of the more militant young people said: "If a lot of us young people don't believe in nonviolence maybe it's the function of the old ones to sort of hold us back"—the way a child wants to be protected from his own anarchic impulses. But if leadership is split this becomes impossible.

in Mississippi the scent of violence has been in the air for a long time, and some people have even longed for it, at moments anyway, as a release from tension. Even a person as committed to nonviolence as Mrs. Harvey could say that many Negroes "feel that they have been patient long enough, and that the Justice Department is not doing anything about their grievances, and that they must take things into their own hands." But such people always have in mind the interposition of a third force: federal force. Ever since the United States Marshals appeared in Oxford to install James Meredith in Ole Miss, there seems to have been a mounting sentiment among Negroes in Mississippi that in such intervention is the only hope.

Before the Summer Project there had been God's plenty of violence in Mississippi. On June 8, 1964, at the National Theater in Washington, D.C., there was a public hearing which produced elaborate testimony to this effect, and later, long excerpts from the proceedings were read into the *Congressional Record* by Representative William Fitts Ryan of New York to support the request made to the Department of Justice for Marshals in Mississippi. Protection, for whatever reasons, good or bad, was not forthcoming. The predicted violence was, however, forthcoming. The disappearance of the white youths Michael Schwerner and Andrew Goodman with, for symbolic completeness, the Negro James Chaney, precipitated, though in a limited fashion to be sure, federal intervention, and at the same time answered the question as to how to get intervention. Plenty of Negroes had suffered violence. So you do not get intervention by violence as such. You get it by violence to white skin.

The Navy assisted the FBI in the search for the bodies—for it was assumed from the first that bodies were what you were searching for. The number of FBI agents assigned to Mississippi was beefed up some tenfold. Governor Johnson of Mississippi was photographed as speaker at the opening of the new FBI headquarters in Jackson, with Director Hoover, arms folded, sitting glumly in the background. With the new headquarters, the FBI was apparently settling in for a long haul, and later remarks by Director Hoover about native law enforcement in Mississippi could give little comfort to the defenders of the status quo.*

* The investigation of civil rights cases in Mississippi, Hoover said, had been hampered by "water moccasins, rattlesnakes, and red-necked sheriffs,

Even if the function of the FBI is not, as Hoover puts it, to protect anybody—including Presidents and "those who go down to reform the South"—the Jackson office is an unmistakable warning that Washington really exists. Meanwhile the Justice Department exists, and any Mississippian who reads the daily paper can find out there is a case catalogued as *U.S. v. Mississippi.*

To bring about federal intervention violence was necessary, but it was not necessary to provoke violence. Violence was built into the Summer Project, for the mere intent to register Negroes, even to prepare them to register, is in itself ample provocation. Undoubtedly Negro leaders wanted, and want, federal intervention, and undoubtedly, not being idiotic, they knew that violence was the only way to get it, but they were in the fortunate—or unfortunate— position of being able to get what they wanted without even having to pray for it, much less lift a finger. Whatever anguish of scruple and tormented casuistry about responsibility there may have been among Negro leaders is not relevant to any objective view of the situation. The volunteers came fully warned of their risks. They took their own responsibility.

There has been some comment to the effect that the Project imported provocative types, everything from Communists, through race-mixing hand-holders, to beatniks. Some of this comment has come from expert observers. David Halberstam, of *The New York Times,* who covered the training period for the Summer Project at Oxford, Ohio, tells me: "I was taken by the fact that a number of the students appeared to me to be very dissident." Some of them, he says, were "so alienated that they might just as well, psychologically, have been Communists—because they hated their own country so much, and distrusted its every word and action. They had moved into the civil rights thing because it was the most tangible way to express their discontent." He added that "some of the Na-

and they are all in the same category as far as I am concerned." As for Neshoba County, where the three youths were killed, he said that "law enforcement is practically nil, and many sheriffs and their deputies participate in crime." (*The New York Times,* November 19, 1964.) Even with the FBI in Mississippi there was no noticeable decline in the number of "incidents," ranging from harassment to murder, tabulated by COFO. According to the COFO report there were more than 450 between June 15 and September 15. During the fall some of the worst bombings occurred.

tional Council of Churches people were somewhat worried about this, and the undercurrent of maneuvering of what they referred to as 'the hotheads from Snick.' " In regard to screening, James Farmer says: "I don't comment on the types who were represented during the Project, but I will state that there should have been more screening, and if there are subsequent projects, then there ought to be more screening. Screening is absolutely essential." But some observers saw things somewhat differently. For instance, one who was at Oxford for the training period, and visited Mississippi in the summer, says that she saw "attractive American youngsters looking much as they do on any college campus."*

In any case, there was no screening to give an acceptable image of the Project. When Mr. Halberstam, who says that other civil rights organizations he had observed had been "quite careful in this regard," asked a leader at Oxford about this, he was told, "and quite proudly too—that they did not screen, that there was room for everyone in their movement and that the commitment of an individual was far more important than his political beliefs—that, after all, was just what they were fighting against."

The leaders of the Project abjured, then, Test Act, barbering, and the psychoanalytic plumb line. They took the straight legalistic view: there should be no thought control and anybody has a right to go to Mississippi. As for motives and states of mind, Negroes in the Movement have, again and again, said to me that, "It's not motive that counts, it's what a man does." For one thing, the Project took the pragmatic view that in action you harness whatever forces you can, and let the state of the soul be an individual's problem. For another thing, the Project had no concern with tact. The leaders argued, presumably, that no amount of tact would get a welcome mat laid outside the door of a registrar's office or put blank cartridges into the chambers of a sheriff's .38. What little provocation a beard or a copy of the *National Guardian* or interracial hand-holding might mean, the big provocation had already been built in.

As for the demonstrable effect on Mississippi the biggest single result would seem to be that the Summer Project decisively pushed the state—that is, those who define public policy—out of their chosen posture. Mississippi had wanted it both ways: it wanted

* Alice Lake, *The New York Times Magazine*, November 21, 1964.

segregation and it wanted law and order. Or rather, it wanted to avoid the things disorder and lawlessness would surely entail: federal intervention, the impairment of business, and alienation from the rest of the country. There was a grimly comic illustration of the official desire to maintain order against over-zealous patriots in the treatment accorded James Farmer when, little more than hours after the Philadelphia murders, he came to Mississippi to investigate the event. The Director of Public Safety took a deeply personal interest in his welfare. In Meridian, whenever he was to enter his hotel room, two police preceded him to look in the closet and bath and under the bed, and while he was in the room, two police stood guard outside the door. When he moved, he moved under guard.*

What the Summer Project finally did, once and for all, was to dramatize the internal contradiction in the cherished policy of Mississippi. The policy had already undergone some shocks. The murder of Medgar Evers, for instance, had not helped matters, even if the hung jury did do something to restore balance. But by massively challenging the system of repression, the Summer Project made disorder inevitable, and it drew lawlessness out from under the guise of law; and now balance could not be restored. The Americans for the Preservation of the White Race and the special home-grown brand of the Klan, the white Knights of the Ku Klux Klan of the Sovereign Realm of Mississippi, had been evoked by the forces that found their climax in the Summer Project; and the random and pathological violence that the Klan and the "Americans" encouraged, and the penetration of the Klan into the law-enforcement agencies, were the last thing the State House, or the Citizens Council —that "uptown Klan" or "reading-and-writing Klan"—wanted; for the bomb-throwing and church-burning ruffians scarcely understood the long-range values of the sophisticated posture.

The Project demonstrated the old truth that so often needs new demonstration: you can't have just some law, you have to have law. The ruffians kicked over the apple cart, and there is no way to pick up the old apples. You have to get a new load.

As for the new load of apples, we find such a statement as that issued in November, 1964, in McComb, Mississippi, a center of

---

* Mr. Farmer had, in fact, been notified by the FBI that he was on the Mississippi "death list" of eight names. When he went to Philadelphia, the state authorities told him that they could not guarantee protection.

bombings, beatings, and general violence. Here six hundred and fifty white citizens—some by their own request—signed a statement calling for an end to "acts of terrorism," for "equal treatment under the law for all citizens," for "obedience to the laws of the land regardless of our personal feelings," for an end to the arrests of harassment, an end to the holding of public office by any person who has any obligation (such as membership in the Klan) "in conflict with his oath of office," and for the "widest possible use of our citizenship in the selection of juries" (that is, the use of Negro jurors). It remains to be seen how much effect such a statement will, in the end, have, but the signers number among them the two local bank presidents, and leading professional men and merchants—in other words, the holders of prestige and the manipulators of credit.

And there was one immediate effect. The next day, Charles Evers, under the watchful eye of local police, led twenty Negroes on a test run of desegregation in McComb, getting service at restaurants, stores, theaters and motels, in one of which, the Holiday Inn, Evers himself spent the night. The chairman of the McComb City Police Committee drew the moral: "Any time the power structure of a community takes a stand against violence, it certainly curtails the possibility of trouble."

Would this statement have been signed—or even imagined—if the Summer Project had not brought confrontation?

Other breaches have been made in the wall of Mississippi. The Jackson Chamber of Commerce advised compliance with the public accommodations provisions of the Civil Rights Act, and the Mayor of Jackson, Allen Thompson—the very man who had bought the police "tank" and mobilized "Allen's army"—rebuked the Citizens Council for urging resistance. Organizations like Mississippians for Public Education and the committee formed to rebuild burned Negro churches—as well as the organization of citizens in McComb—indicate that some focus for action can be found for the broad spectrum of opinion that runs from moderate to liberal. The state government has purged members of the Klan from the Highway Patrol, and significant cooperation between the state and some local law-enforcement agencies with the FBI has occurred. Schools were integrated in September, 1964, without incident. In Ripley, racially a very tough town, local suppliers gave discounts on material bought by the Carpenters for Christmas, a student organization from the North which had come in to rebuild the Antioch Baptist Church burned by segregationists; and this gesture by local merchants was, apparently, spontaneous, without connection with the organized effort by white Mississippians to help in rebuilding churches. Even in Philadelphia, one minister, the Reverend Clay Lee of the First Methodist Church, shortly after the arrest of the twenty-one, preached a sermon on Herod and the Infant Jesus in which he said: "The Herod spirit is also a spirit of bigotry. . . . We blindly adhere to our old ideas and concepts. We want to defend them regardless. . . . Deceitfulness has to be a virtue in the eyes of the bigot."

Whatever change of heart is involved here is being encouraged by the economic situation. The current income from state taxes has fallen significantly. State bonds offered on the New York market in late 1964 found no takers. The Gulf Coast resorts were badly hit by the Philadelphia murders, losing some fifty per cent of their clientele almost immediately; and in December, 1964, in Jackson, a Chamber of Commerce spokesman from the Gulf publicly admitted that hotel and motel use in his area was down to eight per cent.* The national boycott of Mississippi products was having serious psychological effects even before it was launched. And early in 1965 Title VI of the Civil Rights Act became operative; it provides for the withdrawal of federal funds from states or cities discriminating on racial grounds in any project federally financed in whole or in part.

The naïveté of a number of Mississippi white leaders is as great as that of Americans in general; faced with their difficulties, they feel that you can advertise your way out of Hell, and that if you get the right public-relations firm Saint Peter passes you at the Pearly Gates. Hugh L. White, an ex-governor, proposed that salvation lies in buying prime time on TV to present "the true image of Mississippi" to the world. Meanwhile, he had raised seventeen thousand dollars to send the band of the Mississippi Vocational College (Negro) to the Rose Bowl Parade to illustrate the cordiality of race relations in Misssissippi. But the voice of reason and realism can now and then be heard. George Keith, president of the Mississippi Press Association, said in a public speech: "It is time for us to be honest with ourselves."

* *The New York Times,* December 20, 1964.

. . .

However, nothing that has happened to date means that Mississippi has become the City of God. Aaron Henry, for instance, said to me that the "Civil Rights Act of 1964 is woefully deficient in the Right to Vote section," and that in the light of the three hundred to four hundred registrations (excluding Panola County) out of thirty-nine thousand applicants in the summer of 1964, "only federal registrars could do the job." Robert Moses maintains that Washington has not taken the fundamental steps necessary to maintain law and order in Mississippi, and says that papers have been prepared for presentation to a federal court asking that a federal injunction, with federal commissioners in Mississippi, be directed at all law-enforcement agencies in the state to halt violence. He points out that, further, a federal grand jury—such as that which first failed to return an indictment against the alleged murderers of the young men at Philadelphia*—is drawn from a voter list which, under present circumstances, contains the names of only a handful of Negroes. And Robert Moses might have pointed out that the twenty-one men arrested by the FBI in connection with the murders had scarcely been taken into custody before a statewide organization was set up to collect funds for their defense.

Far from being the Holy City, Mississippi is not even desegregated—except in some spotty incidental way that scarcely fulfills the intent of the Civil Rights Act. There has certainly been no universal change of heart. And some white people—who do not, of course, accept the theory of solution by "confrontation"—report that the summer has intensified the split between white and black to such a degree that a settlement is farther off than ever. But one thing is clear: there has been a change in the conception of self-interest and in policy. And such a change of mind can sometimes be a step on the way to a change of heart.

It is hard to believe that the Summer Project, by its very timing if by nothing else, did not have some influence in whatever change has been brought about. And it is hard to believe that some of the

---

* *The New York Times,* November 25, 1964. On January 15, 1965, true bills were returned by the federal grand jury at Jackson. The indictments are based on a statute of 1870 and the charge is conspiring to violate the Federal Civil Rights Code, with a maximum penalty of ten years and a fine up to $5,000. No arrests have been made under a state charge of murder.

forces mobilized by the Summer Project will not occupy the new breaches and widen them. The process would seem irreversible, but there is no reason to expect that the process will continue at an even pace—particularly if a real fragmentation of Negro leadership occurs.

3 ✖ *The Big Brass*

: 1 :

At my request, Adam Clayton Powell has kindly provided me with
the following biographical note, prepared by John H. Young of
Congressman Powell's staff:

In the fall of 1930—in the midst of the Great Depression—Adam Clayton Powell, Jr., a handsome, white-
complexioned, fun-loving and debonair youth of 22, stepped
ashore in New York City packing gifts, champagne and
pleasant memories gathered on a European tour. Welcoming
friends at dockside saw him as a dissipated and sophisticated
bon vivant, pampered and shielded by an eminent father,
and already on his way to success as the youthful business
manager of the large and powerful Abyssinian Baptist
Church of which his father was minister.

The young man and the carload of merry welcomers
dashed away from the pier and swept through the streets
of lower Manhattan up to Harlem, where he lived in a swank
brownstone with his father and mother. Rocking with merri-
ment as they rode, young Adam, the voyager, was oblivious
to the hungry, suffering and pain-ridden Negro masses shuf-
fling along the soon-to-be frozen streets of Harlem.

But a few nights later, fate in the person of five Negro
doctors came knocking at the carefree young man's door.
The physicians, weary from pleading with old-line conformist
Negro organizations to take up their professional cause of
disbarment from Harlem Hospital, had sought out young
Powell. After prolonged persuasion that lasted through the
night, he reluctantly agreed to take up their cause.

There followed a winter of discussions, consultations and indecisions, interspersed with young Powell's first series of mass meetings (later to become his chief weapon as a civil rights fighter). And in young Powell's own mind, a conflict was raging. For during that winter of 1930, two indelibly-etched experiences were turning over in his mind as if they were lights to be followed along roads leading out of the cold darkness of fateful decision.

One bobbing light recalled a teen-age experience as a bell-boy at the fashionable Equinox House in Manchester, Vermont. Young Adam remembered that by passing for white he possessed the remunerative daily privilege of opening the door of Robert Todd Lincoln's limousine, a chore not dared by "Negro" bellboys lest they receive the customary rap on the knuckles from a walking stick wielded by the son of the Emancipator (the son could not tolerate Negroes).

The other, a steadier light, recalled an experience at Colgate University when young Powell's roommate had left a note saying he could no longer share a room with him after his father, the Reverend Powell, making an ardent address before the assembly in behalf of the Negro's rights, had revealed that young Adam was a Negro. "Patterson's note," says Powell, "came as a tremendous shock to me. We had been such good friends. We had drunk out of the same bottle and slept with the same women . . . and to top it all, the University Dean put ME out of the room."

These two burning experiences revolving in young Powell's head during that winter of soul-searching and surging passions offered two roads to the future: to pass for white and escape the privation, realities and pains of being a Negro in America, or, to take up the cross of the "Black Man's Burden." In moments of doubt, young Powell struggled with his decision. For, as he knew, once having committed himself to the road of Negro protest there would be no escape and no turning back.

The decision launched a career and influenced the course of history in the United States. In the spring of 1931, a transformed and fiery young Powell led 6,000 marchers against City Hall and won his first heady victory under mass protest—he had discovered in his first encounter that he COULD fight City Hall AND WIN!

In describing the actions of the demonstrators on that day, Powell says, "they moved as one with me, for in the few short months we had lived together, I had taught them and myself the power of nonviolence." And of the event itself he says: "This was heady wine for a youngster of 22. All my life I had prepared for that opportunity. That day we started a movement which would never be stopped; a rising chorus which would never be stilled. I knew we had within our hands a powerful weapon which if disciplined and mastered would cut through the false veneer of America into the rotting cancer of racial prejudice. We were marching up freedom road now and there wasn't anybody to stop us."

Thus began one of the most publicized and controversial, yet dynamic, fruitful and persevering careers in the entire history of American politics. It was a career whose trail was to lead from a Virginia slaveholding grandparent on his father's side, and from a mother who was the daughter of Colonel Jacob Schaefer of the brewing family and his life-long mistress, to 30 years of service as the minister of the great Abyssinian Baptist Church with 12,000 members; to the New York City Council and on to 20 continuous years in Congress and to a seat there of power never before attained by a Negro, as Chairman of the all-powerful House Committee on Education and Labor; and to the praises of two presidents of the United States—John F. Kennedy and Lyndon B. Johnson—for legislative achievement in the passage of laws benefiting the nation.

Along the way, Adam Clayton Powell became an enigma and an object of hate to some, and a saviour, hero and object of love to others. Among the former can be counted most white newspapers and other news media, and perhaps a majority of white America who have recoiled from what they consider to be bad habits and unjustifiably bitter attacks against them; also to be listed among the opponents of Powell are some Negro intellectuals who have disagreed with the bluntness of his approach and the direct street action of picket lines. Among those who support Powell and find him their hero are perhaps the great majority of the Negro people and Negro news media of the nation who have cheered his fighting utterances from public platforms in practically every state in the Union and over nation-wide television. His most fanatic worshippers are the members of his church and those Negro people of Harlem who have consistently voted him ten consecutive two-year terms in Congress, over strenuous efforts by outsiders to defeat him.

Indeed, it is difficult, if not impossible, to disassociate Adam Clayton Powell from the Harlem he represents, and vice versa. In the sweep of three series of descriptive words one discovers a striking similarity in the portrait of both of them: desperate, bitter, angry and explosive; pulsating, flamboyant, dynamic and vicarious; God-fearing, fanatic, erratic, ambitious, determined and perservering, are but a few of the words which fit both Harlem and her congressman like a snug mantle.

But even *The New York Times,* one of his severest critics, admits that Powell "has done more to dramatize the issue of civil rights than any other man in our time." Critics aside, an objective view is that no one can doubt that Adam Clayton Powell is a real spokesman for the Negro, by and with their own choice; over a span of thirty years, he is perhaps their greatest spokesman.

*   *   *

I wait in Room 409 of the old House Office Building, on Capitol Hill, for Mr. Powell to arrive from a meeting of the House Education and Labor Committee, over which he presides. The outer office of 409 is spacious. The furniture is the institutional mahogany of a successful institution. At a desk in one corner a Negro clergyman, with reversed collar and *rabat,* is reading a newspaper; the secretary-receptionist, Mrs. Harris, an extremely pleasant and cordial young lady, is typing away at her desk, and getting off telephone calls; an assistant or secretary, youngish, heavy, presides over an enormous desk, littered with papers, with the easy air of a man who knows that in chaos is a secret order. He is white.

Somewhat late the Congressman arrives—height 6 feet, 2¾

inches, weight 190 pounds. For all his fifty-six years, he shows not even an incipient belly, and carries himself like an athlete, or a horse Indian. In fact, he has the classic profile of the Indian, and though he is far paler than an Indian, there is a coppery-reddish tint of skin. His hair is black and straight, probably coarse, combed back, scarcely touched by gray. His mustache sprouts vigorous and black. He is wearing a splendidly cut tan suit, something like a gabardine, and a shirt with the bold dark stripes at this moment in style. He is a master of dignified affability, commanding affability.

He leads the way into the inner office, which is larger, with more mahogany, well-stocked book shelves along two walls, the great desk. The chairs are black leather, numerous, enormous and comfortable. The chairs have the aura of the nineteenth-century good living, nineteenth-century statesmanship, and expensive cigars. The Congressman, though not precisely a nineteenth-century type, lets his long frame sink into a chair with graceful, practiced ease and cocks a knee up.

> WARREN: On the telephone the other day you said to me that the old Negro organization leadership is finished.
> POWELL: Like old ladies, they have not kept pace with the times. Let's trace the birth of an idea. It's born as rampant radicalism; then it becomes progressivism, then liberalism, then it becomes moderate, then it becomes conservative, then it's outmoded, then it's gone. And the old leadership has not brought forth new ideas.
> WARREN: What do you conceive as the function of your organization ACT?*

* ACT includes Lawrence Landry, who has been active in the school boycotts in Chicago and in the political insurrection against William Dawson, the Negro who has become a fixture in Congress from the First District in Chicago; Gloria Richardson, with whom the Negro revolt in Cambridge, Maryland, is identified; Isaiah Brunson, of the Brooklyn chapter of CORE, who sponsored the stall-ins at the approaches to the World's Fair; Stanley Branch, chairman of the Freedom Now Committee of Chester, Pennsylvania; and Jesse Gray, who first became newsworthy in organizing the rent strike in Harlem, and has since called for "100 trained revolutionists who are not afraid to die." Malcolm X has met with ACT, but I do not know how close the association is. "ACT," according to a spokesman, "will not function in a manner acceptable to white people. It will do things that are acceptable to Negroes" (Nahaz Rogers, quoted in *Commonweal*, July 3, 1963). The letters ACT are not initials; they merely make a word.

POWELL: I do not belong to ACT. I have said this repeatedly. I only participated in one of its meetings, at the written request of Mr. Landry of Chicago, and in the letter he asked me to come as "consultant," the grand old man of the Black Revolution—because I'll be sixty years old in four years and these are all kids in their twenties. I was there as consultant and I gave them definite advice based on my years of experience, because I led the first successful nonviolent campaign among Negroes in the United States, for eleven years, from 1930 to 1941, and I quit in 1941 because there were no more worlds to conquer, almost like Alexander the Great—no, I don't mean that—now we have new worlds to conquer. The Northern school desegregation, the housing and retraining of the older Negroes, automation, the training of drop-outs and push-outs, and up-grading, and political patronage commensurate with the Negro's balance of power in the key electoral states.

WARREN: In revolutionary situations there is usually a drive toward centralization of leadership.

POWELL: Correct.

WARREN: That has not yet happened here?

POWELL: ACT is only one year old. But I think there's going to be a polarization. ACT may be the catalytic agent in this polarization. There is dissatisfaction with the old leadership. Now with ACT there might be produced a polarization. Eric Severeid commented in a column that in the Negro Revolution the fight is not between conservatives and liberals, the fight is between liberals and extremists.

WARREN: How do you place ACT in this spectrum?

POWELL: As a catalytic, a group fumbling around trying to find something to hang its hat on. They want to be a clearing house. And I said, "What you should try to do is to make your umbrella big enough to include everyone." I pointed

---

The general role of ACT, except insofar as it clearly aims to strike beyond the established organizations for mass support in political, and other, action, and beyond the objective of civil rights, is not yet clear. The only notable program in which ACT seems to have been involved to date is the barrage of telegrams to President Johnson, a program organized by Jesse Gray, supporting the claims of the delegates of the Mississippi Freedom Democratic Party, and threatening to storm the convention at Atlantic City.

at Malcolm X with whom I disagree, but for whom I have great admiration, for some of his insights.

WARREN: He has some great insights.

POWELL: That's right, that's right. I don't agree with the Black Muslims, don't believe in separation, so I did something which sounds like semantics, before the ACT program, which they ate up. I said, "Let's don't fight about integration. Let's fight for desegregation, and once we desegregate let each go the way they want to go." The Black Muslims want to go for separation. I'm an integrationist.

WARREN: You make a sharp distinction between integration and equality?

POWELL: That's right. Desegregation now, then let each one indulge whatever philosophical view they have.

WARREN: But first deal with civil rights?

POWELL: We're not even concerned with civil rights. If the Civil Rights Bill is passed, in its entirety, it would not affect the Black Revolution in the North one bit.

WARREN: Wouldn't it affect the South?

POWELL: Yes. You see, the Black Revolution is two-pronged. In the South it's the middle-class and upper-class Negroes, the preacher, the teacher, the student, and they're fighting for the golf course and the swimming pool and the restaurant and the hotel and right to vote. But when you leave the South, where only one-third of the Negroes now live, you have a revolution of the masses. Not the classes. And that revolution is interested in schools, housing, jobs. And the Civil Rights Bill will not help them at all.

WARREN: Not in a direct way but—

POWELL: It will create a climate.

WARREN: What's the relation of leadership to the mass-based movement in the big Northern cities? Can leadership control and direct this?

POWELL: There's no leadership in either the old-line, or new, organization that can control the masses. One of the shocking statistics is that if you take the so-called Big Six* of the civil rights organizations, they don't have but 900,000

* NAACP, the Urban League, CORE, SCLC, Snick, National Council of Negro Women.

members. And many of those are white. So you have
19,000,000* black people who are uncommitted to the civil
rights movement.

WARREN: What is the problem of leadership then?

POWELL: The problem of leadership is as follows. I have had
here in Washington two summit meetings. They were not
recorded by the press, although the news was released to
the press. Here is the quickest way to get to the heart of the
masses, and if I weren't so extremely busy with this tremendous committee I have that handles forty per cent of the
domestic legislation in the United States, I would do it. I
asked the Bureau of Census to give me the names of all
national organizations with black membership, that are
black-led and black-financed. They gave me the Masons,
the Elks, the doctors, the lawyers—and altogether there
are 51 national Negro organizations, with a membership of
12,100,000. Of course, there are duplications. But that's
where your mass is. So if someone could ever form a council
of Negro organizations, they'd be getting right into the heart.

WARREN: We know there is no social change without power.
What kind of power is involved in the present situation, and
what is the nature of the threat it mounts?

POWELL: The white man is afraid. He has a monopoly of
the instruments of containment—the National Guard, the
police, the electric cattle prods, numerical superiority. All
of a sudden Birmingham explodes. There are demonstrations
all over the country. And these demonstrations are based
on nonviolence. And you cannot stop nonviolence with
violence. So the white power structure stands aghast.

WARREN: The technique of nonviolence is the decisive
factor in Negro power?

POWELL: The day the Negro changes from nonviolence to
violence, he is finished, and the Black Revolution has to
start all over again, at some future date.

WARREN: In any revolutionary situation there is always
competition for power, and the crisis of overreaching—more
and more extreme promises, more and more radical solutions
proposed. How much danger of that do you now see?

* In 1960, the official figure of the Bureau of the Census was 18,871,131.

POWELL: I don't see any danger at all, except in the ranks of those self-proclaimed leaders who are trying to move up the ladder, by virtue of those promises because they have no other method of moving up the ladder.

WARREN: How did you respond to the now well-advertised statement by the Reverend Galamison that the public school system should be wrecked if it did not conform to his time-table for integration?

POWELL: I don't subscribe to that any more than I can subscribe to the white segregationists' destroying the public school system rather than obeying the Supreme Court.

WARREN: In regard to overreach, what about the stall-ins?

POWELL: It's an overreach, but I was in favor of the stall-ins, because to me any form of demonstration that's non-violent necessarily quickens the thinking of people in the power structure.

WARREN: In nonviolent demonstrations, is there a distinction between legitimate and illegitimate? That is, with reference to the effect on society? Say the stall-ins as contrasted with picketing or sitting-in?

POWELL: I don't think there's any difference. I say that any form of nonviolence has its effect.

WARREN: Violence has an effect, too.

POWELL: Yes, but I don't believe in it.

WARREN: What about the difference between demonstrations that have a specific target, as contrasted with those that are merely expressions of anger or discontent?

POWELL: I believe in demonstrations directed at specific targets, because when you have demonstrations of just bitterness and frustration, with no goal, then you're on the edge of something that could turn into violence.

WARREN: Did the stall-ins have a specific objective?

POWELL: They had an objective to me in pointing out to people coming from all over the world the lily-white policy of the Fair itself, the discrimination in the building of it. For instance, the African pavilion was built entirely by white labor. No Negroes worked on it at all. Now if the leaders of the stall-ins didn't have that as their target, I say they were wrong.

. . .

Mr. Powell is always at ease, leaning back, that one knee cocked over the side of the chair. He never hesitates for a word, the rich voice moving steadily in its controlled rhythm. He knows his own mind.

We touch on some of the familiar topics. Apathy, for instance. It had been massive in Harlem, he says, but the "Birmingham explosion" cured that. For instance, in his Harlem district, the support of the school boycott was ninety-two per cent effective, with the next highest the district of the organizer, the Reverend Galamison, with only sixty-eight per cent. When I ask about the Negro's responsibility, he says it is "different than what you are probably thinking about." It is, he says, "to quicken the white man's responsibility into action." The Negro has no other responsibility now—"not all this business of fixing up your house, and not spending money on luxuries, and getting better education." Not in a time of crisis. I mention Dr. King's "street-sweeper" speech, but he will have none of that.

As for the cultural split in the psyche of the Negro American, he has little concern for that. The Negro American doesn't know anything about Africa, and never had any culture of his own in America. "The nearest thing to it is something the whites have adopted, and that is the Negro spiritual." Anyway, now the Negro's impulse is to adopt and use the culture around him: out of a population of roughly 20,000,000 Negroes in the United States there are more young people going to college than out of the 56,000,000 population of England. The Negro newspaper was moribund before the Negro Revolution began, and presumably will not survive the success of that movement. Only the church will survive.

When I mention Myrdal's theory of a workable Reconstruction of the South, Mr. Powell says immediately that he would have had no resistance to the idea of compensating slaveholders. Not only a moral question is involved, but an economic one. He says that he sees moral questions not abstractly but in a social and economic context. And Myrdal's ideas about Reconstruction lead us to Powell's own Manpower Development Training Act, which, he remarks, *The New York Times* predicted "might go down in history as the greatest labor bill of this century." As for Whitney Young's "Marshall Plan," and even the President's Appalachian Program, "that is really old WPA." He thinks that his own war-on-poverty bill—and his vocational-education and manpower-training bills—will take out some of the wrinkles. "These are specifics. These are much more important than the Civil Rights Bill."

We get on the question of where Negroes live in relation to whites, and Mr. Powell recalls that when he married Hazel Scott, "the Chief Justice of Vermont rented me his lakeside chalet, for my honeymoon, and the neighbors of the Chief Justice threatened that they would have my water supply cut off." But he is the only Negro leader ("and I don't count as a Negro leader because I don't have a national organization") who lives in Harlem. The others don't. They live on Riverside Drive, Long Island, Westchester. If he can live in Harlem, why can't they? In Washington he lives in the heart of the slums, in Southeast Washington. "The Negro leadership has got to stay with the Negro masses as he fights to integrate the Negro masses, and for him to go out and be integrated is of no help to the masses." Furthermore, Negroes are somewhat justified in their suspicions of a sellout.

*   *   *

On Hoffa's Trial:

POWELL: I think the article by Fred Cook in *The Nation* is absolutely shocking. *The Nation* devoted fifty pages to an analysis of the way they tried to, and did, hang Hoffa. It's unbelievable: star witness, for instance, who has been on the payroll of the Department of Justice, which is against the laws of Congress—$150 to $200 a week—and the jurors not only were served liquor as they were locked in, but the male jurors —women were procured for them by the Department of Justice, and paid for by the Department of Justice.

WARREN: Gives jury duty a new glamour, doesn't it?

POWELL: If the women were glamorous, it did.*

* Mr. Powell has had his own legal difficulties. He was acquitted, in 1958, of a charge of tax evasion, defended by Edward Bennett Williams, who also defended James Hoffa. In 1963 Mr. Powell was found guilty of defaming Mrs. Esther James, a Negro, by calling her, on a TV program, a "bag woman" for gamblers' pay-offs to police; subsequently, after being cited for contempt of court for failing to pay the judgment of $46,500, a civil arrest

On the Role of the White Liberal:

Joe Barry asked me this same question in Paris, at a press conference I held at the Embassy. And my answer to him was very terse. Not to be abrupt—just to give him the answer: "Follow black leadership."*

On the Bandung Conference:

Until the Bandung Conference I believed that everything I had done, in picketing New York for eleven years, in being the first Negro in the New York City Council, in authoring or co-authoring every civil rights bill in Congress, was for the good of the Negro. But when I got back from Bandung, on April 19, 1955, I said, "No, this now is a fight to save America."

On Lincoln:

I think Lincoln is vastly overrated. I think that he did nothing at all except that which he had to do, and he did it in terms of winning a war.

---

order was issued. In April, 1964, a criminal arrest order was issued on the charge that Mr. Powell had transferred ownership of his estate in Puerto Rico to relatives of his wife; and in July a criminal arrest order was issued in connection with the alleged transfer to his wife of payment received for an article in *Esquire* magazine. In December the New York State Supreme Court refused to prohibit criminal prosecution of Mr. Powell on the charge of transferring funds.

* "Constance Baker Motley, the Associate Chief Counsel of the Legal Department of the NAACP, speaking just last month at a meeting of the Guardians, 1500 men of the Police Department, said that 'Negroes and *only* Negroes should lead their organizations.' The interesting thing is not only that her statement confirmed my view, but that her statement also was not made until after she had been elected a New York State Senator from Harlem, and was independent to speak her mind. Prior to that she had to take orders from a white man, who is the Chief Counsel of the NAACP." (Speech by Powell at Harvard University, April 24, 1964.)

On Southern Congressmen:

I have very good relations with men from the South. People on both sides of the fence would be amazed if they knew how well we get along. Because I know their situation. Right now I have two or three outstanding Southern Congressmen — from the deep, hard-core South who are begging me to attack them in public, because they're afraid they might lose the primary.

* * *

It is easy to understand how Congressman Powell has good relations with, even, his colleagues from the South. He is a man of enormous magnetism. And he does understand their situation. He is a political animal.

: 2 :

In 1905 in answer to a call from W. E. B. Du Bois, twenty-nine delegates from fourteen states gathered at Fort Erie to deny that "the Negro-American assents to inferiority, is submissive under oppression and apologetic before insult." This was the beginning of the Niagara Movement, organized to combat the accommodationist policies of Booker T. Washington and the rising tide of the new Jim Crowism and lynch law. At the second convention in 1906, at Harper's Ferry, in a syntax and tone very familiar to us in late years, Du Bois proclaimed, "We want full manhood suffrage, and we want it now."

Du Bois named some other things that the Negro wanted, and wanted "now"—the end of discrimination in public accommodation, free association, education, the enforcing of the Constitution. This was, in fact, the beginning of the long drive for civil rights—that is, in the organizational sense as we know it now.

The Niagara Movement was short-lived, but by 1910 the durable National Association for the Advancement of Colored People had been founded. Two facts of the founding remain crucial for any understanding of the NAACP. First, the NAACP was bi-racial in its inception. Though Du Bois was important in the founding, it was, actually, Oswald Garrison Villard who, at the suggestion of three other white people, W. E. Walling, Dr. Henry Moskowitz, and Mary White Ovington, called the conference out of which the NAACP grew. Second, the primary concern of the NAACP was the legal definition of the status of the Negro.

These two facts of its founding indicate its special role and, in late years, its special vulnerability. The bi-racial nature of the organization, with white men in positions of responsibility, and the emphasis on legalism clearly relate to a certain conception of an integrated society toward which the Negro presumably aims. But meanwhile the NAACP has been under attack as both "soft" and "narrow"—soft because there is the recollection of white sponsorship, narrow because it is not grounded in the masses. As long ago as 1942 Ralph Bunche said: "There can be no doubt that the Negro leaders in the organization have always kept a weather eye on the reactions of their prominent and influential white sponsors." And more lately we hear Adam Clayton Powell demanding why a white man should be head of the NAACP Legal Defense and Educational Fund, when there are Negroes as well qualified as Jack Greenberg. Or, if the NAACP is bi-racial, he again demands, Why doesn't it stop saying "that this is the voice of the black masses?" The NAACP can win court cases, it is said, but the Negroes, the masses, don't live in a court, they live up in Harlem, or down in Oxford, Mississippi. The NAACP, Louis Lomax further charges, is undemocratic in its internal operation, and externally "cannot decide what, if any role, it should play in the mass movement, and is unwilling to commit itself."*

In 1946, Spencer Logan, then a young man just back from the war, in a book called *A Negro's Faith in America,* said: ". . . a man who fights for the legal recognition, may in the process lose sight of the human values involved."

It is easy to see how Roy Wilkins, president of the NAACP, surrounded by the flashier direct-action organizations that can knock off the headline spots, was stung, in a speech at Alexandria, Virginia, on June 16, 1963, to say that Snick and CORE "furnish the noise," but the NAACP "pays the bill [the bail bonds and court costs]," and that the other organizations are "here today and gone tomorrow," and that there "is only one organization that can handle a long, sustained

* *The Negro Revolt.*

fight—the NAACP." He should be comforted, however, by the glowing testimonial that any member of the Citizens Council of Mississippi will give the NAACP. It is the NAACP that still comes in for the "big cussen."

In the rest of the country it still comes in for the big membership. There are five hundred thousand members, an all-time high, and in 1963 the income was $1,437,675.77, some ninety per cent derived from Negro sources.* It seems here to stay, and if you go up to its offices in Freedom House, at 20 West 40th Street, in New York City, you feel you are entering the portals of a going concern that has been going a long time. As you sit in the big outer office, you face the little brass plates bearing the names of life members: they run from floor to ceiling, in column after column.

*   *   *

Roy Wilkins seems durable, too, in a quiet, graying, balding, somewhat academic way. He is a very busy man, working under pressure, but if you did not know it you would not guess it, for his manner is unhurried, and he has a natural warmth that seems to spring from a simple curiosity about human beings, and a feeling for you, yourself, as a person. Born in St. Louis in 1901, he received his A.B. from the University of Minnesota and was the managing editor of the *Kansas City Call* for eight years, before he became assistant secretary of the NAACP. He is, clearly, a thoughtful man with something detached and professorial in his tone, and his smile has a certain trace of sadness in it, a faintly ironical sadness. You feel that he knows a good deal about human nature, including his own—and yours.

WARREN: May I start with a quotation from a TV interview with Mr. Galamison? He says that he would rather see the public school system destroyed than for it not to conform to his own schedule for integration. And he goes on: "Maybe it has run its course, anyway—the public school system."

* There was an operating loss in 1963 of $107,540.67. The NAACP is organizationally and financially distinct from the NAACP Legal Defense and Educational Fund.

WILKINS: I recall this, Mr. Warren, and I disagree absolutely with every syllable. I know the Reverend Mr. Galamison, he was at one time president of the NAACP chapter in Brooklyn. I have respect for Reverend Galamison's devotion to his cause, for his single-minded attention to the public school system of New York. He knows a very great deal about it and about its deprivations of Negro children, but for any reformer, black or white, to come along and say, "I'll destroy it, if it doesn't do like I want it to do," is a very dangerous business.

WARREN: In a city like Washington, D.C., with the immense disproportion of Negro children, how can integration of the school system be achieved?

WILKINS: It applies not only to Washington, it applies to the Borough of Manhattan. We have a steady trend here. Whether you can achieve what is popularly called integration under such circumstances is a very real question — and I don't know but that then we are faced with the question that we ought to be facing along with the question of integration— that is, the quality of public education. I don't think white people would assert that schools attended by white people are inferior schools with respect to the quality of education— mathematics, history, et cetera. Though they might well admit, as we maintain on our side, that they would be better schools if there were different racial strains.

WARREN: Let's grant that. That's not the point I am raising.

WILKINS: That's right. Well, when you say that you can achieve quality education only through integration, then it seems you go a long way toward admitting that a school composed of your own race from top to bottom could not be a superior school. Personally, I'm not willing to admit this.

WARREN: A Negro of great intelligence and distinguished achievement said to me: "Take Washington—if necessary we will have to go to Virginia and bus them [white children] in" —ignoring all legal problems.

WILKINS: And also ignoring the welfare of the children. You will find Negro parents who also object to busing small children for great distances. Desegregation must be a prime objective of the Negro community, and we of the NAACP in-

tend to work at it persistently. But I think we ought to come to grips with the idea that a school in the midst of a black district which isn't going to melt soon—no matter how much progress you make in housing—that a school in a black ghetto has to be made a good school—so good, in fact, that pupils in other areas will want to transfer to it. When we make this [integration] an absolute condition, then I think we're on the way to *not* achieving what we want to achieve. The reason Negroes made a drive for integrated schools was because it was demonstrably clear that the best education was over there where the white people are—and the bad education over here where the black people are. We have to meet these [issues] with practicality—but never retreat on the idea of equality of opportunity and the absence of racial compulsion.
WARREN: The issue of economic class—that overlaps and confuses the race issue, doesn't it?
WILKINS: Exactly. A city that doesn't have any Negroes still has a school problem. The children from the poor white districts come from homes that don't have books—and it's hard to talk to them. They don't have the same vocabulary, words don't mean the same thing.

There is a vein of hard realism in Mr. Wilkins' thinking. He is prepared to deal with things as they are. He tries, apparently, to keep his mind firmly fixed on the thing, not the word; on the situation, not the shibboleth. He says that "we have to meet these issues with practicality—but never retreat on the idea." That discrepancy, that lag, between "practicality" and the "idea," is what he lives with—is the pervasive irony of his effort; not bitterness, merely a recognition of the human process, of the fact of so much strain and distress for so little gain. It is, even, the wry recognition that, in the long run, willingness to pay this excessive cost is the fundamental glory of the human effort.

A man who knows the hard substratum of our experience needs to be durable. Some can even hate him for his knowledge. It is a knowledge many do not have the strength to put up with.

WARREN: You remember the article by Norman Podhoretz, in *Commentary*—the idea that assimilation is the only solu-

tion of the Negro problem? How do you respond to that?
WILKINS: I don't know. I don't know that I can put it into
words. I've had the feeling that he was trying to say the
unsayable. I don't know.

But what is the "unsayable"? Is it the thing we think too painful
or shameful to admit—that there may be a deep, irremediable, incor-
rigible, hard germ of prejudice in all of us, a real entity and not
something that we can explain away by all the theories of symbolism, or economics, or a shadowy relic of tribal xenophobia, or political manipulation? But if we should admit to such a prejudice, what
is the moral of the tale? Would it mean hopelessness or self-torturing
guilt? Or is the question always, in immediate terms at least, not that
of the extirpation of prejudice but of what to do about it? If put on
this basis it becomes a matter of justice, not sentiment. Is justice to
be scorned? And might not the recognition of justice even be a step
to something else?
In any case, Wilkins is asking a shrewd question about the view
of Podhoretz: is anti-Negro prejudice different from anti-Semitism?
He does not, however, phrase it that way.

*   *   *

WILKINS: I cannot help but think whether he, Podhoretz,
could be found among those who might maintain that the
Jewish-Gentile relationship will never be solved except by
assimilation. I don't think he is of that school. I don't know
how far assimilation will go, or how much is inevitable.
WARREN: There are some white people—*not* segregationists
—who say: "Any price to be rid of this problem." Is something like that between the lines of the article?
WILKINS: Exactly. Now, as the Negro's economic and cultural
position improves—and by cultural I mean his adjustment to
what the lords of culture of our day say is the culture, I don't
mean that his culture is necessarily inferior—but as he ad-
justs, I look for more and more mixture. But not in substantial proportions. I think the Negro is very proud of himself.
He has been proud in a sort of defensive way for many years.
He is now proud affirmatively.

WARREN: That is, the notion of escape has become less important?

WILKINS: Exactly so.

WARREN: And the sense of identity as Negro is more important?

WILKINS: More and more important.

WARREN: Let me read you a quote, sir, in relation to identity, about Negro history: "The whole tendency of the Negro history movement—not as history but as propaganda—has been to encourage the average Negro to escape reality."* This is by Arnold Rose, Myrdal's collaborator in *An American Dilemma.*

WILKINS: Yes, at the University of Minnesota. Well, I've had some disagreement with Dr. Rose's conclusions for some time —some of them—and this strikes me as a little far-fetched. It bends over triply backward to say that the emphasis on Negro history, while it's aimed at race pride, may result in self-depreciation, because it was necessary—and here he makes an assumption—it was necessary to delude oneself as to one's historical accomplishment in order to build pride.

WARREN: But we have seen this principle work in the American South, haven't we?

WILKINS: Yes. But I don't believe that Negro history, as it's taught, is on a par with the playhouse that the Southern white people have constructed for themselves in order to rationalize their position in American life after 1865.

WARREN: What about New England?

WILKINS: The same thing goes.

* The Negro History Movement goes back into the last century. There are items ranging from *Jesus Christ Had Negro Blood in His Veins,* by W. L. Hunter or *The Ammonian or Hamitic Origin of the Ancient Greeks, Cretans and All the Celtic Races,* by Joseph E. Hayne, through *The Story of the Negro,* by Booker T. Washington, on to the massive work of W. E. B. Du Bois. In 1897, in Philadelphia, was organized the American Negro Historical Society, in 1912 the Negro Society for Historical Research, and in 1915 the Association for the Study of Negro Life and History, with its *Journal of Negro History,* founded by Carter G. Woodson, a Harvard Ph.D. The Negro History Movement drew support from every point on the Negro spectrum—from Black Nationalists and separatists to amalgamationists. The inculcation of race pride was a declared purpose, but this, of course, has been modified and sophisticated as Negroes have entered into the mainstream of scholarship. See August Meier, *Negro Thought in America.*

I ask why the Negro Revolution should have occurred now. He sees it as a stage in a long history—"back even in slavery days"—but accents several factors of the recent past: the "cumulative resentment" given a symbolic focus in the centennial year of the Emancipation Proclamation; the creation of "an educated cadre of youngsters"; World War II and the new mobility; the beginning of Negro political power; the bitterness when the Supreme Court decision of 1954 was not obeyed—"the attempt to change the rules after the game had been won." When in 1960 the Negroes took direct action they were, in effect, saying: "We can't depend on legislatures and we go to the courts and we take fifty years to go slowly through the courts and chip away at the separate but equal, and we win in 1954, but we don't win. So let's get out on the streets and take it directly to the seat of government."

In response to his account of the long history behind the Negro Movement, I remark that many Negroes flinch from this sort of explanation in the frame of historical process, because it implies time. He says that, emotionally, he sympathizes with that flinch, that the "Negro shrinks from the use of this word *gradualism,* or even the concept." I observe that *process* is a bad word now. "Yes," he says, "the Negro doesn't like that at all."

But he goes on to say that if the Negro would read the history of the labor movement in this country, just the struggle for child labor laws, or the struggle to get rid of the injunction, "he would understand that while you never, never, never give up or compromise, that things don't happen overnight."

We are now back to that strain of hard realism, the awareness of the grinding process by which "practicality" and the "idea" are brought a little nearer together—this side of the horizon beyond which parallel lines do intersect in the blue haze of distance and daydream and sentimentality.

*   *   *

On the Revolution:

> We are not seeking to overthrow a government or to set up a new government. We are here trying to get the government,

as expressed by a majority of the people, to put into practice
its declared objectives.

On Violence:

I once said about Malcolm X—he was talking about rifle
clubs—if the Negro had believed in that he would have used
it a long time ago when he was much worse off than he is
now. As a matter of fact, the Negro in this country is a very
practical and pragmatic animal, and he has never lost sight of
the elementary facts of survival, and he has never forgotten
that he's a ten per cent minority. He does not have the power,
except the moral power.

The Negro as an Old American:

He's a very old American, and he's an American in his
concepts. I think he's a liberal only on the race question. I
mean, I think he is a conservative economically, I think he
wants to hold on to gains in property and protection. I don't
see him as a bold experimenter in political science or social
reform. He may change once he gets into a period of equality.

On Anti-Semitism Among Negroes:

Basically the Negro is not anti-Semitic, and such anti-Semitism as he ordinarily expresses stems from his personal experience—I knew one once and he did so-and-so to me.
The Negroes who make anti-Semitic remarks are those who
have run into, say, a Jewish storekeeper or a Jewish land-
lord or a Jewish woman who is the boss of domestic servants.

But I have met thousands and thousands of Negroes, and
they have never forgotten, wherever they've been, the Jews
who helped them—some Jews. Even in the Deep South, you

recognize that Jews have helped them—and remember Jews have been vulnerable in the South, too.

* * *

I remember how Harry Golden analyzes the role of the Jew in the South. "The Jew," he says, "missed an opportunity, an opportunity to give the same sort of help he himself had had to ask all through these long bitter centuries. The Jew missed this opportunity not because he lacked sympathy for the Negro and his cause, but because the Jew feared his own security depended upon conforming with the habits, attitudes, and prejudices of the surrounding society."

According to Golden's account, many Southern Jews, even before 1954, opposed the ultra-liberal American Jewish Congress which filed an *amicus curiae* brief in behalf of the NAACP, and told Dr. Israel Goldstein, president of the Congress, that they might cut back their allocations. The more conservative American Jewish Committee, when it tried to establish a liberal stand, met with strong opposition. A delegate from Memphis said: "You Jews from Brooklyn should keep your long noses out of our Southern way of life."

In the Negro Movement, according to Golden, the Negro "understands that the Jew is the weak point in the white power structure of the South. By instinct, the Negro launched his strongest demonstrations in Birmingham, Atlanta, Richmond, and Savannah against the Jewish-owned department store. Tragi-comically, Jews clutch my arm to tell me Negroes are anti-Semitic."

My own observation is that, by and large, both Negroes and non-Jewish whites in the South assume that a sympathetic relation exists between the Jew and the Negro. And in most places which I know, some Jew has given a basis for this assumption.

* * *

On the Role of the White Liberal:

White people—beginning with long before the Magna Carta—were fighting against oppression and for the liberty of the individual, and they have fought, since we have had our country here, many battles not connected with race. They have fought for freedom of the press, and freedom of religion—all the sorts of things they have fought for. We ought to recognize that they have a heritage of protecting and enhancing the Constitution of the United States, irrespective of whether it applies to black people, white people, Northerners or Southerners and that there can be sincere white people who believe in these principles and want to fight for them, and we ought not to shut them out of our movement because they don't fit into every niche and cranny of our thinking and being, and they don't behave exactly as we feel they should behave as blood brothers—we're brothers, after all, in a cause, the cause of liberty.

In the present state of Negro-white relations, and the scramble that's going on to get on record and to be uncompromising and to be militant and demanding and to be all the things that are now regarded as the things you have to be—people say a lot of things in public about white people having to conform to this—white people *must* give up that—white people *must* recognize—white people *must, must, must.* This is a sure way to get on television and to get quoted and to cause tremors in some quarters—or, at least, if not tremors, head-scratching and soul-searching. But I believe that the Negro must recognize that there are sincere white people interested in the cause of freedom.

They don't know us, we say. We know about them, we're so sure, but they don't know about us. Now when they come over and try to find out about us, why don't we teach them, instead of saying to them, "We look on you with suspicion. You're just trying to ingratiate yourselves. You don't know how to get on in the Negro world. You're awkward and you —we look down on you—we laugh at you."

On the Next Phase:

What principally will remain is for the Negro, with the barriers down, to speed up the process of self-development and self-discipline, so that he becomes a contributing, a more con-

tributing member of society. When you come out of a ghetto
—not only a physical ghetto but a ghetto intellectual and
ideological—it takes a while to find out how to function outside. But there are Negroes who already have identification
with the community. You find them assuming their roles and
sometimes suffering derisive comments from their brothers
on how they have removed themselves from racial life.

On Whether the Southern Mob Represents the Southern Majority:

The biggest obstacle in the South is not the white rank
and file, who demonstrate against the Negro, but the Southern
political oligarchy. It has used the Negro to perpetuate control over the entire South.

On Roy Wilkins' Being Called a Moderate:

I know I've been called a moderate, but I always reply
that our position has sponsored the most radical idea in the
twentieth century—the idea of eliminating racial segregation.
So I'm not concerned particularly with these labels that the
latter-day crusaders bring upon us.

On the Speech at Alexandria, Virginia:

When that speech was made it was an accurate statement.
It applied to our unfortunate experience with some members
of CORE in Louisville, Kentucky, where we had a joint
demonstration, which was billed, however, as a CORE
demonstration. I wish I knew the secret of CORE's ability to
get publicity. I'd like to hire whoever they have over there.
In that demonstration two hundred and sixty-seven people
were arrested, and two hundred and fifty-five were NAACP
youngsters. That's another thing that sticks in my craw.
Most of our young people have been involved, but the credit
has gone to other organizations. Anyway, only twelve people
out of this so-called joint demonstration were identified with

CORE, and yet, when all the shooting was over, and all the hooting and hollering was done, we not only got none of the credit, but were left with the legal bill of some five or six thousand dollars. Since that time the picture has changed to some degree.

On Louis Lomax:

I regard Mr. Lomax simply and solely as a recorder, as a writer, who has made a very good thing out of it financially. He has made several references to the NAACP, and his analysis of our role is totally and completely inadequate, because it is based on his own personal, subjective estimate and not upon our records. He has never been here and consulted any records, and I would have to discount sharply his estimate. As for his remarks on the structural organization of the NAACP, a lack of democracy, this is absolutely nonsensical. The only organization that has a democratic structure is the NAACP. I think sometimes we have too much. I can't afford to spend too much time on Lomax. I think he is a sort of parasite on the civil rights movement. I think that other civil rights organizations have found him similarly at fault, if I recall correctly.

On Responsible White Leadership in the South:

Some has emerged. The Tuscaloosa businessmen, for instance, pleaded with Governor Wallace. The Birmingham businessmen. The Norfolk businessmen, in Virginia, took charge of school desegregation. In Durham they did the same thing.

On Overreaching Among Negro Leaders for Power:

I think it's almost self-controlling. I think any irresponsible leadership which genuinely overreaches itself to the point where it inflicts damage on the cause, quickly loses its influence.

On Living Together:

This so-called Revolution must be conducted in an uncompromising fashion, but it must be conducted in a fashion that recognizes that when it's all over, we have got to live here together in mutual respect.

*   *   *

To live together in mutual respect: that, it would seem, is the vision that governs the actions of Roy Wilkins.

: 3 :

The Urban League is as old as the NAACP. Its emphasis has been economic rather than legal, but in late years, as the Negro Revolution has emerged, its economic emphasis has been envisaged in a more and more complicated context. Whitney Young, the Executive Director since 1961, sees the League as complementing the activities of the other organizations. In his view the League provides the social engineers, the planners, the men who can work at a policy-making level, with the highest levels of the corporate, labor, and governmental communities.

To fulfill this function the League must be a "professional" organization. There are some five hundred and twenty-five full-time staff members, of whom three hundred and fifty have an M.A. or above. There are offices in sixty-five communities, where eighty-five per cent of the Negro population lives. Each League is bi-racial, with a board about half-and-half white and Negro. It is this careful balance of black and white plus the heavy support from white philanthropy and business, which has, over and over again, invited the charge of "Uncle Tom-ism."

Whitney M. Young, Jr., is over medium height, and weighs, probably, some 190 pounds. The pounds look like the thickening flesh of the slightly aging athlete, not fat, and his step on the carpet of his office is yet lithe under the bulky burden. When he moves from the big desk, it seems, in fact, that more energy comes into play than is required to carry him to the couch or chair where he will sit to talk. When he stops, he stops abruptly as though applying a brake, then sits down. Above the broad shoulders the head is big. It is a roundish head, with the hair combed carefully back on the heavy skull, the hair streaked with a little gray. The brow is not high but heavy; the eyes are deep, with a hardness, at times even a hint of sullenness, in the glance; the jowls are heavy, and the underlip agressively out-thrust. The whole impression is of persistent, heavy, aggressive force: impatient aggressiveness leashed and controlled by will.

Mr. Young was born in 1921 in Lincoln Ridge, Kentucky, and educated at Kentucky State College, Massachusetts Institute of Technology, and the University of Minnesota (of which Roy Wilkins and Carl Rowan are also alumni). He was once, briefly, a basketball coach. He was Dean of the Atlanta University School of Social Work, from which he resigned to come to the Urban League. During World War II he was a sergeant of engineers in a Negro company with white officers. "Most of our combat was building roads," he says, "but we did get into the Battle of the Bulge when they ran out of infantry."

WARREN: In the light of the bi-racial tradition of the Urban League, let me read a passage, Mr. Young, from a recent book by Charles Silberman:*

In [James] Baldwin's cosmology, in fact, there seems sometimes to be no decent white of any sort, and no way a white man can prove his decency: If you are hostile, you are a racist; if you express friendship or sympathy, you are a fuzzy liberal, part of "the chorus of the innocents"; and if you commit yourself to action, this merely proves that you are a condescending white using Negroes to purge your own conscience, or trying to raise Negroes to your level.

* *Crisis in Black and White,* Random House, 1964.

Well—you see the line.

YOUNG: Yes, I see the line, and my analysis would differ. First of all, I think that neither white people nor Negroes have any monopoly on vice or virtue. The present plight of the Negro citizens—and that plight is serious—results not so much from historic ill will or good will; actually what we've had in our society is about ten per cent of white Americans who have been actively resistant. But about eighty per cent have been largely indifferent. So it hasn't been ill will or good will. It's been *no* will that's largely responsible. White Americans have ignored the Negro. They keep their heads buried in the *Wall Street Journal* as the commuter train stops at 125th Street.

The significance of the Negro Revolution is that America is now forced to look at the Negro. But I think, increasingly, white America, when it's confronted with the tragic consequences of indifference, with the consequence of considering race relations as a spectator sport, will find themselves on the right side. I'm not distressed by the unrest, by the tension, by the conflict. I think this is in many ways healthy, because it's bringing the real attitudes and feelings to the surface where we can deal with them.

WARREN: There are a lot of ideas there, but I'm going back to the question of the Negro's conception—or conceptions— of the role of the white man. We've had all sorts of pronouncements, including that by Lorraine Hansberry, who asks who would want to integrate with a burning house. Your organization assumes a special kind of cooperation.

YOUNG: This is a very basic question. But let me say first that it *is* quite true that the Negro today no longer conceives of his goal in life as simply a replication of white society. He is now conceiving of integration more as a synthesis than as a complete dropping of all that is Negro. He's saying that all that is white is not good—or else we wouldn't have been kept in slavery all these years; there must be some bankruptcy somewhere. The Negro says, "I think I can bring something to a new society, even though I can't bring, certainly, a superior technological know-how, certainly I can't bring money, I can't bring in many cases the same level of education—

but out of suffering one develops something that goes beyond just jazz. One develops compassion, one develops humaneness—certainly the Negro has developed a tolerance, a patience, that maybe the larger society can use. Maybe General Motors can use some of our compassion." What we are working for is a society where we can lift the positives out of both cultures, reject the negatives—and we *do* find negatives in both cultures—and move toward a new society much better than either of the old.

WARREN: Are there Negroes who don't want to integrate—not only Black Muslims—who reject the white man in a number of ways?

YOUNG: Yes, but how significant are they? One of the tragedies of the whole civil rights movement is the inability of the white person to distinguish significant Negro leadership. For example, any Negro who achieves a certain amount of prominence—a Cassius Clay or a Willie Mays—when he utters something about race relations is treated as an expert.

WARREN: A self-designated expert—like the white Southerner?

YOUNG: Yes. It's like asking Primo Carnera about foreign policy. We ought to keep perspective here. While Lorraine Hansberry is a gifted playwright and while Baldwin is a gifted writer, these are not people who either by their experiences or by their training or by their whole emotional orientation, are by any means leaders of the Negro Revolution. They are people who describe it, who react to it, but who themselves are not equipped to suggest strategy or to interpret social implications. It must be remembered that when the struggle was really hard and tough, Baldwin couldn't take it. He left the country—he wasn't even here. There are many people who now are able to write about it, make a wonderful living on it, but let's not confuse this with leadership. You see *Time* magazine making that mistake.

WARREN: But to take Baldwin for an example, his role as a writer has been necessarily and inextricably tied to the question of race.

YOUNG: But again this writing reaches only the intellectual kind of white person who is moved by this because he has a great deal of guilt feeling, people who, as Baldwin well knows, are in a masochistic mood, where they don't do anything but at least will permit themselves to be ridiculed and punished.

WARREN: Who's masochistic—white people or Negroes?

YOUNG: White people.

WARREN: Isn't there something of that in Baldwin? For instance, in his talk about the gas chamber for the American Negro?

YOUNG: But my point is that a great preoccupation of the white press, whether with Malcolm X or Baldwin or Adam Powell, is a kind of guilt feeling, saying, "Beat me, daddy, I feel guilty." About Malcolm X, many white people are saying, unconsciously, "You know, I'm sort of sympathetic with this notion of separation." Many a white person who's irritated by tension and conflict, takes comfort when a Negro comes along who says, "I don't want to integrate your daughters and I'm going to get rid of crime and welfare." That white person unconsciously says, "Look, that's not such a bad idea."

WARREN: "Let's subsidize him," he says.

YOUNG: So the press says, "Let's play this up. Instead of talking about Whitney Young, let's play up the Black Muslims." But there aren't ten Negroes who'd follow Malcolm X to a separate state. The only appeal he has is to give a Negro who's been beaten down all day a chance to get a vicarious pleasure out of hearing somebody cuss out the white people.

WARREN: Like the Ku Klux Klan in reverse.

YOUNG: Precisely. It's the exploitation of misery and despair, and that's easy for the demagogue.

WARREN: Let's get back again to the white man—that white liberal.

YOUNG: Well, today, the Negro is saying to him, "You've had all the institutions in society and an opportunity to do something about our plight. But you haven't done it." Now the one who's offended, the one who's hurting—he's going to be the one to say he's hurting. The Negro is assuming the initiative and he will never again turn it over to anybody else, so that white people, if they want to express liberalism today, must accept the fact that the Negro is going to lead, or that the Negro will accept him only as a peer.

Now what worries me today is that most white people bemoan the methods and tactics the Negroes use, instead of saying, "Well, I don't like the sit-ins or I don't like the blocking of traffic, so I'm going to support the Urban League's massive Marshall Plan."

The Triborough Bridge is an example—three educated white people and three illiterate unemployed Negroes were engaged, and yet the whole civil rights movement and all Negroes get blamed and warned. Negroes, in general, have shown more restraint than any group of people. The white man is concentrating on the inconveniences and disturbances and not on the basic *cause* of the problem: poverty.

WARREN: Yes, the white man may bemoan methods and tactics instead of removing causes, but you—in your position —have to choose among methods and tactics.

YOUNG: I don't think I have to make this kind of basic decision either.

WARREN: I mean in this way: When it comes down to the method of the stall-ins as contrasted with the method of demonstrating against particular pavilions at the World's Fair—

YOUNG: Yes, I'll make a choice there.

WARREN: In terms of a basic policy?

YOUNG: Oh, you'll find responsible Negro leadership. Some things we endorse, other things we certainly will not endorse. We take a public position against the stall-ins. On the other hand we will not oppose picketing the Maryland or Mississippi pavilion. We have to make this kind of choice. But one thing, if nothing else, 1963 did for us—it taught us that no longer can we generalize about our friends and our enemies. In the past we said Northerners are liberal and Southerners are bigoted, and management is bigoted and labor is liberal. We found, in the 1960's, some of the most sophisticated and brutal bigots in the North and in labor than we ever found in the South and in management—and we found the reverse also true. As long as some of those fair-weather friends could express liberalism in terms of indignation about a lynching in Mississippi, this is one thing; when it comes to having somebody move next door to them, this is something entirely different.

WARREN: Let's leave the white man alone for a minute. What about Negro responsibility?

YOUNG: I have been concerned, as the Urban League has for years, with the fact that with rights go responsibilities. I have been inhibited in elaborating on this publicly because so many of the columnists and so many of our newly appointed advisors—

WARREN: You mean self-appointed?

YOUNG: Self-appointed advisors have taken this line about Negro responsibility almost solely, and these are the very people who in the past have been largely indifferent to the plight of the Negro citizen, they've been people who fought against civil rights. I'm thinking of columnists like David Lawrence and Fulton Lewis. Now these are the people who speak of Negroes' assuming certain responsibilities before these rights are to be given.

WARREN: Isn't the question of responsibility somewhat poisoned by the association with Booker T. Washington's self-improvement program, his "Cast-down-your-bucket-where-you-are" program?

YOUNG: Yes, very definitely the word *self-help* has been tied in with the philosophy of Booker T. Washington.

WARREN: So we're dealing with a symbol which carries the wrong connotation?

YOUNG: Yes, but I don't want to leave the impression that even with that reluctance there is an absence of recognition of the Negro's responsibilities. My speech "The March on Washington" is an example. It recognized the responsibility not as an either-or. I spoke about the responsibility of the Negro to do a lot of different types of marching—in front of city halls and five-and-ten-cent stores—to get elementary rights, but at the same time we must also march our children to libraries and the parents must march to adult education centers and to PTA meetings and to other places.

WARREN: I recently heard Dr. King speaking at Bridgeport, and he wound up on the theme "If you're a street-sweeper, be the best, et cetera."

YOUNG: I've heard, I'm sure, a similar speech by Dr. King, but this is always preceded by a most militant posture. I think that's important. In many of the speeches of Negro leaders to all-Negro audiences we deal with this a good deal. Seventy-five per cent of it is a reminder to the Negro citizen that the removal of barriers will not insure first-class citizenship.

But I never want people to forget the amazing sense of responsibility that Negroes have shown through history— remaining loyal to the country, not being taken in by the Communists, not getting violent and being restrained in the face of all sorts of provocation, the responsibility of taking care of their unwed children when white parents would have been able to arrange for abortions or send them off to institutions that were closed to Negroes. This is a kind of higher responsibility and a higher sense of morality.

WARREN: Can you speak about the intersection of class and race in the Negro's situation?

YOUNG: In the centennial edition of *Ebony* magazine I discussed the class situation inside the Negro community. The Negro's choice is too often between bread-and-water or champagne-and-caviar, either sending his kids to slum ghetto schools or to plush prep schools, either living in a hovel or in a suburb. This is creating a vacuum, it is depriving the lower class of Negro of leadership potential. It develops not so much by an attempt to escape the Negro mass on the part of the Negro middle class, as an attempt to escape the ghetto.

WARREN: Is this split between the Negro mass and the middle class getting wider?

YOUNG: Oh, it's much wider.

WARREN: This is not what is said by many Negroes, of course.

YOUNG: Well, I'm talking about an economic fact of life. The figures show that now we have more unemployment and poverty than ten years ago. But we also have more Negroes in the middle class. The gap is there.

There are factors at work here other than the economic to widen the gap, paradoxical factors that arise from the very success, however limited, of efforts to integrate society. For one thing, when a Negro moves into a white neighborhood he leaves some rancor behind him in the black neighborhood from which he has come, a rancor that negates, to some extent anyway, whatever strength he had as a potential leader: he "used to be black."*

Or if a talented, successful Negro moves into some intellectual or artistic world where integration is more advanced than in society in general, he, again, may be cut off, to a degree, from acceptance by the Negro mass. In some cases, a program of integration contains within it certain self-defeating elements. For instance, the open-enrollment plan, which permits a student—a Negro, say—to go to the school of his choice, is a device for integration; yet by and large the student who elects to go outside the de facto segregated school and compete in the white world is superior, and the removal of his leaven from the segregated school is bound to have a bad effect on that school. By the same token, insofar as he succeeds in the integrated school, he is probably removed from his basic contact with the Negro world. This is not an argument against open enrollment—except for Black Muslims; but it is a fact that should be recognized.

WARREN: A question is, what is the spiritual gap? Is there a failure in identification?

YOUNG: Yes. But there are two things happening. On the one hand there is greater sense of pride in race and solidarity as far as goals are concerned, but on the other hand there is developing this economic gap that sets up social and actually geographic distances and makes identification between the lower-class and middle-class Negro more difficult. This means that the lower-class Negro is suspicious of the intervention of the middle-class Negro. And it also means that the rabble-rouser is able to influence the masses easier and discredit responsible leadership.

WARREN: That's a real danger, isn't it?

YOUNG: That is the real danger.

WARREN: Has this led to serious cracks in leadership by bids for power?

YOUNG: It has made it much more difficult for responsible

* See pp. 142, 393–395.

leadership to intervene and to get emotional response from the masses. But another thing in the picture is that the mass media have helped to build up the demagogue. The only person the masses see on TV and on the front page speaking for their hopes and dreams is the demagogue. And this makes it difficult for a responsible leader to get the confidence, or even get the awareness, of the masses that he is working for.

WARREN: How does this relate to Adam Clayton Powell's remark that the leadership of the Negro civil rights organizations is dead, that because they can muster only about nine hundred thousand members they have no political significance?

YOUNG: I think that Mr. Powell is reflecting his own frustration and his own inability to reach national status. What set this thing off was the March on Washington, when he was not called upon in any major role.

WARREN: It's funny how discussion of Mr. Powell provokes considerable evasion in even some quite direct and courageous Negroes.

YOUNG: Usually they pull away—they're afraid to take him head-on.* And if white people didn't attack him so much, Negroes would not rally to his defense so much. Negroes just get defensive any time a white person attacks a Negro.

WARREN: In general, what can the responsible Negro leader do to fill the needs of the masses?

YOUNG: Responsible Negro leaders must be given some victories, because we stand out in the midst of unemployed people and hold up nothing. I don't know how long the white responsible community believes that it can continue to not

---

* One good reason for not taking Adam Clayton Powell head-on can be surmised from the turnout for the Adam Clayton Powell Day celebration in Harlem on September 19, 1964—a parade of sixty cars and four brass bands, crowds on the street waving green and gold pennants saying "I was there— Adam Clayton Powell Day," a rally attended by thousands, with tributes from twenty-three leaders of the civil rights movement and organized labor, and a street dance. The Reverend Richard A. Hildebrand, president of the New York chapter of the NAACP, and Whitney Young were among the notables who paid tribute. Even so, the power of Adam Clayton Powell is not monolithic. In the fall of 1963, J. Raymond Jones ("The Fox"), who had worked with Powell against Tammany in 1958, was elected to the City Council over the positive opposition of Powell.

give any victories to Negro leaders and expect them to continue to be leaders and influence their people.

WARREN: That's clear, I should think.

* * *

On the Liability of White Participation in the Urban League:

I think it's made us vulnerable to certain attacks, but I would think that if it hasn't seriously hurt us, that is because Negroes deep down inside know that they cannot go it alone.

On the Role of the White Liberal:

Now we're at the point where the Negro ought to be able to say to the liberal: "Look, I'm upset about discrimination in the labor movement. I'm upset about some other things, but I know we have to work together on the common goals of better housing, better education, and better social legislation." In turn, the liberal ought to say to the Negro: "I am opposed, maybe, to the activities on the Triborough Bridge or the stall-ins, but I am for these other things, and on those we must keep together."

On the Pressure by Negro "Extremists" to Jockey the Liberal into an All-or-Nothing Situation:

I'm not sure it's pure tactic. I think what we're witnessing here is a new group that finds some power and influence and is able to attract mass attention, and it's a new experience to be able to throw one's weight around and be the source of all the news stories and television, and there's a period of sort of tasting this and getting accustomed to it. I think the Negro is like somebody just learning to walk, he's trying out his legs and doesn't want anybody to help him.

On Myrdal's Plan for the Reconstruction:

I think it would have been very sound.

On Lincoln:

I have mixed feelings about Lincoln. Yet I recognize the limited contact that white people had with Negroes of that period, and probably they were victimized by the kind of anthropology and other things that they were reading which would suggest basic inferiority. I think you'd have to judge Lincoln in the context of his climate, and in that context I still would give him this kind of credit.

A Joke about Historical Context:

Let me tell you a little story I once heard. A group of Negroes was trying to get a mayor of a certain Southern city to employ Negro nurses, and after a great deal of effort, he finally said: "Well, I can get these nurses in here if you will promise me you don't care how I do it." And they all said all right. And he said, "Now don't get angry with me—when you hear how I do it." And they said, "No, we just want nurses in there." Then he publicly went to the hospital people and went to the legislature, and he said: "I think it's a dog-gone dirty shame that our fine white girls from nice homes and nice backgrounds have to rub and scrub and wash the private parts of these black Negroes."

On the American Way of Facing Problems:

We don't act; we react.

*   *   *

The action that Mr. Young regards as fundamentally and immediately necessary is a sort of massive crash program to relieve the Negro's poverty and poor education. According to his statistics, 20 per cent of the Negro workers are unemployed. Family income for Negroes is 53 per cent of white family income and the gap is widening. Family income for 60 per cent is under $3000, for 75 per cent is under $4000. Of one million young people, between sixteen and twenty-one, who are out of school and out of work, 50 per cent are Negroes. In Chicago, for instance, 85 per cent of the welfare caseload is Negro, out of a Negro population of slightly over 20 per cent. Negroes get three-and-one-half years less school than whites. The Negro adult life span is seven years shorter than the white. Infant mortality, like childbirth mortality for mothers, is on the upswing; in Harlem, for instance, it is twice that of New York as a whole. Unless the situation of the Negro can be relieved, and he can be productively drawn into the economic mainstream of American life, civil rights become a travesty.

In other words, within the Negro community, as the talented and the lucky make their way out of the ghetto, the great mass seems doomed to become a lumpen proletariat, with an infinite potential for blank destructiveness. At this moment the drift of evidence is in that direction.

When Mr. Young first promulgated his Marshall Plan it was specifically for Negroes. This raised the cry of "preferential treatment" in some quarters. To this charge Mr. Young retorts: "Papers like *The New York Times,* instead of grabbing hold of the Marshall Plan, called this preferential treatment. Now at the same time, only a few days later, they applaud the Appalachian plan, a special effort for those people; they urge massive help be given to Alaskans after the earthquake, they applaud a special help to the Hungarian refugees and the Cubans. But with the Negro, they come back and say, no, he must be treated as an individual, not as a community."

His basic argument is that equality must be made to mean equality of opportunity if it is not to be mere verbalism. Now the Negro, as he puts it in his book *To Be Equal,* "is educationally and economically malnourished and anemic. It is not 'preferential treatment' but simple decency to provide him with special vitamins, additional food, and blood transfusions." This program he regards as a transitional stage: "I believe we [the Negroes] must receive assistance *until* [italics mine] we can make use of equal opportunities now opening to us because we are Americans, and no Americans ought to be deprived or disenfranchised economically or socially."

In the hearing before the Ad Hoc Committee on the War on Poverty Program, on April 14, 1964, he had already shifted emphasis somewhat from that in his original Marshall Plan proposal: "The Urban League is concerned about *all* of the poor, but we are particularly concerned about the Negro and we think that the facts should reveal that we have every reason not only to be concerned but that all Americans should be very much concerned."

And he returns to one of his favorite arguments. The Urban League, by professional training and by the confidence it enjoys in large sectors of the Negro community, is well prepared to help administer a War on Poverty Program; and this relationship would "buttress Negro leadership and established groups." It would, in other words, head off the irresponsibility of an opportunistic over-reach.

Young's whole approach involves a clear-eyed look at the de facto inferiority of a considerable percentage of the Negro population—a subject which many people, some Negroes and some white liberals, flinch from. They flinch from it for the same reason that white Southerners flinch from the facts and figures on the de facto inferiority of the white South—things like the lag in IQ scores in the armed forces, illiteracy rates, educational standards, poor records in Northern graduate schools, the high incidence of venereal disease, general health standards. People flinch from unpleasant topics. But Whitney Young does not flinch from facing the unpleasant fact of the Negro's condition: "The Negro, if he fails to recognize his deprivation or acts as though it doesn't exist, is guilty of stupid chauvinism. And the white person who ignores this reality or acts as though it doesn't exist is guilty of dishonesty." Young goes further, and generally recognizes that there is a "Negro's Negro problem"—the problem of taking responsibility to raise standards and enter competitively into the general society.

Furthermore, Young is one of the few people who has quite soberly put his mind on the problem of what integration might really mean. He is certainly not unaware of the moral aspects of the question, but he is far removed from the rhetoric and rancor, the breast-beating and Bible-pounding, which, mixed with a pseudo-Pentacostal babble, have too often, on both sides of the color line, been the order of business. What Young comes up with is apt to disappoint the host who have some sort of vested interest in, or emotional need for, the doctrine of the Great Day, when trumpets will blare and we will all rush forth to embrace one another in transports of redemptive joy. "This matter," he says, "of seeing integration as an overwhelmingly complex, delicate, or revolutionary kind of thing must be overcome. In reality, integration is concerned most properly and urgently with the simple, elementary fundamentals of everyday life." He imagines, as it were, some morning just like any other morning, when, on the bus, on the way to work, you think, "My goodness, I guess I'm integrated." Then turn to the morning paper.

I do not mean to imply that Young takes a mechanical view of the matter. He seems to be undergoing a struggle toward a philosophy, scarcely articulated as yet, that would significantly relate the act of "living" to the business of "making a living." He has some instinct for the wholeness of life, and for him, I assume, a job is not merely a means to an end—survival, pleasure, acceptance: the job under ideal conditions is a way of being, one aspect of the human fulfillment. If this is true, then Young is up to more than an attack on segregation and poverty, up to more than a program for integrating the Negro into American society. He is attacking, instinctively perhaps, the great dehumanizing force of our society: the fragmentation of the individual through the fragmentation of function and the draining away of opportunity for significant moral responsibility—the fragmentation of community through the fragmentation of the individual. In the end, then, the integration of the Negro into American society would be, if I read Young aright, a correlative of the integration of the personality, white or black.

: 4 :

James Forman was born in 1928, in Chicago, but passed the first seven years of his life, with later visits, in Marshall County, Mississippi, some thirty miles north of Oxford, on the Tennessee border. But his mother took him back to Chicago, where he attended gram-

mar and high school, graduating in 1947. After that came four years
in the Army, with a hitch on Okinawa in 1949-50; then college—
UCLA and Roosevelt University, from which he received a B.A.,
and then Boston University, where he had a fellowship, was an
assistant in the Government Department, and majored in African
Affairs. Then came a year working at the Illinois Institute in
Juvenile Research, while writing a novel (unpublished), and a
period as a schoolteacher in Chicago. In 1960, just back in Chicago
from the summer school in French at Middlebury College, he became involved by some members of CORE in public relations work
for the campaign to get food down to Fayette County, Tennessee,
to provide for evicted Negro tenants. The next step was logical:
he became a worker on a vote drive in Fayette County—the county
just over the line from his childhood home in Mississippi—and ever
since 1961, has been working, as Executive Secretary for the Student Nonviolent Coordinating Committee.*

Up to that time his life, Forman says, had been "all up for grabs."
There had been something of the same drift and blankness we find
in the account Robert Moses gives of his life before the first sit-
ins. Like Moses, Forman had had an intellectual bent but no clear
goal. He had been ambivalent about many things, he says, "and
this ambivalence revolved, I think, about the whole question of
whatever it is that I do, can this best integrate with the conception
of doing something for the Negro in the United States." And like
Moses, Forman found in activism the thing that gave focus to his
existence.

He does not see the plunge into activism as the result of a sudden revelation, or an overnight decision, but as the ripening of a
long process. "Things have more historical context than that," than

* The founding of Snick came as a result of the first wave of the sit-ins.
Ella Baker, one-time Executive Secretary of the Southern Christian Leadership Conference, suggested to her organization to call a meeting of the leaders
of the various sit-ins. On April 15-17, 1960, at Shaw University, in Raleigh,
North Carolina, at the expense of SCLC, the meeting took place, with some
two hundred persons present, one hundred and twenty-six being students. A
loose organization, without any official connection with any other body, was
set up, at first called the Temporary Student Nonviolent Coordinating Committee. Not until October, at a conference in Atlanta, was the organization
put on a permanent basis. Snick is not a membership organization; workers
move in and out. There is a minimum of structure, a maximum of spontaneity
and fluidity.

an overnight decision, he says. And even the novel on which he had been working had a theme of the "daily frustrations in a Northern city, and one of the characters tries to break through this frustration by developing a nonviolent movement"; this, he says, looking back on the novel, was obviously an expression of something that he had wanted to do.

At lunch, before Forman had told me about his own novel, we had been talking of Ralph Ellison, and he had said that he never understood what a person meant when he said he wanted to be primarily a writer or an artist. Now we return to it:

> FORMAN: . . . or a tennis player or a golf player, and then after that want to be a Negro.
>
> WARREN: And after that a human?
>
> FORMAN: Yes—I just don't understand it. I'm critical of the position, but in being critical I am sophisticated enough to know that I should understand the frame of reference that other people are talking about.
>
> WARREN: Maybe no theory is basically involved—just a compulsion—a need.
>
> FORMAN: I have never understood what is art for art's sake.
>
> WARREN: Well, some of the greatest artists would deny such a theory. Tolstoi, for instance.
>
> FORMAN: I wouldn't want to go on record that I'm opposed to Ellison because Ellison has said—is supposed to have said—that he considers himself as an artist and then as a Negro. If that's his position, then I don't understand what people mean by what's an artist.

Later I say that I don't think Ellison ever said that he was an artist first and a Negro afterward. I want to indicate that though Ellison does aspire to be (and clearly is) an artist, and does not see literature as a mere device for protest, this does not mean being an artist first and a Negro (or a human being) later. But the topic gets lost. And it seems that Forman is firmly committed to the notion that literature must be directly instrumental or degenerate into "art for art's sake." In any case, his interest, his passion, lies elsewhere.

But perhaps I am misinterpreting him. Perhaps he is merely

saying that his interest has its present focus because the world has its present structure; if the world were different his interest would be different. For twice during our period together, he says that he wishes that everything were settled, that we did not have to talk about this topic—the topic of race and society; he wishes that we could talk about other things. Even about novels, he says, and novel writing.

The world is, however, what it is, and we do not talk about novels. I ask him if he can give a profile of the "young Negro" of Snick.

FORMAN: People are always typing individuals and I have just never been of that school, perhaps due to my own inability to give such typings, such generalizations. But I think one can say of these young people that I know best—within Snick—that there is, you know, an awareness among some of them that social change has to come. At the same time, you know, there exist, within this country, many young people, both black and white, or certainly many young Negroes that are motivated by traditional American values, a desire to make a lot of money, a desire to be socially mobile and have a home, two cars, partial payment on traveling abroad, then pay for the rest later on. But at the same time you have people who are rejecting these values. We [in Snick] don't make any money, and the important thing is, you know, working for social change.

WARREN: I've just been reading a dissertation by a young man named Rose on the American Negro student. He is impressed by the large number who don't involve themselves —who follow the standard American middle-class aspirations.

FORMAN: Why is he impressed? I don't see how it could be otherwise. Negroes are a part of this society and they're going to accept these values just as most whites do. But that's not relevant to social change, because you don't have to have a whole mass of people. You just have to have people who are dedicated to working for social change and spreading the message.

WARREN: Among those that are dedicated, what's the relation of activism to two things—first, to an idealistic and intellectual grasp of the social question, and second, to a desperation at having no sense of direction and no clear aspiration—activism as a mere emotional expression?

FORMAN: I don't think there are many involved simply as an emotional—as an outlet for frustrations solely. Now, there's no question about it—myself, I am personally frustrated and that involves my emotions. At the same time, there is a sort of intellectual and idealistic commitment. I don't think the two are separable.

WARREN: I remember Gilbert Moses, in Jackson, Mississippi, remarking on his first shock to find among freedom riders a type he associated with street-corner hoodlumism—the drifters. Then he went on to say that the first shock passes, and you realize this is their way to become people.

FORMAN: It's necessary to understand the frame of reference from which he speaks, because I don't think that it's accurate just to call people street-corner types, you know. They're human beings who may not have had the so-called formal education, the so-called world view that some of us may have. Yet they know that within their own social circumstances there are certain things which are not right. If you're going to have any kind of profound change you must get people whom some would call the lower classes.

WARREN: Adam Clayton Powell says there are two distinct Negro movements. The one in the South is primarily middle and upper class, people claiming the rights appropriate to what they feel their talents to be. In the North it is a mass movement based on the claustrophobia of a ghetto culture.

FORMAN: I don't think he understands—if that's his statement—what's going on in the South. Because the movement in the South is not basically a middle-class movement. In 1960, when the movement first started it was led by students who might be considered middle-class. But it didn't take long to become a mass movement involving very poor people. As a matter of fact, I would say that the so-called middle and upper class in the South are not involved, and sometimes even act as a hindrance.

WARREN: But what about the leadership of, say, Snick itself? All I know are persons of intellectual attainment.

FORMAN: That's very true. Snick is the one movement that has room for intellectuals, and I think it's one of the main strengths that we are capable of absorbing the energies of people of intellectual attainment but who, at the same time, are not snobbish. There's a difference between being middle class and having intellectual attainments. There's a commitment to work with people. We're not working in major cities —we're working in very poor areas in the country, and so whatever your intellectual attainment is, you have to begin working with the masses.

WARREN: Do you find that some of your field workers of intellectual attainment—say, in Mississippi—have a romantic view, a romantic feeling for the purity of experience of, let us say, the field hand, the poor and deprived and ignorant —a kind of Wordsworthian attitude?

FORMAN: Your question—we both come from different backgrounds in a sense—but the fact of the matter is, I understand it sufficiently to say I don't think that that is the case.

WARREN: I could offer you some examples to the contrary, I think.

FORMAN: That may very well be the case. I haven't talked with everybody in the organization. But I don't think there's this romantic attitude. I think that what people may be saying, on the other hand, is that in the Deep South, the issues are clear-cut. In Greenwood, Mississippi, for instance, it's quite obvious who the opposition is. It's different from the West Side of New York when you're trying to get in a Princeton Plan. I mean, where is the opposition? The situation becomes ambivalent because some Negroes may even present a plan counter to that. In Greenwood, Mississippi, it becomes clear-cut.

WARREN: Shotguns are clear-cut.

FORMAN: That's right. But that's very different from a romantic conception of the purity of experience. I may be wrong.

WARREN: Changing the topic a little, what vacuum was Snick created to fill?

FORMAN: First, it decided to go into the small towns and underprivileged areas of the Deep South. Secondly, Snick would fill a need among students to feel a unity that had some type of Southern base. The primary focus is not so much to building the organization itself as trying to develop leadership not only in students but also in these communities. In Mississippi, for instance, we have been trying to create an impression of unity on the part of the civil rights organizations—to the exclusion many times of any kind of projection of Snick. You know, to develop local leadership. Now as for myself—I got involved because I first of all felt that young Negroes who had had Southern experience would have to return and lend their technical skills to the development of the Movement in the South.

WARREN: The other day, when I was talking to Malcolm X, he justified unselective reprisals against whites—shooting, bombing, if necessary—on the ground that in war reprisals are unselective and the present situation is a war between the Negro Movement and society at large. What is your interpretation of the relation of the Negro Movement to society?

FORMAN: The protest movement currently is not depicted by many people as any type of war, because most people are seeking reforms within the structure of American society. In fact, many Negroes are very apologetic, you know, for the society. The values of the society are basically racist values that suppress the dignity of the Negro, and this puts the Negro at odds—which may be a less potent word than *war.** He must struggle to change society, to change the values and structures of society. Now, I don't agree that because one is at odds with society therefore anything goes in order to change it.

---

* Undoubtedly Forman is right in general, but Snick is a very fluid organization, and does not attempt to screen for opinion and attitude. David Halberstam tells me of an episode in Greenwood, Mississippi, during the Summer Project: "In the COFO office there was some kid about twenty-three years old, a copy of the *National Guardian* on his desk, and I introduced myself and got a very favored response—boy, he was glad to see me—and said, 'Oh, Mr. Halberstam, I've enjoyed reading your coverage of our other colonial war.'" The other "war" Mr. Halberstam had covered was in Vietnam.

WARREN: Have you made a public statement about the recent outbreaks of hoodlumism on ferries and in subways?

FORMAN: No, but I have some personal opinions about it. One has to understand the milieu, the structural situation which allowed these people to be so placed [to be hoodlums]. The thing that surprises me is not that we have one or two incidents of violence, but that there is not more of this.

WARREN: The white man and white-dominated society have a responsibility—that is clear. Meanwhile there are two other questions. First, what kind of containment is, at present, possible? And second, what kind of responsibility from the Negro society, as distinguished from over-all society, is desirable?

FORMAN: Well, first of all, it's my feeling that the Negroes, even in slavery, effectively controlled some of the frustrations and anger. The Negro church has been an outlet. Within the civil rights movement itself, the posture of non-violence has helped to control some of the anger and frustration. That goes back to the old problem of, you know, why there hasn't been more [violence]. So I don't think that the Negroes themselves can be indicted for acts of violence that have been committed on the part of Negroes—I read an article or a letter in the *Times* where someone said that you don't blame all the Italians for the Mafia, you know. I think that the basic reponsibility that all Negroes have, and all Americans, is to hurry up and change the conditions that first of all make it necessary for me to be giving you the kind of interview I'm giving. There are other things that we could be discussing, but the racial problem is paramount. In other words, let's get rid of racialism in the society.

*   *   *

Reading over these remarks by Forman I recall the somewhat different tone with which Roy Wilkins expressed his views in *The Amsterdam News* on the outbreak of hoodlumism: "punks," "foul-mouthed smark alecks," who are "selling out the freedom riders" and "undoing the work of hundreds of Negro and white sit-in youngsters," and "cutting and slashing at the race's self-respect." And he attacked Negroes who would "offer the same old thread-bare excuses to cover up for viciousness."* What Forman says is, also, true: in the long-range view white society is substantially responsible, and the viciousness spilling over from the Negro ghetto can be traced to the white man's failure. By the same token a Negro can welcome every piece of Negro hoodlumism as one more indictment of the white man—and one more useful threat to his complacency. This is the view implicitly adopted by Forman, who avoids the question of Negro responsibility. By pushing the same line of thought, one might say there is no personal guilt attached to the killers of the civil rights workers in Philadelphia, Mississippi—nor to those of the community who tacitly defend them—for all are the automatons of social and psychological conditioning.

Forman's view and that of Wilkins are in fact the two poles of the issue—the two inevitable poles of any such situation, both demanding recognition, both relevant, but relevant in very different dimensions.

These are the two poles of any discussion of hoodlumism—as of the riots in Harlem and Brooklyn subsequent to the killing of the Negro youth James Powell, age fifteen, by Police Lieutenant Thomas Gilligan. On July 21 a group of thirty-five leaders of the Bedford-Stuyvesant section of Brooklyn issued a statement that, as Forman would presumably do, views the whole situation in the light of social conditioning: "Violence and disorders do not occur in a vacuum. In dealing with riots and disorders we are dealing with symptoms rather than causes."† This is perfectly true, and any intelligent long-range policy should be directed at the removal of the causes.

But meanwhile the results—the symptoms—have to be dealt with, for they, in turn, are social causes of a very serious order. So we get Wilkins declaring that "the Negro community itself has just got to call a halt to violence," that the riots give "New York a black eye, Harlem a black eye, and the civil rights cause a difficult obstacle." That is, the fact that the riot is socially conditioned does not relieve those who understand that fact from the obligation to

* See *The New York Times,* June 24, 1964.
† *The New York Times,* July 23, 1964.

act to contain the riot. Unless, of course, they see the violence as tactically desirable.

That was, apparently, the view that seemed to be held by some of the Bedford-Stuyvesant leaders who, according to the press, said that they themselves were, in fact, uncertain that their goals could be achieved without violence.* There was no uncertainty, however, about the views of some. For instance, on the afternoon of July 19, the day after the first riot, Jesse Gray, the leader of the Harlem rent strike, addressed a mass meeting: "There are some people who say that the only thing that can solve the problem in Mississippi is guerrilla warfare. I am beginning to wonder what will solve the problem in New York." While the crowd shouted "Guerrilla warfare," Gray went on to say: "The Negroes of New York City can determine what will happen to New York City." Then somebody in the crowd shouted: "When do we start?" And another voice: "Eleven o'clock!"

Jesse Gray is thinking of a dialectic as clean as a whistle: white to black, gun to gun.

Some have said that only out of a total polarization, the full confrontation, can a solution come. And this polarization suggested by Jesse Gray, who asked for "one hundred trained revolutionists not afraid to die," is the kind that is total, and naked. Is this what Jesse Gray—not up on a platform with the crowd cheering, but alone in the dark—would really have in mind?†

*   *   *

Some time ago, before the riots, in a conversation, William Stringfellow, the author of *My People Is the Enemy,* graduate of the

---

* *The New York Times,* July 23, 1964. Some of the group merely declared that they themselves had lost any power to restrain the mob. In the Philadelphia riots, even such leaders as Cecil Moore and Stanley Branch, who could scarcely be called Uncle Toms, were unable to influence the mob.

† The Reverend Dr. W. Eugene Houston, chairman of the Commission on Religion and Race of the Presbyterian Church, while presenting a set of demands from his Commission, said that Jesse Gray and the Reverend Nelson C. Dukes, a Baptist minister (who led the "mob march" on the police station the night of July 19) should have been arrested for inciting to riot. As an indication of the position of Dr. Houston, the demands called for a civilian board of review and, among other things, for the suspension of Lieutenant Gilligan. Dr. Houston is a Negro. (See *The New York Times,* July 22, 1964.)

Harvard Law School, Episcopal layman, seven-year resident of Harlem in what the *Times* has called the worst block in New York, predicted to me such riots, and said that the duty of a white man, confronting a Negro mob, is to accept his fate without resistance. The white man, he said, could at least offer his Christian testimony.

When his predictions came true, and the riots broke, we saw the news photographs of police, steel helmet on head, drawn revolver in hand, advancing up the dark street.

Again two poles, again in different dimension: the expiatory nonresisting acceptance of fate, the drawn revolver.

*   *   *

In slum violence there is perhaps an element other than "racialism" to be considered. I ask Forman what about the white slum boy who goes berserk.

FORMAN: Well, I'm not saying that it's necessarily race, but I do say that we have to remove from society—which is going to be a long process—those conditions that don't produce a good life for anybody. There are many things fundamental to the society—our whole parole system, our prison system, for instance—which are not necessarily racial but do take a racial form.

WARREN: But these things do intersect in a very crucial way, don't they? So that the race question is scarcely to be isolated?

FORMAN: There is a great deal of interlocking in these areas.

WARREN: When you say "crash program"—or Marshall Plan—for the Negro, must you revise it, then, to "crash program for the underprivileged"?

FORMAN: I think that's the most desirable thing. But then on the other hand I am not opposed to saying a "crash program for Negroes," because I think that if the Negro is to ever present legitimately his demands before society, he has to take an interest-group point of view.

Here I had been about to ask Forman to clarify his apparent contradiction. But I think I know what he means: Even though a crash program for all underprivileged is the social desideratum, given the psychology of our arena system of political action, the interest-group pressure of the Negro is the necessary tactic. Or would he say more? That by using the interest-group approach the Negro emphasizes the snarl and tangle where the strand of race intersects that of economics?

* * *

On In-fighting:

One of the troubles in the civil rights movement right now is that there has been a lot of in-fighting.

On Nonviolence and Systems:

I happen to accept nonviolence as a way of life, in a sense. But at the same time, I am sophisticated enough to understand that one has to change systems that breed violence rather than try to change a particular person who may be violent.

On Nonviolence and Moral Effect:

It produces reactions in the consciousness of people who are not even there [at the scene], and it's one of the things that has advanced the Movement to the point where it is.

On the Role of ACT:

I think that ACT is simply a further manifestation in the deepening roots of the civil rights movement—that it was inevitable either that Snick would begin action in the North, or that some other organization would come to the forefront. Because the boycotts [school boycotts of February

1964] were meeting a need that a lot of the traditional organizations in the North just were not fulfilling, you know.

On the Future—After Achieving Civil Rights:

I'm not sure—and maybe this is where I'm pessimistic—that you're not going to have to have some type of militant action to watch over people's opinions. What you'd have to guard against is the subjective opinions of people creeping out and again expressing racial attitudes.

On "Freedom Now":

It's a slogan that is used in terms of motivating people to come out of their apathetic positions and to recognize that social change is possible.

On the Commitment of the Negro Middle Class:

It feels itself committed to certain advantages for that class.

On the Climate of Southern Opinion:

The climate of Southern opinion is changing. I was acquitted in a case in Alabama.

On the Speech of Roy Wilkins at Alexandria, Virginia:

Well, he's wrong.

*   *   *

James Forman is now thirty-six years old. He is of medium height. He seems soft, even fatty; at other times the fattiness seems merely a light sheath over an awkward strength of musculature. His movements tend to be abrupt, nervous, and awkward. The shoulders are heavy, rather hunched, the head set forward, sometimes sinking to a posture of withdrawn and sullen brooding. The face, medium brown, is broad, tending to be broader toward the lower part, the whole head seeming to be somewhat pressed upon from above, to force an unnatural width. Fleshiness hides the bone structure, but the nose is strong.

I should guess that one aspect of his self-diagnosis is correct, that there is an element of anger and frustration and hurt ego along with the element of intellectual and idealistic drive. But I should guess— from the tone of sardonic and bitter humor, sometimes overcharged for the occasion, from the moments of what seems sullen brooding, from the ragged gestures, from a dozen such minutiae, from his aura —that little peace has been made between those two elements of his being. What peace there is has probably been made in the blind moments of action, or in the anticipation of such blind moments, when commitment is, perforce, absolute.

James Forman is very different from those men like Roy Wilkins or James Farmer or Whitney Young, who, in the daily hassle, try to keep in mind the great context of social and economic problems. He is very different from a man like Martin Luther King who sees present action in the light cast by a vision of men living together in spiritual peace. He is very different, too, from a man like Robert Moses, who, in the midst of Mississippi, seems to have found, through his philosophy, a personal peace.

James Forman is a combat officer. His inner peace comes only, perhaps, in the immediate outer clash. He is bitter, or at least impatient, about those who do not have his special kind of total commitment—the Negro middle class ("committed" only to its own "advantages"), anybody who has a concern that Forman cannot immediately tie to his own conception of the race struggle (a concern with art, with literature, a concern with juvenile delinquency, a concern, even, with "society as a whole"). To him such people are "marginal."

He does not, in fact, first think in terms of the moral or psychological question or motivations but in terms of practical effect: "It's what the social effect is of what a person is doing that's important." He tends to speak in terms that imply force: "getting rid of all those Southern Dixiecrats down there," "some type of militant action to watch over people's opinions," etc. In regard to what Dr. King calls the "third phase"—the phase of intensive effort on the part of Negroes, after achieving civil rights, etc., to raise standards—Forman scents the effluvium of Booker T. Washington.*

For instance, he says of King's "third phase": "If you had this third phase and you said, 'OK now, the Negro has got to raise himself up to be accepted in this society, or so that he can be like other people,' then by definition you still have an opinion that regards him as something different"—that is, as inferior. In one sense—in the sense we may cover by the phrase "under the same circumstances" —we have compelling evidence that Negroes are not "different," are "like other people"—that is, are not inferior. But generally the Negro Americans have not been, and are not, under the same circumstances as other Americans. If, as we are told, many of the traits that are said to be "Negro," are merely the traits characteristic of poverty, whatever its color, then we still have to reckon with the fact that poverty itself is massively characteristic of Negroes. They are poor out of all ratio, and the massiveness of their poverty itself makes a difference—being Negro and being poor tend to interfuse in an identity and a doom, in a crippling combination of anger and despair. If, as we are told, the traits of poverty, irrespective of color, tend to be self-propagating, we still have to reckon with the fact that the Negro carries on his brow what seems, sometimes even to himself, the mark of his doom—that is, the mark of his inexpungeable past and his irredeemable future. Race may be, as some say, a superstition, but the consequences of a superstition can be facts with their own persisting, pervasive, and maiming reality. To put matters a little differently, the Negro-ness of the Negro is not in itself a mark of inferiority, but in our superstitious social system it may become a contributing cause of inferiority.

* Another line of criticism of Dr. King's "third phase," and of his remark that if you're a street-sweeper you ought to be the best possible street-sweeper, comes from David Cohen of the Cleveland CORE; "It's no longer appropriate to talk about being the best street-sweeper. What it is appropriate to do is to involve those street-sweepers in a movement where by doing things themselves they achieve a kind of personal excellence that they had never been able to achieve before. If you engage yourself in a movement that's going to open up opportunities for a lot of other people, you're making a much more profound contribution. We're not worried about street-sweepers, but we are worried about building a movement that's going to change things. So I think that what King said is just inappropriate."

The trouble in Forman's statement is that he confuses the notion of congenital inferiority with that of de facto inferiority—that is, he confuses it with low standards of performance consequent on bad environment and training. And here we find a certain grim comedy, for both the segregationist and some of the most radical members of the Negro Movement are guilty of the same confusion of congenital inferiority and of de facto inferiority, each using the confusion to support his characteristic view. For instance, the segregationist says: "Negroes are inferior, and therefore you have to segregate them." And the radical integrationist says: "Negroes are not inferior, and therefore they don't need to raise any standards." Both are talking nonsense, and the nonsense hinges on the fact that the word *inferior* has not been analyzed. And both are dealing in tricky generalizations.

Forman's statement, furthermore, confuses, by implication at least, the question of civil rights, human rights, and human dignity on the one hand, with those aspects of integration related to occupational and social mobility, aspects which have always had, in all societies, regardless of race, to do with standards of performance, morals, manners, and taste. To approach it in another way, we may say that there are no standards to be fulfilled before a man is entitled to equal treatment before the law, but that there are standards to be fulfilled before he can expect to practice medicine or receive certain dinner invitations. This distinction would seem obvious, and it is certainly obvious to a great number of Negroes—for instance, to Martin Luther King, Carl Rowan, and Roy Wilkins. But the failure to grasp it, and grasp its relation to the problem of standards, has constantly and mischievously haunted discussions of the race question.

Often, when the matter of standards appears, people will switch the subject toward the need for a revision of values, toward a change, as Forman puts it, in the "values and structure of society," a "revolution" that will reject white middle-class standards—and therefore, presumably, render the talk of self-improvement irrelevant. Let us grant that middle-class standards are, in many ways, deeply unsatisfying, and grant that the Negro Movement is a "catalytic" in a far-reaching social and economic change. But the question of standards would still remain. For certain technical standards are built into a society—they are not a matter of race or class prejudice. Furthermore, no matter what form a new society may take, it will also have non-technical as well as technical standards, including standards of

morals, manners, and taste. There can be, for instance, a snobbery
of beards, blue jeans, anger, and agony, just as there can be a snobbery of Dior and self-indulgence. And for both technical and non-
technical standards, in any society, the effort of learning is required:
education—i.e., "self-improvement."

If Forman rejects King's third phase, he seems to do so in favor
of some massive federal program of aid, like Whitney Young's
Marshall Plan, to repair the damages wrought by segregation. I am
convinced that some such program (for the disadvantaged of both
the white and black races) is essential, but what I find disturbing is
the implied opposition between "self-improvement" and "aid." All
that aid can ever do is to give the chance (to Negro or white) for
self-improvement. And even if the phrase "self-improvement" floats
in a poisonous aura of association and symbolism, that is no reason
to reject the thing to which the phrase points. This would be the trap
of verbalism or symbolism that all movements tend to fall into. The
trap is a deep one, and the spike at the bottom is lethal.

Forman's opposition between an aid program and self-improvement is related to a tendency to ignore, unless pressed, the individual,
subjective, and moral aspects of a social problem. It should be clear
to all of us that the individual is conditioned by systems—by many
kinds of systems intermeshing and overlaying one another. But at
the same time, unless we assume some purely mechanistic structure
of the world, we count on the more or less free play of the individual
mind, critical and creative, as an agent in the change of conditioning.
But Forman, unlike Ronnie Moore of Louisiana, who talks of
"changing minds and hearts," thinks of changing systems. At the
same time he says that the great value of Montgomery and of Birmingham—and of the student movement—has been to force the issues
surrounding racial segregation into "the area of public opinion." But
what, we must ask him, can effectively come out of such forcing of
the issues into the area of public opinion except by changing minds—
if not hearts?

*   *   *

This whole question of the dynamics of change perhaps implies
another inconsistency in Forman's position. On one hand he is contemptuous of the tepid, the partially committed, the "marginal" peo-

ple. On the other hand, he calls for drastic and comprehensive action by the federal government for racial ends, forgetting that the government is a political agency, and can, and will, act only insofar as a certain number of those marginal people—i.e., the ordinary voters— see fit to act, see a value in such action on the problem of race as will coincide with their "marginal" values. The Negro, for better or worse, is doomed to act with the marginal people.

How?

By educating them and himself to their community of interest. That is, by changing minds, and hearts. There are many ways to change them. Montgomery and Birmingham changed some.

How long before systems can be changed? Forman sees no solution in his own time or in the time of his children. "Anyway," he says, "we may all be destroyed in thermonuclear war, you know." There is a glint of saturnine gaiety in the way he says it. Is there some hint of relief in the thought?

* * *

Much of my reading of James Forman must be based on slim evidence. Certainly, I do not want to make into absolute distinctions and oppositions issues which are merely matters of emphasis. For instance, in regard to the question of federal aid and self-improvement, he will, when pressed a little, say: "The Government can't do anything for people that people are not prepared to do for themselves." But the point is that his mind has a certain cast, a certain bias, that is not uncommon. Perhaps a streak of tragic absoluteness.

His streak of absoluteness, his impatience with marginal people and marginal considerations, his will to locate and strike at the root —these are qualities of a man who lives on the raw edge of experience. He lives with the ulcers that have nearly killed him, with the threat of violence in his daily life, with the mixture of pessimism and grim humor. He lives intensely, I should guess, and painfully, in a strange drama of compulsion, bitterness, and hope. This is what makes him demanding to the imagination. He is engaged in a struggle for reality. For his own reality.

So sitting there in the oak-paneled office of a publisher in New York, in a red leather chair, in the luxurious coolness and dimness removed from the heat and hurry of the summer afternoon, his mind, even as he speaks, seems to be far away. In some place where he can be real.

: 5 :

In *The Negro Revolution in America,* William Brink and Louis Harris say that a significant difference between the ordinary Negro and the Negro with capacity for leadership lies in the attitude toward segregation itself. The ordinary Negro finds in segregation merely a destructive force; the superior Negro finds the challenge, the goad, that drives him to achievement. And they quote James L. Farmer, the founder and national director of the Congress of Racial Equality: "Discrimination increased my determination to do something about inferiority feelings. I felt handicapped, but never doubted my own abilities."

Sitting in his office, a big bare, shabby room with a big desk the only significant furniture, I asked Mr. Farmer about this remark. It was true, he said, that segregation had, for him, been a stimulus; but he wanted to make a distinction between his situation and that of many Negroes. His father had been a college professor, and the son (like the young Adam Clayton Powell, the young Roy Wilkins, or the young Martin Luther King) had been protected from many of the shocks of the system; there had been the challenge, as it were, without the deadening weight of constant contact. We might paraphrase Mr. Farmer by saying that, according to the formulation of Arnold Toynbee, the ratio of challenge to the power of response was benign. And some psychologists tell us that, as might be expected, young Negroes who are raised in solid, well-protected homes tend to set higher goals for themselves than young white people, and to drive at them harder.* But he would not have this situation interpreted, Mr. Farmer said, as any sort of justification for segregation. As for the stimulus in the situation, the greatest one "that I found as a child was to prepare myself to try to get rid of segregation, to oppose the thing and bring it down."

Unlike some Negroes of achievement (and plenty of white men,

---

* B. C. Rosen, "Race, Ethnicity, and the Achievement Syndrome," in *American Sociological Review,* 1959, vol. 29.

too) who carry the distorting scars of some painful situation that goaded them to special effort, James Farmer seems fulfilled in himself, comfortable but solid in his ample coffee-colored flesh, not notable for humor, but ready to smile out of his round face, certainly without any self-irony, not needing any. He gives the impression of fulfillment—of being a free man—for the simple reason that his mind and feelings turn outward, naturally and objectively, to the problems to which he is dedicated. He has, I should guess, as few loose ends of being as most men.

*   *   *

The national headquarters of CORE are at 38 Park Row, in Manhattan. This is far downtown, symbolically set to face that teeming hive of ambiguous and shadowy forces called City Hall. Park Row faces a grubby patch of park, where as I approached—the time being noon—old men sat on benches eating out of paper bags, with the abstraction or picky fastidiousness of old people eating, and young girls drank from Coke bottles, leaned together to whisper secrets that nobody was trying to overhear anyway, and then burst into wild snatches of laughter and waved their Coke bottles in the summer sunshine. After wandering up and down two blocks of Park Row, jammed with the narrow fronts of the predictable kind of stores and restaurants, I finally found the right entrance. It was not conspicuous.

Nothing here reminds you of the headquarters of the NAACP or the Urban League—not the sodden cigarette butts and old gum wrappers on the floor of the hall, nor the creaky elevator, nor the waiting room with bulging and broken cartons stacked in a corner, nor the grime-stained plaster, nor the receptionist herself. At her invitation I sat down in a chair, and the traffic flowed over my feet; people—some Negro, some white—marched back and forth carrying documents and letters. There was a jumble of offices, everything seemed disordered, untidy, improvised, like headquarters just set up in a requisitioned building in an occupied town, but with some sense, all the same, of a busy order in the operation.

A pleasant, smiling woman, fortyish, white, came to say that Mr. Farmer would see me soon. She came back in half an hour with regrets. There was some sort of crisis, somewhere, it seemed. In an hour she came back to say the crisis was past, and led me down a little hall, past offices, each seeming more jumbled than the last, through her own jumbled domain, into the big bare one where Mr. Farmer waited.

There wasn't time to go out for lunch. The pleasant, smiling woman ordered us some sandwiches.

I asked him what vacuum CORE had been founded—back in 1942 —to fill.

Before that time, Mr. Farmer said, he had been working as Race Relations Secretary for the Fellowship of Reconciliation, a pacifist organization, and, naturally, had been studying the work of Mahatma Gandhi. The study of Gandhi, and a tour South in 1941, the first trip South in three years, convinced him that a new approach to the race question was in order, something not to replace, he said, but to supplement the method of the NAACP. The new ingredients needed were, first, the active involvement of the rank and file, not merely the "talented tenth" of the theory of Du Bois, nor professionals and experts; second, a real, not merely a verbal, rejection of segregation, an adaptation of the method of Thoreau; third, emphasis on direct, nonviolent action, "putting one's body in direct confrontation with the evil." The dream was of a mass movement, which, he said, "fortunately we do have now." And the result of such a movement would be to appeal to the "conscience of the majority" and, through boycott and through the scrutinizing by individuals of their investments, to make segregation too expensive to maintain.

At this point, taking a distinction from Eric Lincoln, I ask whether the Negro wants real integration, with the shocks and the sharpened competitiveness entailed by that, or a token, a superficial integration, with the insult of formal segregation removed but a self-imposed segregation maintained, blurred around the edges of public contact but hard at center.

Farmer, unlike many Negroes, emphasizes the fact that a crucial debate on this point is now going on in the Negro community. When I ask for elaboration he says quite flatly that most Negroes—"the ordinary John Does whose skins are black"—are not concerned with the issue of segregation or of separation versus integration. "The real issue for them is getting the heel of oppression off their neck, they know something is hurting them—they aren't sure what it is, but they want it removed. Now Malcolm X and I can address a mass rally the same morning, he can get applause talking about separation, I can get applause talking about integration."

This fluidity, this amorphousness, of Negro opinion—which many Negroes neglect to mention or on which, consciously or unconsciously, they graft their own schematizations—has, of course, great dangers: it invites the talents of any demagogue. But it also offers, Mr. Farmer says, the great challenge to leadership, to analyze the feelings and needs of the inarticulate Negro, define the situation and devise solutions: "and so the debate that is going on among leadership." He himself holds that the solution lies in integration, "but it is important for us now to define that integration." Would it mean the absorption of the Negro into white culture, perhaps even the blood stream disappearing, or would it mean that the Negro, with "pride in culture and history" and with a sense of "identity," could enter as a "proud and equal partner who has something to give, something to share, and something to receive"? He would emphasize "unity through diversity" as the basic American concept, and this, for him, as for King, would be the way to evade the dilemma of the "psychic split" that haunted Du Bois.

As for blood absorption, Farmer says he would not "shrink from it," but that "it should be a permissive absorption"—a matter of free individual choice. In general, for any predictable future he does not see any significant bleeding away at the edges of the Negro group. "Nor do I think that most Negroes will choose to live in what are now lily-white suburbs. If the Negro wants to live in Lovely Gardens or Lovely Lane, then he should do so; but most are going to choose to live in what are now the ghettos."

I remember a prominent Negro lawyer in Nashville, Avon Williams, saying to me with a bitter twist of the lip: "White society will not allow me to escape [from the Negro community], and now I don't want to escape. I wouldn't want to live in a white neighborhood now, because I'm so accustomed to things that go on in my neighborhood that I wouldn't feel comfortable without it. But I don't want my son to be deprived of the freedom of selection."

But James Farmer's lip is not twisted in bitterness as he makes this prediction; he is thinking of free choice, even of the possibility, presumably, of the self-separation characteristic of much minority life in America after "success" and "acceptance." And here I should have asked if self-imposed segregation is not, for practical results, still segregation, and still maintains certain difficulties and liabilities inherent in the imposed ghetto.

But I did ask him about Washington, D.C., where the general racial imbalance seems to make real integration of schools impossible; and to this question he replied that "you do as much as you can, given the situation." In regard to the Washington situation he added that to try to bring in children from Virginia or Maryland to correct the local imbalance—as some Negroes have suggested—is "sheer nonsense."

What is important for him, it seems, is to establish good will and good faith in working toward a solution. He does not find good faith or good will in some of the resistance to pairing and busing in New York. Rather, he sees the sudden discovery by many whites of the sanctity of the neighborhood little red school house as a mask for other motives, racial motives. If in general he would rest on the practical man's formula of "doing what you can," he would, in school balancing, probably say do "a little more than you can," for he sees no possibility for equality under segregation, and in segregation he sees a special danger—a danger no one else has mentioned to me— that of encouraging nationalistic sentiment and anti-white feelings among Negro children. He would count on the mere fact of association to offset this danger; it would be offset "if your children studied in the same schools and became friends." Given the right context, he is willing to trust human nature.

*   *   *

On CORE as Interracial:

Powell included us in his criticism of NAACP for having white people in positions of leadership. With us it's a matter of principle. We don't see how we can fight for an open society through a segregated organization, and this is a policy position we intend to maintain. Of course, we run into difficulty. There are many, many Negroes who will not work with an interracial organization because of their suspicion of whites.

On the Role of White Liberal, and Black:

FARMER: "White liberal" has become a bad word—like "Uncle Tom." I think the white liberal does have a role, but his role cannot be top leader of any organizations—if those organizations are to have any impact in the Negro community. White liberals must be willing to work in roles of secondary leadership and as technicians.

WARREN: What about the white man who is outside of organizations, the person who is concerned with the state of health of the entire society, and subsumes the Negro situation under this?

FARMER: The feeling in the Negro community now is that the Negro question is the key issue and all other issues must be secondary. If there is a conflict between fighting militantly for civil rights and a civil liberties point of view, for example, then civil rights must prevail. My own view is that while the civil rights issue is the key domestic issue, we have got to begin bridging the gap, and showing the relationship between the struggle for rights for Negroes and the struggle for a better America.

WARREN: What about the liberal who puts his views on record but who will not march?

FARMER: I think we have just got through the stage where the feeling was that the only important contribution is in the streets. There are some people who will not be in the streets, for various reasons. In a sense it has been our failure in not pointing out specific things that they can do to help the revolution.

WARREN: You find certain Negroes who come in for criticism. Take Ralph Ellison, for instance, a man of great talent and distinction—did you read Irving Howe's piece on him, in *Dissent?*

FARMER: Yes. Well, in the case of Ralph Ellison, I don't know whether the criticism is only that he hasn't been in the streets—Baldwin, for example, has not been in the streets, but his writing has been oriented toward the streets.

WARREN: *Invisible Man* has had an enormous impact.

FARMER: That is true. I repeat what I said—I think we have got to find roles which will not necessarily be picketing or sitting-in.

On Upgrading the Ghetto:

We realize the ghetto is going to be with us for a long time. Even if Negroes have the freedom to move out, to move elsewhere, many will stay voluntarily while others may stay because they are locked in economically even if there's no discrimination elsewhere. So we've got to upgrade it economically, and this means co-ops, it means credit unions, it means pooling of resources to start businesses and industries and that sort of thing, not in the way the Black Nationalists speak of it as a rival economy but in the sense of urging Negroes to participate fully in every aspect of American life.

On Tension Between the Negro Middle Class and the Lower Class:

We find increasing tension. A number of new leaders are springing up from the Negro working class. Many have not had much education—they have developed a feeling for the struggle—they have developed some facility in the use of the techniques of nonviolent direct action.

The middle-class Negro looks alien. A favorite saying now among Negroes is "So-and-so *used* to be black." What is apt to happen now is a competition among Negro leadership, based on the fastest footwork—whether people are able to adopt the vocabulary of the masses. One man who has fast footwork is Adam Clayton Powell. He has no real relation to the masses—three houses and four cars. He keeps officially a little apartment some place in Harlem—but this mansion in Puerto Rico and a house in White Plains and everything else. Yet Powell knows the masses and he can speak to them, and he becomes a lower-class leader. Malcolm is another one.

Now Malcolm is not lower-class—has a home out in Queens*
—a house and yard, Malcolm drives a new Oldsmobile,
Malcolm wears two-hundred-dollar suits and expensive hand-
made shirts—but Malcolm has the footwork to keep pace—
he doesn't lead the masses, but he reflects them and verbalizes
what they are thinking. I suspect there's going to be an attri-
tion among Negro leadership, based on their ability to speak
the proper vocabulary. Now Baldwin is a writer who has that
vocabulary and thus has appeal to the lower-class Negro.
I have been absolutely amazed to see lower-class Negroes,
working class unemployed, reading Baldwin's books—probably the first books they ever read; I am not sure understanding what he is saying, but getting a feeling—"I dig this guy
because he digs me."

On Centralization of Power:

The present tendency is toward proliferation of leadership,
but there is also a trend toward greater coordination.

On Overreaching:

I don't see any way to avoid it. There will be jockeying
for power—this is inevitable because the stakes are high, and
ambitious men will let their ambition run rampant. I would
say, actually, it is not a bad thing. The competition keeps us
on our toes.

Verbalism as a Substitute for Leadership:

Right now it is easy for a man to become a Negro leader—
or be accepted as one. If he makes speeches which are militant

---

* On February 14, 1965, Malcolm X's home in East Elmhurst, Queens,
was set ablaze by firebombs, which he blamed on the Black Muslims. He was
to be evicted the following day by a court ruling, which was instigated by the
Muslims, who hold title to the house.

enough, which capture the press, then he becomes recognized, at least temporarily, as a Negro leader—on the basis of pure verbalism—without having any following, without having any organization, without taking any action. One example is Malcolm X. Malcolm has done nothing but verbalize—his militancy is a matter of posture, there has been no action. Well, Malcolm can survive a long time on that, because Malcolm happens to be a man of unusual abilities. But there will come a time when Malcolm is going to have to chirp or get off the perch. I am sure that he realizes the dilemma he is facing—he is not an activist, really. I suspect that he is going to come out as an integrationist before long, and I think he was trying to prepare for that when he sent back those letters and postcards from Africa [saying that in the world of Islam color does not matter].*

On the White Press as the Creator of New Negro Leaders:

Whitney Young is absolutely right—the press has been irresponsible [in publicizing the mere verbalism of would-be leaders], partly out of ignorance, and sometimes, I suspect, out of a deliberate attempt to create conflict within Negro leadership.

On Acceptable and Unacceptable Demonstrations:

It is difficult to lay down guide lines as to what is acceptable as a demonstration and what is not acceptable. This fact was pointed up recently in *The New York Times,* when Javits called for Negro leaders to issue statements for the boundaries of demonstrations. I don't think that is possible, because what may be acceptable in New York is not acceptable in Chicago. What is not acceptable today may be acceptable a year hence. For example, the stall-in. I was not opposed

* This prediction about Malcolm X and integration has been fulfilled. See p. 263.

in principle, I was opposed in tactics and timing. I consider a stall-in to be an essentially revolutionary tactic which requires a revolutionary situation—to be in the same category as a general strike, a general work stoppage—and it has certain prerequisites. First, unity in the Negro community. Second, an almost absolute polarization between the races. It would be a desperate measure. For instance, in Plaquemine, Louisiana, I have recommended to the Negro community that they explore the idea of a general strike. There you have the total polarization, and the absolute unity, so that such a measure would be justified; while in New York it would be neither justifiable nor workable. Also there is the extent to which you have been able to get dialogue, and in New York at least we have had dialogue.

On the Relation of Demonstration to Negotiation:

They are not contradictory at all—not mutually exclusive. We find that demonstrations are frequently the catalyst—spur the dialogue. Sometimes demonstrations start the dialogue. Before demonstrations—I mean massive demonstrations—started in Birmingham, there was very little discussion. Without them, it is unlikely that we would have had a Civil Rights Bill.

On Demonstrations and the Affirmation of Identity:

I think that is a very profound point. One of the most valuable functions of demonstration is to weld people together in unity, and to recruit. Many people come because they see action in the street. [But then they join in and] walk and get tired, and they will never be the same again.

We have found, too, that we have to have demonstrations to build a movement. You can't build one on paper, nor can you build a movement on negotiations, and this poses a dilemma for us. Very often our campaigns are successful in the negotiation stage, then you lose your momentum. Then you find another issue and it becomes all the more difficult to regain momentum. That is why it is very hard to call off demonstrations which have been planned. We have learned we have to have some other action for the people to get involved in immediately.

This reminds me of the criticism that Gloria Richardson gave me, in Cambridge, Maryland, of the conduct of Charles Evers in persuading the students of Jackson College off the street, the night of the riot there. Yes, she said, twisting and turning in her chair, he had done right in getting them off, to prevent random violence. But to get them off and leave them, that damped out something it would be hard to rekindle. He should have got them back on the campus, made them sing songs and pray, and then led them out, singing, in an orderly nonviolent march—to face whatever there was to face, without their bricks and Coke bottles.

She kept turning her thin body in the chair, ceaselessly, twisting her handkerchief, her near-ugly, near-beautiful yellow face marked by the tension she had lived with all the months. Her eyes are not on you as she talks. She has learned, it seems, all there is to know about maintaining spirit—her own, the spirit of others—day after day. She turns and turns in the chair, reliving what she knows.

*　　*　　*

Farmer on Leadership and Responsibility:

My only argument with Whitney [Young] is the meaning of "responsible." You see, I have been accused of being irresponsible—and other times I have been *accused* of being responsible. In the current civil rights context this is an accusation—to tell a Negro that he is responsible, because this means that he is alienated, or that there is a gap between him and the people. It becomes a kiss of death! I don't want any reporter to call me "responsible"—or call me a "moderating influence." I'm as militant as the next!

*　　*　　*

But I wonder, as I hear him, if there is any necessary contradiction between being militant and being responsible. Farmer has given deep thought to the kind of society he wants to achieve; he has, clearly, given deep thought to the appropriateness of means to achieve that particular end; and he would not use means irrelevant to that end. He is, in other words, "responsible"—responsible to his conception of society.

What we are dealing with here is a matter of semantics. Particular context, particular usage, has poisoned the word; the emotional aura is wrong. "Responsible," the white man says. And the Negro retorts, "Responsible to whom?" And subtly, or irrationally, the Negro may take "irresponsibility" to be the antonym of "sell-out."

Words are what we make them. We are concerned with things, not words. We can know, it seems, what "things" concern James Farmer behind the words—even behind the words he does not want to use.

There are certain forces implicit in the Movement which make, willy-nilly, for "responsibility," or whatever word one wishes to use. The basic force derives from the fact that the Movement is a revolution that does not aim to liquidate, but to join, a society; therefore, the elements of threat and violence must be balanced, in the mind of any serious leader, with the need to keep open the possibility of a continuity of that society and a reconciliation in it. A clear example of this force making for "responsibility" appeared in the coalition of various factions called the United Council of Harlem Organizations, created as a backwash of the riots of the summer of 1964. The spectrum presented was very broad—ranging from Black Nationalists to Alexander J. Allen, Executive Director of the Urban League of Greater New York. The Council defined its function as "responsible militancy"—and the phrase puts the issue in a nutshell. However shaky and ultimately ineffective the Council may turn out to be, the very nature of the attempt is significant: "militancy" *and* "responsibility."

The same intention lay behind the attempt to get the national organizations to agree to a moratorium on demonstrations until after the Presidential election, and to emphasize political action. Farmer, and John Lewis of Snick, refused to cooperate, but one may guess that Farmer here acted out of tactical considerations. His decision may have been conditioned, in part at least, by the fact that earlier his opposition to the stall-ins had alienated the radical wing of CORE, so that now he had to avoid the label "responsible." But in taking this decision not to cooperate, he did not manage to achieve unity in CORE; for example, Norman Spencer Hill, Jr., third-ranking man in the organization and expert tactician, repudiated Farmer's new policy and resigned to support the "responsible" King-Wilkins-Young line. But the real test, as far as Farmer is concerned, was in what he was to *do,* not say, in the period between the conference of the heads of organizations and the election in November.

On the "Good" White Man in the South:

Negroes used to feel that there were good white people. I look at Plaquemine, Louisiana, and after massive police brutality, the saying in the Negro community then was, "The only good white man is a dead one." For instance, somebody says, "Say, did you know that old Mrs. Johnson's boy was riding one of those horses with the cattle goads. I always thought he was a good white man."

In Plaquemine, after polarization became complete, the Negroes thought all whites were against them. I made it a point to send some of our white secretaries to work there. It succeeded, in a subtle way—these individual white persons were finally accepted by the Negro community—in a sense removed from the white race and accepted into the Negro race. About one young lady I heard some Negroes say: "Well, yes, she is white, but she is the blackest white woman you ever saw."

On the "Devil" Theory of History:

FARMER: I do not believe in the devil theory of history—nor do I think there are angels, and that anybody who happens to oppose us is a completely depraved human being. We try to look at the enemy and say, "There but for the grace of God—"

WARREN: You place the moral issue in the context of the human condition—socially and historically conceived?

FARMER: Exactly—and also recognize the possibility of human change.

Footnotes on History: Lincoln, Kennedy, Johnson:

My own opinion is that Lincoln was not the Great Emancipator.

President Kennedy? Oh, I think he was growing some—but I am nauseated by the current deification, especially on the civil rights issue, because this is not accurate. The President did intellectualize the issue and intellectualize it well, but it was a cold intellectual issue and political issue with him. He moved only when there was pressure and he had to move.

I think that Johnson is much more for civil rights than Kennedy ever was.

On the Obligation of the Negro—After Civil Rights:

First, the walls come down, then the bridges go up. When the thrust changes from desegregation to integration, then one's definition of integration becomes very pertinent. And then one of his [the Negro's] chief responsibilities is to prepare himself to live in an integrated society.

*   *   *

So we are back to the word *responsibility*.

: 6 :

An event is never single and isolated. It is not a bright unit gleaming before the eye of God. It is a complex of various factors. It is

hard to know where accident comes in. It is hard to know where
necessity comes in.

On the evening of December 1, 1955, Mrs. Rosa Parks, age
forty-three, a seamstress at a department store, was seated on a bus
in Montgomery, Alabama. The bus driver asked her to move to
the rear so that a white passenger might have her seat. She refused.
The driver summoned the police and she was arrested.

It is not clear why she did this on this particular night. Was this
the end result of an accumulation of a thousand such requests which
she had, over the years, acceded to? Was it the result of the fact
that already during that year five Negro women and two children
had been arrested and one man shot to death for disobeying a bus
driver? Was it because the climate had changed after the Supreme
Court decision of the year before? Was it merely that her feet hurt?

In May, 1954, Martin Luther King had begun, as a monthly
visitor flying down from Boston, to preach at the Dexter Avenue
Baptist Church in Montgomery. He was not yet *Dr.* King; he was
doing work on the dissertation that was to earn him that degree
from Boston University.* By early fall, however, he, with his wife
and baby daughter, was settled at 309 South Jackson Street. By December of 1955 he had established himself as a preacher, popular in
a small circle, but unknown to the general public, even to the general
public of Negroes in Montgomery.

After Mrs. Parks was arrested it was not the young Dr. King
who organized the first resistance. A number of ministers were involved in trying to find some way to head off the violence that
seemed to be brewing in the poolrooms and bars, but it was the
Women's Political Council that suggested to E. D. Nixon, head
of the local of the Brotherhood of Sleeping Car Porters, that a
boycott might be mounted; and Nixon called on the Reverend Ralph
D. Abernathy and Dr. King to arrange a meeting at the Dexter
Avenue Church. The boycott, originally scheduled for one day, had
a brilliant success—so brilliant that it was almost called off for
fear of a subsequent decline—and in this first flush of success the
Montgomery Improvement Association was organized.

---

* The dissertation was a comparative study of the philosophies of Paul
Tillich and Henry Nelson Wieman. The degree was awarded in June, 1955.

Up to this point, Martin Luther King had in no way distinguished himself as a leader. If anything, his temperament would have slanted him away from the role of action. Then, all at once, immediately upon the founding of the Association, for reasons that remain essentially mysterious, he was offered the presidency.

The first demands of the MIA were mild: for reasonable courtesy; first-come-first-served seating in a segregated pattern but with no requests that Negroes relinquish seats; and Negro drivers on Negro routes. The demands were so mild that the national office of the NAACP at first showed no enthusiasm for the movement. But when negotiations broke down even on this basis, and the Mayor and the City Commissioners announced that they were joining the White Citizens Council, the inner logic of the movement began to unfold. In the same way, the inner logic of the fate of Martin Luther King began to unfold. But in the early stages he met with little success; and at least once—after a breakdown of negotiations—he offered to resign. In the early stages, even though the boycott was nonviolent, he had developed no philosophy of action. Actually, the first reference to Gandhi appeared in a letter in the *Montgomery Advertiser,* on December 12, by a white librarian, Juliette Morgan, who compared the boycott to Gandhi's salt march to the sea. And in those same early days King even applied for a permit to carry a pistol— an application that was refused. For the first two months, though he was president of the MIA, King showed no hint of the greatness to come—except, perhaps, to a few who were already falling under his spell.

Then, on the night of January 30, 1956, his house was bombed. It happened while he was away at a mass meeting, but his wife and children were there. By the time he reached his house, a crowd of Negroes had gathered, angry and muttering as the police tried to clear the lawn and street. Dr. King appeared on the porch and began to speak: "He who lives by the sword shall perish by the sword . . ."

The photographers and newsmen were there.

The bombing began the creation of the image of Martin Luther King and the authorities of Montgomery finished the work. When the MIA, after the breakdown of negotiations, abandoned the original soft demands and brought suit in federal court, with the case of a Mrs. Aurelia S. Browder, to demand the desegregation of buses, the local grand jury indicted 115 Negro leaders under an anti-boycott statute of 1921. Many of the leaders gave themselves up—almost in a spirit of carnival. Dr. King was out of town, but returned. When the trial came, his case was first, and with the town jammed with reporters and cameramen of the national press, he was convicted. At one of the several overflowing mass meetings that night, Dr. King said: "We are not bitter. We are still preaching nonviolence. We are still using the weapon of love."

Though the case of Mrs. Browder in Montgomery was antedated by two years by a suit in Columbia, South Carolina, the boycott in Montgomery, and the revolutionary aura, and the personality and doctrine of Martin Luther King gave the situation an entirely new dimension. The question of the buses had long since been elevated from a literal to a symbolic significance. But as for the literal aspect of things, on November 13, 1956, the Supreme Court ruled that bus segregation violates the Constitution. On December 22, Dr. King, Mr. Ralph Abernathy of the First Baptist Church, and other members of the MIA high command rode a bus through Montgomery; their seats were up front.* Dr. King had already issued an official statement which ended:

Our experience and growth during this past year of united nonviolent protest has been such that we cannot be satisfied with a court "victory" over our white brothers. We must respond to the decision with an understanding of those who have oppressed us and with an appreciation of the new adjustments that the court order poses for them. We must be able to face up honestly to our own shortcomings. We must act in such a way as to make possible a coming together of white people and colored people on the basis of a real harmony of interests and understanding. We seek an integration based on mutual respect.†

* * *

Since then the main outlines of Dr. King's history are fairly clear. He moved to Atlanta. He was instrumental in organizing the Southern Christian Leadership Conference, which, presumably,

---

* Mr. W. H. Wheeler, president of the Mechanics and Farmers Bank of Durham, North Carolina, tells me that in his early days in Atlanta, the elder Martin Luther King would never ride a streetcar because he had to sit in the back. He had carried on a one-man boycott.

† Lawrence D. Reddick, *Crusader Without Violence*, Harper & Bros., 1959.

would apply the techniques and philosophy of the MIA to situations in other communities.

He was summoned to a conference with President Eisenhower.

He was beaten and arrested in Montgomery, tried, convicted, and when ordered to pay a fourteen-dollar fine or go to jail, elected jail; only to be frustrated by the canny Commissioner of Public Safety, who himself paid the fine and ejected King.

He was rotten-egged in Harlem, by toughs who were, apparently, under the spell of Black Nationalism.

He was stabbed, almost fatally, while sitting in a department store in Harlem, to autograph copies of his book *Stride Toward Freedom,* the assailant being a poor deranged woman whose motives were never clarified.

He was in Albany, Georgia, at the time of the protest movement there, in 1961, went to jail, and to the dismay of many, took bail.

He was in Birmingham, in the spring of 1963, the season of the bombings and police dogs and the riots, and went to jail there, and wrote the famous "Letter from a Birmingham Jail."

In October, 1964, he received the Nobel Peace Prize. The award confirmed him as a world figure.

*   *   *

We do not know how the twenty-seven-year-old Martin Luther King, with his new doctorate, feeling his way into his first ministry, was translated into this charismatic leader. Now the prestige is there, the authenticity conferred by both suffering and success— and publicity; and it is easy to recognize the charisma. But, the charisma is not the product of publicity. It is real.

And no matter who in Montgomery first recognized the power and proposed Martin Luther King as President of the MIA, and no matter by what fumbling process he discovered himself in that role, he gave it what it needed. There were other leaders, men of will, intelligence, dedication, and strategic sense, such as the Reverend Ralph D. Abernathy, but what the movement needed, beyond those qualities, was a voice to explain it to itself. It needed a voice to convert short-range outrage into long-range determination, anger into moral authority, and the blind impulse to avenge inferiority into a steady and pitying vision of moral superiority. It needed, in short, a voice to tell it how to win.

*   *   *

Auburn Avenue is a long street, the pulsing artery of what, in Atlanta, used to be generally called "nigger town," and by my taxi driver still is. There are the run-down stores, a few with ambitious patches of new paint and tabs of chrome; hock shops and bail-bond establishments; restaurants and honky-tonks. "Come sundown," the driver says, "and all them places now looks like is closed up will start roaren and shaken—gin and poontang." At Number 334 Auburn Avenue, N.E., not far above the building marked *Brooks Bail Bond,* the glass front, like a store front, announces the Southern Christian Leadership Council.

There is no lobby. You step through a narrow glass door into an L-shaped office, not so large that it doesn't seem cramped by the desks of four typists and two girls who act as receptionists and message-takers and such, one very fat and slow, the other a self-conscious yellow beauty in a loose yellow dress, bare-legged, wearing no-heel soft golden slippers that make no sound. The walls are that dreary institutional green found in slum high schools, county hospitals, relief headquarters, and the offices of small-time, failing realtors. On the wall is a big map of the United States, with pins stuck here and there, as for a military campaign, and with Freedom Flags—red-white-blue in three big stripes with the word FREEDOM on the white—stuck at an angle behind the map. There is a green baize bulletin board. There is, also, a big framed photograph of Dr. King, high up.

In one of the two chairs cramped near the door, where visitors wait, I read some of the hand-out literature, a copy of the *Time* cover-story on Dr. King. Two young Negroes, with a stiff-legged, cocky strut, wearing once-white buckskin shoes now dirty enough to be the pride of a senior in a fashionable New England preparatory school, and pork-pie hats and sport jackets, enter from the street and pass down the hall beyond the office, the second one pinching the fat receptionist's amply inviting bare arm, not even looking down or back in the act, as though automatically. The receptionist does not seem to notice.

The atmosphere of the place is friendly and easy, but with a steady, muted businesslike bustle. A typist asks the little world of the office how to spell *piece*—"Is it *i-e* or *e-i,* somebody say." Somebody says.

The fat, slow receptionist, whose arm had been pinched, tells me that Dr. King will see me now.*

* * *

He looks like his pictures. He is a shade less than medium height, a tidily made, compact man, the head rather large but rounded and compact too, the lips rather full but drawn back at the corners under a narrow close-trimmed mustache to emphasize this impression of compactness, the nose broad rather than projecting, the ears close-set, the hairline already receding, the hair growing close and cut short to define the shape of the skull. Compactness and control—that is the first impression, even in the natural outgoing cordiality at the moment of greeting, when the eyes brighten. At the handshake you notice that the hand is unusually large for a man of his stature, a strong hand. He has the tight-packed skin of a man who will be fat some day if he doesn't watch it, a skin with a slight sheen to its brownness. His dark clothing sits rather close on him, too, emphasizing again that compactness and completeness, nothing loose or shaggy or tweedy—a sheen to things. The shoes are of highly-polished, hard-glazed black leather, with elastic inserts that make them fit as tight and flexible as skin. He has a natural grace of movement as he turns to sit down at his desk. He could, you think, move fast and effectively.

We are on a close schedule. There is a meeting after our interview, and I gather that he is giving up his lunch and rest for me.

* Writing in 1962 Louis E. Lomax had found symbolic the fact that Dr. King then had no office in the SCLC headquarters on Auburn Avenue, but conducted his business from the Ebenezer Baptist Church. The men who came out of the mold of the Negro Baptist Church, Lomax writes, are not disciplined to become executives: "Rather they are emotional men; they think in spiritual rather than practical terms of reference; and as an inevitable result they periodically confuse God's will with their own personal desires and ambitions. . . . Men such as Martin are natural-born revolutionaries; they have what it takes to get people out into the street yelling and dying for a cause. But when the revolution is over, the republic would be better off if somebody else took over the executive leadership" (*The Negro Revolt*).

We plunge in. His father, after many years still the pastor of the Ebenezer Baptist Church in Atlanta, had been a leader of the Negro community, the type to whom the agents of white power, in the old days, had had to turn. I ask Martin Luther King if he sees his own role and his father's role as different historical phases of the same process.

KING: Yes, I do. My father and I have worked together a great deal in the last few years, trying to grapple with the same problem, and he was working in the area of civil rights before I was born, and I grew up in an atmosphere that had a real civil rights concern. It [his father's involvement] is the same historical process.*

WARREN: Saying that your father represented one phase of the Negro Movement, and you the next, can we predict the third phase?

KING: When we move into the realm of actual integration, which deals with mutual acceptance, a genuine inter-group, inter-personal living, then it seems to me that other methods will have to be used. It would be in what Mahatma Gandhi used to refer to as his constructive program, whereby the individuals work desperately to improve their own conditions and their own standards. After the Negro emerges in the desegregated society, then a great deal of time must be spent

---

* The Negro churches have not traditionally been concerned with the rights of the Negro. Simeon Booker puts it in *Black Man's America:* "The reason, perhaps, is because the Church is a victim of its own heritage—segregation. Its strength came from segregation, and its leaders hardly shared any desire to shift the foundations. . . . The Negro Church is big business . . ." He points out that in the Little Rock crisis, Mrs. Daisy Bates had little support from the Negro pulpit, and that "many of the prominent ministers openly opposed her integration effort," that the Reverend J. H. Jackson, President of the National Baptists Convention of America, had refused to support mass demonstrations led by ministers, and that only with the bus boycott in Montgomery did there come an organized effort by the Negro Church to deal with a racial abuse. Dr. King himself, in *Why We Can't Wait,* has discussed the reluctance of many of the Negro clergy of Birmingham to support the demonstration there in 1963: "I suggested that only a 'dry as dust' religion prompts a minister to extol the glories of Heaven while ignoring the social conditions that cause men an earthly hell." And in 1963, when the SCLC held a general conference in Montgomery, no church was made available for a mass rally, not even the Dexter Avenue Baptist Church, where Dr. King had begun his ministry.

in improving standards which lag behind to a large extent because of segregation, discrimination, and the legacy of slavery. The Negro will have to engage in a sort of Operation Boot-strap.

*   *   *

I have mentioned the physical compactness, the sense of completeness, that Dr. King gives. This is related to something else, something more significant, that appears as soon as you put a question to him. Even if it is a question that you know he has heard a hundred times before, there is a withdrawing inward, a slight veiling of the face as it were. There is the impression that for an answer for even that old stale question he must look inward to find a real answer, not just the answer he gave yesterday, which today may no longer be meaningful to him. It is a remarkable trait— if my reading is correct: the need to go inward to test the truth that has already been tested, perhaps over and over again, in the world outside.

Does the charisma inhere in this?

But for some the charisma does not appear. Some critics suggest that it can be truly recognized only in a society where the religious background is still generally significant—that is, in the South as opposed to the secularized society of the great Northern cities. The psychologist Kenneth Clark— who, as has emerged from some of our earlier dialogues, finds in King's philosophy something of emotional instability, even pathology—has more to say:

> It has been argued that the proper interpretation of King's philosophy of "love for the oppressor," must take into account the Christian philosophical and strategic significance. This argument may be perfectly correct for a small minority of educated and philosophically sophisticated individuals. But it is unlikely that it can be accepted with full understanding by the masses of Negroes. Their very attempt to cope with this type of philosophical abstraction in the face of the concrete injustices which dominate their daily lives could only lead to deep and disturbing inner conflicts and guilt.*

* "The New Negro in the North," in *The New Negro,* ed. M. H. Ahmann.

There are, too, other objections to his philosophy, among them
the objection that his soft line flatters the white man's sense of
superiority, encourages him in his sense of security. I ask him about
this.

KING: I don't agree with this, naturally. I think one must
understand what I'm talking about and what I'm trying to
do when I say *love,* and that the love ethic must be at the
center of this struggle. I am not talking about affection and
emotion. I am not talking about what the Greek language
would refer to as *eros.* I'm talking about something much
deeper, and there's a misunderstanding.

WARREN: This misunderstanding persists among a large segment of Negroes and a large segment of whites.

KING: I don't think it can be cleared up for those who refuse
to look at the meaning. I've said it in print over and over
again.

WARREN: Yes, you have.

KING: And I do not think that violence and hatred can solve
this problem. They would end up creating many more social
problems than they solve. I'm thinking of a very strong love,
of love *and* action, not something where you say, "Love your
enemies," and leave it at that. But you must love your enemies
to the point that you're willing to sit at a lunch counter
in order to help them find themselves. You're willing to go
to jail—and I don't think anybody should find this cowardice
or a weak approach. I think that many of the arguments come
from people who have gotten so caught up in bitterness that
they cannot see the moral issues involved.

There are some who see that the moral issues and the world of
practicality intersect. For instance, Stephen Wright, President of
Fisk University, who said to me of King: "He's gifted with the
ability to create an issue in a community, and bring it to a point
where resolutions almost have to take place, and if I were a Southern white segregationist, I would be more afraid of Dr. King than
almost any type of Negro leader." But Dr. Wright is approaching
middle age; thinking of the young, I remember the repudiations,
ironic to bitter, of King's philosophy at the Conference on Non-

violence at Howard University—repudiations even by those who accept nonviolence as a tactic. And I remember the words of James Baldwin: "Poor Martin has gone through God knows what kind of hell to awake the American conscience, but Martin has reached the end of his rope."*

So I turn and ask Dr. King about our most spectacular attempt to solve a social problem by violence—the Civil War and Reconstruction.

WARREN: You recall Myrdal's scheme for what he thinks would have been a reasonable Reconstruction—beginning with compensation to the ex-slaveholders for the emancipation, and the expropriation of land from the planters, with compensation, and the sale of this land, on easy terms, to the freedmen. That's not all of his program, but would you find any emotional resistance to that much?

KING: I don't find too much emotional resistance to it. It was a tragic period because many of the social problems we face today are here because that period was not used properly. The future wasn't looked at then. Maybe this plan would have worked all right because it would have given both [Negroes and whites] a sense of dignity, and maybe the bitterness that we now face—still face at many points—wouldn't be here because the start would have been a little better.

WARREN: This plan of Myrdal's sometimes evokes very violent responses even from Negroes who are thoroughly conversant with history.

KING: Well, mine are the same way. I'm not saying that I agree that this was a way to solve the problem. But I do feel that after two hundred and forty-four years of slavery, certain patterns had developed in the nation and certain attitudes had developed in the minds of people, so everybody had to take some of the responsibility. Consequently in solving the problem it seems to me maybe some things would have had to be done which may not have represented

* Interview with Kenneth B. Clark in *The Negro Protest*, ed. Kenneth B. Clark.

everything that we would want to see. But it might have saved us many of the bitter moments we now have.

WARREN: You wouldn't feel, then, that this program would have been a betrayal of your dignity as a Negro, to have this compensation paid?

KING: I would think the whole system—my revolt or my emotional response is so much over the tragedy of the whole system of slavery, that I wouldn't revolt against that [the compensation] as much as over the fact that slavery had existed for all those years, you see. I don't absolutely feel that this was a way to solve the problem. But yet I don't have this strong emotional feeling of bitterness when I hear it suggested, because we had accumulated a social problem that had to be grappled with.

* * *

I remember his face as he was working to sort out his feelings about Myrdal's scheme. He no longer seemed aware of my presence. His face was drawing together, sharpening inwardly, his eyes seemed veiled. There was some tension, as far as I could determine. But he was not the kind of man to deny one pole of the question. He was sitting there, aware of both, living through the question. Perhaps that is the deepest kind of life he knows. His philosophy is a way of living with an intense polarity.

* * *

WARREN: All revolutions have a tendency to move toward a centralized leadership, to come to focus in a man who embodies both power and a symbolic function. Now in this revolution—if we can call it that—you are stuck in a very special role, but even so, this revolution is not following, to date, that pattern of centralization. Can a movement persist without such a focus?

KING: I think so. But I do think there must be a centralized leadership in the sense that—say, in our struggle—all of the leaders coordinate their efforts, and at least evince a degree of unity. We have had on the whole a unified leadership, although it isn't just one person. There can be a collective leadership.

WARREN: Some informed people now wonder if any leadership, now visible or imaginable, can control the random explosion that might come at any time, say in some center like Harlem or South Chicago or Cleveland.* Violence is being stored up and we know it's being stored up. Is that the big central problem for leadership now?

KING: It's a real problem, and I think the only answer to this is the degree to which the nation is able to go—the speed in which we move toward the solution. If the Civil Rights Bill is watered down, for instance—if the Negro feels that he can do nothing but move from one ghetto to another —the despair will be so great it will be very difficult to keep the struggle nonviolent. It will depend on the recognition by white leadership of the need to get this problem solved and solved in a hurry.†

WARREN: The Reverend Galamison has said that he would rather see the public school system destroyed than not conform to his schedule of integration—based on a massive busing arrangement. Then Galamison adds: "Maybe it has run its course anyway, the public school system." How do you respond to this?

---

* Stokely Carmichael, of Snick, tells me that in some of the demonstrations in Cambridge, Maryland, only a few local Negroes were willing to enter a nonviolent demonstration, but that when the Snick demonstrators, committed to nonviolence, moved into the street they were followed by a crowd of the local people who had refused to demonstrate. Then when the Snick demonstrators confronted the police the local people, behind that screen, threw bricks and bottles at the police. "So we were their patsies," Mr. Carmichael said, "for the cops weren't going to discriminate between the violent and the nonviolent demonstrators, they laid it on the nearest, which was us."

† The shaky control of Negro leadership was well exemplified in the Harlem riots. It was impossible to find a unity of views among the Big Brass; Farmer of CORE and Lewis of Snick refused to follow the policy of a moratorium on demonstration asked for by Wilkins, King, and Young. The recently formed United Council of Harlem Organizations was offended by what they interpreted as King's neglect of them (or perhaps what was interpreted as interference in the local affairs of New York). Certainly it was not clear whom King, at the moment, represented. But a poll conducted in Harlem after the riots showed that King was still the dominant figure.

KING: I don't think the public school system has run its course, far from it. And I don't think we should think in terms of destroying the system. We can rectify the system by constantly bringing this issue [integration] to the conscience of our communities. I think it [the boycott] is one of the creative ways to dramatize an intolerable condition.

WARREN: Let's take Washington, D.C. How do you integrate if you have some eighty-five per cent of the children in public school Negroes? Where do you get enough whites to integrate with them?

KING: You have two problems here. One is the fact that this will never be solved until the housing problem is solved. As long as there is residential segregation, and as long as the whites run to the suburbs, you do have a real problem. Now, the only way it can be dealt with in the transition, while we are trying to solve the problem of housing discrimination, is to transfer students—the busing system.

WARREN: But in Washington where do you get the white children? Can you go to Virginia for them?

KING: In a case like that you do have a real problem. I guess Washington is almost unique.

WARREN: What about New York—where it's moving in the same direction?

KING: But on the whole people are still in New York City— sometimes they're in, say Westchester County, or some area of Queens.* I could see it working a little better in a situation like that.

WARREN: But in dealing with this question of mass transfer as a matter of principle—you can see situations that seem insoluble. Then what do you do?

KING: I agree that the problem will not be solved if we have these situations—we have to see the problem solved in the run of history when we get housing integration on a broad level. However, wherever schools can be integrated through the busing method, and where it won't be just a terrible inconvenience, I think it ought to be done. Because I think the

* But Westchester and Queens are, as a matter of fact, as inaccessible to Harlem as Virginia to Washington.

inconveniences of a segregated education are much greater than the inconvenience of busing students so they can get an integrated quality education.

WARREN: Are you referring to white and Negro students both—both are being short-changed, as it were?

KING: That's right—exactly. When a white child goes to school only with white children, unconsciously that child grows up devoid of a world perspective. There is an unconscious provincialism and it can develop into an unconscious superiority complex, just as the Negro develops an unconscious inferiority complex. If I can't communicate with a man, I'm not equal to him.

WARREN: What do you feel about the danger of the psychic split that Du Bois wrote about—the pull, on one hand, toward Negro tradition, or culture, or blood, and the pull on the other hand toward the white cultural heritage with, perhaps, an eventual absorption of the Negro blood? Does this present itself to you as a real issue?

KING: It's a real issue, and it has made for a good deal of frustration in the Negro community, and people have tried to solve it by various methods. One has been to reject psychologically anything that reminds you of your heritage—this is particularly true of the Negro middle class—and then trying to identify with the white majority. Often this individual finds himself caught in the middle, with no cultural roots, because he's rejected by so many of the white middle class, and he ends up, as E. Franklin Frazier says, unconsciously hating himself and tries to compensate through conspicuous consumption.

This has been a problem, but I don't think it has to be. One can live in American society with a certain cultural heritage—African or what have you—and still absorb a great deal of this culture. The Negro is an American. We know nothing of Africa. He's got to face the fact that he is an American.

WARREN: Some sociologists say that the American Negro is more like the old American—the old New Englander or old Southerner—than is any other kind of American. Does this make sense?

KING: I think so.

WARREN: A young lady at Howard—who stands high in her studies and has been on picket lines and in jails, too—said to me that she has hope for settlement in the South because of the common history on the land of the Southern white man and the Negro—because of some human recognition. And she added that she was frightened by the big anonymous city—the apparent lack of possibility of human communication. Of course, she was raised in Virginia. What about that?

KING: I think there may be some truth in it. In the South you have a sort of contact between Negroes and whites, an individual contact that you don't have in the North. Now this is mainly a paternalistic thing, a law of servantry—

And here there was a change of tape. By the time the new tape was on I was asking how he interpreted the slogan "Freedom Now," in the light of historical process.

KING: The slogan is a good one, it really means that the Negro feels he should have his freedom now. I don't think there's any illusion in the mind of anybody about the fact that you've got to observe the historical process.

WARREN: A very bright boy in a college said to me: "I understand about social process—it takes place in time—" Then he stopped, and burst out: "But I can't bring myself to say it!"

KING: We have lived so long with people saying it takes time, wait on time, that I find it very difficult to adjust to this. I get annoyed when I hear it, although I know it takes time.

And here, with his peculiar candor, his peculiar inwardness, he is dealing with another of the polarities. After a moment he says that time is neutral, it can be used either constructively or destructively.

WARREN: But some words become so symbolically charged that they cannot be used?

KING: Yes—exactly.

WARREN: The word *gradual* has become symbolically charged?

KING: That's right.

WARREN: Would you say that the phrase *historical process*— it looks cleaner but it means the same thing?

KING: It means the same, identical thing. But all the emotions surrounding [the word] *gradualism*—bring about an initial resentment from the Negro.

WARREN: Recently I was talking with a Negro attorney in Nashville, Avon Williams—an able and bitter man. And suddenly he said, "We live in a society where the symbolism of the poetry I read, the Bible I read, everything is charged with the white man's values—God's white robes, the white lights of hope—all these things are an affront to me. I find myself schooling myself to resist all this symbolism and invert it for myself."

KING: Many Negroes go through this, I think now probably more than ever before. My only hope is that this reaction will not take us back into the same thing we're trying to get out of. There's always the danger that an oppressed group will seek to rise from a position of disadvantage to one of advantage, you see—thereby subverting justice. It can lead to the kind of philosophy you get in the Black Nationalist movements—black supremacy.

WARREN: All previous revolutions—if this is a revolution— have aimed at liquidating a class or a regime. How would you define your aim?

KING: This is a revolution to get in. I think you're quite right that revolutions have been centered on destroying something. Whereas in this revolution the quest is for the Negro to get into the stream of American life. It's a revolution calling on the nation to live up to what is already there in an idealistic sense.

WARREN: A revolution to liquidate an idea—an attitude?

KING: To liquidate an idea that is out of harmony with the basic idea of the nation.

WARREN: A new kind of revolution?

KING: It is a new kind of revolution.

WARREN: If the dynamic of a revolution is of hope and of

hate, then you want to drive one horse and kill the other one?

KING: You're saying . . . ?

WARREN: Hate is a great dynamic.

KING: You're right, and part of the job of leadership is to keep the hope alive and yet keep this kind of—I guess the word is *hate* here—the best way to keep the kind of righteous indignation alive, or the healthy discontent alive that will keep a revolution moving.

WARREN: Without a personal focus?

KING: Without a personal focus.

WARREN: How do you interpret the personal assaults on you in Harlem?

KING: The first one—I don't know if we'll ever know what the cause was, here you had a poor demented mind. Maybe she was just so confused she would have done this to anybody who was in the news. But on the other, when they threw eggs, I think that was really the result of the Black Nationalists—you know, they've heard these things about my being soft, my talking about love, and they transfer their bitterness toward the white man to me. In fact, Malcolm X had a meeting the day before and he talked about me and said, "You ought to go over there and let old King know what you think about him." All this talk about my being a sort of polished Uncle Tom. But they don't see that there's a great deal of difference between nonresistance to evil and nonviolent resistance. But even if one didn't want to deal with the moral question, it would be impractical for the Negro to make his struggle violent.

WARREN: On this point, in *The Negro Revolution,* the survey by William Brink and Louis Harris indicates an over-all six per cent of the Negro population of the country does not know the Negro is a minority; and the presumption is that a large part of that percentage is in the big ghettos.

KING: They never get out of Harlem.

WARREN: So the tactical appeal for nonviolence does not apply to them. That's a dangerous fact, isn't it?

KING: That's a dangerous fact. And you see how this bitterness can accumulate. They see no way out. If they could look down a long corridor and see an exit sign they would feel better. I've never thought about it, but it's quite true that if you talk to them about nonviolence from a tactical point of view, they can't quite see it, because they don't even know they're outnumbered.

WARREN: When you were assaulted—the egg incident, I mean —what were your feelings?

KING: I remember my feelings very well. I guess I had a very depressing response, because they were my own people. I guess you go through those moments when you think about what you are going through and the sacrifices and suffering you face, that your own people don't have an understanding —not even an appreciation, and seeking to destroy your image at every point.

But then, it was very interesting. I went into the church and I spoke and I started to think, not so much about myself, but about the very people, the society that made people respond like this. It was interesting how I was able to get my mind off myself and feeling sorry for myself and rejected, and I started including them into the orbit of my thinking, that it's not enough to condemn them for doing this, but what about the society which made people act like this?

*　　*　　*

And here, again, we have the effort to reach out and absorb an antithesis of feeling, the attempt to deal with a polarity: the condemnation becomes, through comprehension, an acceptance.

Sitting there by the desk and hearing Dr. King's voice, I had been wondering how much that voice has to do with his authority, his mystical hold. It is, of course, a rich, resonant voice, with a vibrance of inner force. But it is not only the quality of the voice, I had speculated; it is a rhythm into which it falls. Back at Southern University in Louisiana, a student had said to me of Dr. King: "To hear him speak is enough to rouse the emotions . . . the places where he places the stress, these are the things that arouse people."

Not in ordinary conversation, but as soon as that inward turning begins, as soon as that faint veiling of the face begins, as soon as an idea or feeling must be explored and dealt with, there tends to be a balanced rhythm, a long movement up, then a sharper fall away, this movement balanced by another like it, pair by pair. *Something of a platform rhythm,* I wrote in my notebook when I stood again in the street. Then added: *Or is the platform rhythm itself out of a deep natural rhythm of feeling, of vision?* Then I wondered if that deep balance of rhythm had some relation to the attempt to deal with and include antitheses, to affirm and absorb the polarities of life.

*   *   *

It was nearly two o'clock when I stood in the street, and the notebook says:

Bright sun, newspapers shifting on the pavement in a light breeze, the sound of construction machinery somewhere away from the dinginess of Auburn, the street deserted, and I walk down past beauty parlors, poolrooms and honky-tonks, see a dwarf ahead, some 45 years old, somehow burly in his small twisted way, trousers size of regular man, only ridiculously short with dolorous, bagging seat after the cutting down, dark coat, pink shirt, big full head carried aggressively back, chin up, hat on back of head like a dead-game sport. Walks downs the street ahead of me. Nobody else. Till somebody steps out of a door, a big man. Dwarf reaches up, seizes necktie of man, pulls his head down and pretends to get ready to mash his face in, a parody of ferocity on his own big face down there. Or is it a parody? Friend is grinning.

: 7 :

Of all the associates of Dr. King in the SCLC perhaps the best known are the Reverend Ralph D. Abernathy, the Reverend Wyatt Tee Walker, the Reverend F. L. Shuttlesworth, and the Reverend Andrew Young. The connection with Abernathy dates back to the early days in Montgomery, where he, like Dr. King, had been pastor of a Baptist church. Shuttlesworth, the minister of a Baptist Church in Birmingham, had been important in organizing the protests there in 1963. Walker was, until 1961 when he came to SCLC, pastor of the Gillfield Baptist Church and head of the Petersburg, Virginia,

Improvement Association. If Louis E. Lomax is right, to any signifi-
cant degree, in his impression that the Movement is "being run in
King's name but by somebody else," then, presumably, that some-
body else is among those three who also sit in offices on Auburn
Avenue—Abernathy, Young, and Walker. And the odds are on
Walker. He is Executive Director of the SCLC.*

The office occupied by the Reverend Walker is considerably larger
and considerably better furnished and more tidily maintained than
that of Dr. King. There are several pictures, reproductions of *La
Gioconda*, Rembrandt's *Night Watch*, and Picasso's *Man With
Guitar*. There is a picture of Christ. There is a collection of books,
the library of a man of intellectual tastes. On the wall to the left
above the big desk are a glittering series of brass plaques and
certificates of award.

Walker himself is a young man of medium height, perhaps a little
taller, thinly but strongly built, with a small well-molded head, a
rather handsome face, pale yellow, with a slightly grayish cast, a small
clipped mustache.† He is well-dressed, but not with the flair that
rumor had attributed to him in earlier days.

The Reverend Walker is a voluble and eloquent man. "Once you
get me talking," he said before we settled down, "I might keep you
here all night." He is, it seems, a man of candor, sometimes an
angry and ironical candor, and of self-knowledge, taking relish,
even, in pulling back from himself to look at himself in the diminishment of a new perspective—in pulling out of his own skin to look
at the poor forked radish or featherless biped which is man. He said
to me: "One big piece of evidence about the greatness of Martin
Luther King is that a man as vain as I am is willing to play second
fiddle to him. And I'm not ordinarily ready to play second fiddle
to anybody."

The impulse to self-knowledge, self-scrutiny—which, of course,
can be a very complicated impulse—is something that runs through
our conversation. And it runs through his answer to my question:
Is the Negro's discovery of his identity part of the whole Movement?

---

* Recently resigned to become vice president of Educational Heritage,
Inc., in New York, a publishing house specializing in work of particular
interest to Negroes.
† Since moving to New York, he has shaved off the mustache.

WALKER: It's a very critical part. I can remember being aware of an internal color discrimination in the Negro community, and being a mulatto, I guess I was sensitized to it because I had brothers and sisters who gave to being light-skinned some special value. I think fortunately for me, I rebelled against this. I have seen that change sharply in the last fifteen or twenty years. I had known dark-skinned people in whose presence I would be afraid to say the word *black*—seriously or humorously.

WARREN: Now?

WALKER: No, in the past. Now it's part of the built-in humor of the Movement and we kid each other about it—calling each other half-white Negroes and black Negroes.

WARREN: What about the color symbolism of light and dark in our culture?

WALKER: I know when I am watching television, and reading stories, my antenna is out, maybe, to pick up these little value assignments, on the basis of color. I saw a television story about a good horse and a bad horse—and the bad horse was black. It's so skillfully woven into our value judgments that I think sometimes it almost happens to us unconsciously.

WARREN: What about light-dark value symbolisms in non-white cultures?

WALKER: It's in the Platonic dualism, in the writings of Paul. But we can go back to the business of day and night, with the primitive mind, and the dangers of jungle life.

WARREN: Then we have a strange overlay of social and natural symbols?

WALKER: One has been superimposed upon the other.

WARREN: What reaction, then, is reasonable for a Negro in facing this situation?

WALKER: No matter how much academically I recognize the fallacy of race, so much has been done to my emotional pattern by the system that I am never really free of it. So you get in fleeting moments the reverse response—discrimination the other way. Negroes like myself have developed a mental catalog of the tones of voice, how a white face speaks to them, which in other circumstances—when a Negro speaks

—would get no response whatsoever. But everything that a white person says is interpreted by the nuance of voice, or the hang of the head—you know, things that in a normal frame of reference would have no meaning.

WARREN: In other words, you are documenting the remark made by more than one Negro that to be Negro is to have a touch of the paranoid?

WALKER: Oh, yes, we have almost a total ambivalence. Even in this moment of history, when the Negro really accepts his identity, there is still a retention of this ambivalence, which has many roads by which it has come.

WARREN: Even by Uncle Remus?

WALKER: Yes, poking fun at the master. This runs through the idiomatic expression of the Negro and the Negro spirituals—and the Negro religion, even.

WARREN: We have very violent statements now and then about the relation of the white man to the Negro Movement Baldwin calls the white liberal an affliction. Is this a logical extension of the attitude you have been talking about?

WALKER: Yes—it is.

WARREN: What role, then, can the white man take?

WALKER: I agree with Adam Clayton Powell that the day has come when the white person has no role to play in the policy decision of the Negro Movement. But I do not go all the way with him to say that we do not need white allies. We passed through the stage of the Southern white liberal of fifteen years ago. We are afflicted with outworn white liberals —or worn-out white liberals. Fifteen years ago what they were saying could have cost them their lives, but they're saying the same thing now, and as James Russell Lowell has said, "Time makes ancient good uncouth." We are at a different moment in history.

WARREN: Can the Negro Movement have success without a white consensus?

WALKER: Yes, I do think so.

WARREN: How would you explain that?

WALKER: This is a minority opinion, but I believe that the Negro has just enough pivotal position in the economy, and just enough visible identity, that we could produce so creative a crisis that the consensus might be forced—prodded by practicality.

WARREN: By political and economic force?

WALKER: Yes. This coupled with the guilt burden that the white community must bear—particularly within the frame of reference of white Christianity.

WARREN: You mean you are coupling the guilt burden with the potentiality of consensus?

WALKER: Yes, I suppose so.

WARREN: But guilt is not an external prod, it is in the guts—if you have a feeling of guilt you already have some awareness of a moral issue. Is guilt the feeling of a desire for another attitude in yourself?

WALKER: When a white person says, "I know what the right thing is to do, but I just don't have the power to do it."

WARREN: That's an old story—for any complexion.

WALKER: That's not consensus.

WARREN: But a potentiality of consensus lies in the recognition of responsibility?

WALKER: Yes, I could buy that. But there was something else I wanted to say about the Negro's accepting his own identity. You find now pride taken in being a visible Negro —you know, if you're on the border line, like some of us mulattoes are, you feel a bit embarrassed—kind of like you've been cheated of the respectability of being black and having kinky hair.

This question of the snobbery of being black reminds me of an episode recounted by William Stringfellow in *My People Are the Enemy.* At a rally in Harlem to protest police brutality one of the speakers was a minister known for his reasonable attitudes, a man so light that he might have "passed." At the rally he prefaced his remarks by apologizing for his color. This evoked boos from the crowd. After persisting for a moment, he changed his tactics and took a virulent line of black supremacy and a resort to violence. He appeased the crowd.

In his destructive, irrational way the minister had done exactly what Walker, in his next breath, describes: "He [the Negro] has found identity, not only for *himself,* but he has found identity *with*

the group." The minister had found it, however, at the cost of losing
manhood, not by finding it. His act is an obscene parody of the
process by which, in Birmingham and elsewhere, Negroes have
found identity. It is no surprise to us that Stringfellow reports that
the next time he encountered the minister he was in a Village
restaurant squiring a white girl.

As for Birmingham, the chief meaning of that event, according to
Wyatt Tee Walker, is that it gave Negroes, in dramatic form, a way
to discover themselves.

WARREN: It is sometimes said that the outbreak of violence
in Birmingham by what had been the apathetic poor was a
shock to Negro leadership.

WALKER: You know what my shock was? I was there in both
instances of violence. I was in the motel when it was bombed.
My shock was that we were successful in containing the violence to what it was. And here we are at the mercy of—they
don't do it with malice—of the white press corps, they can
see it only through white eyes. They can't distinguish between Negro demonstrators and Negro spectators. All they
know is Negroes, and most of the spectacular pictures printed
in *Life* and in television clips had the commentary "Negro
demonstrators" when they were not that at all. I could go
through reams of pictures.

On the first Sunday of the demonstration, we had twenty-
three demonstrators in the march. But people began to stand
around, and it swelled to about fifteen hundred, and they
followed us twenty-three down the street, and when the UPI
took pictures they said: fifteen hundred demonstrators—
twenty-two arrested. Well, that was all we had.

So we devised the technique, we'd set the demonstration up
for a certain hour and then delay it two hours and let the
crowd collect. This is a little Machiavellian, and I don't know
whether I ever discussed this with Dr. King. It was the
spectators following upon whom the dogs were turned. It
wasn't until three weeks later that the hoses were actually
used on demonstrators.

The Saturday before the truce there had been some rock-throwing by spectators. So the next morning we began to distribute our demonstrators to other points in the city, to other churches [than the Sixteenth Street Church]. We couldn't let the spectators know. They waited from, say eleven in the morning until about four in the afternoon, waiting to see some action. So they gathered in the park, and firemen set up their hoses at two corners. And the mood was like a Roman holiday—it was festive—there wasn't anybody among the spectators who was angry.

It was beginning to get dark now, so somebody heaved a brick—in fact, they'd been saying, "Turn the water hose on, turn the water hose on!" Then somebody threw a brick and they started turning them on. So they just danced and played in the spray. This famous picture of them holding hands, it was just a frolic, they'd get up and run back and it would slide them along the pavement. This went on for a couple of hours. All in good humor. Not any vitriolic response. Which to me was an example of changing spirit. Where Negroes once had been cowed in the presence of policemen —here they had complete disdain.

WARREN: Who were these people?

WALKER: Mostly marginal and sub-marginal livers.

WARREN: Town or country people?

WALKER: Both, but primarily town people—who were not inclined to get into the Movement per se—to take the training. With all of more than thirty-four hundred people who went to jail, there was hardly an instance of anybody going to jail who was not signed up and who did not receive two hours of instruction. It was a tremendous administrative responsibility. Nobody will ever know, I guess, until I get my Birmingham diary finished, what really went into Birmingham.

WARREN: You know what Louis Lomax has written about the campaign in Albany, Georgia?*

---

* The account by Lomax states that the original attack on the segregation of the bus station at Albany had been begun by the NAACP; that the SCLC had then financed Snick students for freedom rides into Albany, along with

WALKER: Yes—and can I say something about Louis Lomax, one of the most informed chroniclers of the Negro Movement. Mechanically, Lou Lomax is a good writer, but Lou is inaccurate, and I would say this as quickly to him as to you. I can document it, that with all the pages Lou Lomax wrote about Albany, could you believe that he never set his foot in the town? With all the pages he wrote about Martin Luther King, Jr.—could you believe he never once interviewed him? And some people think that my criticism of Lou is because they felt he gave me bad treatment. I did not feel so. I felt he was absolutely accurate in his description of me—he had one or two facts off, but as to my demeanor and attitude, he was as honest as any man could be. So it isn't anything personal. It's a matter of his—what shall I call it—maltreatment of an analysis of the Movement, about which he is generally uninformed. Lou is not knowledgeable about Birmingham. He wasn't there long enough to know or to grasp or to understand all that was involved in Birmingham.

If Wyatt Tee Walker can withdraw from and be critical of Wyatt Tee Walker, he can probably free himself more than any Negro with whom I have talked (except perhaps Whitney Young) from the cagey act of maintaining the impression of a united front of Negro leadership vis-à-vis the outside world.

* * *

other groups of students, to work up local support; that this situation created a "head-on clash with the local NAACP," which was resolved by the setting up of an over-all organization called the Albany Movement; that then King and Walker personally entered the picture—King to be well received, but Walker unwelcome:

"Local Negroes got mad.

" 'Dr. Walker can't come to Albany and take over,' one of the leaders cried.

" 'We can bake our own cake,' another shouted. 'All we need from the Atlanta boys is some flour and sugar.'

"But, as the Negroes across the South are now learning, when you get flour and sugar from Wyatt you also get Wyatt."

As for Birmingham, some informed and detached observers (white) have remarked on the great effectiveness of Walker's operations there.

On the NAACP:

The NAACP has become bureaucratic, it has lost contact with the grass-roots people—if it ever had it. I worked within the structure of the NAACP since I was eleven years old, so I know it pretty well. I was branch president for five years in Virginia, reputedly one of the best branches in the nation per capita. I think I could pretty well document that whenever within the lines of the NAACP energetic and/or ambitious leadership begins to develop, you go to the guillotine. It seems to me that the life of any organization, if it's going to exist in perpetuity, must have some transfer.

On James Baldwin:

I recognize James Baldwin mechanically and artistically as a good writer, but I cannot accept James Baldwin as the last word on Negro expression—what I feel. James Baldwin can speak for James Baldwin and what he feels, but that does not make him the architect of expression for the Negro community. I don't think there's any person who speaks for the Negro community—not even Martin Luther King, Jr.

On Charles Evers and his Statement that Birmingham Was a "Disaster":

First, he isn't knowledgeable about the Negro Movement in the South. He's been away from Mississippi too long. Secondly, you can't measure the results of a revolution altogether in tangible results—it was a direction-turning event, not just for a single city but for the South and even the entire nation.

*   *   *

As for general topics Wyatt Tee Walker has the same readiness to put himself and his opinions on the line. He has a hard, active mind. He has thought many things through to his own satisfaction. Unlike Dr. King, he feels no need to re-test the answers. He has filed them away, and they can be produced immediately, on demand.

On Busing:

I would say, just as a rule of thumb—and this is right off the top of my head—anything more than a half-hour or forty-five minutes would be unusually burdensome. It would only be an interim program—to get certain results and at the same moment dramatize a situation.

On "Passing":

If that's what he [a Negro] wants to do, more power to him. There's always the inevitable question—if you could come back would you come back as a white man or a Negro? I'd come back as a white man every time. I might have been Attorney General of the United States.

On the White Man and this Historical Moment:

I think the white man may [now] feel that he is, in a sense, at the mercy of history, whereas the Negro, in a sense, is guiding or directing.

On the South and Reconciliation:

I have said at different times, and others who have worked in our revolution say so, that we believe that the South is going to be a better place to live for Negroes and whites than perhaps the North. Even though we are passing through a period which is very costly emotionally, after a period of reconciliation Negroes and whites may live here in a warmer relationship than anywhere else because of their common bond. Perhaps because both of us were refined in the cauldrons of the Civil War and Reconstruction and then the nonviolent revolution—maybe because of our common geographical history. I think the level of interpersonal relationships is closer than it could ever be in the North.

On the Black Muslims:

The Muslim movement and its impact on race relations is almost nil. It's a specter, a paper tiger that the white press has created. Fifty per cent of the Negroes never even heard of the Black Muslims, they don't know who Malcolm X is. But ninety per cent know who Martin Luther King is.

On Martin Luther King:

I think we should have to face the practical realities that in these civil rights organizations, with the diversified attacks, the one point at which there is sharp competition is fund-raising. Even though we stay in the red, we have a broader out-reach than any organization, and this is because Dr. Martin Luther King is in it.

There isn't anybody who commands the kind of response —the individual physical response—that he does. This is the symbolism of Martin Luther King, and we translate it into meaningful support for his organization. He raised, by his appearances, last year better than $400,000 for his organization—fifty per cent of the budget or more, for which he himself got one dollar. He gets no personal income from the organization, but yet the stories persist that this man is making a mint. I know more about the personal finances of Martin Luther King, Jr., than any living person except his wife and secretary, and I know of offers that come to him that are legitimate and which he has every right to accept, but because of his unique symbolism he is reluctant. Many people do not know that Martin Luther King, Jr., was born a wealthy man. He has no need.

It is undoubtedly true, as Walker puts it, that there is no Negro leader who commands "the individual physical response" that Martin Luther King, Jr., commands—no one who has his "symbolism." But such a power always meets with resistance. A few days after King had received the Nobel Peace Prize, I shared a seat on a plane from North Carolina to New York with Mr. Walker. The award, he said, would be very useful, it would help to "consolidate Dr. King's position."

"With Negroes," I asked, "or with white people?"

"With both," he said. "Take the power structure of Atlanta, for instance."

"The Negro power structure?"

"Yes," he said. "They have never felt comfortable with him there. There was always the fear that he might 'take over.' And this reflects their provincialism. He would upset things. In the Scott paper, for instance—a Negro paper—there was a directive never to publish his picture or mention his name on the front page."

*   *   *

But to return to that evening in Atlanta, after our interview, Mr. Walker asked me why I was mixed up in this project. I said that I wanted to find out about things, including my own feelings.

"It is very courageous of you," he said.

I said that that notion had never crossed my mind. That was true, and yet at the same time, at hearing his words, there had been, deep down in me, a cold flash of rage.

NOTEBOOK:

At the condescension—moral condescension. The Negro Movement is fueled by a sense of moral superiority. No wonder that some sloshes over on the white bystander as condescension. The only effective payment for all the other kinds of condescension visited on black men over the years. Antidote indicated: humor. And not only self-humor.

: 8 :

That night, my last in Atlanta, I went to dinner at the house of a young Negro lawyer—a new house, bright, commodious, well-designed. For dinner—eaten in the bar—there were two white men as guests, one of them an old acquaintance of the family, a professional associate of the husband. The hostess was in and out, but did not drink with us. The host went out to cook the steaks, and we, the two white guests, were left alone most of that time. The hostess made a fleeting appearance as dinner began and ate a few bites, but soon found occasion to leave, taking her plate with her. She was a very good-looking young girl, toward thirty, graceful and golden-skinned. She was the graduate of a good university.

Later that night, my host drove me through one of the gilded ghettos of Atlanta—a large Negro section of houses ranging in price, I should say, from $60,000 to $90,000, each with a well-laid-out garden, most of the gardens large, some with a swimming pool and bathhouse—some houses, I was told, with an indoor pool to boot. At one o'clock in the morning, lights, discreetly concealed in expensive shrubbery, cast a glow over the lawns. As we drove slowly along, admiring the display, my host, with calculated detachment, fastidiously handling the wheel, said: "It's funny about my wife. The way she is. She just doesn't like to be around white people."

*   *   *

My plane was not to leave until early afternoon. I had a morning to kill, and I had never seen the famous Cyclorama of the Battle of Atlanta. The Cyclorama—reputedly the largest picture in the world, 50 by 400 feet, 20,000 square feet of painted canvas—was executed at the American Panorama Company, in Milwaukee, by a group of imported German artists who were already veterans of a number of cycloramas celebrating the glories of the Franco-Prussian War; and this work was undertaken to celebrate the glory of Yankee arms, not to pander to the sentimentality of the Lost Cause. First exhibited in Detroit in 1887, the cyclorama endured many vicissitudes before a public-spirited citizen of Atlanta bought it and gave it to the city, where now, handsomely housed in Grant Park (no relation to Ulysses S.), it serves, for the sub-literate or visual-minded, as a kind of adjunct to *Gone With the Wind.*

At the door you buy your ticket, and plunge into a bright, hygienic-looking tunnel, to emerge at the foot of a circular platform which is surrounded, at some distance off, by the Cyclorama. The space between the platform and the Cyclorama itself is cluttered with the three-dimensional debris of war—dead bodies and broken caissons, both in painted plaster—life-size if near but at a little distance scaling down rapidly to fade into the illusion of the Cyclorama. There it was—the events of that grim day, July 22, 1864, when Confederate valor and bad judgment undid all the expertise of Joseph E. Johnston, and sealed the fate of Atlanta.

It was a weekday morning, and raining besides. I had expected to be alone for my little ritual visit. I was not. There were some twenty Negroes there—age, upper teens to forty, well-dressed, most of them—silently watching the little ball of light that bounced over the painted canvas to indicate some event or person being referred to by the flat, mechanical voice of the narration, which was occasionally interrupted by canned music—"The Battle Hymn of the Republic" or "Dixie," quite impartially.

When I got back into the cab to go back into town, I asked to be taken to the office of the *Atlanta Constitution.* "Bet you gonna see Ralph McGill," the driver said.

"Yes," I said.

"That old Cyclorama and Ralph McGill," he said, "then you done seen At-lanta. You done seen it all."

*   *   *

At lunch Ralph and Gene Patterson, an editor of the *Constitution,* talked about the symbolism of the Negro's color (darkness, temptation, sexuality) in relation to white puritanical Protestantism; about the paper's support of the Civil Rights Bill;* and about the irony

---

* "The Civil Rights Bill is no panacea but by spelling certain things out it will give a basis for several kinds of operations—legal action instead of demonstration, an orderly attack on de facto segregation in housing, and a consolidation of responsible Negro leadership." McGill, in conversation.

in the fact that while Russell was fighting in the Senate his own version of the Battle of Atlanta—a battle quite as hopeless as the event of 1864—Leroy Johnson, a Negro, sits in the Georgia legislature. In fact, in January of last year, with his wife and four Negro guests, he attended the inauguration ball at the Dinkler Hotel and danced in honor of Governor Saunders.

"Thank God for Martin Luther King," Ralph McGill said.
"Yes, thank God for him," Gene Patterson said.

: 9 :

Unlike any other major figure in the Revolution, Bayard Rustin enters as a worker not primarily for racial justice but for general social reform. Not that the situation of the Negro in America was not, from the very beginning, his concern but, to use his words, he "had felt for some time that certain problems which the American Negro faced could not be solved as race problems, but that many aspects of our society would need some change prior to the Negro's gain of a certain status." In other words, in his youth, he had anticipated the direction in which lately more and more of the Negro leaders have been moving; for instance: Whitney Young, Robert Moses, and most recently, Martin Luther King.

Bayard Rustin's membership in the Young Communist League, back at the time of the Scottsboro Case, when he was in his early twenties, indicates his approach. The other organizations were not "militant enough," he says; but primarily it was the prospect of general social reform that attracted him to Marxism. But in 1941, when he confronted the fact that the Communist Party was not "interested in justice" but in supporting "the foreign policy of the Soviet Union," he broke with Communism and began to pursue the line which has been characteristic of him ever since. His early Quakerism had made him uneasy from the start with Communism, and now he went to work for the Fellowship of Reconciliation—a pacifist organization—as Race Relations Secretary, and he became a socialist. The same year he was youth organizer for A. Philip Randolph's March on Washington, which forced Roosevelt's signature to the famous Order 88020; and he became the first Field Secretary to the new organization CORE. In 1942 he was in California working to protect the property of the interned Nisei. The next year he began a sentence as a conscientious objector.

After the war, Rustin became chairman of the Free India Committee, made several visits there as a guest of the Congress Party, and on one visit worked in India for six months. In 1951, he was in West Africa working with Azikewe and Nkrumah, and later was a founder of the American Committee on Africa. In 1957, in England, he was an organizer of the Aldermaston Peace March, and in 1962 was in Addis Ababa for the All African People's Conference.

But in this general context he had constantly been active in the problems of the Negro in America. There was, of course, the work in CORE. In 1947, as a result of the first freedom ride—to test the decision in the Irene Morgan case which had outlawed discrimination in interstate travel—he did thirty days on a North Carolina chain gang; and his account of this experience, published in *The New York Post,* led to the abolition of the system in North Carolina. He was director of the Committee Against Discrimination in the Armed Forces. In 1955 he assisted Martin Luther King in organizing the Montgomery bus boycott, and, at the request of Dr. King, with whom he was to be closely associated for several years, drew up the original plan for the Southern Christian Leadership Conference. In 1964 he directed the New York school boycott. But his greatest fame springs from the fact that he was Deputy Director of the March on Washington in 1963. A. Philip Randolph called him "Mr. March on Washington."

Bayard Rustin was born in 1910, in West Chester, Pennsylvania, and attended high school there. He is a tall man with wide shoulders and a good carriage. In school, he was a football player and a track man, and even now he has some trace of the athlete's fluidity of movement. His college work was at Wilberforce University, Cheyney State Teachers College, in Pennsylvania, and City College of New York. He is a handsome man, medium brown in color, with a fine brow under crisp graying hair, with cleanly molded features; and the general impression is a strange mixture of strength and sensitivity. His hands are large and strong-looking, but have a delicacy of modeling and the long tapering fingers that we do not ordinarily associate with that size and strength. Sometimes when he talks, especially when he leans a little forward at you, these fine, slick-skinned fingers move on the surface of the desk or on his knee as though on a keyboard. He is, I should guess, not unconscious of the beauty of the hands.

The office where I found Rustin is on the fourth floor of 112 East 19th Street. There is a large bare room, with two white secretaries, and Rustin sits in one of the two inner offices. This is the headquarters of the War Resister's League, an organization of which Rustin has been executive secretary since 1953.

Mr. Rustin, early in our conversation, emphasizes that in the face of automation and a technological revolution it is imperative to think of the over-all problem, and not simply of jobs and training for Negroes. "I reject," he says, "the idea of working for the Negro as being impractical as well as immoral, if one does that alone." Certainly he is not for "preferential treatment," for "next we would find Negroes and whites fighting each other in the streets for the few jobs that did exist"—the basic cause, he believes, of the riot in the summer of 1964, in Newark, New Jersey, "where fifty-two per cent of the city is Negro, with almost three times as many Negroes unemployed as whites." The only answer is a political movement, not "a political party," he says, "but the kind of movement that got the civil rights legislation through Congress, a movement made up of civil rights groups, minority peoples, the best elements in the trade union movement, the religious groups and churches—they played a magnificent role—and the intellectual students." He is speaking of a "great consensus, of the congealing here of all the best elements in our society, which broke the back of the filibuster and got the first important social legislation since 1938."

But mere political action is not enough. There must be a philosophical reorientation. "We have to redefine what work is," he says. "We must recognize that the work of the young people is to develop their minds and skills for the benefit of society. There is no work more sacred. High school and college students who cannot afford it should have not only their books paid for and their tuition paid, but if necessary get a salary in order to make it possible for them to continue their work."

Furthermore, as automation takes over, there must be some basic inspection of old assumptions. "If the private sector of the economy is not capable of keeping people at work with dignity, then the public sector must play a larger role." For instance, there are in Harlem a great number of boys "who because they have not been able to get work have become skilled at taking care of younger children and teaching them to play sports and other things." Why not, he asks, open up more parks and put such unemployed boys to work as recreation directors and supervisors of young children? Or why not put "five hundred young men to work, if only at forty or fifty dollars a week, to make Central Park livable and beautiful again?" Or why not take a number of the poor Negro or Irish or other women who "all their lives have taken care of the children of the rich," and who, though said to have no skills, "have the skill of loving and being able to deal with children, and elevate them to assistant teachers at, say, four thousand dollars a year, to do the housekeeping of the schools"? That is, they would free the regular teachers to teach, taking over the baby-sitting aspects, the lunch supervision, the toilet going, et cetera. All in all, he envisions the possibility of extending personal services, the one thing automation cannot do, in all sorts of fields, from handicrafts to psychiatric counseling.

Though his purpose, Bayard Rustin insists, is not to seek special benefits for the Negro, even though his need is great, the Negro does occupy a special position in the process of reordering society. Originally the Negro's motive was, he says, to seek freedom for himself, to achieve integration, "which means getting his part of the cake, or becoming part of the institutions as they exist. He is not a revolutionary basically."* But he has "unconsciously become a revolutionary, and a catalytic agent," because what he wants cannot be had without basic changes. His own demands instigate larger events than he had envisaged. "When he touches a rent strike, what happens is not merely that a few Negroes get their rent reduced and a few rats and roaches are cleaned up, and hot water is given, but we are finding that more is now occurring around the rent strike: law, which says that human rights must not any longer be subjected to property rights. Here the Negro is a catalyst." But

* Wilkins says that the Negro is "a liberal only on the race question . . . he is a conservative economically. I don't see him as a bold experimenter in political science or social reform." See p. 152.

there is another aspect: the Negro challenges the hearts of people; for instance, the image of the Negro working for civil rights challenged the conscience of the white churches. The War on Poverty comes "not because white people were moving, but because the Negroes had to move." The Negroes are a "chosen people," he says, with a "peculiar mission," but this does not imply that they are "superior" or "better" or "more noble." It is merely that they are now thrust into a special role in history.

And in this connection Rustin discusses the problem of identity. "Our true identity is struggle, and not a lot of foolishness about culture and the like. That culture which is truly new, and to which we will contribute, lies in our struggle."

*   *   *

On Demonstrations With and Without Targets:

A demonstration should have an immediately achievable target. When a demonstration is just against being a black man in America, this is not a demonstration, it is a gimmick.*

Sooner or later even one's own group will not tolerate this, because they have to have victories in order to keep moving, and those victories must be clearly interpreted to them, so that they know truly what they have won. There is nothing you can win by going out on a demonstration because you're black.

* The Reverend J. Metz Rollins, of the United Presbyterian Church in Philadelphia, Pennsylvania: "You don't have to have any specific objectives. This is a protest against being a Negro in this country." Rev. Rollins was referring to the demonstrations in Nashville, Tennessee, in early May of 1964, which, unlike previous demonstrations in that city, did not have a target, and according to the *Nashville Tennessean* (with a "liberal" record on the race question), had been "untrained, misdirected, and without sensitive leadership." The point is not that there were no justifications for demonstrations in Nashville; according to a signed statement by an interdenominational group of ministers, the early policy of desegregation had ground to a halt, or near-halt. The point here is the nature of the demonstrations. The Reverend C. T. Vivian of the SCLC, agreeing with Rev. Rollins in support of the demonstration, said: "We must be more radical than we were yesterday. That means we are going to have to move massively and in such ways that we can be heard." See *The New York Times*, May 3, 1964.

On Action in the Next Phase of the Movement:

We are now in a period where fundamental problems can be solved through assistance from the Federal Government —tearing down slums, public works, putting everybody back to work. That's a political job. And you have to work at it politically. However, demonstrations must still be called upon because they have two objectives, not one. A demonstration, first of all, calls attention to an evil, and simultaneously pricks the conscience of men, and second cures the evil. This will have to be done in the future at many levels. The problem is that in public accommodations, it was possible to do the first and second simultaneously. You can go in front of a restaurant and prick the conscience and integrate it, all in the same act. In the North, however, dealing with jobs, schools, and housing, you cannot simultaneously prick the conscience and solve the problem. This is part of the crisis, and many people do not understand it. Demonstrations will still be valuable for the first aspect.

Another fact about demonstrations in the future is that instead of there being only Negroes parading, we must gear them so that more and more of the white dispossessed feel comfortable in them. The Negro and white will be saying: "We will not fight in the streets over jobs. We know that full employment can be had. We want work. We want no more relief."

On Attitudes and Institutions, and Inherited Guilt:

I think that you do not change attitudes first, that attitudes are gravely shaped by the institutional way of life, and therefore I do not expect every white person to like me, given our history, any more than I can avoid having some bitterness toward some white people. We are both victims of having been trapped for three hundred years, and it wasn't your grandfather's nor my grandfather's fault, really. And if it was, what difference does it make? We're here now, sitting together.

On Martin Luther King and the "Debt" Theory:

I don't think that even a social movement can be based on past sins. It has to be based on the collective needs of people at this time, regardless of color, creed, race. Dr. King knows this is my view because I have said it to him after reading that section of his book [*Why We Can't Wait*].

On the Stages of a Riot:

Number one, the rioting was the result of pent-up frustration, the absence of hope, the confusion one finds in ghettos, the inability to sleep at night in the summer because you sleep in shifts, because the trash is not collected at the proper hours. Now, there was a second stage, the stage all criminal elements use. When something is going on, regardless of what caused it, they move in because they are criminals, black or white.* The third stage is that where certain political groups try to keep the situation stirred up.

If we go back to stage one, the responsibility of black and white people of good will is to relieve as rapidly as possible the frustrations. If we come to stage two, one is then in a very difficult position in regard to the police. They have to maintain law and order. What made a number of people in Harlem angry was that the police used force far beyond what was necessary. I think it is because they are afraid of the ghetto, they are frightened men. This is the ticklish part. What we are trying to do is to get the police to recognize that

---

* In analyses of the riots of 1943 in New York and Detroit, the distinction was observed between the fighters, who were young, and who acted out their frustration and hostility, and the looters, who were older and were exploiters of the situation. (Thomas F. Pettigrew, *A Profile of the Negro American.*)

until we can deal with the fundamental questions, no matter how well they behave it is never good enough. Even if the police behaved well there would be frustrations. If you have a ghetto, which is like a cell, you think of the police as jailers —the man finally responsible for keeping you there.*

So far as the third stage is concerned, when the political folk come in to make hay, as when the Progressive Labor people tried to put a parade on Lenox Avenue, when they knew there would be problems, that has to be dealt with by the Negro community's intelligent leadership. It was not the police who put an end to this, it was those of us who went into the street and got people off, who organized the youth to keep them off the streets. They [the parade] had finally thirty people.

On the Police Review Board and the Riots in Philadelphia:

If it had not been for the police review board, the likelihood is that they would have had trouble earlier and to a greater degree.

On Negro Police:

I know Negro policemen who are among the most brutal. The Negro has all his life been told whatever field he goes into he's got to be better than anyone else. Therefore the Negro policeman is out to do two things, to prove he's a good policeman—which, given the nature of our society and vengeance toward criminals, very often means mistreatment —and secondly, he is trying to prove that he is not being soft because they [the people in the ghetto] are Negro like himself.

* Long ago Du Bois, in *The Souls of Black Folk,* speaking not merely of the Negro in the slum, said that the Negro had come to "look upon courts as instruments of injustice and oppression, and upon those convicted in them as martyrs."

On the Negro in the South:

I hope that [in the South] we can find some means of keeping a number of Negroes on the land. The distribution of the Negro there is conducive to a settlement. Also politically the potential voting power of the Negro, disgraced as he is in the South, is conducive to a settlement. In a situation where both poor whites and Negroes could be uplifted a great deal of prejudice would disappear. And finally—and the only psychological thing I can say—is that when people in the South finally see the light, they are often infinitely more consistent than a number of people in the North, who have never been through the traumatic experience of change. They often come out with more insight, and that is my hope for the South.

On the Disorientation of the Young:

I would call the poverty in Harlem physical poverty that comes from the absence of plenty. There is another form of poverty, the poverty of plenty, which may produce violence. Now at the root of both these is the same thing, the feeling on the part of young people that they don't belong, they don't know what their place in society is, that somehow they are a sub-class which has nowhere to go. There is a great deal of frustration among white youngsters, even rich ones, —children who tear up a house in Long Island and who take dope in Westchester—and it springs from the basic fact that we don't have hope, we don't have a future, we don't know who we are.

On Opposing Injustice:

We have to be certain that we are opposed ourselves not to injustice to Negroes or this or that, but we are opposed to injustice anywhere it exists, first of all in ourselves.

On Malcolm X:

I think there's every indication that Malcolm X doesn't know where he's going, and I think he's somewhat frightened of coming back here.* I feel he's just lost. He has very little in the way of an organization—practically nothing. They're a few frustrated youngsters and a few confused writers and others, but even before he left here these Sunday meetings which he was having got smaller and smaller, because he doesn't have any real answers to the immediate problems which Negroes want an answer to.

*   *   *

Bayard Rustin is now engaged in organizing the A. Philip Randolph Institute. The Institute, according to the prospectus, "is committed to strengthening the alliance needed to insure democratic change; to projecting political, social, and economic programs that will improve the conditions of all Americans; and to stimulating united action on behalf of all of America's oppressed and forgotten people."

What does Bayard Rustin mean by integration? He means working together for a common goal.

: 10 :

The scene is the Theresa Hotel, on the southwest corner of the intersection of Seventh Avenue and 125th Street, in Harlem. It is a large square building of white stone long since soot-smeared, the rigor of its squareness mollified by the fussy, tatting-like carving of the stone. It is the hotel where Castro put up during his visit to New York. It is now the base of operations for Minister Malcolm X.

Minister Malcolm X occupies, for business purposes, Suite 128 on the mezzanine of the hotel. I am admitted by a strong-looking young Negro man, dressed impeccably in a dark suit, white shirt,

---

* From the Near East. The date of this remark is October 5, 1964.

dark tie; he is silent but watchful, smooth-faced, impassive, of ominous dignity. A tall man is standing across the room toward the left, in front of a small door. It is quite clearly Malcolm X: the lithe athletic figure, the high-built handsome head, the horn-rimmed glasses.

I cross to him, over the royal distance of floor, and with the slightest hint of a smile, he gives me his hand. The hand is large and strong-boned, but not heavy, and the fingers are long. The face is a pale yellowish brown, with a somewhat scraggly short beard, with reddish-copper tints, the brow straight, squarish and high. The short-cropped hair of close, crisp kinkiness, set tight on the skull like a cap or casque, is rather light in color, with reddish-copper glints.

The most striking thing, at first, about that face is a sort of stoniness, a rigidity, as though beyond all feeling. When the lips move to speak you experience a faint hint of surprise. When—as I discover later—he scores a point and the face suddenly breaks into his characteristic wide, leering, merciless smile, with the powerful even teeth gleaming beyond the very pale pink lips, the effect is, to say the least, startling. But behind the horn-rimmed glasses always the eyes are watching, pale brown or hazel, some tint of yellow. You cannot well imagine them closed in sleep.

After the handshake he turns to his aide—a replica of the young men you see, over and over, in the photographs of rallies of the Black Muslims, one of the Fruit of Islam, as those guards are called. I am, for the moment, dismissed, and wander across the room, inspecting it. The suite is, simply, a very large room—a banquet room or conference room—not too clean, bare of furniture except for a cluttered desk, a couple of chairs, and a long improvised table parallel to the windows which give over the noisy street. At one end, covering the whole wall, is a big blackboard, with nothing significant now on it except the announcement that the Restaurant Lumumba serves "good Muslim food." But a smaller bulletin board is covered with newspaper clippings from Africa concerning the visit of Minister Malcolm X—from the *Daily Graphic* of Accra and the *Ghanaian Times,* blurred photographs of Malcolm's tall head, assertions of solidarity with Malcolm in his crusade against American oppression, a tribal name for Malcolm, "Malcolm Asibe." I read the clippings, waiting, wondering how far

away, exactly, is Africa from the street below, which is full of
noise and the glint of light on Detroit chrome and the stench of
American gasoline ignited in the heavy June air. How far away,
in fact, from this room.

*   *   *

That question—How far away is Africa?—has always been there.
There were various manifestations of Black Nationalism among the
pre-Civil War Negro colonizationists. Since then we have seen
people like Alexander Crummell, rector in the last century of St.
Luke's Church in Washington, who had spent twenty years in
Liberia; the members of the Liberia Emigration Clubs of Oklahoma
in 1897; W. E. B. Du Bois, who finally died in 1963 in Ghana; the
self-styled Ashanti chief Alfred C. Sam, who, just before World
War I, raised money and bought a ship and took a load of the
faithful on a tragic voyage; Noble Drew Ali, whose "Moorish"
followers believed that the hour of redemption would come when
a star appeared in the sky in a crescent moon. The most sensational
of all was Marcus Garvey, who declared God and Christ black, was
inaugurated as President of Africa, surrounded himself with a re-
splendent entourage of Knights of the Nile and Dukes of Niger
and of Uganda, founded the Black Star Line to transport colonists
to Africa, and wound up in the federal penitentiary in Atlanta. And
now we have Elijah Poole, born in Georgia, but revealed to be Elijah
Muhammad, the Prophet and the Messenger of Allah to the Lost-
Found Nation of Islam in the wilderness of North America—an
aging, pale-skinned, sweet-faced man who, though he did inherit a
few thousand followers from the mysterious Detroit peddler Fard,
now known to be Allah, is the effective founder of the Black Muslims.

How far away is Africa?

Many answers, for more than a century, have been given. But
never the right answer. The right answer is: *It is as far away as a
dream.*

It was, and is, a dream—sad, angry, or vainglorious. And, as is
apt to be the case with dreams, it is dreamed to repair a defect
in reality. The defect in reality which engendered the dream was
the white American's refusal to recognize the black American as

American. The majority of Negroes, from the very first, have preferred to deal with that defect in reality in some real way, by accommodation or by a long struggle in the hope that some day the recognition would be given or could be forced. But sometimes the black man, humiliated or enraged past endurance, or logic, by the white man's all too real contempt, has sought refuge in the unreality of the dream. He has, sometimes, thought the dream real and has tried to act on that assumption.

The Black Muslims have been, presumably, ready to act on that assumption. Elijah Muhammad has prophesied an Armageddon, a great day of reckoning, after 6,000 years of white domination, when Allah will destroy the white race and the black man will inherit the earth. There is, presumably, one way for the white man to be saved—to see his error and give the black man a country for himself. But that way is mentioned only for schematic completeness, as it were, for the white man is a devil—the "white devil" created long after the black man, who is, according to Elijah Muhammad, the "Original Man . . . the first and last, the maker and owner of the Universe." By his nature the "white devil" cannot repent and do good.

The day of reckoning has, in fact, once already been postponed, to give the American Negro a chance to prepare himself. To do so, he must learn his true identity. He must give up his surname, which is a "slave name" put on him by a white man, and take "X" in its place. He must cleanse himself of the white man's habits, appetites, and vices—alcohol, tobacco, pork, corn bread, unchastity, provocative dress, cosmetics. He must work hard, practice thrift, deal honestly with all, respect authority, defend the home and honor the Muslim woman, who has greater beauty than what Malcolm X has called the "false beauty of the slavemaster's leprous-looking women." He must "wake up, clean up, and stand up," and must separate himself from the white civilization in all ways. He must not initiate violence, but must be ready to defend himself or the honor of his women to the death; and he must recognize his brotherhood with all Muslims.

Upon conversion the Black Muslim, in short, becomes a man. The lost identity is found, the never-experienced dignity dawns, meaning enters life. By acknowledging lack of identity, lack of courage and will and productive energy, by acknowledging, in short, the painful fact of inferiority, the convert takes the first step toward the promised superiority. As Elijah Muhammad, addressing the white man, has put it: "We cannot say that we are equal; we can't do it because we are not. We have undergone such treatment that it has absolutely made us inferior to you. . . ." Furthermore, in acknowledging the de facto inferiority, the convert accepts responsibility for changing his own condition; if he has, in the past, been the creature of conditioning, he now becomes a man of insight and will. As Malcolm X says: "The worst crime of the white man has been to teach us to hate ourselves." But now, with insight, self-hate becomes self-respect.

The release from self-hate is associated, though, in a less schematic form, with the Negro Movement in general. For instance: "To be called 'nigger' has once been thought of as derogatory. . . . Within the movement, however, we come to a valuation of our own worth. We begin to see our own role and our responsibility to our country and to our fellow men, so that to be called 'nigger' on the picket line was now an unimportant thing that no longer produced in us that flinch."* In fact, self-hate, which sometimes paralyzes, can paradoxically, in certain contexts, be the preparation for action. As Emile Cailliet, in his book *The Clue to Pascal,* says, "one was well minded to understand Holy Writ when one hated oneself."

The Black Muslim movement evinces aspects of the psychology of redemption which we know well from Christianity, the Communist Party, and psychoanalysis; and it openly offers, in addition, a powerful attraction not officially advertised by those other communions: hate. It has been successful. Drunkards, dope addicts, criminals, and prostitutes are reclaimed in numbers to leave psychologists and social workers and members of Alcoholics Anonymous agape, and thousands of the aimless discover an aim, and Cassius Clay discovered how, he says, "to best that big ugly bear" that was called Sonny Liston. Nobody knows the exact number of the Muslims, but educated guesses run from 7,000 to 200,000. But the fellow travelers—those Negroes who to a greater or lesser degree respond to the promise of glory and vengeance—may run into some millions. Dr. Kenneth Clark says of them: "They are not inventing

* Diane Nash, "Inside the Sit-ins and Freedom Rides," in *The New Negro,* ed. M. H. Ahmann.

nor for that matter are they even exaggerating or distorting the basic fact." The basic fact is there for any Negro, with his basic human nature, to respond to; and the Black Muslims merely state the fact with basic drama.

Such are the psychological assets the Black Muslim movement presents. As for practical assets that now are merely implicit in the situation but might be exploited, we remember the analysis by Myrdal in *An American Dilemma:* "A Negro leader who really accepted segregation and stopped criticizing it, could face the dominant whites with a number of far-reaching demands." Under such circumstances, he maintains, Negroes could get their own governing bodies for many kinds of institutions—lower courts for Negro communities, separate state and national representatives with specially defined functions, a rational policy in housing, job allocations, and so on. Such a system, he finds, would be far less inefficient and cruel than the present hit-or-miss arrangement, and presumably the Black Muslim leadership is not unaware of some of the advantages that might, with luck and cunning, be made to accrue.

To Myrdal, the fact that Negroes have never developed such a rational solution is something of a mystery. Or rather, it would be if there were not an overriding consideration in their minds: "Negroes feel that they cannot afford to sell out the rights they *have under the Constitution and the American Creed, even when those rights have not materialized.* . . ."

By this line of reasoning the Black Muslims are doomed. That is, they are doomed as long as any hope remains in the Constitution and the American Creed.

The question is: what is the date of the breaking point on that hope?

Elijah Muhammad, the Messenger, is aging, and for some years Malcolm X has been enormously effective as what might be termed the executive officer of the organization. He had seemed, in fact, the heir apparent to this great power. Then he found himself out of that role. In five minutes he had talked himself out of it. In a speech in Harlem, apropos of Kennedy's assassination, he had said that "the chicken has come home to roost." This attitude of distrust and animosity toward Kennedy was one commonly found among Negroes for some months before the assassination, but it had not ordinarily been expressed with such glee and pungency, nor, of course, under such circumstances. Muhammad felt compelled to repudiate the orator and order him to silence for ninety days.

Later, in an article in the *Saturday Evening Post* Malcolm X explained that jealousy of his bright prospects in the organization and the fact that he had had the courage and the concern to confront Muhammad himself with rumors of his un-Muslim-like incontinence* were the real reasons for the suspension, which, in fact, Malcolm quickly converted into a definitive rupture. In a letter quoted in *The New York Times,* he said, "I declare emphatically that I am no longer in Elijah Muhammad's 'strait-jacket' "; and in his article in the *Post* he said that the break was supported by a number of "the militant 'action' brothers" of the Black Muslim Mosque No. 7 in New York, who defected with him. It was subsequently confirmed that one of the sons of Muhammad, Wallace, has joined the defectors. Later still, there was word from Egypt that Akbar Muhammad, the youngest of Elijah's six sons, a student of Islamic law at Al Azhar University in Cairo, had repudiated the father's "concocted religious teachings, which are far from and in most cases diametrically opposed to Islam," and has rejected "his politically sterile philosophy of the Afro-American struggle." In general, he said, he was sympathetic to the position of Malcolm. Malcolm, meanwhile, had announced the establishment of an official Muslim center in New York, with the support of the World Muslim Council of Mecca. (It was Akbar Muhammad who gave the low figure of 7,000 for the membership of the Black Muslims.) But according to

---

* Malcolm reports that in expressing that concern to Muhammad, Malcolm affirmed that the "good deeds outweighed bad," and said that he understood how Muhammad's conduct was merely the fulfillment of Biblical prophecy. Muhammad, according to Malcolm's account, quickly embraced this explanation: " 'I'm David,' he said. 'When you read about how David took another man's wife, I'm that David. You read about Noah, who got drunk, that's me. You read about Lot, who went and laid up with his own daughters. I have to fulfill all of those things.' " Even so, the official morality of the Black Muslim is strictly puritanical, no Muslim woman is supposed to be alone in a room with any man except her husband, and any philanderer is subject to the discipline of the Fruit of Islam, the Black Muslim militia.

Malcolm's concern was, apparently, well-justified. Muhammad is now confronted with two paternity suits.

some other Negro leaders, and to the obvious indications, Malcolm is without a real organization.

He is, merely, himself.

*   *   *

Malcolm Little was born in Omaha, on May 19, 1925, the seventh child of Early Little, a Baptist preacher, a "race man" and a supporter of the Garvey Movement, who did not curry favor with the white people. When Malcolm was very young, the family moved to Lansing, Michigan—really driven from Omaha because of the father's Garveyite principles; but there the same trouble followed, the family's house was fired by the Ku Klux Klan, and the firemen, when they did arrive, merely watched the blaze. "The same fire that burned my father's home still burns my soul," Malcolm X has said.* Later, the father was found on a street-car track with his head crushed and his body cut nearly in two, and the son presumes that he had been murdered and then dumped on the tracks.

After the father's death the family underwent dire poverty, and eventually broke up; and Malcolm, who had been involved in petty thefts, was sent to a detention home to await transfer to the reform school. The matron of the home—apparently the only white person he has ever had any affection or respect for—managed to prevent his being sent to the reformatory; and he entered a regular school.

At school, he was the only Negro—and by both students and faculty was called "the Nigger," but, he says, without meaning "any harm." His grades were "among the highest in the school," and he was, in fact, the president of his class. This account in his *Saturday Evening Post* article is somewhat at variance with the accounts presented by Nat Hentoff, C. Eric Lincoln, and Louis Lomax,† who report that the high grades incurred the resentment of both teachers and students—rather than being rewarded by the office of class president; and that when, in the eighth grade, Malcolm Little said he wanted to be a lawyer he was told that a Negro ought to think about carpentry.

* C. Eric Lincoln, *The Black Muslims in America.*
† Nat Hentoff, "Elijah in the Wilderness," *The Reporter*, August 4, 1960; C. Eric Lincoln, *The Black Muslims in America;* Louis Lomax, *When the Word is Given.*

In any case, it was in crime, not carpentry, that he was making a precocious success: in Harlem, still in his teens, "Big Red" was in numbers, bootlegging, dope, hustling, an employer of men, with a $1,000 roll in his pockets. But despite the pay-offs, the law finally had him. He went to prison.

*   *   *

This morning, in Suite 128 of the Theresa Hotel, he is no longer the heir apparent to Elijah Muhammad, he is merely himself. But that fact—as he stands there across the expanse of bare, ill-swept floor, conferring with the ominous attendant—is not to be ignored. I am watching him, and he knows I am watching him, but he gives no sign. He has the air of a man who can be himself with many eyes on him.

Finally he beckons to me. The attendant takes my raincoat and hat and hangs them in a little closet, and acknowledges my thanks with a reserved inclination of the head. Minister Malcolm X leads me into a long, very narrow room made by partitioning off the end of the big room where the blackboard is. The only furniture is a small table and two chairs, set face-to-face, under a series of windows that give over the street. Malcolm X tells me that he has only a few minutes, that he has found that you waste a lot of time with reporters and then you don't get much space. It is the same remark that Whitney Young had made to me at our first interview; only he had said, "enough space for the Urban League to justify it."

I begin by asking if the Negro's sense of a lack of identity is the key for the appeal of the Black Muslim religion.

MALCOLM X: Yes. Besides teaching him (the American Negro) that Islam is the best religion, since the main problem that Afro-Americans* have is a lack of cultural

* For the Black Muslims, the word *Negro* is a white invention, a badge of slavery. Ordinarily the Muslim will, if he uses the word at all, preface it with "so-called." Afro-Americans or Black Men is preferred. As Malcolm X puts it: "If you call yourself 'white,' why should I not call myself 'black'? Because you have taught me that I am a 'Negro'! Now then, if you ask a man his nationality and he says he is German, that means he comes from a nation called Germany. . . . The term he uses to identify himself connects him with a nation, a language, a culture and a flag. Now if he says

identity, it is necessary to teach him that he had some type of identity, culture, civilization before he was brought here. But now, teaching him about his historic and cultural past is not his religion. The two have to be separated.

WARREN: What about the matter of personal identity as distinguished from cultural and blood identity?

MALCOLM X: The religion of Islam actually restores one's human feelings—human rights, human incentives—his talent. It brings out of the individual all of his dormant potential. It gives him the incentive to develop, to be identified collectively in the brotherhood of Islam with the brothers in Islam; at the same time this also gives him the—it has the psychological effect of giving him incentive as an individual.

WARREN: One often encounters among Negroes a deep suspicion of any approach which involves anything like the old phrase "self-improvement" and a Negro's individual responsibility. You take a different line.

MALCOLM X: Definitely. Many of the Negro leaders actually suffer themselves from an inferiority complex, even though they say they don't, and because of this they have subconscious defensive mechanisms, so that when you mention self-improvement, the implication is that the Negro is something distinct and different and therefore needs to improve himself. Negro leaders resent this being said, not because they don't know that it's true but they're thinking—they're looking at it personally, they think the implication is directed at them, and they duck this responsibility, whereas the only real solution to the race problem is a solution that involves individual self-improvement and collective self-improvement.

"Self-improvement," for the Black Muslims, then, carries no stigma of Booker T. Washington or Uncle Tom. And the reason I

his nationality is 'Negro' he has told you nothing—except possibly that he is not good enough to be 'American.' . . . No matter how light or how dark we are, we call ourselves 'black' . . . and we don't feel we have to make apologies about it." (C. Eric. Lincoln, *The Black Muslims in America*.)
But in the course of the conversation Malcolm X begins to use "Negro."

take to be clear: the purpose of the self-improvement is not to become "worthy" to integrate with the white man, to be "accepted" by him—to integrate with "a burning house"—but to become worthy of the newly discovered self, as well as of a glorious past and a more glorious future. The question asked by Lorraine Hansberry and James Baldwin—"Who wants to integrate with a burning house?"—with its repudiation of white values, has some of the emotional appeal of the Black Muslim prophecy of destruction for the "white devils" and the glory of the Black Kingdom to come. In a more subtle form we find the same appeal in the role that some Negro workers in the Movement assume: the role of being the regenerator of society, not working merely for integration into white society but for the redemption of society—a repudiation, and a transcendence, of white values that gives something of the satisfaction that may be found in the Black Muslim promise of Armageddon, and a perfect world thereafter. It assumes, not equality, but superiority—superiority to, at least, the present-day white man.

I am thinking of the freedom the Black Muslim enjoys in accepting the doctrine of self-improvement, and then of the complex—and sometimes unfree—reaction the white man has to Negro's assumption of the role of regenerator, even as I ask Malcolm X about his own conversion.

MALCOLM X: That was in prison. I was in prison and I was an atheist. In fact, one of the persons who started me to thinking seriously was an atheist—a Negro inmate whom I had heard in discussion with white inmates and who was able to hold his own at all levels; and it was he who switched my reading habits in the direction away from fiction to nonfiction, so that by the time one of my brothers [who had become a Muslim in Detroit] told me about Islam, I was open-minded and I began to read in that direction. One of the things that appealed to me was in Islam a man is honored as a human being and not measured by the color of his skin.

I think of Lolis Elie, back in his office in New Orleans, his voice full of controlled violence as he says: "At what point—when will it be possible for white people to look at black people as human beings?"

Elie had said that he was reading Black Muslim literature. And the thing that drives him is what had driven Malcolm X to his conversion.

WARREN: Was your conversion fast or slow—a flash of intuition?

MALCOLM X: It was fast. I took an about-turn overnight.

WARREN: Really overnight?

MALCOLM X: Yes. And while I was in prison. I was indulging in all types of vice right within the prison, and I never was ostracized as much by the penal authorities while I was participating in all the evils of the prison as they tried to ostracize me after I became a Muslim.

WARREN: If Islam teaches the worth of all men without reference to color, how does this relate to the message of black superiority and the doom of the white race?

MALCOLM X: The white race is doomed not *because* it's white but because of its misdeeds. If people listen to what Muslims declare they will find that, even as Moses told Pharoah, you are doomed if you don't do so-and-so. Always the *if* is there. Well, it's the same way in America. When the Muslims deliver the indictment of the American system, it is not the white man per se that is being doomed.

I discovered that that pale, dull yellowish face that had seemed so veiled, so stony, as though beyond all feeling, had flashed into its merciless, leering life—the sudden wolfish grin, the pale pink lips drawn hard back to show the strong teeth, the unveiled glitter of the eyes beyond the lenses, giving the sense that the lenses were only part of a clever disguise, that the eyes need no help, that they suddenly see everything.

He has made his point.

I study his grin, then say: "There's no blood damnation, then?"

MALCOLM X: No, but it's almost impossible to separate the actions—to separate the criminal exploitation and criminal oppression of the American Negro from the color of the skin of the oppressor. So he thinks he's being condemned because of the color of his skin.

WARREN: Can any person of white blood—even one—be guiltless?

MALCOLM X: Guiltless?

WARREN: Yes.

MALCOLM X: You can answer it this way, by turning it around. Can any Negro who is the victim of the system escape the collective stigma that is placed upon all Negroes in this country? And the answer is "No." Well, the white race in America is the same way. As individuals it is impossible to escape the collective crime.

WARREN: Let's take an extreme case—your reaction to it. A white child of three or four—an age below decisions or responsibility—is facing death before an oncoming truck.

MALCOLM X: The white child, although he has not committed any of the deeds that have produced the plight the Negro finds himself in, is he guiltless? The only way you can determine that is to take a Negro child who is only four years old—can he escape, though he's only four years old, can he escape the stigma of segregation? He's only four years old.

WARREN: Let's put the Negro child in front of the truck, and put a white man there who leaps—risks his own life— to save the child. What is your attitude toward him?

MALCOLM X: It wouldn't alter the fact that after the white man saved the little black child he couldn't take that little black child into many restaurants right along with him. That same white man would have to toss that child back into discrimination, segregation.

WARREN: Let's say that white man is willing to go to jail to break segregation. Some white men have. What about him then?

MALCOLM X: My personal attitude is that he has done nothing to solve the problem.

WARREN: But what is your attitude toward his moral nature?

MALCOLM X: I'm not even interested in his moral nature.

Until the problem is solved, we're not interested in anybody's moral nature.

How close is this, I wonder, looking back, to what James Forman had said? "It's what the social effect is of what a person is doing that's important," he had said. Does he mean to imply that moral value equates, simply, with consequence? Many people have believed that. Machiavelli, for one; Bishop Paley, who wrote *Evidences of Christianity,* for another; Stalin, for another. I wonder if —and how deeply and in what sense—Forman believes this. I do not need to wonder about Malcolm X.

For behind all his expert illogic there is a frightful, and frightfully compelling, clarity of feeling—one is tempted to say logic. Certainly a logic of history. Of history conceived of as doom.

So, even as I ask Malcolm X if he could call that white man who goes to jail a friend, I know that his answer will be "No."

MALCOLM X: If his own race were being trampled upon as the race of Negroes are being trampled upon, he would use a different course of action to protect his rights [different from going to jail].

WARREN: What course of action?

MALCOLM X: I have never seen white people who would sit—would approach a solution to their own problems nonviolently. It's only when they are so-called fighting for the rights of the Negroes that they nonviolently, passively and lovingly, you know, approach the situation. Those types of whites who are always going to jail with Negroes are the ones who tell Negroes to be loving and kind and patient and be nonviolent and turn the other cheek.

He would not call him a friend. And I think of an article in the *Village Voice*—"View from the Back of the Bus" by Marlene Nadle —reporting the dialogue on a bus to Washington for the March, in August 1963:

Frank Harman (a young man, white, member of the Peace Corps) was asked why, since he was white, he wanted to go to Nigeria. He replied, "I want to help those people because they are human beings."

Suddenly Wayne (a Negro) shouted, "If this thing comes to violence, yours will be the first throat we slit. We don't need your kind. Get out of our organization."

Completely baffled by the outburst, Frank kept repeating the questions, "What's he talking about? What did I say?"

Wayne, straining forward tensely, screamed, "We don't need any white liberals to patronize us!"

Other Negroes joined in. "We don't trust you." "We don't believe you're sincere." "You'll have to prove yourself."

Frank shouted back, "I don't have to prove myself to anyone but myself."

"We've been stabbed in the back too many times."

"The reason white girls come down to civil rights meetings is because they've heard of the black man's reputation of sex."

"The reason white guys come down is because they want to rebel against their parents."

Poor Frank Harman, he doesn't know what kind of test he has to pass. But Malcolm X could tell him.

> MALCOLM X: If I see a white man who was willing to go to jail or throw himself in front of a car in behalf of the so-called Negro cause, the test that I would put to him, I'd ask him, "Do you think Negroes—when Negroes are being attacked—they should defend themselves even at the risk of having to kill the one who's attacking them?" If that white man told me, yes, I'd shake his hand.

But what would this mean, this hand-shaking? If the demand Malcolm X makes is merely that the white man recognize his right of self-defense (which the law already defines for him and which the NAACP supports), then he might go around shaking hands all day and not exhaust the available supply. If by "defend themselves" he means the business of Armageddon, then he will find few hands to shake. But in any case, what does the hand-shaking mean if he maintains that the white man, and the white man's system, can't change from the iniquity which he attributes to him?

> MALCOLM X: It is the system itself that is incapable of producing freedom for the twenty-two million Afro-Americans. It is like a chicken can't lay a duck egg. A chicken

can't lay a duck egg because the system of the chicken isn't constructed in a way to produce a duck egg; and the political and economic system of this country is absolutely incapable of producing freedom and justice and equality and human dignity for the twenty-two million Afro-Americans.

WARREN: You don't see in the American system the possibility of self-regeneration?

MALCOLM X: No.

We come to the separatism, the independent nation, to Africa—the dream or the reality.

MALCOLM X: The solution for the Afro-American is two-fold—long-range and short-range. I believe that a psychological, cultural, and philosophical migration back to Africa will solve our problems. Not a physical migration, but a cultural, psychological, philosophical migration back to Africa—which means restoring our common bond—will give us the spiritual strength and the incentive to strengthen our political and social and economic position right here in America, and to fight for the things that are ours by right on this continent. And at the same time this will give incentive to many of our people to also visit and even migrate physically back to Africa, and those who stay here can help those who go back and those who go back can help those who stay here, in the same way as the Jews who go to Israel.

WARREN: What about the short-range?

MALCOLM X: Immediate steps have to be taken to re-educate our people—a more real view of political, economic, and social conditions, and self-improvement to gain political control over every community in which we predominate, and also over the economy of that same community.

WARREN: That is, you are now thinking of localities—communities in the United States—being operated by Negroes, not of a separate state or nation?

MALCOLM X: No. Separating a section of America for Afro-Americans is similar to expecting a heaven in the sky after you die.

WARREN: You now say it is not practical?

MALCOLM X: To say it is not practical one has to also admit that integration is not practical.

WARREN: I don't follow that.

MALCOLM X: In stating that a separate state is not practical I am also stating that integration—forced integration as they have been making an effort to do for the last ten years—is also just as impractical.

WARREN: To go back—you are thinking simply of Negro-dominated communities?

MALCOLM X: Yes, and once the black man becomes the political master of his own community, it means that the politicians will also be black, which means that he will be sending black representatives even at the federal level.

WARREN: What do you think of the Negroes now holding posts at the federal level?

MALCOLM X: Window dressing.

WARREN: Ralph Bunche too?

MALCOLM X: Any Negro who occupies a position that was given him by the white man—if you analyze his function, it never enables him to really take a firm, militant stand. He opens his mouth only to the degree that the political atmosphere will allow him to do so.

In my opinion, mature political action is the type of action that enables the black people to see the fruits that they should be receiving from the politicans, and thereby determine whether or not the politician is really fulfilling his function, and if he is not they can then set up the machinery to remove him from the position by whatever means necessary. He either produces or not, and he's out one way or another.

WARREN: There's only one way to put a politician out, ordinarily—to vote him out.

MALCOLM X: I think the black people have reached the point where they should reserve the right to do whatever is necessary to exercise complete control over the politicians of their community by whatever means necessary.

I ask him if he believes in political assassination, and he turns the hard, impassive face and veiled eyes upon me, and says: "I wouldn't know anything about that."

He has only said: ". . . reserve the right to do whatever is necessary to exercise complete control . . . by whatever means necessary." What is "reserve the right"? What is "complete control"? What is "whatever means necessary"? Who knows?

Malcolm X has always been a master of the shadowy phrase, the faintly shaken veil, the charged blankness into which the white man can project the images of guilt or fear. He is also a master of parable.

WARREN: What about the matter of nonselective reprisal?
MALCOLM X: Well, I'll tell you, if I go home and my child has blood running down her leg and someone tells me a snake bit her, I'm going out and kill snakes, and when I find a snake I'm not going to look and see if he has blood on his jaws.
WARREN: You mean you'd kill any snake you could find?
MALCOLM X: I grew up in the country, on a farm. And whenever a snake was bothering the chickens, we'd kill snakes. We never knew which was the snake did it.
WARREN: To read your parable, then, you would advocate nonselective reprisals?
MALCOLM X: I'm just telling you about snakes.

*   *   *

On the Police State:

Whenever you have to pass a law to make a man let me have a house, or you have to pass a law to make a man let me go to school, or you have to pass a law to make a man let me walk down the street, you have to enforce that law—then you'd be living in a police state. America right now is moving toward the police state.

On the Civil Rights Leaders:

I don't think that anyone has been created more by the white press than the civil rights leaders.

On Abraham Lincoln:

He probably did more to trick Negroes than any other man
in history.

On Kennedy:

Kennedy I relate right along with Lincoln.

On Roosevelt:

The same thing.

On Eleanor Roosevelt:

The same thing.

*   *   *

Malcolm X, as we have pointed out, has broken with Elijah
Muhammad and lost the succession. But has he lost power? As far
as New York is concerned it would seem that he has not lost power;
and it would seem that Elijah Muhammad has. When Muhammad
appeared in Harlem in early July, 1964, for a rally that had been
liberally advertised in advance, the turnout was, by all report, not
more than eight thousand. If that was all he could muster, then New
York would seem to be Malcolm's parish.

Malcolm X still presents himself as a Muslim—even if not
a Black Muslim. He announces that he is opening an official
Muslim center in New York. But if he succeeds in this project
the key to his future is still in his personality and his instinct for
leadership. When he broke with the Black Muslims he said he was
able "to approach the whole problem with a broader scope." And
he continued: "If you look only through the eye of an organization,
you see what the organization wants you to see, you lose your ability
to be objective."

With or without the Muslim center, chances are that Malcolm X will continue to be "objective"—that is, to tack with the wind. There is no indication that he will go back on his statement: "The problem is so broad that it's going to take the inner working of all the organizations—going to take a united front of all the organizations —to come up with a solution." And he would, he says to me, even work with Martin Luther King—for they disagree, he says, only on the method.

The remark is, of course, preposterous, for with King the method and the end are inseparable. But the presposterousness appears in other quarters. Shortly after the riots in Harlem and Rochester, in the summer of 1964, a group of leading Negro artists and intellectuals held an informal meeting in New York City. Among them was Clarence B. Jones, legal counsel of Martin Luther King. In the discussion with the press after the meeting, Mr. Jones predicted eventual cooperation between Dr. King and Malcolm X. He said: "I think it an irony and a paradox in terms of the national Negro community that two Negroes of such opposing views as Dr. King and Malcolm X should have such great mass appeal. I personally believe that Malcolm could engender the same feeling in the lumpen proletariat as Dr. King does in other classes of Negroes . . . Malcolm cannot be corrupted, and the Negroes know this and therefore respect him. They also know he comes from the lower depths, as they do, and regard him as one of their own."

The irony and paradox that Mr. Jones remarks on are certainly here, and more deeply set than he indicates; but they may be resolved, and Malcolm X may be even now in the process of resolving them. As early as the spring of 1964, when he was on a visit to the Near East and wrote back to America saying that in Islam color does not matter, he laid the groundwork for the rapprochement with the integrationists, with the white man himself. By the time of the article in the *Saturday Evening Post,* he was saying: "Once I was a racist—yes. But now I have turned my direction away from anything that's racist." Malcolm X is, bit by bit, purging himself of his association with violence and rifle clubs, and as for "snake-killing," proposes only a little guerrilla warfare against the Klan.

With his change of views Malcolm X is in a position to enter into any centralized grouping of the various elements in the Movement that may be managed. He will, in fact, be in a position to be the center of such a centralized grouping.

At the same time, Malcolm X must be aware that the basic appeal he has had is not merely his incorruptibility or his origin in the lower depths; it inheres in his racism, his celebration of blackness, his promise of vengeance. And here is the irony and paradox for Malcolm X himself: Can he maintain that appeal and at the same time move toward a commanding central position?

We may remember that, in the past, even at his most intransigent, Malcolm X has never committed himself. A man like Jesse Gray is committed, and there is no sawdust trail he can take, no matter how much he might bedew the sawdust with tears of repentance. But for Malcolm X there are highroads leading in all directions. In fact, he speaks of his "direction"—and for all his heels-dug-in and grim-jawed intransigence, he also presents himself, in one avatar, as a seeker, a quester, he is "going somewhere," toward some great truth. This fact, this role, has a fundamental appeal, too; we are all "seekers." Therefore his appeal is double. How long can the balancing act continue?

But Malcolm X has, in fact, never had any association with actual violence in behalf of the Negro cause. He has always, by happy accident or clever design, been somewhere else. In the summer of 1964, for instance, when the bad troubles broke, he was not around, he didn't have to put anything on the line—except his trans-Atlantic rhetoric. Perhaps this is what Wyatt Tee Walker meant—and not merely that Malcolm X was a creation of the press—when he said that he is a "paper tiger." James Farmer, as we may remember, said flatly that "Malcolm has done nothing but verbalize—his militancy is a matter of posture . . . he is not an activist, really." And Farmer added: "But there will come a time when Malcolm is going to have to chirp or get off the perch."

That time is, apparently, not yet. And it may not come for a long time, for Malcolm X has, again to quote Farmer, "the footwork to keep pace," and may "be able to survive a long time." He may indeed, for he is a man of great talents and great personal magnetism. He knows that psychologists, and not philosophers, rule the world. He is, like all men of power, a flirt; he flirts with destiny. He conceives of the general situation as fluid and he has made his own situation fluid. He is free to tack, to play the wind. He trusts his magnetism—and his luck. He may end at the barricades. Or in Congress. Or he might even end on the board of a bank.

Meanwhile Malcolm X, however willing to work with other organizations, and however much he may yearn to enter the world of politics and respectability, still carries over, in his doubleness, some hint of the orthodoxy of the Black Muslims, a weapon and a lure that no other national leader, except the failing Muhammad, can exploit: the stance of total intransigence, the gospel of total repudiation, the promise of hate, the promise of vengeance. Even as late as December 20, 1964, at a Harlem rally, Malcolm X could say: "We need a Mau Mau to win freedom!" With this emotional appeal, which even the coolest-headed and most high-minded Negro, in some deep corner of his being, is apt to admit to responding to, Malcolm X stands prepared to undercut and overreach the leaders of those very organizations which he, with one hand, beckons to a "united front." Beneath all the illogicalities there is the clear logic of feeling: the black powerful current beneath the crazed and brittle ice.

It may be argued that the personal fate of Malcolm X—how much power or what kind of power he attains—is not what is important about him. What is important may be the mere fact of his existence in this moment, his role, his symbolic function.

I may approach this notion by a story told me by Dr. Anna Hedgeman of the National Council of Churches. In a seminar she was conducting on race and religion there was a serious-minded and idealistic young girl, from, I think, Alabama. Among various guests who spoke to the seminar was Malcolm X, who pronounced his usual repudiation of the white devils. The girl asked him if there wasn't anything she could do—not anything—to be acceptable. "Not anything," he said. At that she burst into tears. Later Dr. Hedgeman said to her: "My dear, don't you think it strange that you couldn't stand for one minute to be repudiated by that Negro man, when I, like all other Negroes, have had to spend my whole life being repudiated by the white race?"

There is something of that little white girl in all of us. Everybody wants to be loved. The member of the White Citizens Council always gets around to telling you how Uncle Billie just loved the kids, would have cut off his right hand for 'em, and how Aunt Sukie or Sallie just loved the whole family and they all loved her right back and when she died they all cried and buried her in the family burying ground. But Malcolm X, even now, will have none of this. That stony face breaks into the merciless, glittering leer, and there is not anything, not a thing, you—if you are white—can do, and somewhere deep down in you that little girl is ready to burst into tears. Malcolm X makes you face the absoluteness of the situation.

But Malcolm X, in his symbolic function, does something else, quite paradoxical. Besides the little girl, there is in you too that hard, aggressive, assertive, uncompromising and masculine self that leaps out of its deep inwardness to confront Malcolm X with a repudiation as murderous as his own, saying, "OK, OK, so that's the way you want it, let her rip!" We must confront that wild elation in ourselves: "Let her rip!"

So, for the white man, Malcolm X can bring the unseen, even the unsuspected, into light. The white man can know what he has to deal with, in himself.

And it is so for the Negro.

It is reported that Martin Luther King, a few years ago, remarked to a friend: "I just saw Malcolm X on television. I can't deny it. When he starts talking about all that's been done to us, I get a twinge of hate, of identification with him."* This despite the fact that, during Birmingham, Malcolm X had called Martin Luther King "a chump, not a champ," despite the fact that the Muslims called his doctrine "a slave philosophy," despite the fact that the rotten eggs thrown at him in Harlem had, for all intents, come from the hand of Malcolm X. And this despite all of Dr. King's own principles. For principles or no, Malcolm X can evoke, in the Negro, even in Martin Luther King, that self with which he, too, must deal, in shock and fright, or in manic elation.

Malcolm X has one other symbolic function. He is the unspecified conclusion in the syllogism that all of the "responsible" Negro leaders present to the white world: "If you do not take me, then . . ."

Then you will have to take Malcolm X, and all he means.

Malcolm X is many things. He is the face not seen in the mirror. He is the threat not spoken. He is the nightmare self. He is the secret sharer.

And we may recall that once, in explaining the "X" in the Muslim name, he said it stands for "the mystery confronting the white man as to what the Negro has become."

* Nat Hentoff, *The New Equality*.

NOTE ON THE ASSASSINATION OF MALCOLM X

On Sunday, February 20, 1965 (when this book was about to go on press), Malcolm X addressed a meeting of his Organization for Afro-American Unity, in Harlem. He was cut down by a shotgun and two revolvers. One of the alleged assailants was wounded and captured on the spot, and soon two other men, both reported to be Black Muslims, were arrested. Meanwhile, on the night of February 23, while the body of Malcolm lay on view in the Unity Funeral Home, the Black Muslim Mosque Number 7 was burned down, presumably in revenge for the killing of Malcolm X.

In Chicago, addressing the annual meeting of his cult, Muhammad described Malcolm X as "a star gone astray," and said that he had "got just what he preached." At the same meeting, Wallace Muhammad, one of the defecting sons of Muhammad, recanted and begged forgiveness; and two of Malcolm's own brothers denounced him.

In Washington, D.C., Carl Rowan, Director of the United States Information Agency, stated that in Africa and Asia, the death of Malcolm X, despite the efforts of his agency, was being interpreted as the martyrdom of a great integrationist.

In London, where he had gone to promote the publication of his novel *Another Country,* James Baldwin told the press that no matter who had pulled the trigger, the white community would have to share the blame. "Whoever did it," he said, "was formed in the crucible of the Western World, the American Republic."

Malcolm X had something of the scale of personality and force of will that we associate with the tragic hero. And he finally found himself caught on the horns of the classic dilemma of tragedy.

4 ✗ *Leadership from the Periphery*

Success breeds success. The individual who has had one success has one leg up on the next. This is even more true of the group. The man of the group who has succeeded gives the boy of the group that indispensable thing: the model of action, the target of ambition, the promise of effectiveness. The Negroes, as a group, have been depressed and trammeled. But there have always been individual Negroes who succeeded. Before the Civil War, Frederick Douglass was, for example, a success. Now there are many, and every Negro who has "made it"—the Ralph Bunche, the Ralph Ellison, the Lena Horne, the Jackie Robinson, the Dick Gregory, the Joe Louis—is a promise to the slum child or to the thin, bent little figure down yonder at the end of the cotton row, a mere dot in heat-haze and distance, that he can make it, too. That he can, in fact, make it in competition in the white world.

But let us grant that the world of the child may be so hermetically sealed that the boy has not heard of, even, Joe Louis, or the girl of Lena Horne. And grant that, sometimes, the apathy and the odds are so great that the child cannot cluster his own fantasies about such a figure. Let us grant that now, despite the new affluence, or in a sense because of it, the gap between the world of the Negro mass and the world of Negro success is widening. Let us grant that the successful Negro (the whole upper group of Negro society, in fact) may find in success the last irony, for success itself is not legal tender for the crucial transaction: it won't buy acceptance. Even so, for the more intelligent, the bolder, the stronger, the luckier, the image of the Negro who has made it is a cloud by day and a pillar of fire by night.

Negroes have often sadly said that invidiousness is the characteristic Negro sin. The complaint is that as soon as a Negro is a success the cutting-down-to-size process begins, that as soon as a Negro breaks out into the great world, they—the Negroes back on the dirty door steps by the unlidded garbage can, or in the gloom of the honky-tonk, or at the cross-roads shack—begin to say that he, the success, has sold out, is an Uncle Tom, is a "white-folks' nigger." The image of success may, in other words, be a mortally invidious reproach to our own failures, and may stir all our spite and envy and sense of inferiority. But at the same time the image of success may flatter us because he is "one of ours." We are all ambivalent, and the success of another person, in the very moment that it hurts our ego, may extend it, hearten it. Even white Mississippians are ambivalent—those who refer to the "successful" Leontyne Price as a "Mississippi girl." And on January 27, 1965, at 7 P.M., in the Dinkler Plaza Hotel, in Atlanta, 1,500 people, including pillars of the white society and power structure, attended a dinner to honor Martin Luther King, Jr., the first "Georgian" to win a Nobel prize.

The Negro who goes into the big world and becomes a success is not only what is called a "role model" for the young Negro, an example of the will to compete with the white man. He is, in a deeper and more subtle way, a role model of another sort: once success is realized, he must exhibit the will to confront the painful consequences of success. The phobia of success belongs, of course, to the white world as well as to the black, but the socially determined self of the Negro may make him, in this way, as in so many others, far more vulnerable. For one thing, the successful Negro must exhibit the will to risk that special invidiousness which is, as many Negroes say, the inevitable accompaniment of Negro success, and the toughness to endure the special spiritual isolation which it entails. There may be, too, a guilt as of the betrayal of the father, of the clan. And perhaps for some, there may be a sense of betrayal of the self—at least, of the black self as presumably determined by white society, the slow, stupid, passive self for whom success was never meant and to whom success will bring the anxiety of a mystic, ineffable vengeance. To some degree, the Negro who has achieved success has faced the risk of replacing the Self-as-Negro (which is another way of saying the Self-as-Failure) with the Self-as-Man. This achievement, however dimly perceived, may be the greatest service that he can perform.

: 2 :

The listing in *Who's Who* reads:

HASTIE, William Henry, federal judge; born Knoxville, Tenn., Nov. 17, 1904; s. William Henry and Roberta (Child) H.; A.B. Amherst Coll., 1925, A.M. (hon.) 1940; LL.B. Harvard, 1930, S.J.D. 1933, Ohio Wesleyan 1951, Knoxville Coll. 1952, Rutgers U. 1953, Howard U. 1955, Yale 1957, Central State Coll. 1959, Amherst Coll. 1960, Temple U 1961, U. Pa. 1961; m. Beryl Lochart, Dec. 25, 1943; children—Karen Roberta, William Henry. Admitted to Bar 1930; practiced law 1930-33; assistant solicitor Dept. of Interior, 1933-37; Judge of Dist. Court of Virgin Islands, 1937-39; dean Howard U. Sch. of Law, 1939-46; civilian aide to the sec. of war, 1940-42; Gov. of Virgin Islands 1946-49; judge, 3d U.S. Circuit Court of Appeals since 1949; mem. Caribbean Commn., 1947-51. Trustee Amherst Coll., Fellow Am. Acad. Arts and Scis; mem. Phi Beta Kappa, Omega Psi Phi, Mason. Home 804 West Sedgwick St., Phila. 19. Office: United States Courthouse, Phila.

Judge Hastie's name is not infrequently mentioned for the next vacancy on the Supreme Court. His career would seem to justify his elevation. He would be, in that case, the first Negro to sit on that bench.

*   *   *

Judge Hastie is a rather tall, well-formed man, who carries his years easily. He would be called handsome, the features clear-cut. His complexion is very light brown. His manner is gracious, in a calm, cool fashion. In the big office—or study—of his chambers in the Federal Building in Philadelphia, he sits among the pieces of massive mahogany, with the books of his library solid as masonry on wall after wall. He wears a soft tan corduroy jacket, not too new, which has replaced his coat, and listens with a relaxed patience to what you have to say. But if you watch his eyes you sense the unflagging alertness. You remember that this listening belongs to his trade, an art honed and developed by years on the bench, long since as natural as breath.

I ask him in what sense the Negro Movement can be called a revolution.

HASTIE: In the sense that it is a movement for more rapid social change than would take place in the normal course of events. Actually the drive for the modification or correction of our basic law, and for equality of status and rights under law, the drive in an organized form goes back to the early 1930's. It is the acceleration in the last ten years, the fact that more Negroes, and whites as well, have aggressively identified themselves with the demand for change, that has caused the continuity of the effort to be described as a revolution.

WARREN: Dr. Aaron Henry, of Clarksdale, Mississippi, says that for years the effort of the NAACP, and other agencies and individuals, was to define the legal basis of life for the Negro, and that now the attack can be made on laws that are not laws, and practices that are not legal, because the citizen—the Negro citizen—knows what the law means. He says that basically this is a revolution within the terms of law.

HASTIE: Part of the problem is the definition of words. One can define revolution as an effort to bring about change *inconsistent* with the legal order—and of course there are persons now who urge that. But the gentleman you are referring to is using *revolution* as perhaps most people do in this connection, to mean rapid change through popular pressure, within the national constitutional framework.

WARREN: A revolution—a popular movement—is driven, they say, by the twin emotional charge of hope and hate. When the hate has a clear target in the liquidation of a society or class its function is clear. What about now when it is assumed that the society will be maintained?

HASTIE: Hate drives people to tear and rend the object of hate. But a movement remains constructive so long as the hate is depersonalized. I suppose this is really a translation of the Christian ethic—hate the evil in man without hating the man himself. I think it has been possible to maintain drive with that kind of hate, as distinguished from personalized hate, because most Negroes do not have the feeling that they are deserted by the entire white community.

At this, I think of the view held by some Negroes that there must be a total polarization of black and white, a stark confrontation, before the issue can be resolved. Clearly Judge Hastie does not hold that view. His whole legal training, his whole experience, his awareness of the role of institutions in history, his sense, as I take it, that American institutions *are* America and have the possibility of self-rectification—all these things preclude that view. But I ask him what he makes of Negro repudiation of the white "liberal."

HASTIE: I'm a poor man to judge, because I am not in a position to get the grass-roots reaction. But I think that the amount of hatred for everything white, the rejection of white liberal assistance, is probably exaggerated. Maybe the wish is father to the thought. It is sensational, and therefore makes headlines, when a Negro takes this position. But my guess is that, as of now, there is not as much rejection of the support of whites as the headlines might cause one to believe. Take the March on Washington. It was a prime indication of what happens when it's necessary to get as wide-based support as possible. But certainly it [this rejection] has a potential of getting greater, and this is the importance of civil rights legislation, if only to prevent the spread of this very dangerous, potentially catastrophic point of view.

Judge Hastie takes his time with his answers, turning them over in his mind. He is concerned about the inadequacy of evidence for grounding a notion, and the limitations imposed by his position. When I ask him if he observes any tendency toward centralization of leadership, he says: "Again, I doubt whether I can give you a meaningful answer." But he goes on to analyze what evidence is available to him, including the psychology of the situation that might lead to unitary leadership. Such a leadership would appeal, he says, "to those who are convinced that there is no satisfaction, no solution, to be found within the present order, under leadership of the sort that we have experienced in the past." He hazards that, for the moment, there is only a small minority of Negroes in that condition. The success of that centralized leadership would, he says, "be in direct proportion to the hopelessness or desperation of the potential followers."

Which, it would seem, implies two things: first, that centralization of leadership would be a step toward revolution outside of law, not within law; and second, that the responsibility of avoiding such an eventuality lies, in the end, with the white man—he can avoid it by recognizing the basic justice of the Negro's grievances.

Analysis of context—over and over that is the pattern his thinking takes. For instance, in regard to the problem of integrating public schools in a great city—such as New York or Washington—with a high proportion of Negro children, with all the ancillary problems of busing and transfers, Judge Hastie begins by raising the prior question of the place of the neighborhood school in a great city, without reference to race. Into this context would be placed the problem of special requirements of all under-privileged children, and the special problem of racial and cultural isolation; and always he would ask "what is the really most advantageous thing for the development of the youngsters." As for integration, though recognizing it as a great good, he would say that it has "to be evaluated in the context of other goods."

And this leads him to a comment on the "nature of revolution." People, he says, "do not get stirred up over a complicated group of ideas. They get stirred up when they struggle for a very simple concept; in Africa you use one word—the Swahili word for freedom —*Uhuru*. Revolution always oversimplifies ideas. And, of course, one of the great problems of leadership is that, though ideas be oversimplified in the minds of people, the leadership, with more sophisticated thinking, attempts to adjust itself to the total need, viewed in a sophisticated way." Related to this problem is the danger of "the tyranny of labels"; for "characterizations that analytically don't mean what they say are, I think, characteristic of all social struggle."

When I ask about several figures in American history—Jefferson, Lincoln, Garrison, and Lee—Judge Hastie distinguished between the symbolic role and the psychological and ethical complications of the individual. Of Lincoln: "It does not seem to me ironic that one can find in an examination of Lincoln's utterances, many things that are contrary to the symbolic figure that we have built." Not ironic, I presume, because Judge Hastie's mind is so steeped in an awareness of human complexity and of the dynamic function of symbolism that there is no surprise in one more piece of documentation.

And this leads to the following interchange, in reference to William Lloyd Garrison:

HASTIE: There are certain stages [in history] when persons like that represent the spark to a movement and we can recognize their value as that, without having a necessary admiration for the intemperate, even violent, personality, yet we recognize that throughout history, those personalities have been catalysts of great changes, some good, some bad.

WARREN: In other words, we put ourselves outside of history, and say add a little salt and pepper—and maybe a dash of evil for spice—to make the stew?

HASTIE: I think so.

WARREN: We don't make ethical judgments on that basis, do we?

HASTIE: Oh, no—no—we don't make ethical judgments that way, no.

*   *   *

On Respect and Demonstrations:

A quotation comes to mind—"Nothing that the white man can give the Negro is as important as the respect he withholds." So many acute situations would not be acute if the Negro had the feeling of being genuinely respected. Many of the demonstrations which, to some people, may seem pointless, or at least misdirected—and here I am playing the psychologist—are expressions of an inward urge to do something that both helps one's self-respect and wins respect from other people. As the Negro wins the white man's respect, regardless of fondness or affection, it becomes easier for the two to deal with each other.

On One Responsibility of the Negro:

One of his responsibilities is to deal with his fellow men as individuals, just as the white man would have the same responsibility. The Negro will have to come out of his protective shell, because there is no question that today you find many situations in which members of the white community are willing to meet Negroes more than halfway in human relationships that generally ignore race, yet find Negroes not responsive.

On a Remark by James Baldwin:*

I understand the statement being made, but to me it's a meaningless statement. Of course, he has no reason to be apologetic to any "white man," but he has reason to be apologetic to himself and to society.

On Nonviolence:

Since we are pragmatists in this country, I would suggest that we look at the experience of other people who have practiced such an approach—that of nonviolence. We know that it was not all—perhaps a relative few—of the people of India who thoroughly accepted Gandhi's counsel. Indeed, the epoch of Gandhi in India saw a tremendous amount of violence. I would suspect that many people,

* "The lowest Negro drunk or dope-pusher has no reason to feel apologetic to any white man." Made at the Conference of Nonviolence at Howard University, November 5 and 6, 1963. This is from notes and not a recording.

rather than have their personalities bruised by an unnatural acceptance of nonviolence, just reject it when it goes too much against the natural human reaction.

*   *   *

Malcolm X would, of course, say that Judge Hastie is nothing more than "window dressing." And many more than Malcolm X—in fact, a whole school of psychologists, sociologists, and activists—would say that a Judge Hastie, an individual absorbed, by reason of personal talent, into the general structure of white-dominated society, is irrelevant, ultimately, to the whole race problem. Such a school of thought sees the individual achievement as relatively insignificant, and holds that "the rights and privileges of an individual rest upon the status attained by the group to which he belongs."*

But let us think of him sitting there in his office, so detached and calm and courteous, with the masonry of law and learning from floor to ceiling behind him, with the distinctions of his honorable career worn as easily as the loose corduroy jacket. His feelings seem so purged of anger and his mind so firmly fixed toward a norm of social good, of justice—in an old-fashioned way, toward the *res publica*. Let me remember, however, that before we began our interview, he said, in the simplest way, with no irony, not even a trace of sadness: "You know, all Negroes spend at least a little time hating white people."

There is, here, a candid will to look at the complexities of a situation. He talks of the relation of historical process and ethical judgment, of the symbolic role and the psychological complication of individuals, of the necessary simplification of issues in revolution and the obligation of leadership not to oversimplify. He has, for example, some of the insights, something of the cast of mind, that make Roy Wilkins, for instance, unacceptable to many militants. Women, children, and revolutionists, one of Conrad's characters says in *Under Western Eyes*, "hate irony"; it seems to strike at the taproot of total commitment.†

* David Danzig, "The Meaning of Negro Strategy," in *Commentary*, February, 1964.
† Sophia Antonova, to Razumov. Part III, chapter iv.

But must it? When the act of commitment is seen as fully as possible in its context, does not the pinch of glory, the flicker of tragic dignity, which is implicit in any human commitment—any real commitment—show more suddenly, like "bright metal on a sullen ground?" And I remember my conversation with Robert Moses, for one. With Gilbert Moses, for another.

Or is it even irony that we are thinking of when we see Judge Hastie sitting there? Is he not merely trying to eschew what William Blake thought of as the great evil, the "single vision and Newton's sleep"—a mechanical, schematic, dehumanizing vision, that violates the density of experience?

Is it traitorous for a Negro to try to be as broadly human and humane as possible?

Is it even irrelevant?

: 3 :

James Baldwin has often been called a "voice"—the voice of a generation, the voice of a revolution, the voice of an age, the voice of conscience, the voice of the New Negro, the voice of this and the voice of that. He has not been called the one thing he really, specifically, and strictly is: *the voice of himself.*

What is that self?

James Baldwin was born August 2, 1924, in Harlem Hospital. The first house he remembers was on Park Avenue, uptown, "where the railroad tracks are," and as a small child he played on what he calls a garbage dump near the East River, but the family, he says, still carried the tone of the rural South. He went to Public School 24, where the principal, a Mrs. Ayer, was a Negro—"the only Negro school principal," he says, "as far as I know in the entire history of New York"—and "was a living proof that I was not necessarily what the country said I was."* Later he went to PS 139, a junior high

---

* This remark was made on May 24, 1963, in an interview with Kenneth B. Clark, from which the quotations in this paragraph are drawn. (*The Negro Protest,* ed. Kenneth B. Clark.) In this interview, in response to Baldwin, Dr. Clark said: "We do not have a single Negro principal in the New York public school system today." That was true as of that date, but there were three Negroes in executive positions outranking the position of prin-

school, and graduated from DeWitt Clinton High School, where his literary talents were recognized in contributions to the student literary magazine. The recognition by the outside world began early, with grants and awards: the Saxton Award, a Rosenwald Fellowship, a Guggenheim Fellowship, a Ford Foundation Grant, an award from the National Institute of Arts & Letters, a *Partisan Review* Fellowship—conscience money, some would say, paid out by the white world. He lived in Paris for some years. He has published three novels and three books of essays. With the last book of essays, *The Fire Next Time,* he became famous. He has become a voice.

So much for the objective version of the career. But Baldwin has written that "the interior life is a real life," and the interior life, with no shadowy screen of fiction or sociological analysis, is sometimes presented almost nakedly and painfully, as in this extract from an interview†:

> . . . I think she [his mother] saved us all. She was the only person in the world we could turn to, yet she couldn't protect us.
>
> *She doesn't sound like that consoling black-mammy figure that we whites are so enamored of. The maids we knew, for instance.*
>
> Yes, who's all wise, all patient, and all enduring . . . I'm sure all the people my mother worked for thought of her that way, but she wasn't like that at all. She was a very tough little woman, and she must have been scared to death all the years she was raising us.
>
> *Scared of what?*
>
> Of those streets! There it is at the door, *at the door*. It hasn't changed either, by the way. That's what it means to be raised in a ghetto. I think of what a woman like my mother knows, instinctively has to know . . . : that there is no safety, that no one is safe, none of her children would ever be safe. . . . You can't call the cops.

---

cipal: Dr. Joseph B. King, Deputy Superintendent of Schools, in charge of instruction, appointed February, 1963; Mrs. Margaret S. Douglas, Assistant Superintendent of Schools, appointed September, 1960; and Frederick H. Williams, Director of Human Relations, appointed August, 1961. Since the date of Clark's interview with Baldwin there have been three appointments of Negroes: Francis A. Turner, Board of Examiners, appointed February, 1964; Mrs. Elizabeth Gaines, Principal of Junior HS 118, appointed May, 1964; and Mrs. Henrietta B. Percell, Principal of PS 24 (the school which James Baldwin once attended), appointed September, 1963.

† "Disturbers of the Peace," by Eve Auchincloss and Nancy Lynch Handy, published in *Mademoiselle,* May, 1963.

What about your father?

He was righteous in the pulpit and a monster in the house. Maybe he saved all kinds of souls, but he lost all his children, every single one of them. And it wasn't so much a matter of punishment with him: he was trying to kill us. I've hated a few people, but actually I've hated only one person, and that was my father.

Did he hate you?

In a way, yes. He didn't like me. But he'd had a terrible time, too. And of course, I was not his son. I was a bastard. What he wanted for his children was what, in fact, I became. I was the brightest boy in the house because I was the eldest, and because I loved my mother and I really loved those kids. And I was necessary: I changed all the diapers and I knew where the kids were, and I could take some of the pressures off my mother, and in a way stand between him and her—which is a strange role to play. I had to learn to stand up to my father, and, in learning that, I became precisely what he wanted his other children to become, and he couldn't take that and I couldn't either maybe.

Did he affect your ideas of what you could do in the world?

My father did one thing for me. He said, "You can't do it. . . ."

Why couldn't you do it, according to him? Because you were black?

Because I was black, because I was little, because I was ugly. He made me ugly. I used to put pennies on my eyes to make them go back.

But out of that an identity emerged.

Yes, all those strangers called Jimmy Baldwin.

Who are some of them?

There's the older brother with all the egotism and rigidity that implies. That tone will always be there, and there's nothing I can do about it except know it's there and laugh at it. I grew up telling people what to do and spanking them, so that in some way I will always be doing that. Then there's the self-pitying little boy. You know: "I can't do it, because I'm so ugly." He's still there some place.

Who else?

Lots of people, Some of them are unmentionable. There's a man. There's a woman, too. There are lots of people here.

It's been said that you have two obsessions: color and homosexuality.

I'm not absolutely sure that I have two obsessions. They're more than that.

. . .

There is one person whom Baldwin does not mention here as a component of the completed self. When he was in his early teens, attending a church service, he was struck down to the floor: "Over me, to bring me 'through,' the saints sang and rejoiced and prayed. And in the morning, when they raised me, they told me I was saved." And he goes on, in *The Fire Next Time,* to describe the boy preacher which he then became: "Nothing that has happened to me since equals the power and the glory that I sometimes felt when, in the middle of a sermon, I knew that I was somehow, by some miracle, really carrying, as they said, 'the Word'—when the church and I were one. . . . and their cries of 'Amen!' and 'Halleluiah!' and 'Yes, Lord!' and 'Praise His Name!' and 'Preach it, brother!' sustained and whipped on my solos until we all became equal, wringing wet, singing and dancing, in anguish and rejoicing, at the foot of the altar."

James Baldwin has, long since, left the church. But when he left, he smuggled out the Gift of Tongues. The magic, however, does not work at his every whim. Perhaps it does not work at the times when he most desperately wants it to work. But it does work when, among all the persons who make up "Jimmy Baldwin," that person whom we shall call the Boy Preacher takes over for his moment.

*　　*　　*

We began our conversation by talking about the nature of the Negro Revolution. He distinguished it from the Algerian revolution, a nationalistic revolution, by saying that this one "in order to succeed at all, has to have as its aim the reestablishment of a union, and a great—a radical—shift in the American way of life." What complicates this revolution is the fact that "here it's your brothers and your sisters, whether or not they know it, they are your brothers and sisters. It complicates it so much that I can't possibly myself quite see my way through this. As for the hope, that is fuzzy, too. Hope for what? You know the best people certainly don't hope to become what the bulk of Americans have become. So the hope begins then to ask me to create a new nation under intolerable circumstances and with very little time and against the resistance of most of the country."

The powerful rhythms of the Boy Preacher have flickered up for a moment—and the tone, we may hazard, of the Elder Brother. Here, too, just as a flicker, there is another element of Baldwin's force: the focus on the personal drama. The Voice of Hope does not ask the Negro, or the Revolution, or us to do so and so; it asks *me*—asks James Baldwin, or rather, asks the Elder Brother, who is "the brightest boy in the house"—to create a new nation, "under intolerable circumstances and with very little time and against the resistance of most of the country." This "interior life" of James Baldwin and the exterior fate of the country are, for dramatic purposes, merged, identified. And each gives the other a new urgency, the beat of blood. And that beat is a long way from the ectoplasmic abstraction of charts and statistics and sociological jargon and school zoning and crash programs.

Even as Baldwin, sitting there before me, enters upon the words which, suddenly, have that inner vibrance, his eyes widen slightly, a glint comes in them, he sits up in his chair, and the nerves, you are sure, tighten, and there is the acceleration of pulse beat and respiration. He is not looking at you now, or talking at you, at all: his eyes are fixed on something over yonder, across the room. He is talking of the change that would have to come over American life: "It is simply not possible for the church, for example, to accept me into it without becoming a different institution, and I would be deluded not to realize that."

It is *me*—the drama of James Baldwin, again. And the drama goes on: "In order to accommodate *me,* in order to overcome so many centuries of cruelty and bad faith and genocide and fear—simple fear—all the American institutions and all the American values, public and private, will have to change."

As for the public drama, precipitated, as it were, by the catalytic introduction of James Baldwin, it must be of apocalyptic intensity. We are not to think of a Civil Rights Bill, of FEPC, of housing, of social adaptations, of economic adjustments, of legal process, of education, of the slow growth, painful and wavering, of understanding and a sense of justice. We are to think of the blaze of light that rends the roof and knocks us all—all America and all American institutions—flat on the floor while the "vertical saints" sing and rejoice and the whole continent rocks like Pentecost.

The drama Baldwin preaches is shot through with the awful choice: the Fire Next Time or the Great Redemption. The drama is powerfully appealing. It appeals to some of our deepest needs. It promises to carry us beyond the daily nags and nocturnal dubieties, beyond the dusty burden of self and self-accusation, beyond niggling responsibilities and, even, our shop-worn virtues, to the great moment when we, the lost children, the wandering "brothers" and "sisters" who do not even know their brotherhood, shall be recognized, received, and forgiven.

Forgiven for what? For our crimes, even our most secret and unspeakable crime, against the black man? Yes—but for another and greater crime: the crime of being our unfulfilled and inchoate and fragmented selves. On that Great Day when "ultimately race would count for nothing," we shall be made whole, and there will be a kind of cosmically exfoliating pun on the word *integration*: racial integration and personal integration at the same apocalyptic moment.

We are even promised, as a kind of bonus, better orgasms.

For we are told about the "poverty of the white cat's bed or the white chick's bed," about "this anti-sexual country," about the "brave and sexless little voices" of white people, about the defect of sensuality, that capacity "to respect and rejoice in the force of life, or life itself, and to be *present* in all that one does, from the effort of loving to the breaking of bread." True, the long indictment of the white cat (and of American middle-class society) in this department does not carry the specific label of a promise of redemption, but the promise is, by implication, there. For the indictment is set in the context of the other indictments which, in the great drama of redemption and reconciliation, can be quashed; and specifically the Negro, who "with love shall force our brothers to see themselves as they are, to cease fleeing from reality and begin to change it," is the carrier of the redemptive "sensuality."

But there is one more thing, he says, in speaking of the Great Day: "Americans simply—not so simply—would grow up enough to recognize that I don't frighten them."

On that day *he*—in the happy ending and purgation of the personal drama—will not frighten them.

*   *   *

On Africa and Identity:

WARREN: If we can believe the figures of the falling sales in
bleaching creams and the avowed sentiments of many
Negroes, there is a movement toward an acceptance of, and a
pride in, Negro identity.

BALDWIN: For the first time in American Negro history, the
American black man is not at the mercy of the American
white man's image of him. This is because of Africa. For the
first time in the memory of anybody now living, African states
mean Africa. It's still, you know, very romantic for an American Negro to think of himself as an African, but it's a necessary step in the recreation of his morale.

*   *   *

But as a matter of fact, the Afro-Cuban literary movement and the
emergence of African themes in the literature of the French and
British West Indies and Haiti, in the period between 1920 and World
War II, did not depend on the rise of the African nations, but was,
rather, a reflection of a popular feeling as well as a backwash from
the vogue of primitivism in European art and letters and, ironically
enough, from the new Negro writing in the United States. Africa,
particularly for the Haitian writers and those of the French and
British Indies, was the home, the womb, as in "Nostalgia," by the
Haitian Carl Brouard:

> Drum
> when you sound
> my soul screams towards Africa.
> Sometimes
> I dream of an immense jungle
> bathed in moonlight
> with hirsute, sweating figures,
> sometimes
> of a filthy hut
> where I drink blood out of human skulls.

Sometimes, as in "Racial Drum," by Maurice Casséus, Africa is the
"murdered land":

and let me embrace to my soul that savage song
which you dedicate to the murdered land,
which in myself I secretly adore.

Africa to some, as to Aimé Césaire, in "To Greet the Third World,"
is the future:

I see Africa, multiple and one
vertical in the tumultuous events
with its swellings and nodules
rather apart, but within reach
of the century, like a heart in reserve.*

* * *

WARREN: What about the split in the psyche of the American
Negro, that Du Bois talked about?
BALDWIN: In my own case, it was very hard for me to accept
Western European values, because they didn't accept me. Any
Negro born in this country spends a great deal of time trying
to be accepted, but nothing you do works. No matter how
many showers you take, no matter what you do, these Western
values simply—absolutely—resist and reject you. So that inevitably at some point you turn away, then perhaps you re-
examine them.

And here I remember Robert Moses telling of the years at Hamilton College, at Harvard, and of his feeling. Baldwin is talking like
Moses. And like many others.

* * *

On a Return to Africa:

BALDWIN: In the case of the American Negro, which part of
Africa would you be thinking of? We've been away from

---

* See G. R. Coulthard, *Race and Colour in the Caribbean.*

Africa for four hundred years and no power in the heavens would allow me to find my way back. I can go back, and maybe even function there, but it would have to be on terms which have not yet been worked out.

WARREN: Richard Wright didn't find it very happy, did he?

BALDWIN: No, not at all. I think Richard went there with the wrong assumptions, but there's no way not to go there with the wrong assumptions. I did, too, in a way, you know—not Richard's assumptions, but—I don't know—I just didn't know what I would find, and what I found surprised me, and I must say, sort of gladdened me, but I still would not be able to say exactly what it was, and I still less would be able to tell you what my own relationship to it is.

WARREN: Do you remember what your assumptions were?

BALDWIN: No, I guess I blocked them out. I did realize, but I realized it before, you know, that I was, in some ways, very European, because that was the way I had been—that's what I had been stained by—and also that I was a Puritan in the sense that Africans are not: of being distrustful of the flesh and the celebration of it, and of being afflicted with the Western kind of self-consciousness which I will always have. I realized, too, that the reality of castration had been uppermost in my mind, as it has been in the minds of almost any American Negro male—since you realized—from the time I realized I was a male. And this has done something to my psyche, no matter how I adjusted myself to it, or failed to adjust myself to it, it has been a reality for me in a way that it has not been, so far as I could tell, for them.

On the Romantic Attitude Toward "Simple" People and the Riddle of Personality:

WARREN: I have heard young Northern Negroes who have gone South to work on voter registration say that the salvation is in meeting the purity of feeling, the purity of expression, in some poor half-literate field hand who has just come awake to his manhood.

BALDWIN: I would tend to agree with that.

WARREN: That is the real revelation?

BALDWIN: I've seen in my own way—myself—some extraordinary people coming, just coming out of some enormous darkness, and there's something indescribably moving and direct and heroic about those people. And that's where the hope, in my mind, lies—much more than in, let's say, someone like me, who is, you know, much more corrupted by the psychotic society in which we live.

WARREN: This impulse, this feeling, you have is a very common one in many different circumstances, isn't it—this kind of romanticism about a simpler form of life—the hunter, the Indian, the farmer—

BALDWIN: Or the worker.

WARREN: Or the worker. I mean the romantic impulse that many people of some inner complication, living in a relatively complicated world which they don't quite accept, or can't accept, feel when they encounter some simpler life.

BALDWIN: I'm not sure it's simpler, though. I'm not convinced that some of the old ladies I talked to down there [in the South]—I know they aren't simple—they're far from simple —and what the emotional, psychological make-up is which allows them to endure is something of a mystery to me. They are no more simple, for example, than Medgar Evers was simple, you know.

WARREN: He was, apparently, a different cut from—

BALDWIN: There was something very rustic about him and direct, but obviously he was far from a simple man. I think it has something to do with, you know, what one takes—it has something to do with what one thinks the nature of reality is. And especially in this country now, it's very hard to read the riddle of the human personality, because we've had so little respect for it.

*　　*　　*

And I remember some of the types I knew in my childhood and early youth—tenant farmers in Tennessee and Kentucky, white and black, or hill men or hill women on some rain-gutted ridge, or back-country blacksmiths or moonshiners. And I remember how, after I had been away to school and read the books, these people took on a new meaning for me, a romantic meaning, if you will. I sought out their society, a society I had had only by accident in the years earlier. Now they were, perhaps, the living stuff of poetry for me—a kind of poetry different from the dazzling images of Eliot and Pound, which haunted my imagination in another dimension. These people were more like the poetry of Thomas Hardy, who, I may guess, had helped reveal them to me.

Was it because they represented, to me, a life simpler than my own? Not merely simpler, anyway. Perhaps, as Baldwin says, they were not simple at all, more complicated in some deep way than I, the person who looked at them with romantic fascination. Perhaps what evoked my feeling was a sense that they were more of one piece, in self and in fate, than I could be. Than I could be, anyway, unless I worked very hard and had very good luck.

And now, again, I remember the Reverend Joe Carter, standing naked in the jail cell, in West Feliciana Parish.

*   *   *

On the Difference Between the White Sharecropper and the Negro:

I have the feeling that the difference between the Southern white sharecropper and a black one is in the nature of their relationship to their own pain. I think the white sharecropper, in a general way, would have a much harder time using his pain, using his sorrow, putting himself in touch with it, using it to survive, than a black one. One thing that is not true of the Negro, in this context anyway, is he is not forbidden, as all white Southerners are, to assess his own beginnings. A white Southerner, I think, suffers from the fact that his childhood—when his relationships to the black people are very different than they become later—is sealed off from him, and he can never dig it up on pain of destruction, nearly.

*   *   *

Aaron Henry, sitting in his room at night, with the curtains tight to cut off any light that might advertise him to the prowling car and the war-surplus Garand, had told me of the never-forgotten pain when he and the little white boy, the companion of his babyhood, could not go to school together. Does that white boy—forty years later, now—remember the little Aaron?

*　　*　　*

On the Effect on Leadership of the Fact that the Negro Has Hit the Streets:

It has created a tremendous struggle for power, but that's not yet such a menace as a split in the leadership—as a real split which is, you know, an open secret.

On the Young on the Streets and Martin Luther King:

Martin Luther King can't reach those people. I think he knows it. I think he's determined to—he can't abandon them—and his influence is absolutely negligible, but he is still the national leader and the national figure.

On Leadership:

Some figures in the Movement impress me as being opportunistic. But the problem is more complex than that. It's involved with the pressure being brought to bear on everybody, by the people in the streets, by the poor and the young, so that one is always having to assess very carefully one's tactics, one's moves, in terms of the popular desire, because if the people feel betrayed you've opened the door on a holocaust.

On the Civil Rights Organizations:

They're certainly either on their way out or in the process of radical changes.

On Irving Howe's Essay, "Black Boys and Native Sons":

WARREN: Have you read the essay in which Irving Howe says that you and Ralph Ellison, in your ambition to be artists, have betrayed the heritage of protest left by Richard Wright?

BALDWIN: No, but I think I can imagine some of the things [in it]. There's a tendency—I'm not talking about Irving Howe, because I haven't read the piece—but there's a tendency on the part of a great many of the Negro's friends, unconsciously—and really unconsciously—they don't mean to say the things they say—that somehow if you don't fit into, don't take the road to do this or that, that you've somehow—well, you've betrayed something. What you've betrayed is their image of you.

WARREN: And in this case betrayed Richard Wright, too.

BALDWIN: How?

WARREN: Well, you and Ralph Ellison want to be artists instead of keeping angry enough, you know, and—

BALDWIN: Ralph is as angry as anybody can be and still live. And so am I.

On the North and the South:

They had different techniques of castrating you.

On the Responsibility of the Negro:

BALDWIN: I can only answer for myself, because I'm not altogether sure I know what a Negro is.

WARREN: Well, I mean—

BALDWIN: You know what I mean—but I suppose I consider the responsibility to be something like this—to take upon oneself a very hard responsibility, which is something you do with the morale of the young, which has to do with a sense of their identity and a sense of their possible achieve-

ments, a sense of themselves. One has to take upon himself
the necessity of trying to be an example to them—to prove,
you know, something by your existence.

In other words, Baldwin sees himself as what the sociologists
call a "role model." It is a function which, as we have said, is
scorned by some Negroes as trivial or irrelevant in its effect.
But isn't the role of the role model something we all—black or
white—for better or worse—are stuck with?

*   *   *

Baldwin's particular role is that of a "voice." The voice is heard—
as is indicated by packed auditoriums and stacks of books in college
stores. Some critics, in fact, see the audience of Baldwin as primarily middle-class, primarily white, primarily young, primarily
people touched by guilt and masochism, and seeking the titillation
of moral significance in rebellion and adventure, not always vicar-
iously; and there was, in fact, a certain grisly comedy in the first
public appearance of *The Fire Next Time* coyly nestling in the pages
of the *New Yorker* among the advertisements for $12,000 diamond
clips and the Bentley automobile, which is to be preferred to the
Rolls by those of a retiring disposition.

But the books are found, too, in hands other than those of the
literate beard-and-pony-tail set or those of well-heeled suburban
matrons whose social idealism is being needled by the approach
of menopause. Baldwin remarked to me that his brother, "who lives
in Harlem, says that the whores and junkies and people like that
steal the books and sell them in bars—there have been a lot of hot
things sold in Harlem bars before, so I gather that means something."

When, on the day of our conversation, Baldwin and I were
having a drink before lunch, the Negro waiter came over, timidly
asked if he were James Baldwin, and receiving the answer, stood and
stared reverentially for a full minute. A little later, walking up Fifth
Avenue, we encountered a young woman, white and well-dressed,
who stopped, stock-still, right in the middle of the crowd, blocking
us, and stared into his face and burst out: "Oh—you're James
Baldwin—oh, thank you, thank you!" The waiter and the girl—
they came from different worlds.

. . .

What does the voice say? It would say, certainly, very different things to the waiter and to the young woman who stopped us. But the difference in what the voice says does not depend merely on the wave length to which the receiving ear is tuned. The voice, as can be discovered by a little exercise in logic, says, or seems to say, very different, even contradictory, things. There is, for example, a very strong ambivalence about the white man, especially the white liberal. Baldwin looks forward to the great day of reconciliation when "race will not matter," and meanwhile lives very successfully in that marginal world of arts and letters where the integration is most nearly, though imperfectly, realized. And in which he is something of a hero and darling. But in his pronouncements, the white man who is sympathetic with the Negro's aspirations—i.e., the liberal—is an "affliction," is "one of the chorus of the innocents"; he carries with him, mystically and inexpungeably, the communal white guilt, and even when acting in the cause of justice, is regarded as doing so out of condescension and with impure motives. Even those white activists who work for CORE and similar organizations —even, by extension, those two young white men, Michael Schwerner and Andrew Goodman, whose bodies were found buried in the dam with that of the Negro James Chaney—are scarcely acceptable: "You can't say they're accomplishing nothing, really, because they're indispensable on a certain level. But their work has no resonance"— and presumably they do not bleed when blade or bullet bites.* The racist is, of course, damned already. So any white man is caught in a cleft stick—damned if he does, damned if he doesn't.

Now, it is perfectly true that the white man is due to be called up short, made to look in the horrifying mirror: you must see yourself as a worm before redemption is possible. This is always the technique of the preacher—and of the Boy Preacher. But whatever the theological and spiritual overtones may be, the intensity of the relish with which the indictment of sin is made is sometimes uncomfortably reminiscent of the old accent of Malcolm X. And certainly, in the crude world of social arrangement, the theological absolutism may sometimes seem, at least, inappropriate.

On the matter of sex, too, some of Baldwin's pronouncements are

* Interview with Eve Auchincloss and Nancy Lynch Handy, in *Mademoiselle.*

difficult to reconcile with one another. All his comments on the defect of white sexuality, etc., clearly carry the implication of some happy norm of Negro success in this department. Yet elsewhere he presents us with the image of the young Negro sitting stoned and apathetic, beyond desire, with the shadow of "the Man" between him and "love and life and power"; and we find the recurring idea of the "castration" of the Negro. In the essay "The Black Boy Looks at the White Boy," in *Nobody Knows My Name,* Baldwin is quite specific: ". . . that myth of the sexuality of Negroes which Norman [Mailer], like so many others, refuses to give up. The sexual battle-ground, if I may call it that, is really the same for everyone. . . ."

Baldwin very directly leads us to the question of Negro sexuality in general. What studies have been made would seem to indicate a considerable rate of sexual disorder among the Negro population of the United States. Abram Kardiner and Lionel Ovesey, in a famous pilot study called *The Mark of Oppression,* write: "The Negro is hardly the abandoned sexual hedonist he is supposed to be. Quite the contrary, sex often seems relatively unimportant to him. The factors that weigh heavily to make this the case are the uniformly bad relations [among those tested by the authors] with females on an emotional level. This has many determinants. If the male comes from a female-dominated household, the relation to the mother is generally one of frustrated dependency and hostility. This does not conduce to good relations with the female. The sexual function does not occupy an air-tight compartment in the mental life of man; it is tied to many other aspects of adaptation. It is, therefore, consistent with the general hardships of the adaptation of the male that his sex life suffers as a consequence. He fears the female much more than is apparent for intrinsic genetic reasons, and also, because his economic opportunities are worse than the female's. Hence, he is not infrequently at the mercy of the woman. Masculinity is closely tied to power in every form in our society. The male is much more vulnerable to socio-economic failure." The effect of the matriarchy is indicated in a number of studies. One study finds that five-to-fourteen-year-old Negro boys without fathers do not readily distinguish between male and female roles. Two other studies, using the same tests (Minnesota Multiphase

Inventory), one of jail prisoners in Alabama and the other of Wisconsin lower-class veterans with tuberculosis, find that Negro males score higher than whites on the feminine index. Another study, in Boston, of two groups of lower-class Negroes indicates that thirty-three per cent of those raised without a father are in adult life single or divorced as against four per cent of those raised in stable homes; and as might be guessed, there are significant differences in feelings of victimization, of hostility in environment, and of distrust of other people. Furthermore, there is strong evidence to indicate that when illegitimacy is added to the absence of the father, the destructive effects are increased. To compound the effect of the matriarchy, there is the fact that the Negro father who remains with the family is often presented to his son's eyes in a menial or feminine role: hospital orderly, dishwasher, cook, janitor, domestic cleaner or window-washer—in other words, as some sort of broom-or-rag-wielder. Then, too, the daughter is apt to take on the contemptuous or bullying attitude toward the male which the mother, being economically more solid, is apt to evince, and will continue to accentuate the pattern.* Kenneth B. Clark, in *Dark Ghetto,* summarizes the matter: "Because, in American life, sex is, like business advancement, a prime criterion of success and hence of personal worth, it is in sexual behavior that the damage to Negro adults shows up in especially poignant and tragic clarity." And he adds: "It has long been an 'inside' bit of bitter humor among Negroes to say that Negro men should bribe their wives to silence."†

The bulk of the instances above refer to lower-class Negroes, but E. Franklin Frazier, in *Black Bourgeoisie,* analyzes sexual disorder in the middle class and refers to the "tradition of female dominance, which is widely established among Negroes." He goes on to say that "in middle-class families, especially if the husband has risen in social status through his own efforts and married a member of an 'old' family or a 'society' woman, the husband is likely to play a pitiful role." He may take refuge in extra-marital relations (as the lower-class Negro man, rejected at home, becomes a vagrant or a "tom

* Thomas F. Pettigrew in *A Profile of the Negro American* and Bertram P. Karon in *The Negro Personality.*

† Some psychiatrists say that the matriarchal nature of the Negro family is probably a difference of degree and not of kind in American society.

cat"), or "sits at home alone, impotent physically and socially"—
and, we may add, thus presents an unsatisfactory model to a son.
The middle-class Negro male is also vulnerable to the effects of status
struggle on his general emotional life. As one of them puts it: "I
think it makes for conflicting loyalties in almost all aspects of
living." Such a "marginal man" feels himself on the periphery of
two worlds; "I and all Negro professionals have a hemmed-in feeling.
That's why we drink too much. You just can't forget being a
Negro."*

What all the studies show is that Negroes, given the same psychic
strains, react exactly as white people do. For instance, Pettigrew
cites the studies of white American boys whose fathers were away
in the service in World War II, and of Norwegian boys whose
fathers are away at sea for long periods of time. Even without the
race pressure you get the same product.

But the mere fact of the race pressure is providing the frame
within which develops what one Negro psychiatrist has told me is a
"male revolution." Here the Negro male can assert himself, can undo
the past, as it were, both the social and the personal past. But it
seems that almost all Negro leaders come from stable backgrounds in
which their powers of personal assertion and their certainty of self
had been able to develop normally.

Two other aspects of this whole question are interesting. Why do
the whites cling to the "myth" of Negro sexuality? And why are
Negroes ambivalent toward it?

As for the first question, there may be a complex of answers, but
one is certainly that sexuality is taken to equal animality, and therefore inferiority and a justification for segregation. Segregation protects
the white woman from the debasing animality of the Negro man, and
at the same time, by defining an inferior and dependent status for
the Negro, puts the Negro woman in a position where she, with the
attraction of her special sexuality, is presumed to be sexually available—even if only to the imagination.

As for the second question, no doubt Negroes tend to exploit the
myth out of ordinary pride and as a claim to superiority over the
white man. At the same time Negroes recognize in the notion the
white man's interpretation of animality and consequent inferiority,

* Kardiner and Ovesey, *The Mark of Oppression.*

and therefore reject it. There is, in fact, a propaganda to prove that the Negro is "just like everybody else"—even in his limitations.

* * *

In general, in Baldwin's utterances, written or spoken, there is a tendency to pull away from the specific issue which might provoke analysis, toward one more general in which, in a shadowy depth, the emotion coils. For instance, when I asked him about the obligations of the Negro, he countered by saying he wasn't sure what a Negro is. What is a Negro? That is, indeed, a more charged and fascinating question than the one I had asked; and a legitimate riposte to my generalized cartoon use of the word. There is no reason, in fact, why one should not ask, What is a white man? The Negro in Charleston who, in 1822, gave information of the plan for the Denmark Vesey insurrection, was promoted to be a white man. "It may be well and proper, that a man of worth," uttered the court that certified the promotion, "should have the rank of a white man." Clearly, the South Carolina court would have answered our question in social, not biological, terms.

To take another example of Baldwin's tendency to undercut a specific issue and plunge into the shadowy depth, we may refer to a round-table discussion in which Sidney Hook said that the case against discrimination rests on ethical premises. Baldwin retorted that there is no use in talking "about ethical considerations in a society which is essentially *not* ethical"; and here the swing is toward the absolute, the eschatological—which is not relevant, for in this same sense, no society has ever been "ethical." And in this process Baldwin sometimes is trapped by his own rhetoric, becomes the victim of the Gift of Tongues which he has smuggled out of the House of Spirit onto the hustings. When Baldwin says that no matter what the white worker for CORE or Snick does (go to jail, be beaten, be crushed under a bulldozer, be shot and flung into a bayou or buried under a dam), his "work has no resonance," we are tempted to wonder just what that word *resonance* is supposed to mean.

My point is not that what Baldwin has to say in any one instance is not interesting and significant; it is that he instinctively makes this shift of the center of gravity of a discussion, toward an undercut, toward the more general and more charged, toward the absolute. He is, in fact, impatient of the nagging problems of ordinary situations, of the half-measures and compromises, of the slow grind of adjustment and improvisation. He must turn toward that "interior life" which is real, turn inward to be refreshed at the fountain of his own being. But some people—including many Negroes—must deal with the nag and the slow grind. They must try to discipline their interior life to some sad facts of the exterior world in order to change those facts. Perhaps this was something of what Wyatt Tee Walker had in mind when, back in Atlanta, he somewhat tartly said to me that "James Baldwin can speak for James Baldwin and what he feels, but that does not make him the architect of expression for the Negro community."

Walker is right, in one perspective. But he is wrong if he thinks that the fact that Baldwin speaks for himself is a limitation. It is, rather, the source of Baldwin's power. Whatever is vague, blurred, or self-contradictory in his utterances somehow testifies to the magisterial authenticity of the utterance—it is the dramatic image of a man struggling to make sense of the relation of personal tensions to the tensions of the race issue. In his various shiftings of ground in treating the race issue he merely dramatizes the fact that the race issue does permeate all things, all levels; and in the constantly presented drama of the interpenetration of his personal story with the race issue he gives the issue a frightening—and fascinating—immediacy. It is *his* story we finally listen to, in all its complexity of precise and shocking image, and shadowy allusiveness.

Baldwin, in his essay "Faulkner and Desegregation," has applied the method of simple logical analysis to Faulkner and has exposed the untidiness of the *thinking* of the "Squire of Oxford." But the point is here that the Baldwin who writes this essay is Baldwin the abstract polemicist, and not the Baldwin who wrote *The Fire Next Time;* and he is dealing with the "Squire" and not with the man who wrote *The Sound and the Fury* or *Light in August* or *Absalom, Absalom!* The point is that the real Baldwin and the real Faulkner are, in one way, very much alike: both are concerned with "truth" as lived, are concerned with the density of experience and the inevitable paradoxicality of feeling, with the shifting depth of being. Both are willing to recognize the tearing self-division that may be implicit in experience, to recognize that the logic of experience is multiphase and contradictory; and are yet willing to submit themselves, without reservation, to this risk of experience. "The intellect, anyway," Baldwin says, "is one more way of avoiding yourself. One must find a way to get through to life or to experience, but that can't be done intellectually."* It can be done through the willing acceptance of the pathos of drama.

But here a difference appears. The drama in which Faulkner sought his knowledge emerges in forms that constitute an enormously complicated intellectual as well as imaginative structure, an objective structure. We think of Benjy and Jason and Caddie, and Christmas, and Sutpen, but we do not think of Faulkner; Faulkner remains taciturn, enigmatic, sealed, his reality absorbed into the objective thing created. And this is why, when he did give an opinion or express a personal view, we may feel let down and defrauded; what the "Squire" says is sometimes thin, or contradictory.

The drama in which Baldwin seeks his knowledge is, on the contrary, subjective. When we mention the name Baldwin, there is no parade of characters speaking and gesticulating as they swing across the mind, the fictions created. What appears is the face of James Baldwin, a fiction too, for what Baldwin has most powerfully created is a self. That is his rare and difficult work of art.

Harry S. Ashmore has remarked that Baldwin sometimes seems to confuse himself with Job. That is true when the Gift of Tongues is not working right, and when all we have to look at and listen to is the James Baldwin who was born on August 2, 1924, in Harlem Hospital, and not the one created. The created James Baldwin—the "real" one, shall we say?—is a voice that says: "I am the man, I suffered, I was there." And we believe him.

It is a wandering voice. It reaches, as Whitney Young said to me, "the intellectual kind of white person who is moved by this because he has a great deal of guilt feeling, people who, as Baldwin well knows, are in a masochistic mood, where they don't do anything but at least will permit themselves to be ridiculed and punished." It also reaches, as James Farmer said, "the lower-class Negro—working class unemployed . . . not understanding but getting the feeling—'I dig this guy because he digs me.' "

We all hear, with whatever differences of interpretation, and

* Interview with Eve Auchincloss and Nancy Lynch Handy, in *Mademoiselle*.

appealing to whatever different needs, the disturbing timbre, the urgency of accent, the choked cry of rage, of self-pity struggling in a last inner anguish to become pity, of outraged self-love to become *love*. For that is the healing word we hear over and over again— the talismanic utterance, the promise of redemption.

The white girl who, on Fifth Avenue, in the crowd, in the blaze of summer sun, stopped James Baldwin and me, had heard the promise. "Oh!" she cried. "You're James Baldwin—oh, thank you, thank you!"

* * *

James Baldwin has become a public figure, involved in a matter of great public concern. But he knows that, for him, that is not where reality lies. In the course of our conversation he said: "I've got to get away from here. I've been associating with all these civil rights people, the kind of people you wouldn't ordinarily see. I've got to get off somewhere and be by myself and do some work."

: 4 :

We have spoken of the people who must deal with the nag and slow grind of the world, who must discipline their "interior life" to the detailed analysis of some of the sad facts about the exterior life in order to change those sad facts. Let us think, again, of Judge Hastie. Or of Dr. William Stuart Nelson, who was born in Kentucky, almost 70 years ago, but after Howard University studied in Paris, Berlin, Marburg, and Yale, and has traveled in Africa and India investigating the philosophy of nonviolence. Dr. Nelson, for all his devotion to philosophical and theological study, is a vice president of Howard University, in charge of special projects, and in that capacity must deal daily with problems of institutional organization; and it is only natural that his conversation on the new Africa should be interrupted by a telephone call from one of the major foundations. Or take Robert Weaver, head of the Federal Housing and Home Finance Agency in Washington, or Clarence Mitchell, who plans political strategy for the NAACP.

Such men are very deeply engaged in manipulating the sensitive machinery of the over-all society and are aware of the complexity of the intermeshings of social forces. Clearly the attitudes of a man in such a position must be, to a greater or lesser degree, conditioned by his recognition of the complexities of society; and there is bound to be a difference between such a man and the man who moves unhampered by commitments to, or sometimes even by knowledge of, the inner nature of institutions.

You do not have to go to Malcolm X to find cynicism about the Negro who is committed to working within the existing institutions. The hostility that greeted Clarence Mitchell from some quarters of the floor of the Conference on Nonviolence in November, 1963, was evidence enough of such cynicism. In a fairly charged atmosphere, after discussion by previous speakers of the "brinkmanship of violence," and "violence short of the lethal," and the technique of the race strike, Mr. Mitchell's discussion of the then pending Civil Rights Bill seemed, to a number of people, tame and irrelevant. Mr. Mitchell, not a man reputed to shrink from the unpleasantness of a collision, demanded of his audience if they even understood the nature of political action—and then demanded a show of hands of those who had even done such a simple thing as writing a Congressman. There were not many hands. Now, the point was not that Mitchell was arguing for the exclusive use of political action; the point was that to a number of people, mostly young people, political action was regarded as irrelevant.

It is well known that Negroes have not used their political potential.* There are many reasons for this. But one reason was evident in that room. They had not tried to—or had not tried hard enough. Mr. Mitchell made his point, picked up his brief case, and stalked off the platform to go to a meeting, I seem to remember, on Capitol Hill. To some people, the mere fact that he was off to Capitol Hill at all would smack of something not too much short of treason—or at least a sell-out.

*   *   *

* "Negroes have traditionally positioned themselves too far from the inner arena of political decision. Few other minority groups have maintained a political aloofness and nonpartisan posture as rigidly and as long as the Negroes." (Martin Luther King, *Why We Can't Wait.*) But the present tendency is toward greater political participation. The margin for Kennedy in 1960 was given by the Negro vote, and in 1964, Johnson carried several Southern states only by the Negro vote.

On West Parish Street, in the middle of the downtown section of Durham, North Carolina, is a six-story yellow brick building, with the ground floor of limestone, heavy plate glass, and stainless steel—the traditional architecture of finance. The upper floors are occupied by the North Carolina Mutual Life Insurance Company, the ground floor by the Mechanics and Farmers Bank.

In this same block, on August 1, 1908, the bank opened for business. The capital funds were $10,000. By 1935 the resources had broken $1,000,000. As of June 30, 1964, they were $15,157,423.06. In addition to the home office on West Parish Street, there are three branches, in Durham, Raleigh, and Charlotte. Permission has been granted for a fourth branch, this too in Durham. The Mechanics and Farmers Bank is a Negro institution.

The president of the bank is John Hervey Wheeler. He was born in 1908, on a college campus, at Kittrell, North Carolina, attended public schools in Atlanta, was graduated (*summa cum laude*) from Morehouse College, in Atlanta, in 1929, but did not receive his LL.B. (from North Carolina College, at Durham), until 1947. He was admitted to practice in the Circuit Court of Appeals in 1950, and in the U. S. Supreme Court in 1955. Meanwhile, since 1929, Mr. Wheeler had been employed by the Mechanics and Farmers Bank. In 1952 he became president.

Mr. Wheeler has the air of authority. Like almost all of the Negro leaders of every echelon, he is a fine physical specimen. He is tall, with good shoulders, and carries himself well. On the day of our conversation, he was wearing a dark suit, white shirt, dark tie. He has great courtesy, but in the early stages of acquaintance he is apt to regard you with cold assessment from under partially lowered lids, a habit that gives a slightly oriental quality to his yellow face. He speaks fluently, sometimes eloquently, in a strong voice.

He has been a director, trustee, chairman, or member of dozens of institutions and organizations—Atlanta University, Morehouse College, the United Negro College Fund, United States-South Africa Leader Exchange Program, the Executive Committee of the North Carolina Fund, the Urban Redevelopment Commission of Durham, the President's Committee on Equal Employment Opportunity, the National Citizens' Committee for Community Relations, the General Board of the AME Church, the NAACP Legal Staff for North Carolina, Governor Sanford's Good Neighbor Council, the Executive

Committee of the National Council of Churches, the Southern Regional Council. And the list could be extended.

In other words, Mr. Wheeler knows the nature of institutions. He knows how the machinery of the world works. But how has his involvement, his knowledge, affected his attitudes on the question of the Negro in America?

We began our conversation with my asking why the achievement of Negroes in business has lagged behind that in other fields. There is, of course, the matter of Negro income, the lack of the margin to provide investment capital. But, he says, there is another factor. Particularly since the turn of the century, artificial barriers have kept the Negro from the total market, and not only in the South. For example, there had been Negro businesses on the main street, even in Mississippi, before the great reaction set in. Here in Durham, as recently as his boyhood, there had been Negro stores on the main street. I remark on the fact that his bank is in the very center of the city. With a wry look, he says that West Parish Street had not been the center when, back in 1908, the bank was founded, that the city had simply grown out to them. So I ask if a Negro business could now come into that block. "I think a great many people would say it would be quite possible," he says, "but I am convinced that it wouldn't be as easy to do as if the prospective purchaser was a white person, or group of white persons, and this is 1964." And he adds: "This is true all over the South still."

And I: "I heard it's true in Harlem, too."

And he: "It is."*

In segregation both residential and business areas are involved. There are understandings between real estate boards, of which, until recently, no Negro could be a member. "Location," he says, "is extremely important," and location is controlled by white people. Negro business has succeeded only when it could find a chink in the

---

* According to Arnold P. Johnson, president of the Small Business Chamber of Commerce of Harlem, less than fifteen per cent of the small businesses in Harlem are operated by Negroes. Mr. Johnson asserts that most of the whites who have businesses in Harlem evince no interest in the community that "sustains" them. As for larger business operations, all the banks (except one organized in late 1964) are branches of white banks. The one considerable department store is white-owned. Property, in general, is owned by non-resident whites. Dope and "numbers" are basically white operations.

structure—where there was a "special need among Negro people."
For instance, insurance companies (because of high rates charged
by white companies for Negro risks) and the funeral business. As
for banking, there is "great need for Negro people to pursue a
policy of thrift," and there had been at one time well over fifty
institutions in the country "that called themselves banks," that
were operated by Negroes. And here he turns to the sad, old story of
the Freedmen's Bank, and says: "Of course, you know the story
of how even with federal—the color of federal—protection, the
bank failed, and Congress refused to restore the savings of the
depositors." And in the context I take it that he regards the failure
of the Freedmen's Bank as the catastrophic blow to the old Reconstruction dream of building up Negro capital by Negro thrift. But
now, he says, wherever there are Negro financial institutions, "they
have done a great deal to create a sense of pride." In other words,
the success of a Negro financial institution gives the individual Negro
a new picture of himself, of his own capacities. It makes thrift
psychologically possible.

The line of talk about Negro business moving into nooks and
crannies of the over-all economic structure, to fulfill "special needs"
among Negroes, makes me ask his view of the theory that a considerable segment of Negro businessmen want the protection of
segregation. He stiffens at the notion. He points out that before the
system of segregation Negro undertakers buried both whites and
Negroes. That the Negro stores had been on the main street. "If the
coming of integration would give him [the Negro] a free market,"
he says, "then he would have no complaint."

Then he analyzes a case in which it is said that Negroes are refusing integration. "I know of two hospitals in a town where the
white hospital is very irritated that the Negro hospital doesn't fold
up, because they want—they need the Negro patients in their clinics
for their internes and residents. And they need some of the appropria-
tions they think the Negro hospital is getting, and some funds, federal
funds, that they can't get if they are segregated. So they—the white
people—want to integrate the hospitals."

And I ask precisely why the Negroes object.

"They [the whites] want to take over the Negro hospital. When
the question was put to the Negroes, they said, 'Well, all right, if
we're going to put the two together, the director of the Negro

hospital is a graduate of one of the big schools of the country in his field, and he outranks the director of your hospital. Who's going to be director?' "

Wheeler goes on to say that it's not a matter of wanting to perpetuate segregation. "The Negro who is in a segregated set-up that someone wants to swallow up—to sweep out all the professionals and hire only a few [Negro] clerks—he is naturally going to oppose. No overtures have been made to recognize the professional's abilities. And further, the Negro client of the new institution isn't going to have protection. They're going to use him and exploit him in every possible way. And as a smoke screen they're throwing out the charge that we want to protect segregation."

Then he analyzes the situation of the Negro in the banking business. There are Negro clerks in Northern banks, but very few who have even junior officer status. And the end result of this is that Negro banks are forced to maintain segregation in employment. For instance, he had taken back one of their own trainees who had gone to a big banking system, had done brilliantly, but could not be promoted. The white banker said to Wheeler: "Really if it were ten or fifteen years further along, he'd have all sorts of opportunities in our organization [of about one hundred branches], because we don't have many men his equal. But I can't advance him."

Ten or fifteen years further along, the white banker says. But meanwhile there is in North Carolina the vice-chairman of a housing authority who is passed over year after year, even though he is the treasurer of a big and successful insurance company and is by far the best qualified man. There is the trained and experienced assistant director of recreation for a park system who is passed over for a twenty-three-year-old boy from Georgia. There is the doctor not allowed into the white hospital—who then leaves the South.

There is the fact that "the U. S. Employment Service operated by the several states is by design a complete block to the Negro's entering into industry." There is a movement, which he says he thinks he could document, "to eliminate every Negro from the employment service in this state. There's too much going on there [racial discrimination in the Employment Service] that a Negro shouldn't have a chance to know."

There is a long way to go, despite the gains in civil rights, "before a Negro has the same invitation to training or promotion that a white person would have. This is what integration means to me—complete freedom of movement in the society. We're whacking away at the periphery."

John Hervey Wheeler trusts in the reordering of society—by whacking away at the periphery—because he believes in the possibilities of the society. He understands institutions, and because he understands them he is a "success." As a success he understands the long process of change, the fact that the success of a Negro insurance company draws white insurance companies to compete for the Negro policy and therefore affects the structure of society. The fact that a Negro bank is there to make loans means that white banks will liberalize their policy of loans to Negroes.* He sees the precise limits of the campaign for civil rights, but also the precise gains. He trusts in the reordering of society—by the whacking away —because he believes in the possibilities of society: "All people are alike essentially." He understands institutions, and because he understands them he knows how to whack away at them. Success is one of the things you whack with.

Does success corrupt or emasculate a Negro? Does it draw him from his integrity and obligation as a Negro?

He puts the answer very simply: Not if your thinking is straight.

During our conversation about "thinking straight," Wheeler said: "I'm going to a dinner tonight involving the Democrats of the state, they invited me. Well, I told them I would not go unless they invited eight other people. I'm not so sure how it would have been with some other people [if they had been invited alone].

The Woolworth's store of Durham is on West Parish Street, directly facing the Mechanics and Farmers Bank. Back in 1960, Woolworth's was the target for the first sit-ins in Durham. The siege of Woolworth's lasted weeks, and during that period, there was much cold weather. Because the pickets were invited to come into the Mechanics and Farmers Bank to warm up and rest,

---

* As a matter of fact about ten per cent of the business of the Mechanics and Farmers Bank is white, both for deposits and loans. This has been the percentage from the beginning.

Wheeler received protests and threats from "responsible" members of the "power structure." He ignored the threats.

In fact, on one occasion he walked across the street and marched with the pickets—just to be sure nobody could make a mistake about his thinking straight.

: 5 :

Carl T. Rowan was born in 1925 at Ravenscroft, Tennessee, he studied at Tennessee State University, Washburn College, Oberlin College and the University of Minnesota, from which he received an M.A. in Journalism. Like Mr. Wheeler and Judge Hastie and James Baldwin, he is a success. He has been a distinguished journalist, he is the author of five books, and as a public servant, he has been Deputy Assistant Secretary of State for Public Affairs, Ambassador to Finland, and, currently, Director of the United States Information Agency. He is in a position to know some of the problems of success. He says:

> Now one of the problems of the Negro community is that the demagogues tend to use this argument [that success equals sell-out, Uncle Tom-ism] against anybody who happens to disagree with them or their particular tactic. Fortunately we've now got more Negroes of success who feel themselves in positions that are secure enough that they don't feel they have to run with the demagogues, and I think when we have more of them we'll find that the Negro as a whole is better off.

And Rowan refers to an interview he had with a *Time* reporter when Rowan was Ambassador to Finland:

> I pointed out to him that every Negro in a position of responsibility who does his job well is aiding immeasurably in the civil rights struggle, because he is carrying along with him a segment of public opinion—of white public opinion. Now one of the things that distresses me about

some of these people who style themselves the new militants, who are replacing the NAACP and the Urban League and so forth, is that they would have you believe that somehow or other by their militancy alone they can force a solution to this business. Well, it just isn't feasible in a society where the Negro represents a ten per cent minority.

And he goes on to say that "you have to have many approaches" simultaneously—the attack on conscience, the attack on law, the attack on "the white man's concern about his economic posture," the attack on concern with "this country's position in the world," the attack on and through "the public-opinion media." All this, he adds, "has to go along with the street demonstrations or the street demonstrations will produce nothing but bloodshed and bitterness."

Mr. Rowan is unequivocal, however, in stating that he has supported the sit-ins and various other demonstrations, and he doesn't particularly relish the fact, he says, that in the Senate during the debate on the Civil Rights Bill, "a hundred white men were making all the decisions." He doesn't think, he says, that "that's good for the Negro, and I don't think it's good for the country."

The demonstrations have done something, he argues, to bring the Negro out of the long night of brain washing and crushed pride, and have given him "a new realization of the possibility of making decisions about your own fate." But the situation is more complex than that. "Some people would have you believe," he says,

> that a so-called angry speech, or an angry article, or violence in the streets, has pulled up the Negro's ego and self-respect to where it ought to be, but I would maintain that this is an exercise in self-deception, that this may move the Negro in the other direction,* that nothing is going to move that ego and self-respect up to where it ought to be until the Negro gets all the other things that make it possible for him to live with assurance that he can compete with the American white man.

· · ·

* See Arnold Rose on the effect on the Negro of self-delusion in regard to Negro history. p. 150.

There are three basic patterns of reaction by Negroes toward white society—movement away from, movement toward, and movement against.* We may find an apathetic cotton picker or a slum dweller who conforms in a fairly pure form to the type of "movement away," or a rioter or criminal to the type of "movement against," but ordinarily, in the complexity of human nature, the pure form is hard to come by. If we take the basic pattern of, even, a Black Muslim to be a movement away, we recognize immediately a strong element of hard aggressiveness that means the movement against. Or if we take James Forman to represent a movement toward, we again recognize the aggressiveness there not only in a mood and aura, but in a will to revise and reorder the very society he would move toward.

But Carl Rowan represents, in at least a superficially pure form, the will to move toward white society.

> A Negro youngster out on the street participating in a demonstration who is not doing anything in his school work, who is gaining nothing in the way of a cultural background and who knows it, is going to go home that night and know that he is still just as much an outcast from American society as he was before he went out on that street and expressed his anger. Heaven knows, when people are talking militancy, and some are even talking violence, you aren't necessarily the most popular man in the world when you say, "All right, go and participate in that sit-in, but when you get through go home and do your homework, because you may ram open the door to the table where the white man is feasting, but if you go in and sit down at that table and are uncertain as to which fork to pick up, you're still going to feel like a man on the outside."

And here Carl Rowan is far from Adam Clayton Powell, who flatly says that now, in the crisis, the young Negro should act—not be concerned with Martin Luther King's version of self-improvement, "not all this business of fixing up your house . . . and getting a better education." Carl Rowan, again on the matter of the Negro

* Thomas F. Pettigrew, *A Profile of the Negro American.*

youth, is also far from the absolutism of James Baldwin, as suggested in this dialogue that Baldwin reports:

"What would you do if your teacher told you that instead of picketing and engaging in sit-ins, you should get an education first?" one boy asked me. And I said, "I would tell my teacher that it's impossible to get an education in this country until you change the country." And the boy said, "Thank you."*

We have said that Carl Rowan represents in a fairly pure form the "movement toward." We have seen his defensiveness against the charge of "sell-out" and of "Uncle Tom-ism." But let us look more closely. It is true that Rowan represents a "movement toward"—but toward what? Toward white society and, presumably, its basic cultural values. Yes—but he would have entered that society to compete, as he puts it, "with the American white man." What we might call the cultural self and the personal self are playing very different roles—one of acceptance, and one of aggression. This may be worth remembering.

*   *   *

On Southerners and Negroes and Paranoia:

ROWAN: Let's talk about how people respond to feelings of persecution. I would say that millions of white Southerners feel that they and the South have been persecuted. Some will carry it all the way back to before the Civil War, or back to what was done in the Reconstruction, et cetera. Others will bring it right down to today, when they swear that magazine *X,* for example, is always writing about the faults of the South, or that the press of the nation has tried to say that racial discrimination is a Southern and not a Northern problem. This feeling of regional persecution makes a man feel defensive and feel more Southern than he may really feel on other terms alone.

WARREN: It's very unfortunate to stake your identity on that, isn't it?

* Interview with Eve Auchincloss and Nancy Lynch Handy, in *Mademoiselle.*

ROWAN: Yes, indeed. You get the other factor, of course, in just casually reading statistics showing, for example, that the number of white Southerners rejected for the draft is considerably higher than the number of white Northerners. You get the economic, cultural, and other indicators of a lower level of society than in the North. People who read this are naturally inclined to look for things to bolster their prestige, and therefore a man in New Orleans, for example, may get a subtle boost to his ego by going to a hotel where he knows Ralph Bunche can't stay the night.

WARREN: That is, the white Southerner feels defensive vis-à-vis the North, in the way the Negro feels vis-à-vis the white society?

ROWAN: That's right. And you will see it reflected to a degree in the fact that many Negroes react almost automatically to a white man with a Southern drawl.

WARREN: They do indeed.

ROWAN: And it's only after a considerable experience and the attaining of a degree of intellectual sophistication that a Negro is honestly able to say that he doesn't judge white men by where they come from.*

WARREN: Or by the color of their skins.

ROWAN: Yes, that's true.

WARREN: You would say, then, that this "paranoia" is shared by both the Southern white and the American Negro?

ROWAN: There being one significant difference, that in the case of the Negro it is not nearly as often a false feeling of being persecuted as in the case of the white Southerner. Any Negro alive can recall enough real incidents.

*　　　*　　　*

We find the same observation made by Kardiner and Ovesey, as a result of a psychological study of Negroes: ". . . in our Rorschach records, mutilation fantasies with considerable fear of the external environment are extremely common. Such anxieties mean one thing

---

* A Northern Negro, the graduate of a good university, tells me that when he went South to do social service work, it took him several years to come to the conclusion that everybody who "talked like that" wasn't a fool.

in the white and another in the Negro. In the white, they mean paranoid tendencies; but not in the Negro. For the latter to see hostility in the environment is a normal perception. Hence we must guard against calling the Negro paranoid when he actually lives in an environment that persecutes him."

Here I remember the last interchange with one of the Negroes I interviewed. I had just said that the interview was very valuable to me. He replied: "I've been interviewed before. When the troubles were going on here, the TV people spent half a day with me, and that night I told my wife, how I'd be on TV. But they never used any of it. I don't expect you to."

* * *

WARREN: Right. But I'm thinking about the way it works psychologically, afterwards, in assessing new situations.
ROWAN: Absolutely. And this is a big factor in this revolution we're talking about. This is particularly true of the demagogue who likes to throw around the term *Uncle Tom*. That may be merely a measurement of the degree to which he's afflicted by this thing we describe as paranoia.

On the Southerner Again:

The vast majority of Southern white people would like nothing better than to get out from under this burden of supposedly being a different breed of Americans. A certain kind of stigma is attached to being a white Southerner, just as there is a stigma attached to being a Negro.

On the Psychic Split:

I've run into a Negro who would complain about racial discrimination, and then turn around and criticize another Negro for moving into a white neighborhood on the grounds that that Negro was showing a lack of pride in his own race.

On the Lack of White Leadership:

Men are more inclined to hate trouble than to hate injustice.

On Northern Capital in the South:

These are the people who have abdicated responsibility.

*   *   *

On this point we have had at least one clear statement from Northern capital. In answer to criticism that the United States Steel Corporation had not fulfilled its social obligations in Birmingham, Roger M. Blough, chairman, said that "for a corporation to attempt to exert any kind of economic compulsion to achieve a particular end in the social area seems to be quite beyond what a corporation should do, and I will say also, beyond what a corporation can do." The criticism had been that the corporation could have helped race relations by "warning the city it did not want its management people to live in a tension-ridden atmosphere, and by making it clear to banks and suppliers that it intended to give more business to those who favored better Negro opportunities."

Some comedy may emerge in the context of Northern capital in the South. The Reverend Kelly Smith, who conducted negotiations with businesses in Nashville, said to me that they "found the Southern owners of businesses were, in the final analysis, more easily convinced than the Northern." He relates that among the outside-owned theaters in Nashville was one of the Martin chain, with headquarters in Columbus, Georgia. "The president of the chain chartered a plane," Mr. Smith says, "and came for a conference. In the first session he agreed to desegregate. Yes, they came through first and then they offered their assistance [to persuade New York owners of other Nashville theaters to desegregate] and made a kind of joke of it. They said: 'Here we are, Georgia white people, trying to convince the New Yorkers they ought to integrate.' Which is what they did."

* * *

On Race Pride:

I would encourage the Negro to work on individual pride, rather than on race pride.

On Color Symbolism:

I would suspect that you could carry it back to the time when men feared the dark. The symbolism would be there, no matter what.

On the Negro's Using Race as an Alibi:

ROWAN: It was used a lot more in times past than now. When it's used today it's often used without the Negro's being aware that he's doing so.
WARREN: Would you say it's even more destructive when unconscious?
ROWAN: Yes, I think so.

On Rhetoric and Slogans:

Negro leaders have got to fight this business.

On the Mystic Bar the Successful Negro Encounters:

It's this bar that can be more frustrating in terms of a man's emotions and his mind and his heart than some of those other barriers.

* * *

Carl Rowan, in 1961, when Deputy Assistant Secretary of State for Public Affairs, was blackballed when proposed for membership in the Cosmos Club, Washington, D.C. The Cosmos is a club of high intellectual, literary, artistic, and, presumably, liberal pretensions.

: 6 :

On May 17, 1954, Chief Justice Warren, in delivering the opinion of the Supreme Court of the United States in the case of *Brown v. Board of Education,* said: "To separate them [Negro children] from others of similar age and qualifications solely because of their race generates a feeling of inferiority as to their status in the community that may affect their hearts and minds in a way unlikely ever to be undone." In support of this view the Chief Justice cited a series of psychological studies. The first item is: "K. B. Clark, 'Effect of Prejudice and Discrimination on Personality Development' (Midcentury White House Conference on Children and Youth, 1950)."

Kenneth Bancroft Clark was born in 1914 in the Panama Canal Zone; he received his B.A. from Howard University in 1935, and his Ph.D. from Columbia University in 1940. By the time Chief Justice Warren cited Clark's study, Clark had won a respected place in his profession, was on the staff on the City College of New York, was research director of the Northside Center for Child Development, and was associated with the Legal and Educational Department of the NAACP; the reference in the decision *Brown v. Board of Education* put him in the way of becoming a public figure. Later developments, especially in New York, in the problems of race and education, and his head-on collision with Adam Clayton Powell about the administration of HARYOU ACT—the Harlem Youth project, massively financed by Washington—have done nothing to shrink his news value.*

* In commenting on the resignation of Dr. Clark from the board of directors of HARYOU ACT, *The New York Times* (July 31, 1964) reported: "Dr. Clark has asserted that Representative Powell was trying to hand-pick the executive direction in order to control the HARYOU-ACT program. He conceded that he had been a bit naïve in underestimating the influence of politicians in the anti-poverty program."

As a professor and researcher, Dr. Clark is still to be found in his office at the Northside Center for Child Development, in the building of the Lincoln School, overlooking 110th Street, on the edge of Harlem. He is not, he says, a "leader." But an official black Cadillac may sometimes be found at the curb waiting to whisk him away from teaching and research to some coign in the power structure where policy is made. Dr. Clark moves, too, among other contradictions and paradoxes. He works for, and presumably believes in the possibility of, the betterment of society. But sometimes he talks as though life and history were little more than a tragic vision of blind and irrational impulse, as though not the wise and good are effective, but only the compulsive and violent. Again, he strikes one as a man of warmth and courtesy, who wants to like and be liked. But sometimes he seems to withdraw into a world shadowed by a bitterness not easy to define.

Perhaps this last division is merely a mark of our common humanity.

*   *   *

Sitting in his sixth-floor office, overlooking 110th Street, where a spring drizzle fell, we begin talking with reference to the Reverend Galamison's outburst about the public school system's having, perhaps, run its course. Dr. Clark says that we have to "make a distinction between emotional statements, and sometimes hysterical slogans which people use in the heat of battle, and sound judgments which are the basis for the long-term program." And he adds that one of the most disturbing things to observe is that "emotional, irrational appeals are much more likely to be effective in bringing about initial concern with a social problem." For example, he says there had been, for many years, a city-wide committee on Harlem schools, but all the reports—some of which he himself had worked on—had been "graciously accepted and, in effect, filed and forgotten." Then came the boycotts and demands for immediate, absolute solutions; and "one must face the fact that Mr. Galamison has had more impact than all the previous years of patient, reasoned, factual study." Speaking from the perspective of a Negro and a psychologist, the thing that really appalls him, he says, is "that one does not get to the point of seeking rational solutions for long-standing ills—racial injustices—unless these injustices are dramatized, more often than not by irrational methods." The danger lies in confusing the methods effective for dramatizing the ills with methods that would be "necessary for the long-term resolution of the problem."

Dr. Clark goes on to say: "One of the difficulties with the civil rights struggle is that such confusion occurs in certain communities. We are in danger of having that confusion in New York City." This cuts both ways, he says, for white and black.

Only once in our discussion did Dr. Clark and I engage one of the practical aspects of a specific problem—the transporting of white pupils into ghetto schools. "My own reaction," he says, "is that this is unrealistic, is not likely to be implemented and is likely just to be a bone of meaningless controversy." It is unrealistic, he says, "because the bulk of white parents would not permit their children to be transported," because the schools in Negro communities are "woefully inferior"—"so inferior that no child should be required to attend them." The Negro slum family has no choice— and this is "criminal." But the middle-class whites would have a choice, private schools or the suburbs, and the insistence on busing-in would, "at this level of development in race relations," have the effect of making "the public school almost totally a minority group—and the poor whites." It would accentuate segregation and, in fact, the class split.

Dr. Clark points out that certain Negro leaders who push for integration in the public schools—even the Reverend Galamison— have children in private schools: they simply refuse the inferior education for their own children but, at the same time, fight for the "democratic education of all children."*

* The Reverend Galamison, in reference to his son's being in a private school, said to me: The fact "was not at all related to this struggle in the beginning. I don't think I was involved in this struggle, if I remember correctly, when we first put our youngster into private school. He started in a nursery school. It was simply a matter of having him in school, and my wife was working and we felt it was time to wean him away from home. Now, when he got to the age when he was ready to enter public school, there came a question of whether he should go to my wife's school where she taught, or whether he should go to some other public school. Well, now, if he had gone to another public school there would have been no one home for lunch and that sort of thing. And my wife didn't feel that it would be an

And here I ask if this argument wouldn't cut both ways, if a white parent, objecting to the bus-in, would not be using the same argument as the Negro leader.

> CLARK: Exactly. And there would be no more basis on the face of it to accuse the white parent of racial prejudice than to accuse the Reverend Galamison of racial prejudice.
> WARREN: That point is not often recognized, is it?
> CLARK: But it's no less real.

Dr. Clark's general position on integration is clear and on the record. I quote this passage to indicate that he does not seem to make integration a touchstone of virtue, but is willing to think about it in a general context, in the context of human motivations, including the white man's, which he wants to evaluate fairly and in the context of the social process—"process" because he qualifies his discussion by the phrase "at this level of development in race relations," a stage to be gone through. In fact, he says, in *Dark Ghetto,* that the educational crisis of Harlem, or of any other ghetto, "is not primarily, and certainly not exclusively, one of the inequitable racial balance in the schools." Furthermore, he recognizes the fact that seventy-three per cent of the public-school pupils in Manhattan are non-white, and the grimmer and less well advertised fact that segregation is increasing. He finds pairing schemes superficial, though of some limited value, and agrees with the Allen Report on the New York school system that busing would be a self-defeating program in that it would, under present circumstances, accelerate the flight of whites from the public schools. Boycotts run the real risk of building up counter-forces, and this process may force the issue totally into the realm of politics.

The key to the whole question lies, Dr. Clark would maintain, in the quality of education. If the ghetto schools give a high quality of education, as good as or better than that of the "white" schools, then the ghetto itself changes and the white resistance to integration, for

objective situation to have him in her school. So we continued him in private school. Then by the time he got to the age when he might have gone to public school, I was so involved in this struggle and I was being so vilified by many people in the school system that I did not feel that I should expose my child to the kind of attitude which I knew prevailed against me among many principals and teachers."

many reasons, declines. He answers those who accept the notion of an environmental doom in the ghetto and who see no hope except a reordering of the context of the ghetto—probably in the Sweet Bye-and-Bye—by insisting that immediate results can be achieved by proper teaching. The actual decline in I.Q. in the ghetto schools is not a social doom; it is merely the result of bad and/or cynical teaching. The sensational results he points to in the Banneker Project in St. Louis, to take only one example, and the moral of the HARYOU studies, give grounds for real optimism—if society is willing to pay the price.

Dr. Clark does not make integration a shibboleth. Nor does he interpret it, as some do, as a device of punishment, a way to spread the grief around, "to wake the white man up." His considered views are incorporated in the report prepared by Harlem Youth Opportunities Unlimited:

> . . . children cannot be sacrificed on the altar of . . . semantic rigidities. . . . Heroics and dramatic words and gestures, over-simplified either/or thinking and devil hunting might provide a platform for temporary crowd pleasing, ego satisfactions, or would-be "leaders" but they cannot solve the fundamental problem. . . . Meaningful desegregation of the public schools in New York City can occur only if all of the schools in the system are raised to the highest standards, and when the quality of education is uniformly high.

There is, it seems, a candor and a willingness to confront tangles and endure tensions without taking refuge in verbal solutions, or solutions that would falsify some aspects of his own feeling.

We turned to talking about ethical judgments in historical contexts, about Jefferson and Lincoln (whom Clark sees as "one of our best examples of the inescapable turmoil, conflict, confusion within thinking Americans"), and then, by way of a discussion of the slogan "Freedom Now," we got on to the following dialogue:

> CLARK: Unfortunately—oh, I don't know that it's unfortunate—there are many people who are mouthing the slogan, who have a rather simplistic, literalistic view of it—and maybe this has always been true historically, the cutting edge of any movement must be by virtue of—I mean men like

John Brown—the cutting edge has to be literalistic.

WARREN: What do you think of John Brown, by the way? Morally and psychologically? Or both?

CLARK: Well, psychologically, the simple designation of John Brown might be too simple—he was a fanatic, a neurotic, a literalist, an absolutist, a man so totally committed that nothing, including reality, stood in his way.

WARREN: How do we treat a man like that in ordinary society?

CLARK: Society can take care of itself with men like that, it always has—see what it did to Christ.

WARREN: Do you equate Christ and John Brown?

CLARK: Unquestionably.

WARREN: In their values or simply in their neuroses?

CLARK: In their values, in their neuroses, and of course, in their end.

WARREN: Christ came as the Prince of Peace, and Brown lived in a dream of bloodshed. He loved the text: "Without the shedding of blood there is no remission of sins."

CLARK: But Christ ran the money changers out of the temple.

WARREN: Do we equate that with the Pottawatomie Massacre?

CLARK: Don't push me too far. But look, Christ was clearly a person committed to values other than those prevailing in his time.

WARREN: Or in our time, either.

CLARK: The depth and reality of his commitment was expressed by his life. All right—Christ was alienated, Christ had values he was willing to run the risk for, and he paid the ultimate price. Christ, Socrates, John Brown—these people are irritating.

WARREN: Suppose a man like John Brown, with the same burning eye, came into your office and said, "I'm tired of this fooling around, I'm going down to Mississippi, take six or seven determined men with me, and I am going to slaughter the Governor and his entire staff in the Capitol and come out and say 'Rise, follow me!'" What would you do about this man who came and asked for a hundred dollars to help finance his trip?

CLARK: First, I wouldn't give him a hundred dollars.

WARREN: Fifty?

CLARK: I wouldn't give him anything.

WARREN: Would you call the police or would you wish him well?

CLARK: I don't think I would do either.

WARREN: Would you call the doctor?

CLARK: I would probably see what I could do to help this man, if it would not inconvenience me too much—or if it would not involve me with him too much.

WARREN: But such a man, with the wild eye and Biblical texts, did go into the offices of certain gentlemen in Boston, some hundred years ago.

CLARK: That is the difference—me and time, you see.

WARREN: You know more about psychology, and more about history—and therefore wouldn't want any part of it?

CLARK: Not only that, I am frank to say to you, I am a professor—I have a vested interest in "either/or-ing," you see—in maintaining issues on a level of discussion rather than action, and certainly anybody who says anything to me about bloodshed is not going to get a sympathetic response.

WARREN: John Brown was like Christ, psychologically?

CLARK: In the totality of his commitment, his alienation, his willingness to run risks.

WARREN: Some mad men are that way, too—but we don't take men as equal in virtue, automatically because of this mere resemblance?

CLARK: No—except that it isn't always that easy. It isn't always easy to differentiate between a madman and a martyr, or the person who irritates the status quo.

WARREN: If the madman happens to tie in with a moral cause and happens to have the bad, or the good, luck to get bumped off in the process, then—

CLARK: Who else does this except madmen?

WARREN: We must trust the madmen to be our moral guardians?

CLARK: Let us back up a little. Of course you could define madness as daring to believe that something which you value is so important that it is worth risking your security, your comfort, and your stagnation—you could define madness as any alienation that brings you into open conflict with the prevailing values and patterns. So defined—who else but madmen defy constituted authority?

WARREN: You are defining them clinically?

CLARK: I am not defining them clinically.

WARREN: Suppose a man also clinically mad—let's just assume that—then what do you do about his relation to an idea, or to action?

CLARK: I am more concerned with Van Gogh's painting than I am with the fact that he was mad. I confess I will probably be more concerned with what a man stands for and does.

WARREN: Would you judge the morality of an act by its consequences?

CLARK: I'm not always sure that I would judge only by the consequences. Even if one sought to rationalize consequences on the grounds that they were morally valuable, these consequences might be contaminated by the immorality of the act.

WARREN: John Brown is almost a test case for this.

CLARK: Boy, you certainly are fascinated with John Brown, and he is one of the most—

WARREN: You brought him up—I didn't.

I had not brought up the topic of John Brown, but Dr. Clark was right, I am fascinated by him. My first book, written while I was in graduate school, was a biography, *John Brown: The Making of a Martyr*. It is far from the book I would write now, for that book was shot through with Southern defensiveness, and in my ignorance the psychological picture of the hero was presented far too schematically. But even so, the work on the book was my real introduction into some awareness of the dark and tangled problem of motives and values. Long after, a French novelist and critic, in writing an introduction to his translation of one of my novels, remarked that the mythic Brown figure recurs again and again in my fiction, in various disguises, the man who at any cost, would strike for absolute solutions—a type toward which, I suppose, I am deeply ambivalent. In any case, how callow I was, in that old biography, to think that I could make a formulation that would, even then, satisfy me!

John Brown was, indeed, mad, and not always nobly mad—he was arrogant, sometimes unscrupulous, sometimes contemptuous of the truth, ambitious, angry, blood-obsessed; but, in the end, he spoke and died nobly. What do we make of a poet who, out of the ruck of a confused and obsessed life, creates the beautiful poem?

If Brown was mad, we may, I suppose, say that a mad society—which America certainly was in the 1850's, and may be today—gives the terms and form for the madness of the individual. The Secret Six, who backed Brown's raid on Harper's Ferry, were incapable of diagnosing the condition of the old man with the basilisk eye, and they were certainly out of touch with reality when they supposed that such a project might succeed in any of its expectations. (When the blow-up came, they quickly regained touch with reality and, with one exception, went into blue funk.) But Governor Wise and the other officials of the Old Dominion, like most Southern politicians and most newspaper editors, were mad enough to compound Brown's madness and the minor aberration of the Secret Six, by putting Brown on the gallows in the cow pasture outside Charlestown, when there was adequate legal and clinical justification to retire him to an asylum. But all this is a mere detail of a general madness for which the shock treatment of 1861-65 has given only the illusion of a cure.

As for Brown, we still live with the split in the interpretation which, long ago, was so clearly exemplified in Concord, Massachusetts, where Emerson said that Brown "had made the gallows glorious like the Cross," and Hawthorne retorted, somewhat tardily, in the middle of the Civil War, that "no man was ever more justly hanged." And both, no doubt, are right.

In any case, I had not brought up the topic of John Brown.

CLARK: All right, I brought him up—I'm not going to abandon John Brown. You're right, John Brown was mad, John Brown was a murderer, John Brown was clearly not respectable.

WARREN: How much does this use of the word *respectable* take back from the other words? You're a psychologist.

CLARK: A great deal—I suppose I put "not respectable" at the end to—

WARREN: To disinfect "murder"?

CLARK: Not necessarily to disinfect "murder" but to deal with the fact—the reality—that respectable abolitionists were talking quite a bit, and while I would not join John Brown's party of murderers, any more than I would join Malcolm X's call for a—what did he call it?—a rifle club—and I personally recoil from bloodshed, because I think it just another form of human idiocy—the fact still remains that major social changes toward social justice in human history, have almost always come—if not always—through irrational and questionable methods.

WARREN: That is, we have to play the double game of making somebody else pick up the dirty marbles for us—a white man in a nice house in the Belle Meade section of Nashville, or in a nice suburb of Jackson, Mississippi, lets those cops and rednecks pick up the marbles down Charlotte Avenue or Lynch Street? You and I are playing the same game with history, is that it?

CLARK: That's one way of putting it—but I should prefer not to put it that way. I should prefer to put it that apparently rational, reasonable men, who are for making a change in the status quo, are generally ineffectual. Changes in the status quo are more likely to come from irrational, unreasonable, questionable men.

WARREN: We are all the beneficiaries of violence, aren't we?

CLARK: Isn't this horrible? It is horrible that irrational, vile, and cruel, horrible things have to be done to prepare the way for the possibility of a little bit of change, or justice.

WARREN: Thomas Jefferson said that liberty is won by inches.

CLARK: Yes, and the costs stand high.

*   *   *

After the interview was over Dr. Clark stood quiet for a moment, his face tense, looking out the window. Then, almost irrelevantly, he said: "I wish I could be as optimistic as Jimmy."

He was referring to James Baldwin, about whom we had been

talking earlier. He could not accept the promise, it would seem, of the Great Day. Any more than he could believe that Martin Luther King's doctrine of love would touch the heart of the man on the street in Harlem.

Certainly, Martin Luther King's doctrine did not touch all the hearts on the streets or in the bars or honky-tonks of Harlem, or Brooklyn or Rochester or Philadelphia. And so the mobs came out, night after night, to pick up the marbles of history for Dr. Clark. And for me.

No doubt the cops have picked up some, too. For us both.

*   *   *

On the Role of the Leaders of the Established Civil Rights Organizations:

I think their role is going to become increasingly important as the more dramatic techniques run their course.

On James Baldwin and Integrating with a "Burning House":

Baldwin is to me one of the most disturbing, irritatingly incisive critics of our society at this time, you see. But this doesn't mean that Baldwin has the answers all the time. I mean, Baldwin expresses anguish, Baldwin expresses frustration, concern—and a wish for something better, in the sense of a totality of betterness; and he also expresses the feeling that maybe he isn't going to get even the minimum, so therefore [he'd] forget everything else, in a sense. I want to continue about Baldwin because I think that what he is expressing is his—his desire, what he would like human beings to be like, what he would like society to be like. Maybe what Baldwin has not yet understood and probably never should understand—maybe he should never accept the possibility that there might be a tremendous gap between what he would like and what can be, because this might reduce his potency, his power as a passionate incisive critic of what is. Lorraine

Hansberry and James Baldwin have no choice other than to be incorporated within this society and this culture, pretty much as it is.

On the Effect of the Incorporation of the Negro:

If America is capable of including the Negro this will on its face strengthen the society—not necessarily change its values but make the existing values less liable to internal decay.

On Adam Clayton Powell and the Civil Rights Movement:

If he is important in the civil rights movement it is because the civil rights movement itself is important. Yet he is no longer a primary power source in the civil rights movement, but rather a successful fellow traveler with the ability to act as if he is directing a movement he is merely following. He attempts always to align himself with the more dramatic sources of power. When the Muslims seemed to be the cutting edge of the Negro Movement, he rejected the NAACP forces in their behalf. When the Milton Galamison-sponsored school boycott in New York City was considered a potent effort, he associated himself with it. He attempted to join with Martin Luther King in the early stages of the Montgomery bus boycott, but King and his admirers were shrewd enough to recognize the tactic, and the liaison failed to materialize. In the genuine thrust of the civil rights movement, Powell is a hasbeen.*

On Powell and the Ghetto:

As long as the predicament of Negroes in American cities endures, just so long will Powell. The amorality of the larger society makes the amorality of the ghetto possible. Those who oppose Powell must oppose the ghetto first, for Powell is a

* This, like the quotation following, is not from tape but from *Dark Ghetto.*

creature of the ghetto, and for Powell to survive the ghetto itself must survive. To transform the ghetto would lead to Powell's political destruction.

: 7 :

In 1952, *Invisible Man* was published. It is now a classic of our time. It has been translated into seven languages. The title has become a key phrase: the Negro is the invisible man.

Ralph Ellison is not invisible and had done some thirty-eight years of living before the novel appeared, and the complex and rich experience of those years underlies the novel, or is absorbed into the novel, as it undergirds, or is absorbed into, his casual conversation.

Ralph Ellison was born in 1914, in Oklahoma City, of Southern parents. His father, who had been a soldier in China, the Philippines, and in the Spanish American War, was a man of energy and ambition, and an avid reader; he named his son for Emerson. He died when Ralph was three years old, but Ralph's mother managed to support the children and encouraged them in their ambitions.

As a boy, Ralph sold newspapers, shined shoes, collected bottles for bootleggers, was a lab assistant to a dentist, waited on tables, hunted, hiked, played varsity football, conducted the school band, held first chair in the trumpet section of the school orchestra. "Was constantly fighting," he says, "until I reached the age when I realized that I was strong enough and violent enough to kill someone in a fit of anger."

With some help from his mother, whom he describes as an "idealist and a Christian," he worked his way through Tuskegee, as a music major. But there he read Eliot, and that fact, though for some years he was to keep his ambition as a composer, was the beginning of his literary career. In 1937, during a winter in Dayton, Ohio, where he had gone for the funeral of his mother (who had died, he says, "at the hands of an ignorant and negligent Negro physician"), and where he was living in poverty and making what money he could by hunting birds to sell to General Motors officials, he took up writing seriously: "This occurring at a time when I was agitating for intervention in the Spanish Civil War, my personal loss was tied to events taking place far from these shores. Thus the complexity of events forced itself to my attention even before I had developed the primary skill for dealing with it. I was forced to see that both as observer and as writer, and as my mother's son, I would always have to do my homework."

Ralph Ellison has traveled widely and lived in many parts of the United States; he has known a great variety of people, including "jazzmen, veterans, ex-slaves, dope fiends, prostitutes, pimps, preachers, folk singers, farmers, teamsters, railroad men, slaughterhouse and roundhouse workers, bell boys, headwaiters, punch-drunk fighters, barbers, gamblers, bootleggers, and the tramps and down-and-outers who often knocked on our back door for handouts." He might have added that he has known the academic world and the world of the arts, has lived for two years in Italy as a Fellow of the American Academy, and has traveled in Mexico and the Orient.

*   *   *

Ralph Ellison is something above medium height, of a strong, well-fleshed figure not yet showing any slackness of middle age. He is light brown. His brow slopes back, but not decidedly, and is finely vaulted, an effect accentuated by the receding hair line. The skin of his face is unlined, and the whole effect of his smoothly modeled face is one of calmness and control; his gestures have the same control, the same balance and calmness. The calmness has a history, I should imagine, a history based on self-conquest and hard lessons of sympathy learned through a burgeoning and forgiving imagination. Lurking in the calmness is, too, the impression of the possibility of a sudden nervous striking-out, not entirely mastered; and too, an impression of withdrawal—a withdrawal tempered by humor, and flashes of sympathy. It is a wry humor, sometimes self-directed. And a characteristic mannerism is the utterance of a little sound— "ee-ee-"—breathed out through the teeth, a humorous, ironical recognition of the little traps and blind alleys of the world, and of the self.

His voice is not deep, but is well-modulated, pleasing. He speaks slowly, not quite in a drawl, and when he speaks on a matter of some weight, he tends to move his head almost imperceptibly from side to side, or even his shoulders.

He does this as he sits on a couch in his study high above the Hudson River, where the afternoon sun strikes and a string of barges moves leadenly against the current. I have just quoted the passage to him from Du Bois on the split in the Negro psyche.

ELLISON: It's a little bit more complicated than Dr. Du Bois thought it. That is, there's no way for me not to be influenced by American values, and they're coming at me through the newspapers, through the books, through the products I buy, through all the various media—through the language. What becomes a problem, of course, is when you turn from the implicit cultural pluralism of the country to politics, social customs. But it seems to me that the real goal of the pressure now being asserted by Negroes is to achieve on the socio-political level something of the same pluralism which exists on the level of culture. The idea that the Negro psyche is split is not as viable as it seems—although it might have been true of Dr. Du Bois personally. My problem is not whether I will accept or reject American values. It is, rather, how can I get into a position where I can have the maximum influence upon those values. There is also the matter, as you have pointed out, of those American ideals which were so fatefully put down on paper which I want to see made manifest.

WARREN: One sometimes encounters the Negro who says he regrets the possible long-range absorption of the Negro blood, the possibility of the loss of Negro identity.

ELLISON: That's like wishing your father's father wasn't your grandfather. I don't fear Negro blood being absorbed, but I am afraid that the Negro American cultural expression might be absorbed and obliterated through lack of appreciation and through commercialization and banalization. But as for the question of diffusing of blood—it isn't blood which makes a Negro American: Adam Clayton Powell's reply to a white TV interviewer's query, "I hear that you have quite a lot of white blood," was "Yes, probably more than you, Mike.*" If it should suddenly become true that being a Negro rested on the possession of African blood alone, without reference to culture, social experience, and political circumstance,

* Mike Wallace.

quite a number of people who are white and who enjoy the privileges of white status would find themselves beyond the pale.

Anyway, I don't think the problem of blood absorption works so simply. There are principles of selection which have little to do with the status accorded to whiteness, and these assert themselves despite the absence of outside pressure. On the aesthetic level alone there are certain types you like, certain sensibilities, certain voices—a number of other qualities. Another factor is that Negroes, despite what some of our spokesmen say, do not dislike being Negro—no matter how inconvenient it frequently is. *I* like being a Negro.

WARREN: Then it's not merely suffering and deprivation, it's a challenge and enrichment?

ELLISON: Yes, indeed—these complete the circle and make it human. And as I was telling the kids this morning at Rutgers, I have no desire to escape the struggle, because I'm just too interested in how it's going to work out, and I want to impose my will upon the outcome to the extent that I can. I want to help shape events and our general culture, not merely as a semi-outsider but as one who is in a position to have a responsible impact upon the American value system.

WARREN: Some Negroes—some leaders—say that there is no challenge or enrichment in the situation of Negroes. Of course, it may be a matter of strategy to insist on the total agony.

ELLISON: Perhaps I can talk this way because I'm not a leader. But I understand that this has become part of the strategy of exerting pressure. There is a danger in this, nevertheless. The danger lies in overemphasizing the extent to which Negroes are alienated, and in overstressing the extent to which the racial predicament imposes an agony upon the individual. For the Negro youth this emphasis can become an excuse and a blinder, leading to an avoidance of the individual assertion. It can encourage him to ignore his personal talent in favor of reducing himself to a generalized definition of alienation and agony. Thus is accomplished what the entire history of repression and brutalization has failed to do: the individual reduces himself to a cipher. Ironically, some of those who yell loudest about alienation are doing it in some of the most conservative journals and newspapers and are very well paid for so yelling. Yet, obviously, the agony which they display has other than racial sources.

Actually, I doubt the existence of a "total" agony, for where personality is involved two-plus-two seldom equals four. But I agree that agony and alienation do form a valid source of appeal.

However, there's another aspect of reality which applies: The American Negro has a dual identity, just as most Americans have, and it seems to me ironic that the discipline out of which this present action is being exerted comes from no simple agony—nor simple despair—but out of long years of learning how to live under pressure, of learning to deal with provocation and with violence. It issues out of the Negro's necessity of establishing his own value system and his own conception of Negro experience and Negro personality, conceptions which seldom get into the sociology and psychology textbooks.

WARREN: The power of character, of self-control—the qualities that are making this Movement now effective—did not come out of blind suffering?

ELLISON: Nor did they come out of self-pity or self-hate—which is a belief shared by many black and white sociologists, journalists, by the Black Muslims, and by many white liberals. But even though some of these elements—the Negro being human—are present within the Movement—the power of character, of self-control—these qualities are no expression of blind suffering or self-hate. For when the world was not looking, when the country was not looking at Negroes, and when we were restrained in certain of our activities by the interpretation of the law of the land, something was present in our lives to sustain us. This is evident when we go back and look at our cultural expression, when we look at the folklore in a truly questioning way, when we scrutinize and listen before passing judgment. Listen to those tales which are told by Negroes among themselves. I'm so annoyed whenever I come across a perfectly well-meaning person saying of the present struggle, "Well, the Negro has suddenly discovered courage."

*   *   *

In all of Ellison's conversation and writing there is the impulse re-inspect, to break through, some of the standard formulations of the Revolution which are in constant danger of becoming mere stereotypes. One is that the Negro has been deprived of a sense of identity and is a "self-hater." When James Baldwin says that "for the first time in American Negro history, the American black man is not at the mercy of the American white man's image of him," he is referring to the question of identity; as he is when he goes on to say that, though it is "very romantic," the American Negro finds it "a necessary step" to think of "himself as an African." Martin Luther King says that he recognizes "the psychic split" as a "real issue," and Wyatt Tee Walker says that only now the "Negro really accepts his identity." Izell Blair says that the young Negro, in facing the dominant values of white society, says: "Well, what am I?" And then: "You feel rubbed out, as if you never existed." The question arises in a number of case histories; for instance, in one of the persons studied by Kardiner and Ovesey: "I know I don't want to be identified with Negroes, but I am identified regardless of how I feel." And, as we have seen, the Black Muslims, including the defector Malcolm X, take the recognition of the problem of identity and self-hate as the beginning of redemption.

In the past, in the essay "Harlem Is Nowhere," written in 1948, Ellison accepted the notion of self-hate among Negroes in connection with what Dr. Frederick Wertham calls the "free-floating hostility" which the Negro senses, and sometimes takes "as a punishment for some racial or personal guilt." Ellison is quite specific: "Negro Americans are in a desperate search for identity . . . their whole lives have become a search for answers to the questions: Who am I?, What am I?, Why am I?, and, Where?" But later (as in the present interview), Ellison insists, over and over again, on the Negro's will, even under slavery, to develop discipline and achieve individuality. For instance, in a review of *Blues People* (1964), by Le Roi Jones, he writes:

"A slave," writes Le Roi Jones, "cannot be a man." But what, might one ask, of those moments when he feels his metabolism aroused by the rising of the sap in the spring? What of his identity among other slaves? With his wife? And isn't it closer to the truth that far from considering themselves only in terms of that abstraction, "a slave," the enslaved really thought of themselves as *men* who had been unjustly enslaved?

What are we to make of these apparent contradictions? In the first place, we have to grant that a man is the final authority about his own feelings. If Izell Blair says that, at a certain time, he felt "rubbed out," he ought to know. By the same token, Ralph Ellison ought to know what he felt, or how he feels. The trouble only starts when one generalizes, and attributes a certain feeling to that abstraction "the Negro"—that is, to all Negroes—and creates a stereotype. But, of course, we would be nearer the truth if we thought not of "the Negro" but of pressures and tendencies implicit in the situation of oppression and of an enormous variety of persons upon whom they act.

Ellison, in thinking of those Negroes who set models for resistance, puts his emphasis on the individual, on the achieving of personal identity. On this point, some psychologists, in discussing the situation of the Negro under slavery, will distinguish between the personal ego and the social ego. For instance, Kardiner and Ovesey say that there were "among the slaves powerful and resourceful leaders," that slavery was not accepted with docility, and that "individual protests were many." But they distinguish such protests from group action, organized action. The fact that rebellions were so few and so promptly failed they attribute to the destruction by slavery of "the fabric out of which social cohesion is made." Under slavery the individual might have "enormous self-confidence," but such confidence would not be available for common use; its reference would remain almost strictly individual.

The explanation for this they would take to be complex. There would be, of course, the breakup of cultural bonds, the inability to form permanent and dignified family ties, the spy system, the use of Negro "drivers" and pace-setters, the system of special privilege for house-servants and "pets." Furthermore, Kardiner and Ovesey emphasize the nature of work under slavery: "No slave can take pride in his work, except perhaps in that it may serve another form of self-interest through ingratiation"—and this would be a bid for discrimination in favor of oneself, to the implied disadvantage of everyone else. The slave—except among favored craftsmen—did not plan work and had no opportunity to cooperate in work, and this fact would also have had a deep psychological effect. And, always, there would have been the pressure to accept the master's values. Under such pressures individuals might, and clearly did, achieve "identity," but with a special struggle—and a struggle that might have emphasized the special personal nature of that identity, an identity that might be expressed in individual acts of resistance or by flight.

As we have said earlier in discussing Samboism, we must think in terms not of absolutes, but of pressures inherent in the situation. And in this instance, common sense would dictate that the distinction between the personal self and the social self cannot be taken as absolute. Certainly, the example of resistance or flight would fire something in those who to that moment had not resisted or fled; and such examples, entering the local folklore, might have continuing effect. And on this point Ellison was continuing, telling of a man who, long after slavery, had entered folklore as the intransigent, individual discoverer of the self:

ELLISON: I remember that when I was riding freight trains through Alabama to get to Tuskegee Institute there was a well-known figure of Birmingham, called Ice Cream Charlie, whose story was also told over and over again whenever we evoked the unwritten history of the group. Ice Cream Charlie was an ice cream maker and his product must have been very good (Negro folklore has it, by the way, and erroneously, I'm afraid, that a Negro slave woman invented ice cream) because the demand for it led to his death. His white competitors ordered him to stop selling his product to white people, but the white people wanted it and, believing in free enterprise, he ignored the warning. This led to his competitors' sending the police after Charlie, and it ended with his killing twelve policemen before they burned him out and killed him. Now there are many, many such stories which Negroes keep alive among themselves, and they form part of our image of Negro experience—nonviolence notwithstanding.

Many people don't even bother to know or care about this part of Negro history. They project their own notions—or prefabricated stereotypes—upon Negroes—they make a slow and arduous development seem a dramatic event.*

The freedom movement, such a person assumes, exists simply because *he* is looking at it. Thus it becomes an accident or an artistic contrivance, or a conspiracy, instead of the slow development in time, in history, and in group discipline and organizational technique which it actually is.

I shouldn't be annoyed, of course, since Americans know very little of their history and we tend to act as though we believed that by refusing to look at history there'll be no necessity to confront its consequences. And we have so many facile ways of disguising the issues, of rendering them banal.

Sometime back I saw a revival of an old Al Jolson movie on television. This was about the time of the summer riots in Harlem, and in one of the big scenes Jolson appears in blackface singing a refrain which goes, "I don't want to make your laws, I just want to sing my songs and be happy!" Well, whatever the reality of the Negro attitudes or whatever the stage of the Negro freedom struggle at the time the picture was originally released—yes, and no matter how many white people were lulled into believing that Jolson's "passing for black" granted him the authority to express authentic Negro attitudes—this piece of popular culture tells us more about Jolson, about Hollywood, and about American techniques for converting serious moral issues into sentimental and banal entertainment than about Negroes. Anyone who bothers to consult history would know that not only were Negroes anxious to change the laws but were trying even then to do so. By 1954 they had helped to discover how— with Charles S. Houston's mock supreme court cases held at Howard University Law School.

Viewed from this perspective of Al Jolson, America has

* In this connection we may remark that Ellison's great admiration for Faulkner stems, in part, from the impulse that made Faulkner more willing perhaps than any other artist to start with the stereotype of the Negro, accept it as true, and then seek out the human truth which it hides." See "Twentieth Century Fiction and the Black Mask of Humanity," in *Shadow and Act*.

been terribly damaged by bad art. Perhaps those Negro writers who wish to be praised for shoddy work, and who regard serious literary criticism as a form of racial prejudice, should remember that bad art which toys with serious issues is ultimately destructive and the entertainment which it provides is poisonous, regardless of the racial background of the artist.

WARREN: What do you think of the suggestion that part of the Southern resistance is not based on the question of race as such but on the impulse to maintain identity? A white Southerner feeling that his identity is involved may defend a lot of things in one package as being Southern, and one of those things is segregation. He feels he has to have the whole package to define his culture and his identity. Does that make any sense to you?

ELLISON: It makes a lot of sense to me, because one of the areas that I feel, and which I think I see when I look at the Southerner who has these feelings, is that he has been imprisoned by them, and that he has been prevented from achieving his individuality, perhaps more than Negroes have. And very often this is a tough one for Northerners to understand—that is, Northern whites, and sometimes even for Northern Negroes.

WARREN: I think it is too—some of the people I know.

ELLISON: Yes, it is very difficult to get that across and I wish it could be spelled out. I wish that we could break this thing down so that it could be seen that desegregation isn't going to stop people from being Southern, that freedom for Negroes isn't going to destroy the main current of that way of life, which becomes, like most ways of life when we *talk* about them, more real on the level of myth, memory and dream than on the level of actuality anyway. The climate will remain the same, and that has a lot to do with it, the heroes of Southern history will remain, and so on. The economy will probably expand, and a hell of a lot of energy which has gone into keeping the Negro "in his place" will be released for more creative pursuits. And the dictionary will become more accurate, the language a bit purified, and the singing in the schools will sound better. I suspect that what is valuable and worth preserving in the white Southern way of life is no more exclusively dependent upon the existence of segregation than what is valuable in Southern Negro life depends upon its being recognized by white people— or for that matter, by Northern Negroes. Besides, from what I've seen of the South, as a musician and as a waiter and so on, some of the people who are most afraid of Negroes' invading them will never be bothered, because their way of life is structured in a manner which isn't particularly attractive to Negroes.

WARREN: There's an interlocking structure, I sometimes think, supported by just one thing—segregation.

ELLISON: Yes, and their fear is so unreal, actually, when you can see the whole political structure being changed anyway. And when the political structure changes and desegregation is achieved, it will be easily seen where Negroes were stopped by the law and where they would have been stopped anyway, because of income and by their own preference— a matter of taste. There is, after all, a tiny bit of Negro truth in the story which Southern whites love to tell, to the effect that if a white man could be a Negro on Saturday night he'd never wish to be white again.

That bit of consolation aside, however, I don't think it sufficiently appreciated that over and over again Negroes of certain backgrounds take on aristocratic values. They are rural and Southern and not drawn to business because business was not part of the general pattern. This is one reason— over and beyond the realities of discrimination by banks, suppliers, poor training opportunities, and even individual lack of initiative—that we've developed no powerful middle class. Here again a cultural factor cuts across the racial and political appearance of things. Southern whites were also slow to take to business.

WARREN: That's been one of the things that have been commented on by observers from the eighteenth century on.

ELLISON: But over and over again, my intellectual friends— they have no conception of this. They can't understand—I mean, it appears ludicrous to them when I say that so-and-so is aristocratic in his image of himself and in the values which he has taken over from the white South. Nevertheless it's true, and some of the biggest snobs that you could run into are some of these poor Negroes—well, they might not be poor actually, they might be living very well—but there are just certain things, certain codes, certain values which they express and they will die by them. And there's quite a lot of that.

WARREN: In Washington I was talking to a Miss Lucy Thornton, in the Howard University Law School, and she's been through the demonstrations, she's been in jail and so forth. She said, "I'm optimistic about the way things are probably going to go here—or may go here—about getting a human settlement after the troubles are over." I asked, "Why?" She said, "Well, because we have been on the land together. We have a common history which is some basis for communication for living together afterwards."

ELLISON: Well, it is true that when you share a common background, you don't have to spell out so many things, even though you might be fighting over recognizing the common identity, and I think that that's part of the South's struggle. For instance, it's just very hard for Governor Wallace to recognize that he has got to share not only the background but the power of looking after the State of Alabama with Negroes who probably know as much about it as he does. Now, here in New York I know many, many people with many, many backgrounds—and I have very often found people who think that they know me as an individual reveal that they have no sense of the experience behind me, the extent of it and the complexity of it. What they have instead is good will and a passion for abstraction.

WARREN: That's a human problem, of course, all the way. It can be special in a case like this, I presume.

ELLISON: It can be special because suddenly something comes up and I realize, "Well, my gosh, all the pieces aren't here." That is, I've won my individuality in relation to those friends at the cost of that great part of me which is really representative of a group experience. I'm sometimes viewed as "different" or a "special instance"—when in fact I'm special only to the extent that I'm a fairly conscious example, and in some ways a lucky instance, of the general run of American Negroes.

WARREN: I encounter the same thing, I suppose, in a way. I've been congratulated by well-meaning friends who say, "It's so nice to met a reconstructed Southerner." I don't feel reconstructed, you see. And I don't feel liberal. I feel logical, and I resent the word—I resent the word *reconstructed*.

ELLISON: It's like this notion of the culturally deprived child —one of those phrases which I don't like—as I have taught white middle-class young people who are what I would call "culturally deprived." They are culturally deprived because they are not oriented within the society in such a way that they are prepared to deal with its problems.

WARREN: It's a different kind of cultural deprivation, isn't it? And actually a more radical one.

ELLISON: That's right, but they don't even realize it. These people can be much more troubled than the child who lives in the slum and knows how to exist in the slum.

WARREN: It's more mysterious, what's happening to him— the middle-class child?

ELLISON: Yes, it's quite mysterious, because he has everything, all of the opportunities, but he can make nothing of the society or of his obligations. And often he has no clear idea of his own goals.

WARREN: It's twice as difficult to remedy because you can't see how to remedy it.

ELLISON: He can't see how to remedy it, and he doesn't know to what extent he has given up his past. He thinks he has a history, but every time you really talk to him seriously you discover that, well, it's kind of floating out there, and the distance between the parent and the child—the parents might have had it, they might have had it in the old country, they might have had it from the farm, and so on, but something happens with the young ones.

WARREN: Do you think there's a real crisis of values in the American middle class, then?

ELLISON: I think so. Perhaps that is what I am trying to say.

WARREN: I think there is, too.

ELLISON: I think there's a terrific crisis, and one of the events by which the middle class is being tested, and one of the forms in which the crisis expresses itself is the necessity of dealing with the Negro freedom movement.

WARREN: Is this why there are some young white people who move into it—because it is their personal salvation to find a cause to identify with, something outside themselves, outside the flatness of their middle-class American spiritual ghetto? Several people, including Robert Moses in Mississippi, have remarked on the resistance of Negroes there to white well-wishers or even courageous fellow workers. One thing, some whites try to absorb arbitrarily the Negro culture, Negro speech, Negro musical terms, Negro musical tastes—move in and grab, as it were, the other man's soul.

ELLISON: Yes, and the resentment has existed for a long time now. But what is new today is that it is being stated, articulated. It is important to recognize, however, that the resentment arises not from simple jealousy over others' admiring certain aspects of our life style and expression and seeking to share them, but because all too often that idiom, that style, that expressiveness for which we've suffered and struggled and which is a product of our effort to make meaning of our experience—is taken over by those who would distort it and reduce it to banality. This happened with jazz, resulting in great reputations and millions of dollars for certain white musicians while their artistic superiors barely got along. Worse, the standards of the art were corrupted. But another aspect of Negro resentment arises because all too often whites approach us with an unconscious assumption of racial superiority. And this leads to the naïve, and implicitly arrogant, assumption that a characteristic cultural expression can, because it is Negro (it's American too, but that's a very complex matter), simply be picked up, appropriated, without bothering to learn its subtleties, its inner complexity, or its human cost, its source in tradition, its idiomatic allusiveness, its rooting in the density of lived life.

WARREN: Grab an apple off the cart and run—

ELLISON: It's like Christopher Newman, in James's *The American,* going over and trying to move into French society and finding a dense complexity of values and attitudes. But to get back to the other point, I'm sure that there must have been quite a lot of resentment even among the Negroes who encountered certain Abolitionists, because they displayed a tendency to use other people for their own convenience.

WARREN: It's awful human, isn't it?

ELLISON: It is, it's awful human.

WARREN: Let's turn to something else. Here in the midst of what has been an expanding economy you have a contracting economy for the unprepared, for the Negro.

ELLISON: That's the paradox. And this particularly explains something new which has come into the picture; that is, a determination by the Negro no longer to be the scapegoat, no longer to pay, to be sacrificed to—the inadequacies of other Americans. We want to socialize the cost. A cost has been exacted in terms of character, in terms of courage, and determination, and in terms of self-knowledge and self-discovery. Worse, it has led to social, economic, political, and intellectual disadvantages and to a contempt even for our lives. And one motive for our rejection of the old traditional role of national scapegoat is an intensified awareness that not only are we being destroyed by the sacrifice, but that the nation has been rotting at its moral core. Thus we are determined to bring America's conduct into line with its professed ideals. The obligation is dual, in fact mixed, to ourselves and to the nation. Negroes are forcing the confrontation between the nation's conduct and its ideal, and they are most American in that they are doing so. Other Americans are going to have to do the same thing. Well, I say "have to"—I don't mean that we're in a position to force anything, except the exertion of—

WARREN: Well, let's say force.

ELLISON: Yes—a matter of pressuring—keeping this country stirred up. Because we have desperately to keep it stirred up.

WARREN: What has been historically proved—not just in America but elsewhere—social change doesn't happen automatically—something has to happen.

ELLISON: One can only hope about these things. We've had the luxury of evading moral necessities from the Reconstruction on. Much of the moral looseness from which we suffer can be dated back to that period. It just seems to follow that you have to learn how to be morally correct and when you have so much mobility, as Americans have, and so much natural wealth, then you come to believe that you can eternally postpone the moment of historical truth. But I think that as a result of becoming the major power in the world, we are being disciplined in the experience of frustration, and the experience of being found inadequate. We're slowly learning that the wealth does us little good, that something more is needed. We're in trouble simply because we've compromised so damned much with events and with ourselves. Something is wrong and it isn't the presence of Negroes. It isn't even the presence of the civil rights problem, although this is an aspect of it.

WARREN: I agree with you immediately that that is not the central fact. But it flows into an American national situation and aggravates it.

ELLISON: The national values have become so confused that you can't even depend upon your writers for some sense of the realism of character. There is a basic strength in this country, but so much of it is being sapped away and no one seems to be too much interested in it.

WARREN: Let me switch the topic, if you will. You know Dr. Kenneth Clark's view of Martin Luther King's philosophy —this will lead us back to the whole question of the nature of violence and nonviolence.

ELLISON: Well, Dr. Clark misses the heroic side of this thing —perhaps because he has an investment in negative propaganda as a means of raising funds with which to correct some of the injustices common to Negro slums. But he seems so intent upon describing the negative that he forgets that there is another side, and in doing so he reveals how much he doesn't know about Southern Negroes. Where Negroes are concerned, the *open sesame* to many of the money vaults in this country seems to be a description, replete with graphs, statistics, and footnotes, of Negro life as so depraved, hopeless, and semi-human that the best service that money could perform would be to stuff the mouths of the describers so that the details of horror could stop. I'm reminded of the Black Guinea disguise in which Melville's Confidence Man blackened his face and twisted his limbs and then crawled about the ship deck whimpering like a dog begging and catching coins in his mouth.

Getting back to King and Clark, I think this—and it might sound mystical, but I don't think so because it is being acted out every day: there is a great power in humility. Dostoevski has made us aware—in fact, Jesus Christ has made us aware. It can be terribly ambiguous and it can contain many, many contradictory forces, and most of all, it can be a form of courage. Martin Luther King isn't working out of yesterday nor the day before yesterday. He is working out of a long history of Negro tradition and wisdom, and he certainly knows more about the psychology of his followers than Dr. Clark. He knows that these people have been conditioned to contain not only the physical pressures involved in their struggle, but that they are capable, through this same tradition, of mastering the psychological pressures of which Clark speaks.

WARREN: Do you mean conditioned by their training or by their history?

ELLISON: I'm talking about the old necessity of having to stay alive during periods when violence was loose in the land and when many were being casually killed. Violence has been so ever-present and so often unleashed through incidents of such pettiness and capriciousness, that for us personal courage had either to take another form or be negated, become meaningless.

Often the individual's personal courage had to be held in check, since not only could his exaction of personal satisfaction from a white man lead to the destruction of other innocent Negroes, his self-evaluation could be called into question by the smallest things and the most inconsequential gesture could become imbued with power over life or death. Thus in situations in which courage appeared the normal response, he had to determine with whom he was involved and whether the issue was as important as his white opponent wished to make it. In other words, he has always to determine at what point and over which specific issue he will pay the ultimate price of his life.

This has certainly been part of my own experience. There have been situations where in facing hostile whites I had to determine not what *they* thought was at issue, because in any case they were bent upon violence, but what *I* wanted it to be. "This guy wants me to fight, most likely he wants an excuse to kill me—what do I have to gain? And am I going to let *him* impose his values upon my life?"

WARREN: To let him determine your worth to you, is that it?

ELLISON: Yes. So, Dr. Clark notwithstanding, if I couldn't love my would-be provocateur as Dr. King advises, I could dismiss him as childish and, perhaps, even forgive him. This, even though at the time I ached to meet him on neutral ground and on equal terms.

One thing that Dr. Clark overlooks is that Southern Negroes learned about violence in a very tough school. They have known for a long time that they can take a lot of head-whipping and survive and go on working toward their own goals. We learned about forbearance and forgiveness in that same school, and about hope too. So today we sacrifice, as we sacrificed yesterday, the pleasure of personal retaliation in the interest of the common good. And where violence was once a casual matter, it has now become a matter of national political significance. Clark regards the necessary psychological complexity of Southern Negroes as intolerable, but I'm afraid that he would impose a psychological norm upon Negro life which is not only inadequate to deal with its complexity, but implicitly negative.

WARREN: Let's go back to what you said a moment ago—you said he lacked a conception of the basic heroism involved in the Negro struggle.

ELLISON: Yes, I'm referring to the basic, implicit heroism of people who must live within a society without recognition, real status, but who are involved in the ideals of that society and who are trying to make their way, trying to determine their true position and their rightful position within it. Such people learn more about the real nature of that society, more about the true character of its values than those who can afford to take their own place in society for granted. They might not be able to spell it out philosophically but they *act* it out. And as against the white man's indictments of the conduct, folkways, and values which express their sense of social reality, their actions say, "But you are being dishonest. You know that our view of things is true. We live and act out the truth of American reality, while to the extent that you refuse to take these aspects of reality, these inconsistencies, into consideration—you do not live the truth." Such a position raises a people above a simple position of social and political inferiority and it imposes upon them the necessity of understanding the other man and, while still pressing for their freedom, they have the obligation to themselves of giving up some of their need for revenge. Clark would probably reply that this is too much to ask of any people, and my answer would be: "There are no abstract rules. And although the human goal of a higher humanity is the same for all, each group must play the cards as history deals them." This requires understanding.

WARREN: Understanding themselves, too?

ELLISON: Understanding themselves, too—yes—in terms of their own live definition of value, and of understanding themselves in relationship to other Americans. This places a big moral strain upon the individual, and it requires self-confidence, self-consciousness, self-mastery, insight, and compassion. In the broader sense it requires an alertness to human complexity. Men in our situation simply cannot afford to ignore the nuances of human relationships. And although action is necessary, forthright action, it must be guided—tempered by insight and compassion. Nevertheless, isn't this what civilization is all about? And isn't this what tragedy has always sought to teach us?

At any rate, this too has been part of the American Negro experience, and I believe that one of the important clues to the meaning of that experience lies in the idea, the *ideal* of sacrifice. Hannah Arendt's failure to grasp the importance of this ideal among Southern Negroes caused her to fly way off into left field in her "Reflections on Little Rock," in which she charged Negro parents with exploiting their

children during the struggle to integrate the schools. But she
has absolutely no conception of what goes on in the minds of
Negro parents when they send their kids through those lines
of hostile people. Yet they are aware of the overtones of a
rite of initiation which such events actually constitute for the
child, a confrontation of the terrors of social life with all
the mysteries stripped away. And in the outlook of many
of these parents (who wish that the problem didn't exist), the
child is expected to face the terror and contain his fear and
anger *precisely* because he is a Negro American. Thus he's
required to master the inner tensions created by his racial
situation, and if he gets hurt—then his is one more sacrifice.
It is a harsh requirement, but if he fails this basic test, his life
will be even harsher.

WARREN: White Southerners have been imprisoned by a
loyalty to being Southern. Now, there's a remark often made
about Negroes, that they are frequently imprisoned, or the
genius of the Negro is imprisoned, in the race problem. I am
concerned with a kind of parallelism here between these two
things.

ELLISON: Well, I think that the parallel is very real. We're
often so imprisoned in the problem that we don't stop to
analyze our assets, and our leaders are often so preoccupied
with an effort to interpret Negro life in terms which sociology
has laid down that they not only fail to question the validity of
such limited and limiting terms, they seem unaware that there
are any others. One reason seems to be that they exclude
themselves from the limitations of the definitions.

Now, we know that there is an area in Southern experience
wherein Negroes and whites achieve a sort of human communication, and even social intercourse, which is not always
possible in the North. I mean, that there is an implacably
human side to race relationships. But at certain moments a
reality which is political and social and ideological asserts
itself, and the human relationship breaks up and both groups
of people fall into their abstract roles. Thus a great loss of
human energy goes into maintaining our stylized identities. In
fact, much of the energy of the imagination—much of the
psychic energy of the South, among both whites and blacks,

has gone, I think, into this particular negative art form. If I may speak of it in such terms.

WARREN: Just from the strain of maintaining this stance?

ELLISON: I think so. Because in the end, when the barriers are down, there are human assertions to be made, whatever one's race, in terms of one's own taste and one's own affirmations of one's own self, one's own way and one's own group's sense of life. But this makes a big problem for Negroes because there's always the dominance of white standards—which we influence and partially share—imposed upon us. Nevertheless, there is much about Negro life which Negroes like, just as we like certain kinds of food. One of our problems is going to be that of affirming those things which we love about Negro life when there is no longer pressure upon us from outside. Then the time will come when our old ways of life will say, "Well, all right, you're no longer kept within a Jim Crow community, what are you going to do about your life now? Do you think there is going to be a way of enjoying yourself which is absolutely better, more human than what you've known?" You see, it's a question of recognizing the human core, the universality of our experience. It's a matter of defining value as one has actually lived reality. And I think that this will hold true for white people. It certainly shows up in the white Southerners who turn up in the North, as with the hill people who are now clinging to their own folkways in the city of Chicago.

WARREN: You are thinking simply of a pluralistic society, without—

ELLISON: Yes, without any racial judgments, negative or positive, being placed upon it. I watch other people enjoying themselves, I watch their customs, and I think it one of my greatest privileges as an American, as a human being living in this particular time in the world's history, to be able to project myself into various backgrounds, into various cultural patterns, *not* because I want to cease being a Negro or because I think that these are automatically better ways of realizing oneself, but because it is one of the great glories of being an American. You can be somebody else while still being yourself, and you don't have to take an ocean voyage to do it. In fact, one of the advantages of being a Negro is that we have always had the freedom to choose or to select and to affirm those traits, those values, those cultural forms, which we have taken from any and everybody. And with our own cultural expressions we have been quite generous. It's like the story they tell about Louis Armstrong teaching Bix Beiderbecke certain things about jazz. It was a joyful exchange and that was the way in which Negro jazzmen acted when I was a kid. They were delighted when anyone liked their music—especially white Americans—and their response was, "You like this? Well, this is a celebration of something we feel about life and art. You feel it too? Well, all right, we're all here together; let the good times roll!"

I think their attitude reveals much about Negro life generally which isn't recognized by sociologists and journalists who consider Negroes powerless to make choices. We probably have more freedom than anyone; we only need to become more conscious of it and use it to protect ourselves from some of the more tawdry American values. Besides, it's always a good thing to remember why it was that Br'er Rabbit loved his brier patch, and it wasn't simply for protection.

WARREN: I know some people, Ralph, white people and Negroes, who would say that what you are saying is an apology for a segregated society. I know it's not. How would you answer such a charge?

ELLISON: There's no real answer to such a charge, but I left the South in 1936. My writing speaks for itself. I've never pretended for one minute that the injustices and limitations of Negro life do not exist. On the other hand I think it important to recognize that Negroes have achieved a very rich humanity despite these restrictive conditions. I wish to be free not to be less Negro American but so that I can make the term mean something even richer. Now, if I can't recognize this, or if recognizing this makes me an Uncle Tom, then heaven help us all.

WARREN: How do you relate this, either positively or negatively, to the notion that the Negro Movement of our time invokes a discovery of identity?

ELLISON: I don't think it's a discovery of identity. I think rather that it is an affirmation and *assertion* of identification. And it's an assertion of a pluralistic identity. The assertion, in political terms, is that of the old American tradition. In terms of group identity and the current agitation it's revealing the real identity of a people who have been here for a hell of a long time. Negroes were Americans even before there was a United States, and if we're going to talk at all about what we are, this historical and cultural fact has to be recognized. And if we're going to accept this as true, then the identity of Negroes is bound up intricately, irrevocably, with the identities of white Americans, and especially is this true in the South.

WARREN: It is, indeed.

ELLISON: There's no Southerner who hasn't been touched by the presence of Negroes. There's no Negro who hasn't been touched by the presence of white Southerners. And of course this extends beyond the region. It gets—the moment you start touching culture you touch music, you touch dance attitudes, you touch movies—touch the structure anywhere —and the Negro is right in there helping to shape it.

*   *   *

In the Introduction to his collection of essays *Shadow and Act,* Ralph Ellison says of his struggle to become a writer:

> . . . I found the greatest difficulty for a Negro writer was the problem of revealing what he truly felt, rather than serving up what Negroes were supposed to feel, and were encouraged to feel. And linked to this was the difficulty, based upon our long habit of deception and evasion, of depicting what really happened within our areas of American life, and putting down with honesty and without bowing to ideological expediences the attitudes and values which give Negro American life its sense of wholeness and which renders it bearable and human and, when measured by our own terms, desirable.

In other words, the moral effort to see and recognize the truth of the self and of the world, and the artistic effort to say the truth are seen as aspects of the same process. This interfusion of the moral and the artistic is, for Ralph Ellison, a central fact and a fact that involves far more than his literary views: for if "truth" moves into "art," so "art" can move backward (and forward) into "truth." Art can, in other words, move into life. Not merely, Ellison would have it, by opening our eyes to life, not merely by giving us models of action and response, but by, quite literally, creating us. For him, the high function of technique is "the task of creating value," and in this task we create the self. For style is the very "instrument of freedom," and in technique lies the "greatest freedom."

This process is a life process—a way of knowing and experiencing in which is growth: a growth in integrity, literally, a unifying of the self, of the random or discrepant possibilities and temptations of experience.

The very paragraph quoted above on the difficulty of being a Negro writer is pregnantly infused with that honesty which it celebrates. We all know, alas, the difficulty of being humanly honest about our feelings. But Ellison clearly means more than that. He means the special dishonesty engendered by what "Negroes are supposed to feel," "encouraged to feel."

"Encouraged" by whom?

By the white world, of course—but also, as he has added, "by Negro 'spokesmen' and by sociologists, *black* and white." But in so far as the Negro writer does have this particular problem of truly knowing his feelings, it means that he has accepted the white man's expectations as his own. It is, then, his own expectation, however derived and even wickedly subsidized, that he must penetrate to the truth. Worse, it is "our" long habit—the Negro's own long habit, however derived and subsidized—of deception and evasion that must be broken before the Negro writer can report "what really happened."

Now, "ideological expediency" would have Ralph Ellison say things somewhat differently. It would prompt him to so slant things that the special problems of the Negro writer would be read as one aspect of the Negro's victimization by the white man. A very good case—in one perspective, a perfect case—can be made out for that interpretation. But Ellison refuses that gambit of the alibi. In various ways, Ellison rejects the "Negro alibi" for the Negro writer. For instance, in the essay, "The World and the Jug," he says, ". . . when the work of Negro writers has been rejected they have all too often protected their egos by blaming racial discrimination, while turning away from the fairly obvious fact that good art—and Negro musicians are present to demonstrate this—commands attention of itself. . . . And they forget that publishers will publish almost anything which is written with even a minimum of competency. . . ."

In regard to the alibi, Ellison is more concerned with the way man confronts his individual doom than with the derivation of that doom; not pathos, but power, in its deepest inner sense, is what concerns him. He is willing, pridefully, to head into responsibility. But in the last half of the same sentence, he flouts even more violently "ideological expediencies" which dictate that the Negro advertise the blankness, bleakness, and misery of his life. Instead, Ellison refers to its "wholeness," its desirability, and elsewhere in the same Introduction he refers to "the areas of life and personality which claimed my mind beyond any limitations *apparently* imposed by my racial identity."

This attitude, which permeates Ellison's work, comes to focus in two essays, which are probably destined to become classic statements,* written as a reply to Irving Howe's essay "Black Boys and Native Sons." Howe's essay takes Richard Wright's work to be the fundamental expression of the Negro genius. The day *Native Son* appeared, he says, "American culture was changed forever. . . . A blow at the white man, the novel forced him to recognize himself as an oppressor. A blow at the black man, the novel forced him to recognize the cost of his submission." Though Howe admires the performance of both Baldwin and Ellison, he sees them as having rejected the naturalism and straight protest of Wright, as traitors to the cause of "clenched militancy"; and then, as Ellison puts it, Howe, "appearing suddenly in black face," demands: "What, then, was the experience of a man with a black skin, what *could* it be here in this country? How could a Negro put pen to paper, how could he so much as think or breathe, without some impulsion to protest . . . ?" And he goes on to say that the Negro's very ex-

---

* The two appeared originally in *The New Leader* (December 9, 1963, and February 3, 1964), and now in Ellison's collection of essays are fused under the title "The World and the Jug." Howe's essay had appeared in *Dissent*, Fall 1963.

istence "forms a constant pressure on his literary work . . . with a pain and ferocity that nothing could remove."*

This, to Ellison, is the "ideological proposition that what whites think of the Negro's reality is more important than what Negroes themselves know it to be"; and this, to Ellison, is Howe's "white liberal version of the white Southern myth of absolute separation of the races." That is, the critic picks out the Negro's place (i.e., his feelings and his appropriate function) and then puts him in it; with the result that Ellison says: "I fear the implications of Howe's ideas concerning the Negro writer's role as actionist more than I do the State of Mississippi." Howe's view is another example of a situation that "is not unusual for a Negro to experience," as Ellison says in a review of Myrdal's *An American Dilemma,* "a sensation that he does not exist in the real world at all—only in the nightmarish fantasy of the white American mind." Howe's attitude represents, Ellison says in "The World and the Jug," a violation of "the basic unity of human experience," undertaken in the "interest of specious political and philosophical conceits." And he continues:

> Prefabricated Negroes are sketched on sheets of paper and super-imposed upon the Negro community; that when someone thrusts his head through the page and yells, "Watch out there, Jack, there's people living under here," they are shocked and indignant.

We must not fall into the same error and take his attack on the white liberals' picture of the Negro to be Ellison's concealed version of the common notion that no white man can know a Negro. By his theory of the "basic unity of experience" and by his theory of the moral force of imagination, such a view—except in the provisional, limited way that common sense prescribes—would be untenable. What Ellison would reject is the violation of the density of life by an easy abstract formulation. Even militancy, if taken merely as a formula, can violate the density of life. For instance, in "The World and the Jug" he says: ". . . what an easy con game for ambitious, publicity-hungry Negroes this stance of 'militancy' has become." He is as ready to attack a Negro on this point as a white man. In a review of Le Roi Jones' study of Negro music, *Blues*

---

* This is, of course, a totally abrupt and therefore necessarily distorted summary of Howe's essay, but the present concern is with the significance of Ellison's response in terms of the principles underlying it.

People, he says that Jones "attempts to impose an ideology upon this cultural complexity" and that even when a Negro treats this subject "the critical intelligence must perform the difficult task which only it can perform."

The basic unity of human experience—that is what Ellison has found; and he sets the richness of his own experience and that of many Negroes he has known, and his own early capacity to absorb the general values of Western culture, against what Wright called "the essential bleakness of black life in America." What he is saying here is not that "bleakness" does not exist, and exist for many, but that it has not been the key fact of his own experience, and that his own experience is part of the story. It must be reckoned with, too:

> For even as his life toughens the Negro, even as it brutalizes him, sensitizes him, dulls him, goads him to anger, moves him to irony, sometimes fracturing and sometimes affirming his hopes . . . it *conditions* him to deal with *his* life, and no mere abstraction in somebody's head.

Not only the basic unity, but the rich variety, of life is what concerns him; and this fact is connected with his personal vision of the opportunity in being an American: "The diversity of American life is often painful, frequently burdensome and always a source of conflict, but in it lies our fate and our hope."* The appreciation of this variety is, in itself, a school for the imagination and the moral sympathy. And for Ellison, being a "Negro American" has to do with this appreciation, not only of the Negro past in America, but with the complex fluidity of the present:

> It has to do with a special perspective on the national ideals and the national conduct, and with a tragicomic attitude toward the universe. It has to do with special emotions evoked by the details of cities and countrysides, with forms of labor and with forms of pleasure; with sex and with love, with food and with drink, with machines and with animals; with climates and with dwellings, with places of worship and places of entertainment; with garments and dreams and idioms of speech; with manners and customs, with religion and art, with life styles and hoping, and with that special

---

* In many places Ellison insists on his love of diversity and a pluralistic society: "I believe in diversity, and I think that the real death of the United States will come when everyone is just alike." (See *Shadow and Act,* "That Same Pain, That Same Pleasure: An Interview.")

sense of predicament and fate which gives direction and resonance to the Freedom Movement. It involves a rugged initiation into the mysteries and rites of color which makes it possible for Negro Americans to suffer the injustice which race and color are used to excuse without losing sight of either the humanity of those who inflict that injustice or the motives, rational or irrational, out of which they act. It imposes the uneasy burden and occasional joy of a complex double vision, a fluid, ambivalent response to men and events, which represents, at its finest, a profoundly civilized adjustment to the cost of being human in this modern world.

Out of this view of the life of the Negro American—which is a view of *life*—it is no wonder that Ellison does not accept a distinction between the novel as "protest" and the novel as "art"— or rather, sees this distinction as a merely superficial one, not to be trusted. His own approach is twofold. On one hand, he says that "protest is an element of all art," but he would not limit protest to the social or political objection. In one sense, it might be a "technical assault" on earlier styles—but we know that Ellison regards "techniques" as moral vision, and a way of creating the self. In another sense, the protest may be, as in *Oedipus Rex* or *The Trial,* "against the limitation of human life itself." In another sense, it may be—and I take it that Ellison assumes that it always is—a protest against some aspect of a personal fate:

> . . . that intensity of personal anguish which compels the artist to seek relief by projecting it into the world in conjunction with other things; that anguish might take the form of an acute sense of inferiority for one [person], homosexuality for another, an over-whelming sense of the absurdity of human life for still another . . . the experience that might be caused by humiliation, by a hair lip, by a stutter, by epilepsy—indeed, by any and everything in life which plunges the talented individual into solitude while leaving him the will to transcend his condition through art.

And the last words of this preceding quotation bring us to the second idea in his twofold approach to the distinction between the novel as protest and the novel as art: the ideal of the novel is a transmutation of protest into art. In speaking, in "The World and the Jug," of Howe's evaluation of his own novel, Ellison says:

> If *Invisible Man* is even "apparently" free from "the ideological and emotional penalties suffered by Negroes in this country," it is

because I tried to the best of my ability to transform these elements into art. My goal was not to escape, or hold back, but to work through; to transcend, as the blues transcend the painful conditions with which they deal.

And he then relates this impulse toward transcendence into art to a stoical American Negro tradition which teaches one to master and contain pain; "which abhors as obscene any trading on one's own anguish for gain or sympathy"; which deals with the harshness of existence "as men at their best have always done." And he summarizes the relevance of this tradition: "It takes fortitude to be a man and no less to be an artist."

In other words, to be an artist partakes, in its special way, of the moral force of being a man. And with this we come again, in a new perspective, to Ellison's view of the "basic unity of experience." If there is anguish, there is also the possibility of the transmutation of anguish, "the occasional joy of a complex double vision."

For in this "double vision" the "basic unity" can be received, and life can be celebrated. "I believe," he says to Howe, "that true novels, even when most pessimistic and bitter, arise out of an impulse to celebrate human life, and therefore are ritualistic and ceremonial at their core." The celebration of life—that is what Ellison sees as the final function of his fiction—or of any art. And in this "double vision" and the celebration which it permits—no, entails— we find, even, the reconciliation possible in recognizing "the humanity of those who inflict injustice." And with this Ellison has arrived, I take it, at his own secular version of Martin Luther King's *agapē*.

*　　*　　*

If, in pursuing this line of thought about Ralph Ellison, I have made him seem unaware of the plight of the Negro American in the past or the present, I have done him a grave wrong. He is fully aware of the blankness of the fate of many Negroes, and the last thing to be found in him is any trace of that cruel complacency of some who have, they think, mastered fate. If he emphasizes the values of challenge in the plight of the Negro, he would not use this, any more than would James Farmer, to justify that plight; and if he applauds the discipline induced by that plight, he does so in no spirit of self-congratulation, but in a spirit of pride in being numbered with those other people who have suffered it.

No one has made more unrelenting statements of the dehumanizing pressures that have been put upon the Negro. And *Invisible Man* is, I should say, the most powerful artistic representation we have of the Negro under these dehumanizing conditions; and, at the same time, it is a statement of the human triumph over those conditions.

5 ❧ The Young

The statistics crowd in from all directions, and the statistics are appalling. Secretary of Labor Willard Wirtz estimates that 350,000 boys unemployed (of the present total of more than 1,000,000) have given up any idea of looking for work, and will be unemployable for the rest of their lives, at an annual cost to society for insurance or institutional guardianship of at least $1,000 per capita. But that cost is small: the real cost is in the loss to society of productivity and in the destructive effect of this group which Secretary Wirtz calls "the outlaw pack." James B. Conant calls this increasing horde of unemployed boys "social dynamite." The massing of "drop-outs" to constitute this "social dynamite" is on the increase, and it is nearer a geometrical increase than an arithmetical one. Secretary Wirtz predicts an addition of over 6,500,000 drop-outs by 1970, and it becomes increasingly clear, year after year, that a drop-out is an unemployable in the making. Of the drop-outs, Negroes constitute a percentage far out of scale to their percentage of population.

There is little reason to be lulled by the fact that the number of Negroes in high school has almost doubled in the last ten years. Every other one will, in fact, become a drop-out—or, as some sardonically put it, a "push-out." In the present tensions of society, all the drop-outs—white and black—are, of course, social dynamite, but for the black dynamite the fuse is already lit. We see the face of that Negro boy in the news pictures of riots, and on TV.

As for those Negroes who do finish high school and thus contribute to the comforting statistics, we may ask exactly how well prepared they are to deal with—not "life"—but simply the ordinary jobs of the modern world. We know what their segregated, or near-segregated, high schools too often are. We know the disorganized, nonverbal, blank environment from which many Negro pupils come. We know the Negro pupil's cynicism about his own opportunities. We know that the lag, which has lengthened every year from the first grade on, between his basic intellectual achievement and that indicated by the national norm, is a handicap which no fine diploma with seals and ribbons can rectify. We know that the Negro (or white) graduate is often little better prepared than the "push-out"; by luck, or the law of averages, the "push-on" merely got pushed on and not out.* He has simply been promoted to vacate the seat for the next victim of the great con game. He has been promoted to misery.

The increasing number of Negroes who attend college, like the number of those graduated from high school, is, at first glance, a comforting piece of statistics. But only at first glance. Of more than 4,000,000 college students in the country, only some 220,000 are Negro—5½ per cent. Of this 220,000 only some 130,000—that is, a fraction over 3 per cent of the total college population—attend integrated institutions outside the South, with California showing the highest ratio and New England the lowest with less than 1 per cent.† These students are, of course, competing with the white students, and are, in the classroom at least, subjected to the same standards. But this cannot be said of the 90,000 Negro students in

---

*U.S. Commissioner of Education Francis Keppel, in an article called "The Pass-Along," reports on the reading skill of the eighth grade of a school in one of the large Middle Western cities: 80% were under the national norm, and over 50% were rated from fifth-grade level down to third-grade level. They had all been promoted—and presumably would be promoted to high school. The real horror of this dawns when we think of the level of the national norm to which the 80% do not reach. (*The New York Times,* January 16, 1964.)

† Many Negroes attribute this low percentage in the North and West to discrimination—even those who themselves are students in, say, some of the better New England colleges. In a recent dissertation, *The Negro Student U.S.A.,* by Tom Rose (unpublished), the claim is made that 70% of all institutions of higher education practice some form of discrimination, and ask for some form of description of the applicant. In the North 33% ask for a picture, a statement of race, or some information that would presumably be relevant to determining race. Some Negro students in Northern colleges complain of the "tokenism." In response to charges of discrimination and tokenism, certain institutions assert—honestly, I think—that they are merely maintaining their academic standards. Whether they should go and seek, and even help to train, promising young Negroes is another question. Perhaps colleges might even give special training after admission.

the Negro colleges. Recognition should be made of exceptions, but in general, and especially in state-supported institutions, the Negro colleges are drastically inferior in competence of instruction, standards of performance, and quality of equipment; and in the South they are inferior by Southern standards. E. Franklin Frazier, the distinguished Negro scholar, has said in *The Negro in the United States* that the average student who enters a Negro college has had little contact with books, and when he enters college "he does not find an atmosphere where educational values of scholarship are highly respected." Even the students from prosperous homes contribute to this intellectual laxness, for "the mass of the student body is generally dominated by non-educational values, cultivated by the children of the business and professional classes," which facilitate social mobility.* The anti-intellectualism is increased by the classroom atmosphere of paternalism and, especially in state-supported institutions, the administrative atmosphere of autocracy. As J. Saunders Redding said, in 1951, in *On Being Negro in America*— a very powerful and remarkable book that should be universally known—this atmosphere "engulfs students, who grow into maturity with personalities habituated to submission and who are likely to believe in the infallibility of the dictatorship principle."

That atmosphere had long engulfed the students in the state-supported Southern colleges, but some at least did not suffocate in it, and paradoxically enough, it was out of a state-supported Negro college that, for all practical purposes, the sit-ins originated. And we find another paradox in the fact that the early student movement largely sprang from the Negro middle class, or from those who aspired to the middle class, the class of which E. Franklin Frazier so despaired. We may have here another example of the submerged and concealed possibilities in Negro life. As Dr. Stuart Nelson, in an interview, puts it: "Of yourself you can't lift yourself out of the situation in which you have been thrown for generations; you tend to yield to it. There comes along, however, a prophet, or there comes along a friend, or there comes along a parent, who says: 'Move out of this!' "

* As for white college students, the Educational Testing Service reports that a survey of 13,000 freshmen indicates that 50.8% give their major interest as social life, extra-curricular activities, athletics, or "carrying on college traditions"—whatever that last may mean. (*The New York Times,* October 29, 1964.)

: 2 :

Izell Blair, now in his twenties, is a slightly built but well-formed, dapper young man, light brown in color, with a slight slur of speech, and a faintly distracted air—as though he is trying to remember something but doesn't want to appear impolite while ransacking his head for it. He is now in the Law School of Howard University. I had heard him speak on the last afternoon of the Conference on Nonviolence, and some months later had arranged a group interview involving him. We sat in a disheveled and none-too-clean basement apartment, with walls calsomined a bilious green. The air was hot and sticky from the bare steam pipes in the ceiling. Some of us sat on chairs, some on a cot, some on a pallet on the floor, leaning back against the wall. We had whiskey and water in jelly glasses or paper cups.

BLAIR: The sit-ins originated, the idea originated with my roommate Joseph McNeil. Right now he's a Second Lieutenant in the Air Force in Texas, but we were all freshmen [at Agricultural and Technical College, at Greensboro, North Carolina]. One day Joe came into the room and he had a disturbed look on his face, and I asked what was wrong, and he told me he had just come from, I think, the Greyhound station in Greensboro, and he asked to get served at the lunch counter and he was refused. So I told him, I said: "You know how things are. It's just been there all the time. There's nothing you can do about it."

WARREN: Was he from the South?

BLAIR: He was also from the South—Wilmington, North Carolina, and he graduated from the Wilmington High School. I asked him, and he said: "Well, we ought to have a boycott." And I said: "A boycott?" And he said, yes, that we should go in and sit down—and he named Woolworth's—and ask for service, and "if they refuse us then we can continue to sit there. And if we're thrown in—we'll go to jail and then we'll ask people not to buy at the place."

WARREN: Then what happened?

BLAIR: Well, we told our friends David Richman, who's from

Greensboro, and Franklin McCain, who's from Washington, and they liked the idea. So in the ensuing week we talked about plans, things like the rights of man and how we felt, you know, about being Negro and what rights we felt should be ours. And finally on January 31, 1960, the night before we went down, Joe came into the room and he asked us were we ready to go. At first I thought he was kidding, so did the rest of us. So Frank was the largest guy in the group, and he said: "Are you guys chicken, or not?" And we said: "No, we're not chicken."

We told a local merchant, in the NAACP. He's always acted as a go-behind, with maybe revolutionary ideas, and most of the students who had served in the NAACP didn't like him because people said he was too much of a radical. We talked to him about the idea and he said he would give us some money to buy articles downtown in Woolworth's, and after we sat in, he would contact the reporters and the Police Department and everything like that. So the scene was set, and around four-fifteen there we were. So that's how the idea started.

Joseph McNeil, it develops, had only one model for his idea, a boycott in Wilmington of a local soda-pop firm that, in a "townfolk show" had neglected to give any prizes to Negroes. The only other "movement" they knew about was in Montgomery. The Greensboro sit-in was, for all practical purposes, their own invention, and it was only natural that they were jealous of it. We may remember what Robert Moses, back in Mississippi, had said of the young Negroes: "Negro students, you know, actually feel this is their own movement . . . this is the one thing that belongs to them in the whole country."

WARREN: CORE came in to back you, is that right?
BLAIR: On the second day we called in the NAACP. Dr. [George] Simpkins, who was president of the NAACP at the time in Greensboro, called in CORE, and Gordon Carey came down and he offered his assistance to our Students' Executive Committee for Justice. At that time we told him that we didn't want any outside organizations to come in be-

cause of what the townfolk might say, that the movement was taken over by outside people. And the next day, Herbert Wright, who was youth secretary of the NAACP, came down; he only gave us more support like "Good luck, we're with you." But Gordon Carey, we understood, had experience with—CORE had experience with sit-ins and so forth. But we passed up both.

WARREN: Some accounts say CORE came in immediately and was accepted.

BLAIR: I was there, and our executive committee went on record as having declined his offer, and he thanked us, and he went on to Durham, I think, the next day.

WARREN: But you had called on Dr. Simpkins. And instead of going to the NAACP, as might have been expected, he called in CORE because he assumed that the NAACP might not be militant enough—that's the interpretation sometimes given in print.

BLAIR: To a certain extent, it's true. I think the Greensboro chapter of the NAACP was sort of written on the blacklist by the national office, after Dr. Simpkins did this, and at a convention I went to in 1960 Greensboro was the last city to be recognized. Oklahoma City was given recognition for starting a sit-in, so we were told, back in '58. We found out later, after we started the movement, that Oklahoma had a similar demonstration. We got a CORE information book and found out that these demonstrations, even though they were NAACP groups, were organized by CORE. But we didn't know anything about it at the time, and so the NAACP tried to write in its minutes at this convention that the demonstrations were spontaneous and were started back in 1958. The organization at that time didn't want to give credit to the Greensboro movement.

WARREN: The national organization?

BLAIR: Yes, and I think the reason was that of CORE—and Dr. Simpkins' actions and our actions, for on February 1, 1960, when we left the store, we were asked by a reporter, were we sent by the NAACP, and we told the reporter no. Although some of us had been proud members of the NAACP in high school, at the time none of us were members.

WARREN: You had repudiated both organizations as far as help was concerned?
BLAIR: We wanted to sort of destroy the old idea that Negroes had to be told everything we do, by the NAACP or CORE.

And that will to independence among the students, not any competition on in-fighting between CORE and the NAACP, is the nub of the matter: to prove the capacity to act alone. We may find it in the attitude of Negroes toward white leadership in any aspect of the Revolution. We find it in the attitude of local Negro leaders toward the national organizations. We find it specifically in the protest, after the Harlem riots, of the United Council of Harlem Organizations at the intervention of Martin Luther King. We find it in the student resistance, as at Greensboro, against friendly adult organizations, against college administrations, and against parents. Sometimes this involves, of course, the garden variety of jealousy, ambition, or rancor, but the constant factor is the will to prove independence.

: 3 :

In the non-state-supported Negro institutions, the rebelliousness against the administration has not, ordinarily, been provoked. For instance, in the midst of the student demonstrations in Nashville, in February, 1960, Dr. Stephen Wright, of Fisk University, issued the following unequivocal statement:

As president of the University, I approve the ends our students are seeking by these demonstrations. From all I have been able to learn, they have broken no law by the means they have employed thus far, and they have not only conducted themselves peaceably, but with poise and dignity. As long as this is true, I have no present intention of instructing them to discontinue their efforts. . . .

It is true, too, that even in state-supported institutions in the South, faculty members have been involved.* But in such cases the adminis-

* As Dr. Wright said to me: "There are any number of teachers who have walked the picket line, some from state colleges—that I know as a matter of fact. And I can't think of a single college community where there has been a sit-in or demonstration where the Negro teacher, particularly the college teacher, has not been involved, and this has been true even in some of the state colleges in the South."

tration of the state-supported institution is always over the barrel if facing a segregationist board or legislature for funds; and to date, no president has been willing to take a firm position and suffer the predictable consequences to his institution—or to himself. Yet in one such state-supported institution in a peculiarly vulnerable position, Jackson College, in Mississippi, I interviewed two groups of students, with several faculty members present and participating, and found free expression of the usual spectrum of opinion, with at least one of the faculty members present perfectly explicit in militant sympathies. And as for the relation to the administration the following bit of dialogue, which took place in the presence of those faculty members, is generally indicative:

FACULTY MEMBER: You don't have the masses of Negroes with you in Mississippi—when I say *you,* I mean the people concerned with civil rights. You don't even have the masses of your students with you.

STUDENT A: You're right. And there's the fear of losing jobs —the chief professional job is the teaching profession, and everybody's afraid. They just decide, "I'll sit back. I agree with you, I'm with you wholeheartedly, I'll give you a donation, but I can't speak out."

WARREN: Is it true that students in this college cannot participate in local civil rights organizations?

STUDENT B: This is not true at all, because I am very active in the NAACP, and I am a student here and I live on campus. The president said that it's perfectly OK if what you do does not interfere with your class attendance.

STUDENT C: I disagree. I have had a personal experience. We went to the President's office here on campus to get his approval on having Reverend Shuttlesworth come to the college and speak to us on an objective basis. And while we were there the President, hearing the name Shuttlesworth, became angry—he became so frustrated that he ordered us out of the office before we had finished talking to him, but nevertheless we stayed on for a moment. After three or four words, he ordered us out again, and still we stayed on. And after that I heard that in a faculty meeting the President raised a question concerning instructors who were instructing their students to do things that were not in order with the college, and he told us in his office that if we were to do anything like that again we would have to be dismissed.

*   *   *

In an interview with students at Southern University, in Baton Rouge, I found the same thing true as at Jackson College, the usual spectrum of opinion and apparent freedom of expression, and here, for a time, a dean was present.

On Malcolm X:

ROBERT WATSON: I think the Black Muslims are here to stay. Malcolm X presents to a Negro a chance to settle his grievances.

On the Meaning of "Integration":

MARTIN HARVEY (Dean of Students): Do you want this black identification or do you want to be lost in the Caucasian population, so there won't be any more brown people?

WATSON: Those who are educated will say, "Just let me acquire my knowledge and let me be a man, let me be hired on the basis of my ability and forget the color." Whereas the least educated will constantly go toward the Black Muslim point of view. But those who are educated—"Let's move toward total integration, into the mainstream."

BYRON SAUCHER: Will you encourage intermarriage?

WATSON: I wouldn't just pinpoint intermarriage, I would encourage one preparing himself and competing—period. Whatever comes as a result of his competitive position, let it be.

DOTTIE DAVIS: I do think a person should retain his identity and there shouldn't be such a hard problem in letting things be open in regard to color.

On the Goal of the Struggle:

WATSON: What am I struggling for? I'm struggling for the heights of a man. Regardless. I think that if I reach the heights of a man in a limited all-Negro society, I have not reached the heights of a man by world standards.

On Black as Alibi:

RITA BARNARD: I think now is the time for Negroes to stop saying, "Because I am black I have a strike against me."

On Martin Luther King:

WATSON: I can partially agree with Dr. Clark [Kenneth Clark on Martin Luther King], because one thing we know about Dr. King is that he is not a great man, but he does have fortitude and stamina—large amounts. And he has worlds of strategy, though he's not exceptionally brilliant. But that is what it takes to be a leader.

SAUCHER: To hear him speak is enough to rouse the emotions. His choice of words, the places where he places the stress—these are the things that arouse people. I dare say if Dr. King had come here [to Baton Rouge] to spearhead the movement, it might have been as great as Birmingham.

On Leadership and Selling Out:

VOICE (unidentified): I had contacts with the students who spearheaded the thing. There was a bit of selling out, and the implications were that they [some of the leaders] were selling out to the administration, and the administration in turn sold out the sellers—do I make myself clear?

On Leadership and the Need for a Unifying Symbol:

WATSON: I did a lot of traveling around the state, helping to establish NAACP youth chapters, and I found that there was a breakdown in the cohesiveness of the leadership, and that one sold the other out, and then he in turn sold the one out, and the discipline broke down and there was no unifying force.

GIRL'S VOICE (unidentified): [To give unity to Negro feeling and action] it need not necessarily be one individual—just one personality—but maybe just personality in the sense that it's something unifying, something individual, so you know what your goal is, and this person can symbolize what you are following.

On Violence:

WATSON: People get tired of being pushed around. It's as simple as that. They say, "Heck, if I have to pick up weapons to defend my nation, why in the devil don't I go ahead and pick up weapons to defend my dignity as a man." And you have to give an ear to this particular point of view.

On Parents:

GIRL'S VOICE (unidentified): It's the general opinion of the younger people [in New Orleans] that their parents are wrong.

*   *   *

As for parents, here is a letter sent by Clarence H. Graham, a student at Rock Hill College, South Carolina. Graham was sentenced to serve thirty days on the York County chain gang, for participating in a sit-in on February 1, 1961.

Dear Mom and Dad:

By the time you read this, I suppose you both will be upset and probably angry, but I hope not. I couldn't tell you but this morning I wanted to, but just didn't know how.

I want you to know that this is something that I really and truly want to do. I just have to. I want you both to be proud of me, not angry. Try to understand that what I am doing is right. It's not like going to jail for a crime like stealing, killing, etc., but we're going for the betterment of all colored people.

You must realize it's time I made some decisions for myself now. After all, I'm almost grown and I do want you both to try and understand this is something that I've thought about very seriously.

Really, I just couldn't be at ease with the rest of my friends and classmates up there and my knowing I should be there too. So try to see things my way and give us, the younger generation, a chance to prove ourselves, please. And most of all, don't worry. Pray for us.

> *Your son,*
> *Clarence**

There must be other letters like this. I know that there are other people like this.

: 4 :

It is not to be denied that, among the young Negroes in general, and students in particular, there is a considerable apathy, indifference, or selfishness. In regard to both national and international politics, a recent study (Tom Rose's thesis, *Negro Student, U.S.A.*) indicates that "most Negro students in the South are almost totally uninformed and without personal involvement."

---

* From *The Student Voice*, the newsletter of the SNCC; reprinted with their permission.

At Howard University, a student at the Law School said to Rose: ". . . the students want to disassociate themselves from the Negro struggle. They feel that they are comfortable, that they don't have to push for anything. 'My father's a doctor, we are comfortable—or a professor and we don't have any worries, we don't want to associate —and anyway we're associating with whites as it is. That's your problem, you work it out, we'll send you some money when you need it.' There were some students from the South there who were working for the cause, but they weren't the kind of outstanding people—either academically or socially—who could be very effective." And of the college students in Atlanta, "George," who had done his undergraduate work at Clark College there, reports to Rose: "Many students participated in the movement just to be participating. Many of them didn't even realize the importance of what they were doing. Some of them didn't even realize the objectives. They would be walking on campus one day, see the gathering, and then join in. But I think this type of participation is representative of any mass participation, any mass activity." And of Negro students in general E. Franklin Frazier (in *Black Bourgeoisie*) has said:

> The second and third generations of Negro college students are as listless as the children of peasants. The former are interested primarily in the activities of Greek-letter societies and "social" life, while the latter are concerned with gaining social acceptance by the former. Both are less concerned with the history or the understanding of the world about them than with their appearance at the next social affair . . . money and conspicuous consumption are more important than knowledge or the enjoyment of books and art and music.

Frazier might, with equal justice, have been describing a large segment of white college students, for, as James Forman said to me: "Negroes are a part of this society, and they're going to accept these values [of the middle-class version of personal success] just as most whites do."

I have heard, over and over again, from Negro students, much the same sort of diagnosis. The majority of them fall into two groups: the "insiders," who represent various forms of the American success dream and who, because of family background or intelligence, have some hope of achievement; and the "outsiders," who without background or ability or any real—or realistic—sense of direction drift through a term or a year or two of college, and then disappear into the blankness and torpor—or into violence—beyond the campus. Even those of ability—especially those in segregated suburbs and colleges—frequently have no way of assessing their own potentiality or the standards they will be required to meet in, say, a graduate or professional school, or in a job. Many sense that, somehow, they live in a dream—or a series of dreams—and they shrink from submitting the dream to the test of reality. It is easier just not to finish school, and thus keep the luxury of the dream.

According to this diagnosis both the "insiders" and the "outsiders" are, for their own distinct reasons, "apathetic" to the Movement. But in considering this indictment, we must be aware that usually the student giving the diagnosis is, in my experience, a militant who is more or less deeply committed to the Revolution. Anything short of total commitment looks like apathy to him—even a student devoting himself ferociously to history or physics is "apathetic"—just as anything short of James Forman's own kind of commitment makes him reach for the term "marginal people." The question of "marginality" occurs again and again among students. In *Columbia College Today* several Negroes express their uneasiness on this matter. Fitzgerald Bramwell, a junior, says, "Most of us are torn by the civil rights demonstrations. . . . To my way of thinking the good I can do picketing seems small beside what I could do with a full education behind me. I like to think that I could be most effective in the Negro cause after I finish my education." And James Alexander, another Columbia student: "I do worry what role I should play in the civil rights movement. I have to work long hours to keep up with my courses, so there's no time left to picket and get locked up in jail." Then he adds: "But then we see white students who do these things for us. This is not entirely a good thing; for no matter how well whites express our ideas, we want to —and should—say it ourselves."

Is it an individual matter?

Sometimes there is a self-contradiction in the testimony. At one moment the committed person makes his complaint about general apathy, but at the next will say that even the students from the "black bourgeoisie" know that they will never be really accepted and therefore have, even though secretly and unacknowledged, a deep

rancor ready to be tapped. As for the "outsider," who does not belong
to the "black bourgeoisie," his frustrations make him ready to hit the
streets. If he can't realize his dream, he can at least avenge that fact.

The number who can, on whatever grounds, be charged with
apathy is not important. Most of the younger people with whom I
have talked, though sardonic about the marginal people, are not
concerned with numbers as such. They have read the books and they
know that social action depends on the "hard core," on the "dedicated
spirits," on tough and realistic leadership.

: 5 :

How fully dedicated are these young people of the "hard core."
We know how dedicated were Michael Schwerner, 23, Andrew
Goodman, 20, and James E. Chaney, 21. The first two were white,
the last Negro, and skin color did not, apparently, make any difference in the way they accepted their risks. And we have the record
for others, black and white, more than we can name. It is the record
of those who have already accepted their risks that gives solidity
to the words of others.

Here are some words spoken in the basement room, with the
scaling plaster of bilious green calsomine, by a group of students
who have long since accepted their risks:

On White Values:

> JEAN WHEELER: I don't think all of the white man's values
> are good for Negroes.
> WARREN: Or for white people?
> JEAN WHEELER: Or for white people. Not such things as
> giving a monetary value for all things.

On Being Southern:

> LUCY THORNTON: Few Negroes would say they are Southern.

On Being Black:

BLAIR: Black is a symbol of evil. Everything that is white is good. If you go to heaven it's in a white gown. If you're an angel, the angel's white. This is the image I faced in growing up in American society. Everything white is pure. So you begin to wonder. You say, "Well, what am I?" You feel you're rubbed out, as if you never existed.

On the Black Man as Regenerator:

LUCY THORNTON: If the black man does in fact achieve his goals, he is actually strengthening the theories on which the nation's founded—also it might strengthen white people, those who are talking in terms of a lost theology or lost ideals, lost goals; in fact, it might even help to reiterate what we once said is the nation's basis for existence.

On Being Hated:

JEAN WHEELER: I have sat in jail and thought, "What is happening? Do all these people hate me that much?" I think it was probably every one of them [every white person] that ever lived [that hated me that much].

On Violence:

JEAN WHEELER: I'm not against violence.
LUCY THORNTON: I've been reading about revolutions, and I'm sort of disappointed because they're not mass things. I think ordinary violence is going to be led, and we're going to be among the leaders—I think there will be a conscious decision to change the tactic. Any large-scale Negro violent movement is going to be organized, it's going to be somebody's fault.

BLAIR: If we have violence, it would definitely be against [the interest of] the Movement, unless there was some aid from countries abroad. Now I don't think we'll get this from Cuba, from Russia, or anybody else. Negroes are pretty much alone in their own country. Violence would not work—except to a limited degree.

JEAN WHEELER: I know that we would be outnumbered, but I say that as soon as you say we're beaten before we start, then the whole—the depth of what you are doing—has been lessened, because you're not willing to take it all the way. Personally, I am willing to take it all the way. If I've got to get shot, then I've got to get shot.

BLAIR: I'm in it all the way, too—if I had no other way to protect my home. I don't read it the same way as Martin Luther King, I read it more from the political standpoint. I think there comes a time when a man has to stand up. If this leads to violence, let it come. As Frederick Douglass said, these people who run away from violence, who want social change, might as well be asking for it to rain without thunder and lightning; it's impossible for crops to grow without rain. It's impossible. Or you can't have the sea without its mighty roar. These things are impossible. And so I say, if violence comes, let it come. I'm here. I'm not going to stay away from it, but I don't advocate the situation.

In saying this last Blair had risen up from the pallet by the wall. He stood there—a not very large, lightly built young man, rather dapper as he pulled his blue jacket straight and drew the wrinkles smooth—speaking in his slurring voice, not looking at us, saying let it come, he was there.

: 6 :

Izell Blair, like many other students, may be ready for violence if it comes, but nonviolent protest is the characteristic method of the students—though not, clearly, of all the young. Presumably the example of Martin Luther King was of enormous importance. As King gave to the Negroes of Montgomery the image that made unity and discipline and dignity possible in the face of violence, so he gave an image to a generation then just entering adolescence and fumbling toward some sense of its role in the world.

One Negro has said that every Negro woman who sees Martin Luther King on a platform, looking, for all his youthfulness and unimpressive stature, so dignified and in command of himself, so well-dressed and graceful, feels that there, somehow, is a son; and more than one Negro, plus some assorted psychiatrists, have said that, for the very young Negro whose own father had probably been powerless or apathetic before the white world, this man who could successfully challenge the white world would become the model, the image of the father-that-might-have-been. In this model, too, there would, presumably, be another element. The young Negro is bound to feel, in some reach of his being, that success in the white world is the real success; and Martin Luther King had not only challenged the white world, he had made a large segment of the white world like it. He was respected by the far-off white world, he was admired, he was an idol, he was on the cover of *Time*.

It was a new kind of success. It combined the best of Joe Louis and Ralph Bunche. It was mass and elite in one package. It was power, black power, but black power revered by the white power that it confounded. So the image was a double one, not only offering a model of aggressive assertion, but a model for public acceptance. The image was, in fact, the answer to the question which Izell Blair had put to himself: "Well, what am I?" It was the image that gave identity. No longer, to use Izell Blair's words again, need you "feel you're rubbed out, as if you never existed." The image gave you a place, a profile, a program, and a promise.

But there is one more element in the image which Martin Luther King afforded the young. It converted the inferior outsider—the Negro stranded in the shallows beyond the mainstream of American life—into the superior insider; for the Negro, by appealing to the fundamental premises of American society, to the Declaration of Independence and the subsequent muniments, puts the white community in the position of the betrayers of the dream. The Negro becomes the defender of the faith for the salvation of all. He not only affirms his right to join society; he affirms his mission to redeem society by affirming the premises of society. He is not only an "old American" in the cultural sense; he becomes, as Stokely Carmichael has said of Negroes, "more American than the Americans." He also becomes, if he chooses to play it that way, more Christian than the Christians, and there are enough professing white Christians left in the country to make this line embarrassing —especially in Mississippi, which is a praying country. So, in either social or theological terms, the Negro can enjoy the superiority of being "the conscience of the community and [can] act out for it the work the community is reluctant to do."*

This notion of the Negro as redeemer is, of course, a cliché of the Movement; it was, of course, developed and emphasized by King himself, from whom, no doubt, the young derived it, but it appears in Farmer, and is common to both the thinking and the rhetoric of Baldwin. Without the theological overtone, it is important for Ellison. But it is easy to see why, psychologically, the idea has such great appeal to the tragic sense of the young, to their thirst for absolutes, to their idealism.

In setting forth that Martin Luther King was the father-image that caught the young, I do not imply that he was alone in having effect, or that his philosophy was without history, or that there was not a social matrix ready to receive it. The people who listened to him in the churches of Montgomery or the pool halls of Birmingham or from TV in a college dormitory lounge had had more than one kind of preparation for his message and his method. The Christian tradition had done its work—even, sometimes, on the young hoodlum with the switchblade. And besides, after three hundred years of white domination, the Negro had learned that he could take, as Ralph Ellison says, a good deal of "head-whipping" and keep control, keep the right to put his own evaluation on his life, to achieve an inner freedom through self-knowledge and self-control. In an interview conducted by Drs. Solomon and Fishman with a student demonstrator from a Northern city we find in slum fighting

* "Nonviolence in the South," by Frederick Solomon, M.D., and Jacob R. Fishman, M.D., read at the convention of the American Psychiatric Association, May 6, 1963, St. Louis, and at the Conference on Nonviolence, at Howard University, November 5, 1963. Drs. Solomon and Fishman call this type of behavior in nonviolent demonstration "prosocial acting out."

a strange school for nonviolence: "When kids on the street want to beat you and pick on you, the natural thing to do is to hit back. But if there are too many of them . . . you'd better just stand there and take it. . . . They may call you a lot of names but it is pretty hard for them to keep beating you up when you aren't hitting back."

At the same time, the Negro had learned a thousand subtle and disguised ways to express his natural resentment—the slovenly broom stroke, the crooked nail, the idiotic "yassuh," the misplaced tool, the Uncle Remus story*—in which the defenseless Br'er Rabbit outwits all the powers, thrones, and dominions arrayed against him. The nonviolent movement has absorbed and readapted all these elements into a complex amalgam of aggression and *agapē*.

But the philosophy of Dr. King does not carry universal conviction among the young. Some young people who have been deeply involved in nonviolent demonstrations are unconvinced of its continuing usefulness. One student, Stokely Carmichael, in summarizing for me discussions with his friends, says that as a mass movement of Negro protest develops there will be no hard core of well-disciplined students to set the model for nonviolence; that as the gains made by nonviolent activities taper off, as some predict, those who had acted out of pragmatic reasons will abandon the method; and that as the novelty and publicity wear off it will be harder to mobilize new people. Furthermore, as the full objectives of the nonviolent movement are unmasked and the effectiveness of the movement's own kind of aggression ("as we push harder . . .") is recognized, many white people who have been sentimentally sympathetic or have been lulled by the idea of an easy solution through nonviolence, will become "alienated." The upshot of the protracted conversations was, according to Carmichael, the question "whether or not Martin and his philosophy could transcend the problems that he would soon have to face. I don't think we came to a conclusion, although my own feeling is that he will certainly have to modify his philosophy."

By all accounts the Deep South, with its closer association with the church and the rural tradition, tends to provide a preponderance of those Negroes (young and old) who accept nonviolence as a way

* For an interesting analysis of this see Bernard Wolfe, "Uncle Remus and the Malevolent Rabbit," in *Commentary*, July, 1949.

of life. Martin Luther King is, of course, from the South, as are many of his associates.* And certainly I have been struck by the number of young Southern Negroes—I have talked with many— who do accept nonviolence as a total philosophy and believe in the "beloved community," that society in which men are reconciled in love. But, clearly, there are a number of very vocal practitioners of nonviolent demonstration who do not accept nonviolence as a way of life, but do recognize the moral value, not necessarily as a means of converting Bull Connor (though, by some accounts, the Birmingham police were actually affected), but as a means of evoking and swaying the moral sense of the uncommitted and the moderate in local situations and, through the national press, that of the general public. As one boy in Tougaloo College in Mississippi said to me: "Morally, it looks better having a nonviolent protest than it does to be waiting in the woods, with a gun and bombs and things to destroy human life." And a girl at the same college: "Most segregationists seem to think that Negroes are really nothing but cannibalistic savages, and if we start fighting this would give them more reason to believe this."

Involved here is the "image" of the Negro as presented to the white world. And there is a large body of testimony to the fact that the dignity of the demonstrators has had its effect on the white world.

* There are, of course, significant exceptions. Bayard Rustin is from West Chester, Pennsylvania. James M. Lawson was born in Pennsylvania, too, at Uniontown, the son of a Methodist minister. He studied at Oberlin and at Boston University as well as at Vanderbilt University Divinity School. While at Vanderbilt he was expelled for his participation in the sit-ins, despite the fact that a large number of the faculty of the Divinity School, including the Dean, resigned, and a number of the members of the faculties of Law, Medicine, and the Physical Sciences were prepared to resign in protest. Mr. Lawson had been a student of nonviolence and a firm believer in the philosophy as a way of life. In discussing with me the speech by Charles Evers at Nashville, he sharply distinguished his views from those of a man who, like Charles Evers or Medgar Evers, "has weapons in his own house," even for self-defense. He was not putting blame, he hastened to say, "but most of us who are involved in this business do not have weapons even in the house— including at least two men that I know of whose lives are definitely marked, and they know it and we know it. Moses is one of them, and Ed King, in Jackson, is the other." He went on to say that some believers in nonviolence as a way of life, even in Mississippi, had disposed of their hunting rifles, to be totally clean. Mr. Lawson is now the pastor of a church in Memphis. He is not to be confused with James R. Lawson, founder of the United Nationalist African Movement and organizer of "Buy Black" drives directed at the economic self-sufficiency of Negro communities.

Here is one piece of testimony from the *Richmond News Leader,* an editorial of February 22, 1960, concerning the then current sit-ins:

> Many a Virginian must have felt a tinge of wry regret at the state of things as they are, in reading of Saturday's "sit-downs" by Negro students in Richmond stores. Here were the colored students, in coats, white shirts, ties, and one of them was reading Goethe and one was taking notes from a biology text. And here, on the sidewalk outside, was a gang of white boys come to heckle, a ragtail rabble, slack-jawed, black-jacketed, grinning fit to kill, and some of them, God save the mark, were waving the proud and honored flag of the Southern States in the last war fought by gentlemen. Eheu! It gives one pause.

It does, indeed.

Another practical, rather than moral, argument for nonviolence is that even if violence is acceptable morally and is workable in the present context, it would make reconciliation and the creation of a practical society almost impossible in any foreseeable future. This notion, of course, can be connected, at times, with the notion of the Negro as the "redeemer" of society, the vicarious sufferer who will bring on the "beloved community." But the argument can be taken on simple pragmatic grounds, as one more point on the spectrum.

At the far end of the spectrum there are those who refuse, in any sense, to be the keeper of the white man's conscience. As Ruth Turner, of the Cleveland CORE, says: "I'm not saying that the Negro should be a suffering servant for the American conscience." For some people, nonviolence is about as much a way of life as it is for the gipsy boy Pablo in Captain Marryatt's *The Children of the New Forest:* "Yes, Missy Edith," Pablo says to his instructress in Christian charity, "you tell me all that and so I do; I forgive pussy 'cause she bite me, but I kick her for it."

For such people forgiveness is only pro forma; and nonkicking becomes merely a technique, a device that has no intrinsic moral significance, though it may be used to exploit the moral sense of some segment of the public. It is thought of as a necessary device for a minority of relative powerlessness, but a device to be laid aside as soon as power, in any other form, is available.

For power is the key. But there are two questions. First, what is the nature of power? Second, how do you gain it? So the debate about the nature and function of nonviolence, which, according to many informants, is constant among the students—and among many others of the young—is really a debate about power: about the relation of physical and spiritual power.

The fact that power is the key becomes shockingly clear when Martin Luther King, who is committed to spiritual power, admits the appeal that Malcolm X, and his vision of physical power, has for him. Ruth Turner says that in moments of depression she has to fight off the temptation to turn toward the Black Muslims. And Lolis Elie, of the CORE chapter of New Orleans, told me that he sees little hope, that he had begun to read Black Muslim literature.

How could things be otherwise?

In the debate among the young on violence against nonviolence, there often emerges the question of the effect, not on the movement or on the future of society, but on the individual. For some the public appearance in a nonviolent demonstration is a proof of personal courage—and this has a special importance in the South, where the Negro sometimes suspects, sometimes with justification, that the old notion that the Negro is a coward, can't take it, "can't face the cold steel" (to use the old Confederate formulation), is still afloat. Charles Evers, for instance, sets store by the fact that the new Negro demonstrates courage and in so doing wins respect, however grudging, from the Mississippi white man, who, presumably, is bred to put that virtue at the top of his list; and though Mr. Evers is speaking of the Negro in general the notion might apply with special urgency to the young who are trying to find their place in the world.

And the Reverend Kelley Smith, who was one of the most important figures in the Nashville sit-in and boycott in February, 1960, says: "Courage has met great respect. We have some interesting stories to tell here. Like the night the two boys, one white, one Negro, were going back in the paddy wagon together—the Negro boy talked to him and before they got to jail the white boy was sorry, he felt guilty and wrong."

It is interesting that Mr. Smith has put the respect for courage as the cause of this reconciliation; other interpretations are possible.

But there are more subtle, deep, and complicated effects on record. Drs. Solomon and Fishman, in the study already referred to, report that many young demonstrators speak of a "strange calm" that is experienced just before a great test or risk. Sylvia Davis, a student at Tougaloo College, at Jackson, Mississippi, said to me, after remarking that anybody can fight, that "it takes a person who has strong emotions to really withdraw from this"; and this sense of power in one's own control—of a calm and a detachment— is what, over and over again, is said to be a peculiar personal achievement, and prize.

But there is not only risk, there is pain and injury to be confronted. When I asked one group, which included several activists of Tougaloo College, about the psychological effects of violent experiences nonviolently accepted, one young man said: "Take for example that demonstration I was in. I was beaten to the floor, and it didn't bother me. No—not psychologically. There was no frustration or anything like that. I was completely normal afterwards. I was completely normal, and—well, for my part it has given me personal strength, I think, to—well—withstand things—emotional things —that I would get upset about emotionally—it seems to have helped out some."

And here, after some discussion of Kenneth Clark's criticism of King's philosophy, is an interchange:

WARREN: Well, do you think this practice of nonviolence is creating "an intolerable psychological burden" for you— making you mentally sick?

BETTY POOLE: It possibly is. Maybe I'm taking my aggressions out on members of—well, John Dollard says that Negroes take out their aggressions on other Negroes.

WARREN: The Saturday-night fight?

BETTY POOLE: Right. But I don't do this. Maybe I take it out on myself—I don't know. But I really do agree with King, I want to achieve integration through brotherly love.

UNIDENTIFIED BOY: If this brings psychological confusion and frustration would you be willing to make that sacrifice so that the generations after you would live in a better society?

BETTY POOLE: It wouldn't be possible to have a better one if we achieved integration through violence.
UNIDENTIFIED BOY: But I mean by nonviolence.
BETTY POOLE: Yes—yes, indeed.
UNIDENTIFIED BOY: Even with physical injury *and* psychological frustration?
BETTY POOLE: I really would.

This same girl, who had been on a freedom ride "all the way from Mississippi to Tampa, Florida," tells of her sudden involvement with the Movement: "I was in a situation once where a boy was beaten up. I wasn't in the Movement and this is what brought me to the Movement. I saw this boy fall to the floor in nonviolence, and it touched me somehow, and from then on I was very active."

"It touched me somehow," she says, and more than once we get the record of this *suddenness*, this *somehow*. When Stokely Carmichael, who is very intelligent, subtle, and introspective, came back from Mississippi, where he had been on the first freedom ride, he could not define the nature of his own experience: "I had everybody on my back, calling me, asking me why, why, why—people from all over the country—and I couldn't answer why, and I still can't answer why."

And another student told me that "really seeing the problem"— seeing nonviolence before his eyes—was the way "I had to find myself, and I couldn't let one person be beaten while I stood around and did nothing." And a girl telling of her first march in a demonstration: "I marched with the people—we were headed toward town—and really, at that moment it wouldn't have mattered to me what happened, even—I felt I was ready to give my life." And she added: "I thought this nonviolent movement was all we had."

"Finding oneself" or being "un-selfed"—is it the same thing?

* * *

Dr. Stephen A. Wright, the President of Fisk University, who has had considerable opportunity for observation, said to me: "Some fulfill themselves through their adoption of nonviolence as a philosophy and a way of life. I've seen young people, who, for example, come to believe in this, undergo all sorts of things. And those that I've had a chance to talk with in depth, I think are better people, by virtue of this. Here I can speak with some degree of authority; not as an authority but as a layman, of what I have seen. I may not have had psychological insights of sufficient depth into the neurotic effects on certain people, but some have developed their poise, they have decided for the first time in their lives that something is worth sacrificing for, and sacrificing for in personal terms."

: 7 :

Ruth Turner was born in Chicago, attended public school in that city, was graduated from Oberlin with a major in German, went on a scholarship to the Free University of West Berlin, and then took an M.A. at the Harvard Graduate School of Education. She taught school briefly in Cleveland, Ohio, but is now a full-time worker for CORE, at the very center of the Negro Movement in that city, which has lately had a violent history of race relations. She is in her middle twenties, a rather small, delicately formed young woman, of dark brown color, with a calmness of manner which is sometimes belied by a sudden intensity that comes over her pleasant face. She wears glasses.

I talked with her in one of the rooms of the CORE headquarters in a decrepit apartment house. The room where we talked had dilapidated straight chairs and a big table cluttered with papers and odds and ends. To one side was the open door to an abandoned kitchen.

When I asked Miss Turner how she had left teaching and become a full-time worker for CORE, she said that "Birmingham brought about the rather sudden decision," that she "could no longer continue teaching German in a time like this." As for Cleveland, she says that there is now "a polarized community by virtue of the fact that a vacuum has been created in the white community through apathy, and that vacuum has been filled by people who would rather scream Communism than address themselves to the real grievances that lie behind the protest now." The outlook for the immediate future is, in her word, "bleak."

The apathy, as she calls it, exists in Cleveland in spite of the fact

that there has been very forceful support from many of the clergy—
a fact dramatized when the Reverend Bruce Klunder was crushed
to death by a bulldozer. She admits that this is a strange situation
—that in Cleveland a courageous body of white "leaders" have not
been able to break the apathy, or to have any political effect, or
to instruct in the meaning of the Negro Movement those people who
seem to be polarized against it but who might welcome a chance to
"re-think their position." At the same time that she deplores the
absence of a liberal, malleable sentiment, she comments on
"liberals":

RUTH TURNER: We have had quite a bit of discussion about
whether the people who are involved in our Movement are
liberals. We think that perhaps another word is more appropriate.
WARREN: You want to save the nasty word for other people
—is that it?
RUTH TURNER: We would call them the "white committed,"
and we feel that their role is a very strong supportive role.
There is a definite role for the white committed person, the
person who is willing, as the Reverend Bruce Klunder was,
to lay down his life. There certainly is a role for that person.

And here we have again the old question. A person like James
Forman or Ruth Turner, who is fully committed, has a natural
contempt for the white person (or black) who is not willing "to lay
down his life." (Although for Malcolm X, even that total commitment is unacceptable as a token of good faith.) Yet, at the same
time, in talking about those who need "to be given a second chance
to think over their position," in talking about white leadership that
might change the climate of opinion and instruct the apathetic or
hostile in the meaning of the Negro Revolution, Ruth Turner is
pointing to the crucial position of the very person who, at the best,
would have to be called by that nasty word *liberal*, but more likely
by that truly horrid word *moderate*; for that person, though no
philosopher or hero, is the citizen who must cast the vote for the
decent mayor, or vote for the right bond issue, or accept an open
enrollment plan, or not panic when a Negro family moves next
door. This is one of the sad basic facts of political life in a democ-

racy; you have to live with people whom you regard as marginal, and who, as marginal, may merit your contempt—but who have power. It is hard, sometimes, for heroes to grasp the fact.

Perhaps if they did grasp this fact they would no longer be heroes. And the world cannot do without heroes.

*   *   *

The Reverend Bruce Klunder was acting in a "supportive role" when he was killed. He was participating in a demonstration, aimed at preventing the construction of a new school that, it was alleged, would further segregation. When Klunder, to stop the operation of a bulldozer, flung himself down behind the machine, he was merely acting on the order of a Negro who was serving as combat officer. The driver of the machine—whose name, by the way, was White— drawing back from a group in front, and not seeing Reverend Klunder, crushed him. It was, you might say, an industrial accident.

As I sat there in the grubby room, Ruth Turner and David Cohen—a friend and active white CORE worker who teaches history at Cleveland's Case Institute of Technology—almost forgetting my presence it seemed, began to go over the event. The dead man had been their friend, and the widow was their friend, and you could tell now that this conversation was not new; it was an extension of a painfully unresolved conversation that had been going on for weeks. How did the ideal values relate to the brute human fact? That was the question, or one of the many questions, that made Cohen burst out: "What was he dying for, then? He wasn't dying for free-dom or anything else then, he was just crying out, 'I'm hurt, I'm hurt and dying, get me to a hospital.'"

Then, more calmly, Cohen said: "We can go on asking the question from now on until the day we die—whether his death was in vain or not in vain, and whether the ideal of this Movement was in some sense in concert [with the event]. But there is the ideal of preserving life—his life, which was very much worth preserving."

And then Ruth Turner said: "We are not in the position to de-cide one way or the other. That was a matter of fate and we ac-cepted the results of that and interpreted them. I mean, we are not, and we did not put ourselves, in a position to decide for Bruce."

And he: "There's more to it than that, because in a sense we did help to decide what would happen to him, even though, you know, tracing responsibility is a very tenuous business. We did help to decide what happened to him and that's what we all felt—and I think probably still feel to a certain extent."

But she had, apparently, settled the matter in her own way, in her own soul. She had written off the human cost. As she had, no doubt, long since written it off for herself.

I asked her if she had been present at the event.

RUTH TURNER: I didn't see it, but I was at the scene at the time.

WARREN: I understand that you did a great deal to quiet the mob at the time of the attack on the driver of the bulldozer.

RUTH TURNER: Well, that occurred around three thirty or four o'clock, when the construction had stopped and the policemen were attempting to send the mob home, and we knew they were angry—they were justifiably angry—they had been provoked considerably by the actions of the police that day. And yet we felt there was no cause to be served at that point by exploding there in the community. We attempted to send them home.

WARREN: The attack on the bulldozer driver—that occurred immediately?

RUTH TURNER: Yes—and it was not a mass attack. There was one young man who went—who became hysterical after seeing the Reverend run over.

WARREN: Only one person?

RUTH TURNER: That's right—in a bodily attack. There were some sticks and stones thrown at the police too, but in attacking the driver there was only one person involved.

WARREN: Was that the way the press reported it?*

RUTH TURNER: No, it wasn't. *Time* magazine carried a deliberate distortion.

WARREN: You saw the event with your own eyes?

---

* According to newspaper men, stones and other missiles were thrown at him. Wes Lawrence, of the Cleveland *Plain Dealer,* tells me that the driver, White, was so shattered by the killing of Klunder that he did not feel he could ever operate another machine.

RUTH TURNER: This was reported to me by eyewitnesses. There was one person who attacked the driver—a young man who went berserk.

WARREN: Did any sticks or stones find their way to the driver?

RUTH TURNER: Not to my knowledge—most were thrown at the policemen.

WARREN: Could you imagine the situation where this explosive violence which you helped to stem could serve a useful purpose?

RUTH TURNER: This is the whole purpose of nonviolent demonstration and protest action. We try to channel justifiably intense feelings of people who have lived under this system—try to channel them in ways which will be creative and bring about constructive changes.

WARREN: I notice—again from *Time* magazine—that Mr. Lolis Elie, of CORE, in New Orleans, says that if violence now comes there, he will take no steps to curb it.

RUTH TURNER: I think there's a point at which the curbing can no longer be done. I feel that it is primarily the duty of the law-enforcement agencies to curb violence. I feel we should take those steps that we can, but I'm also realist enough to know that if wide-scale violence breaks out I would no longer be in a position to curb it, and I think this violence has to be seen as an expression of tremendous frustration that has built up over a long period of time. No one person can stop it.

WARREN: What should the cops do?

RUTH TURNER: The police, if they behave in other places like they do here, are unfortunate tools of a power structure which has failed to understand the dynamics of protests, and not understanding anything about the people with whom they deal, have not been able to deal with the situation in any constructive way. That's why police brutality takes place, and of course, police brutality breeds more violence. I feel that, clearly, the police ought to step in to prevent loss of life and limb, but they should not be there to prevent loss of life and limb on one side only, as had been the case. At

Murray Hill, where a mob rioted—a white mob, I'm happy
to say—the police made no attempt whatsoever to curb them.
This exemplifies the double standard of the police.

*   *   *

On Ethnic Complications:

WARREN: I understand that here much more is at stake than
a mere white-Negro collision, that it's Italian-Negro and
Polish-Negro, for instance.

RUTH TURNER: This is quite true, that we have in Cleveland
ethnic pockets which jealously guard their own traditions
and their view of doing things. Often this way of doing things
runs counter to the mood and progress of the entire community, and this, of course, complicates the situation.* But
I don't think it can be said that these people are responsible
for the violence. I think white ordinary Americans who don't
belong to those ethnic groups will respond the same way if
challenged.

WARREN: But the challenge now is to, say, the Polish and
Italian enclaves?

RUTH TURNER: Through the education issue the challenge has
been primarily at those pockets.

* Elsewhere, in regard to ethnic enclaves, Miss Turner says that the Italians,
and presumably the Poles, "offer the example that sharing in more than one
culture does not necessarily broaden. In fact, their knowledge of their origins
seems to contribute to a sense of inferiority because they are not quite
American (or so they feel). These feelings of inferiority contribute to their
feelings of insecurity and sense of being threatened by other groups such
as the Negro community. Hence their reaction is to go the WASP Americans
one better in dealing with other minority groups." This analysis would raise
two considerations: First, it might be only an attack on the concept of the
society enriched by a continuing of its pluralistic base—it "does not necessarily broaden." (But in the interview she questions the value of the melting
pot). Second, it questions the value of a sense of historical identity among
minority groups—say the Italians, Poles, Jews, Irish—a sense which the
Negro, it is often said, does *not* have, and which the Muslims, for instance,
try to create synthetically.

WARREN: Is this an unfortunate necessity, or would there have been ways to avoid this collision?

RUTH TURNER: If the commitment of the School Board was to city-wide integration and to plans to bring it about, I don't think that these ethnic groups would feel as though they are selected and isolated, that this would be something to involve the West Side as well.

WARREN: They feel they've been discriminated against, is that it?

RUTH TURNER: I guess that's their feeling, yes.

On Negro Enclaves:

RUTH TURNER: My supposition is that if all the barriers were lifted, Negroes, after having the experience of equal opportunity, would still choose to live together.

WARREN: Because there was nothing to prove?

RUTH TURNER: That's right.

On the Older Generation:

We now have a generation markedly different from the generation that preceded. That's like talking about my father. He was a hard worker, he struggled to raise a family of five, and was so engaged in the struggle for survival that he could not give attention to problems which he felt deeply about and met every day. But he made it possible for me. There is a certain backlog of security which our parents did not have.

On "Freedom Now":

"Freedom Now"—this is perhaps one of the most frustrating experiences for someone who is committed to it— is to a certain extent relative.

On the Melting Pot:

The melting pot has had a pretty homogeneous and un-interesting flavor to me. It has become a gray mass of medi-ocrity, and I reject the melting-pot idea if it means that everybody has to come down to the same standard.

On Liquidating Injustices:

It, the Revolution, is liquidating injustices. I don't think these injustices are carried necessarily by a particular class of people in this country. Although it is quite true that the wealthy are in control, I don't think the problems to be solved are in liquidating the wealthy, but in changing the socio-economic system which permits these injustices.

On Martin Luther King:

WARREN: Do you think that Dr. King's influence in the North is now waning?
RUTH TURNER: I do, because I do not feel he addresses him-self to the basic problems that Northerners are in a better position to grapple with than Southerners. He is not polit-ically aware and sensitive. I don't think he's a politician, nor does he think like one. I think you have to [think polit-ically], because we are playing, in a sense, a game of power, and we have to understand the dimensions and implications of it.

On Regeneration of the Country:

Those who concentrate on integration have much too nar-row a goal, because the basic issue is restoring to this country—no, implementing for the first time—economic justice, social justice, political justice.

On Symbolism:

There are all kinds of symbolisms—black sheep and white sheep—yes, it's very clear, and in fact it was possibly done purposely at some time.

On Blackness and Beauty:

A tiger or a panther is appreciated for his blackness, but a Negro woman is not. Negro girls are not encouraged to participate in beauty contests, because somehow being black does not mean that you're a candidate for beauty.

On Myrdal's Scheme for the Reconstruction:

WARREN: Supposing that Myrdal's scheme would have worked—would have given us a decent society by, say, this time—would you accept it?

RUTH TURNER: It's so difficult here in our Movement to plan from one week to the next—no, I'm just saying the complexity of the issue is such that you can't give an on-the-spot answer.

WARREN: But we are assuming that there had been, as a consequence, a decent society—all coming out beautifully.

RUTH TURNER: I question that it would all have come out beautifully.

WARREN: But that is the term on which the question is put.

RUTH TURNER: In so doing [compensating for slaves and for expropriated land] you would re-enforce the slave-owners' attitude about the Negro, that he was something that was property.

WARREN: I didn't state the question that way.

RUTH TURNER: You ask me if I would compromise my ideal for the end result?

WARREN: There are two different ideals that compete——your end desire for a decent society and your desire not to compromise, in any way, your notion of the Negro's dignity as a man?

RUTH TURNER: I know it. I really just can't answer, because you're making assumptions that—

WARREN: But I'm entitled to do that in terms of the game —to set up the terms hypothetically.

RUTH TURNER: But your making assumptions means that I can't answer the question.

WARREN: Does this mean that you find it too painful to answer? A real split, is that it?

RUTH TURNER: That's right. That's about the best assessment of it. It's too painful to answer the question—and it's also—the relevant premises are not agreed on.

*   *   *

Ruth Turner is not alone in this feeling. Vernon Jordan, a graduate of DePauw University and of the Howard University School of Law, a member of the staff of the Southern Regional Council, says: "This was one of Lincoln's theories—that they [slaveholders] ought to be compensated. This nauseates me." Even when I press the question:

WARREN: Let us suppose that Myrdal's plan had been put into operation, with compensation, etc., and had worked— that long before now all our race difficulties had been reasonably solved. Would you still prefer things the way they are now—with no compensation having been paid to slaveholders?

JORDAN: I expect so.

WARREN: You'd rather have it the way it is?

JORDAN: I expect so, and that's a kind of a hard thing to say.

*   *   *

On Hate and Hope and Despair and Love:

RUTH TURNER: Hate and hope? I would say that in the particular movement in which I am involved, hate doesn't have much function. Hope does. Despair does—if you're acting on despair with hope—acting on frustration with hope. None of us really have time to hate. It's too all-consuming. Similarly, we don't have time to love, not in any intense, personal way.

WARREN: You mean in the ordinary sense of personal attachment?

RUTH TURNER: That's right.

*   *   *

Ruth Turner is an idealist, and she knows the anguish of her role. If she were set in Cordelia's shoes, facing the foolish, vain old man, would she change the story?

: 8 :

Stokely Carmichael was brought by his family from Trinidad to Harlem in 1952, when he was eleven years old. Now twenty-three, he is tall, of fine athletic build, quite dark, with well-modeled features. His manner is calm, with occasional streaks of ironic humor, often self-humor. He was graduated from Howard University, with a major in philosophy, in June, 1964. He will continue at least another year as a full-time activist in Snick, for he feels he is needed, although he has the offer of a full scholarship in one of the best colleges, for supervised reading and advanced study in whatever field might interest him.

In Trinidad, some ninety-six per cent of the population had been Negro; all immediate authority—police, teachers, ministers, civil servants—and the storekeepers and entrepreneurs in general were Negro. The four per cent white population lived in "mansions," but then many Negroes lived in "mansions" too, and the question of exploitation of the black by the white had not occurred to the boy. In America all was different. Immediate authority was white, and the storekeeper was white. His parents, who had no friends among the Negro Americans and saw only West Indians, said that in America Negroes were "unambitious" and pointed to the number of West Indians in Harlem and Brooklyn who owned their own homes, while American Negroes "do not own anything except a Cadillac."

They had a profound distrust of all white people, too. But, in the complexity of things, the father aspired to escape from the ghetto into "a good neighborhood"—which meant white. They finally succeeded in moving to the East Bronx, "an old Italian neighborhood balanced by a Jewish neighborhood and an Irish neighborhood." Here they were the only Negroes. The first week the boy had a fight: "Everybody had heard Negroes were tough and they wanted to see how tough I was."

Now in the nice neighborhood, he had to prove "all the bad things" to prove his point: "By the time I was in the eighth grade I knew all about marijuana, and pot. I had heard from my cousin but never touched the stuff, but now some friends from school wanted to show me how to do it. Before I knew it, I was putting on a demonstration for about thirty people in the bathroom—how to blow up."

The white friends of the new neighborhood had long since taught him "the tricks, how to break into stores, how to steal cars," but his parents still touchingly held to the belief that they were, at last, in a "good neighborhood," and the son did not disillusion them.

In the good neighborhood they owned their own house—"a shack," but the father spent long hours after work remodeling it. He was a man of prodigious energy and honesty, a carpenter who was "always being screwed by the union" because he didn't believe in giving a bribe to the union representative to get assigned to work. He was ambitious, and after regular hours was moonlighting as a taxi driver or at other jobs. In the winter, when carpentry was slack, he was a seaman. He aspired apparently, in some devious way, to white middle-class standards. At the same time he kept the old distrust of whites, and when the son brought white friends home, the parents would ask: "What's your social life going to be? They don't really accept you." In the old tension of values, the father wanted the son "to be respectable, speak, do all the things the white kids were doing." But the son, who was keeping ties in Harlem as well as with the local white kids, had his own tensions; as for doing what the white kids did, and talking like them: "I wasn't sure I wanted to do all that." For one thing, at this stage anyway, the boy "never dated but two white girls. It seemed that there were too many barriers and too much conflict to be bothered with."

By 1956 he was in the elite Bronx High School of Science. Here he found out that "people do more than fight each other, they didn't swear, and were respectable, and read a lot, good books, and discussed these things at the lunch table." It was hard, he says, for him to adjust; but even though he still went out to do a little gang fighting, he worked hard, because his mother kept saying: "Remember one thing, those guys are white, they'll all make it, and you won't unless you're on the top." So he read—"to get her off my back," and she "didn't care what I read as long as my grades were good."

At the same time, he was discovering how inadequate his "intellectual background was." He didn't know who Marx was or about dialectical materialism, and his fellow students told him about relativity and Einstein, who, he thought, was only an old nut who went out in the sun with an umbrella: "My parents never finished school, we had no intellectual background. All these students' fathers had been Harvard, Yale, doctors, dentists, Ph.D.'s. They had what I didn't have, but I tried to develop my own—just beginning to read as quickly as I could, anything that anybody mentioned. It was naïve at the time, but it was sincere."

He was repairing the deficiencies in his background, and one way was to associate with a "lot of people on the Left, young Socialists." He began reading "on the Left," too, studying social problems. His parents had always wanted him to be a doctor, but he had no inclination for that, and he "just let them assume." He was being told at school that he would be "a brilliant Negro leader," and he says: "I thought I was going to be brilliant, I was going to solve the race problem."

In Bronx Science there were only some fifty Negroes out of two thousand pupils. But, he says, everybody was his "best friend," and he was always invited to parties; they leaned over backward because he was a Negro. As for one party: "on Park Avenue with a friend of mine, I think he's in Yale now, he invited me, he kept asking me. So I went to the party, and was very impressed with the place, doorman at the door, and the elevator went up and opened on the living room, sunken living room, open fire, stereo all over the place, rugs about that thick. Never seen this before, only in the movies."

When his friend's mother came in, he insisted that everybody meet.

her, especially Carmichael: "I didn't particularly care to meet his mother, I was so fascinated with the place. He was living on about the fifteenth floor, and I was looking out the window, just enjoying myself being there. But he insisted and I thought I would appease him. Well, his mother had a group of ladies there, and it was like I hit it off right away. She said: 'Oh, I've heard so much about you, you've got such a sense of humor, Jimmy is always talking about you, you're such a good-looking boy, what features you have . . .' and on and on. Finally, when I was leaving, the door was just about closed, his mother turned to the other ladies and said, 'Oh, yes, we let Jimmy hang around with Negroes.' I didn't like that."

Nor did he like a lot of other things: "It was a continual thing, everybody would ask me, 'Whose party are you going to? We'll be there.' And 'Oh, you dance so well'—when I can't dance. All the stereotypes were carried over leaning backward. Everyone telling me how well I could sing—when I can't carry a tune. All the stereotypes, and what a good sense of humor."

But he is inclined to think that there was some sincerity mixed, maybe they really wanted to be his friend, and not merely the friend of "the Negro." But he resented being taken as a type and not a person.

Meanwhile he had his own way of exploiting the white condescension. For instance, whenever there was a racial conference, he was "always consulted as the spokesman"—the "brilliant Negro leader," as he ironically describes himself: "I went out to the NSA conference. I took the floor and said just any ridiculous thing, you know, about Negroes, about the race conference. Here were students from all over the country, and they would never have attacked me no matter what I said, because I was a Negro. The whole thing is shifted so much, if you're a Negro and among a white group, you're good, you're great, you're—but I am sure you know Negroes are bastards, too. But you know, I was good no matter what I did."

But a crisis had come as early as the summer after freshman year at Bronx Science. That year he had been trying to cut himself off from his old associations, both those of the tough white neighborhood and those of Harlem, but in the summer he slipped back into the old pattern: "I stayed in New York City and hung around with all the fellows—the gang—stole cars, gang fighting, and all that nonsense. By about the middle of the summer, I kept thinking, 'I'm going to get into real trouble if I keep this up.' So I started alienating myself from them. And I started calling up people from Science, started to hang around with them more, and go swimming, play tennis. Of course, all my old friends would call me fag. By about the middle of the sophomore year I had completely broken all the old ties."

All in all, there was a deep conflict of loyalties, one that was, in various forms, to continue. Here is a passage on "integrity," "identity," the "psychic split":

CARMICHAEL: I used to hang out down in the Village, because that's where everything is happening. I used to see a complete reverse of the usual—white kids jumping into Negro neighborhoods, becoming Negro-fied. "Yeah, man—yeah, baby," you know, everything out of context, just dropping words that come from Negro neighborhoods. I always thought, "This isn't right," and I wondered if I went into the white world, wouldn't I do the same thing. That bothered me quite a bit, because I didn't want to do that.

WARREN: You thought you would lose integrity, is that it?

CARMICHAEL: I wasn't sure if it was a loss of integrity, it was a loss of being yourself.

WARREN: Your identity being betrayed?

CARMICHAEL: Yes—like Negroes and whites, teenagers dance entirely differently. Now I've danced both ways, and I find myself, at a party for instance, beginning to Lindy—now Lindy, I don't know if it's still around, is probably a white dance. Negroes slop. And when everybody would start looking at me, they said, "You dance just like a white boy." And then I'd stop, and catch myself, and I'd say, "Yeah, I do." And they'd say, "You hang around with them white kids there?" And I said, "Yeah, I hang around with white kids." And they said, "Man, you ought to be square, don't know what's happening." Then I'd go to a white dance and do a slop, and, "Oh, man, that's cool! That's real cool, show me how to dance!" You know, leaning over backward.

Then I wondered whether or not, in Harlem, they were being completely fair when they said I was square when I was hanging around with white kids. That was an internal conflict. I resolved the problem with myself just going wherever I wanted to go. If I felt like going to Harlem, if I felt like going down to the Village, I'd do what I wanted to do. But there certainly was a cutting off of culture.

WARREN: Several Negroes have told me that white students coming into Mississippi to work in voter registration sometimes try to assume vocabulary and stances that are Negro, and that this is resented, or if not resented, it becomes a matter of satire. Have you encountered this?

CARMICHAEL: Quite a bit. There are a few white people in the Movement who are what we call completely Negrotized. But there's still a difference; you can tell people who come into the Movement and try and say there is no difference. Also, the other conflict, you get Northern whites, all committed to equality, on a humanitarian and intellectual level, but they themselves don't know a Negro, they don't even have Negroes in their own neighborhoods, have never known a Negro. They don't know a Negro is really different. When they come South and find out that it's different, they jump right in, to accept it.

WARREN: To assume the culture without understanding the experience behind it?

CARMICHAEL: Right. Then they say things without realizing what they're saying. You know—"Yeah, man, I really dig that," and *dig* can be used in two ways, sarcastically a lot of times. They use words out of context. They want to be accepted right away, without being accepted for their work.

WARREN: Social climbing?

CARMICHAEL: That is it. They want to be accepted as a Negro, not as an individual. "Look, I'm not like the other whites you know, I dig you." Snap their fingers out of tune: "I dig Ray Charles." Once a white fellow came in and started playing Ray Charles. "Ray Charles," he said, "he's swell, man, too much!" And after he walked out, one of the Negroes, out loud, said, "You know that white boy don't even understand, 'cause Ray Charles play like white boy don't

even think." And everybody laughed. The white boy putting
on a show was resented. As much as it would be resented if
I put on a show to show how white I was—how much I had
absorbed the culture.

WARREN: How commonly do you think the Negro may accept
some derogatory stereotype of himself?

CARMICHAEL: At one point—I was about a sophomore in
high school—I realized that I was really ashamed of being a
Negro. I was really ashamed of it, and would stop saying
things that I would say in the Negro neighborhood, and I was
afraid of Gospel music, which I had always liked. I remember
thinking about that for two weeks, and then I decided to go
back to my Gospel music.

WARREN: How common do you think this is?

CARMICHAEL: It's very common, because whether Negroes
admit it or not, they are one hundred and fifty per cent
American. They think, they act, they accept America without
even questioning it.

WARREN: Including the white man's version of himself—the
Negro?

CARMICHAEL: Including that, I'm afraid. Because you're not
sure how much truth there is in it, if you really want to be
honest. You have to admit if you walk through Harlem, it is
about the dirtiest place, there're always drunks on the street,
people are always cutting each other, there are prostitutes on
every corner, bars on every corner, and you want to be careful that you're not just rationalizing. You start off with the
basic premise that Negroes aren't really inferior, and you
wonder, have the conditions really been thrust upon them, or
are they—the Negroes—really lazy? This bothered me for a
time too. But you do accept it unconsciously.

WARREN: What is the psychological solution?

CARMICHAEL: For me it was to read as much as I could to
show—maybe I do it even now, I think I still do it—as soon
as I meet a white student I want to prove to him that he isn't
any smarter than I am. This is what Baldwin talks about in
"The Black Boy Looks at the White Boy": play a game of cat-
and-mouse, let's see how much you know, because I know
you think that because I'm a Negro I don't know very much,

and I'm going to prove to you that's not true. You see, I even
caught myself playing this last September. I met a white boy
from Yale, and kept playing the game. Then I caught myself:
"What do I have to prove to him? Why am I doing it?"
WARREN: In other words, you were acting like the Yale boy
who goes to Mississippi?
CARMICHAEL: Yah, yah—in the reverse.

Carmichael's original involvement with the Movement was not
immediate. It did not come out of the undefinable force that later put
him in the freedom ride. In 1960, he happened to pick up the paper
and read about "Izell Blair's Four Companions." His first reaction
was that the sit-in was the wrong way. He threw the paper down.

WARREN: Why this reaction?
CARMICHAEL: Actually what I said was, "Niggers always
looking to get themselves in the paper, no matter how they do
it." My opinion was that they didn't know what they were
doing, and I'm convinced now that they didn't know what
they were doing.
WARREN: You mean they stumbled on it?
CARMICHAEL: Yeah. About three weeks later, *The New York
Times* documented that the sit-ins had spread all over the
South. My reaction was: "Niggers are just like monkeys—one
do, all do." Threw the paper down again. About a month
later TV interviews began to appear. I'd heard students from
A and T, students from Greensboro, and I was distressed
about this—you know, you don't want a revolution, you want
to be intelligent. At the same time you can't just talk about
how badly you've been treated; I get tired of seeing that stuff
all the time. By mid-April I thought there were possibilities.
In May, 1960, I met a number of people who were involved in
the sit-ins.
WARREN: You were still in high school then?
CARMICHAEL: Right. I went on a sit-in in Virginia. Very impressed with the kids, their courage. I had always been
oriented to the Left, from an economic point of view—not an
economic determinist but certainly a great proclivity for that
sort of thing. And now I realized that a lot of the kids weren't

talking about what I thought they would be talking about.
They said—"We have the right to human dignity."
WARREN: This, as opposed to an economic approach?
CARMICHAEL: Right.
WARREN: You mean a human approach, a moral approach?
CARMICHAEL: It seemed to me this is euphemistic, I think
men always cover up their actions with moral issues. So I
began to think seriously whether this was an economic problem or whether these students were right, whether nonviolence
and love was the thing. I never took the approach we've got
to teach them to love us. I thought that was nonsense, from
the start. But I was impressed by the way they conducted
themselves, the way they sat there and took the punishment.
WARREN: You mean not just by their fortitude, but by self-
discipline and personal power, inner power?
CARMICHAEL: Right. I was really impressed, because when I
lived down in Harlem, I learned, you know, that you don't
get tapped on the shoulder without turning around.

Carmichael had already begun, in any case, to drift from the Left.
He had begun to feel that the Communists who expected the Negroes
to start a civil rights revolution which could be developed into
"The Revolution" weren't really sincere about Negroes, "were just
trying to use Negroes." And he made no sense out of any Communist
attempt to outline a program. The first dip into the sit-ins had shaken
his economic theories; and now he elected Howard University, even
though he didn't want to go to a Negro university and "wasn't sure
that Howard could give me a good education," because there he
could keep working in the Movement.

In December, 1960, he went, in fact, down to Fayette County,
Tennessee (where James Forman was also working), and there received further confirmation of the courage and moral force of people
involved: "I was cold, hungry, and freezing, the ground was hard,
when it wasn't hard it was muddy, ankle deep. And the kids would
go out and chop firewood, then come back and sit around and sing
songs in the evening—a very, very moving thing."

Then came the freedom ride. He knew that this was serious. He
had seen violence, had seen "what people can do to people." In his
old neighborhood in New York, "five guys could jump on someone

and beat him up, and I was sometimes the victim of that." So he knew that the ride was serious: "Do I really want to put myself in a position where I can die?" He got rid of that by saying: "Well, somebody will die, but it won't be me, it will be the guy next to me."

So he went. He saw a mob. He was arrested. He heard a chief of police tell him: "You're not going to change anything, we'll keep throwing you in jail, we'll beat you, and furthermore, those people will kill you." He was released, made it to Jackson, and confronted the mob there: "one old lady in particular, she was about seventy years old, shaking a cane viciously, just trembling all over, and I just kept looking at her, not because I wanted to antagonize her, but because I really couldn't believe this."

People in the mob yelled, "I'll kill you, I'll kill you!" Carmichael had been threatened before, but for once he really believed it. "I wondered whether I really thought these people meant it or whether I was scared because I was in the South." He stared at the faces, holding his hands up to keep from getting cigarette butts in his own face: "And I kept thinking, why, why. A naïve question, but it's something that still comes back, because you can't find the answer to questions that bother you—really a problem."

He, with his group, was in the City Jail of Jackson. There the other Negro prisoners thought the riders were "great, you know—heroes." On the night before they were to be removed to Parchman, the penitentiary, the jailer came and held on to the bars, to talk:

WARREN: What kind of a man was he?

CARMICHAEL: An old man, early fifties, believed in the Southern way of life—whatever connotation that brought him—but he was an honest man, and he thought at first that we were just a bunch of troublemakers, we were Communists, and so forth, and he was going to rule with a ruthless hand. We'd still keep singing, when he'd say not to sing. And after a while it became a little petty game, you know. He'd do certain tricks to try to keep us in line, and there'd be soup for a meal one day, and let's say there were about thirty of us in there. He would pass thirty hot bowls of soup, with about three spoons, you know. So if you were at the end of the line, you'd just have cold soup. All these simple little things.

But he found out that we wouldn't break. Then he got so

that he'd even joke a little, and laugh, and he'd say, "You gonna be here for a long time." And then we'd say, "Yeah, but you gotta be here with us, don't forget that."

But I think we got to respect each other. Anyway, I got to respect him. After a while, the respect grew. And we got to respect each other very well, sort of. It grew because I respected him as a man, you know, forgot that he was a white Southerner, that he was my jailer.

Well, it came that we could really talk—you know, about issues—and he'd tell us about what we didn't understand about the Southern way of life. Of course, he'd say the same stereotypes, of Negroes being treated well, and so forth. We finally came to some understanding, I guess a sort of unspoken understanding. I found out a lot from him about Mississippi and the way of life, you know, how he used to go fishing with Negroes, and so forth. He thought it was on an equal footing. I didn't think it was an equal footing. I don't know, it might have been, it's something that bothered me.

But anyway, the night we were leaving, he came to the bars, and he held on, very, very tightly, you know, and all of a sudden he started talking about his life, and started talking about his maid. "Annie was good," he said, "she brought up and raised all my five kids, and we loved Annie dearly." A deep introspective thing, about how when Annie died the whole family cried, how they went to Annie's funeral. Every year he places a wreath on Annie's grave. And he wanted us to understand that we were all wrong, about race relations in the South. That they were really very good, and gonna be better, and the Negroes really liked it that way.

But he was shaking, visibly shaking, and he said that we had our points of view as far as he was concerned, and he had his. He didn't want us to try and change them, he was gonna keep his way of life, he believed in God, and he believed in the way of the life of the South, he believed in human beings for what they were worth. He started crying. Tears dropped. And finally he said: "I want you to know that whatever happened to you, you know that you caused me a lot of trouble." He said, "I can't go along with the trouble you caused me, but you're still human beings, you have your beliefs, and

I have mine." And he left. I thought about that for a long time. Everybody else felt that he was just putting on a show.
WARREN: I doubt it.

* * *

On Black Nationalism:

I knew Malcolm X and I told him, "You keep your talk, and you can say what you want, I don't even think you put me in a better bargaining position, you know, because you don't say anything."

On Goodbye to Liberals:

Everybody is afraid to attack him [Malcolm X]. The funniest thing was an article by Loren Miller, on the West Coast, vice president of the NAACP. An article in *The Nation* called "A Farewell to White Liberals," which was a ridiculous article. He got hopped up with this Black Nationalism, and said goodbye to white liberals—"We don't need you—you don't do anything for us." The NAACP put out reprints and passed them all over the country. Ridiculous. When they were attacked by Malcolm X, instead of standing their ground, they absolved him, and said, "We're friends." You know, people just jump on bandwagons.

On Being an Opportunist:

I don't think he [Reverend Galamison] is a very intelligent leader. If you're really serious about it, it seems to me you've got to think about whether or not you're opportunistic. It bothers me a lot. If I see my name in the paper, I'm not sorry it's there. When you write me and say you want to interview, I'm not sorry, I sort of feel good. That's one of the things you have to be worried about. The trouble is that you get an opportunist, and he becomes a rhetorician, he says things that are going to appease people, he's not going to really look for solutions.

On Busing into Harlem:

I've worked in Harlem and I know the schools, how the schools are. We have the poorest teachers, the schools are run down, and so forth. I'd agree [with protesting] if you were to dramatize that [situation]. But now when you bring in the question of busing kids, it seems to me you're being unfair, because I think—let's face it—Harlem is no picnic ground, you know. It's not a bad neighborhood just because white folks get beat up—because Negroes get beat up in the neighborhood, too. Negroes get beat up in Harlem all the time, so just because you're white and get beat up, it doesn't mean that all the Negroes are beating up white people. But it's a bad neighborhood—let's face it—whatever conditions produce it. And you can't really and truly ask anybody to send their kid in there.

On Nonviolence and on Conversion:

I think the issue of nonviolence is very important in the question of solving certain things, but it's not true that it necessarily brings us closer together and makes us love each other. It does in certain cases, I'm not going to deny this.

Eddie Dickerson, from Cambridge, Maryland, a white fellow, two years ago, dragged me off a stool, and kicked me in the stomach about seven, eight, nine times. Really gave me a good roughing up. One of the roughest times I've ever spent was at the mercy of his hand. The same night he came back to church, apologized, said he was sorry, and started working in the Movement. Last summer, he was the fellow— a white owner was smashing the eggs over his head, the white restaurant owner, and kicking—he was the same fellow. He joined. We sent him to New York to CORE, and CORE gave him some sort of nonviolent training.

On Bob Moses and a Mississippi Episode:

There were three cars, the men in the cars had guns hanging out of the windows. George started off driving. Bob asked
why he was driving so fast. George said: "God dammit,
Moses, we're being chased." Bob looked back and could see
the headlights. He said: "Well, they won't bother us." And
Bob turned over and went to sleep. James and I were scared,
and Bob went to sleep.

On the Debt to the Negro and Communal Guilt:

It's a drip from the Muslims, you know—you owe us dues.
I don't know that anybody owes me anything. I can't hold
you guilty. And I don't want you to hold me guilty. For what
my father did.

On "Freedom Now":

It's a funny thing—if you just ask somebody what they
mean by "Freedom Now."

*   *   *

Stokely Carmichael is now a veteran of many campaigns. He has
spent the crucial summer of 1964 in Mississippi. But he remembers
his first visit to Mississippi. He remembers Parchman, which was
tougher than the Jackson jail, and remembers Sheriff Tyson, who
made it tougher. He remembers, in fact, a number of things:

I can go on freedom rides, with people around me, and I can
say, "Oh, yes, nothing is going to happen to me, it will be
the guy next to me." But when you get alone, and you're sitting on that stool by yourself, and somebody's behind you,
and you hear the knife clicking, hot coffee being poured down
your back, and you're alone, you really begin to feel, "Why

am I here, when is it going to end?" But just before that first punch, just before you get hit, that little period there just before, when tensions are building and you can't control your stomach, and it's jumping, you start thinking over and over again, "You know, maybe this is the way it is, when you're really alone." When you really want to sit down and talk to people, when you really got to say, "Let's just sit down and talk this out, Sheriff Tyson, just me and you, and let's see, you know, where we go from here." And you say, "Why can't I sit down and talk with Sheriff Tyson?"

: 9 :

Ruth Turner, Stokely Carmichael, Izell Blair, Lucy Thornton, Jean Wheeler, Betty Anne Poole, Byron Saucher, Dottie Davis, and all the others—there are many of them. There will be more.

There will be many more, and with their coming something else will happen. There will be a great release of energy. That energy now must spend itself against blank negation—like Sheriff Tyson—and against resistance that does not even know itself to be resistance. Suppose that that energy could be creatively directed—as it certainly will be some day directed—against those resistances that the human condition proposes, and not against resistances that human beings, tragically, think are the human condition. History has seen such moments when energy, long suppressed, has suddenly found a way. We sometimes look back on them as great ages.

*   *   *

: 10 :

One recollection: At Jackson College, in one of my group interviews, there was a silent lad named William Lucky. At the very end of the interview one of the teachers present asked him which Negro leader he most admired. After a little, when he still couldn't answer, the teacher demanded: "Well, which one would you rather be?"

He managed to say: "I'd rather just be William Lucky."

6 ✖ Conversation Piece

Somewhere back in the mind of many people there is an image of *the* Negro leader—a glare-eyed robot propelled by a merciless mechanism to stalk forward over the smiling landscape, where good clean American citizens (including well-adjusted Negroes) go happily about their constructive business. Many of us who are white— in our moments of stereotype and cartoon thinking—share that vision. In those moments we do not realize that there is, in one sense, no Negro leader. There are, merely, a number of Negroes who happen to occupy positions of leadership.

A number of those Negroes, some of the best advertised, did not seek such positions; neither their training nor temperament nor aspirations had seemed to point in that direction. Robert Moses, sitting in the graduate seminar in philosophy at Harvard, would scarcely have been dreaming of the hot, straggly street of Liberty, Mississippi, and the knife handle splitting his scalp. Gilbert Moses wanted—and wants—to write and direct plays. Ruth Turner was a teacher of German. James Forman, who wanted to be a novelist, said to me that he wished he could be talking about something other than the Revolution—that he wished the whole thing were over. The young Martin Luther King, with the be-ribboned and be-sealed sheepskin, proclaiming his new doctorate, to hang on the wall of his study in his first parsonage, could not well have foreseen the Montgomery Improvement Association, the cover of *Time*, and the Nobel Peace Prize.

The whirl of history created a vacuum, and they were sucked in.

Some of them have, indeed, found in leadership a natural fulfillment. Here the unsuspected talent and the unsuspected self have blossomed, and it is no crime for a man to feel at home with, and take pleasure in, what he can do well. Nor is it necessarily a crime to seek leadership. The will to power, grisly as it appears in certain lights, can mate, if uneasily, with love of justice and dedicated self-lessness. Even in the bloody in-fighting among Negroes (usually well screened from the prying eyes of white folks) more may be at stake than organizational aggrandizement or personal vanity; principles and policies may be involved, too. And one should not, in fact, be too ready to risk an *argumentum ad hominem* in dealing with, even, the most ambition-bit demagogue bidding for fame, or some pathologically compulsive headline-grabber. On any particular issue, they may be right, after all.

One should not, in other words, be appalled by the human complications. Certainly, one should not be more appalled by complications among Negroes than by those among white people. Regardless of complexion, social movements are always powerful magnets for some of God's more peculiar creatures; and it would, on second thought, seem only natural that, in California, a group of self-styled space-travelers claiming the planet Venus as their point of origin should have—as was rumored—applied for a charter from CORE. If it seems natural that the Movement should have attracted the space-travelers, it is certainly natural that it should attract its quota of self-anointed prophets, spiritual DPs and deviants, sufferers from footless ambition, masochists, blood-lusters, and common pilferers from the poor box. What is remarkable is that it has attracted so few —or that so few have risen to the threshold of public mention.

In general, the Negro leadership has given the public little reason to be appalled, for in a situation as complicated as this it would not be easy to imagine a higher level of idealism, dedication, and realistic intelligence. If leadership of that quality is supplanted by other, less savory types that are already lurking in the wings, and that certainly do not have any vision of a reconciled society, the white man has only himself to blame. Mayor Wagner had only himself to blame if his European vacation, in the summer of 1964, was cut short by riots in Harlem and Bedford-Stuyvesant; everybody knew there would be riots (except perhaps the Mayor), and everything he did afterwards by way of appeasement or amelioration (including the trip to the White House to beg money) could have been done before hand and as part of a program that would have inspired the Negro community to some hope and confidence. Then, if there had been disorders, the issues would have been more clear-cut: looters would have been looters and not liberty-looters. If now in Mississippi—with no convictions for the Neshoba County killings —terrorist organizations, like the Russian nihilists or the Stern Gang of Palestine, emerge among Negroes, then white people must, at one level, hold themselves responsible. Such a romantic, ruinous, and desperate gesture is, as we have said, one of the possibilities implicit in the situation. In reference to such a gang of "dedicated retaliators," the Reverend Galamison says: "I refuse to advocate violence as a principle, but almost all oppressed people have had such a group that will retaliate in kind, and this might serve some kind of purpose in bringing about a swifter resolution of a problem that exists." How delicately the issue is here balanced!

Whitney Young is right when he says that the leaders need victories in order to contain the danger of overreach and to forestall violence; they need something solid and negotiable in the Negro power market. If in the summer of 1964 they had had something a little more solid and negotiable, James Farmer of CORE and John Lewis of Snick *perhaps* could have strung along with Wilkins and the others in proclaiming a pre-election moratorium on demonstrations. But under the circumstances, Farmer certainly could not risk it, for, in the spring of 1964, following a policy of sweet reason, he had put himself on the defensive in repudiating the stall-ins; so, at the time of the riots and after, he had to insist on a stance of militancy or feel the jerk as the wild boys snatched the rug out from under his feet. If Farmer found himself forced to adopt the new stance, the white people helped force him. They had given little reason for the Negro to believe that they would surrender anything except under pressure. As the Reverend Galamison put it, there was the fear that LBJ would go Right if he thought he had "the Negro people in his vest pocket."

But in any case, the Negro leaders know enough about power to know that power frozen is not power. Maneuverability is of the essence, and at no time can the white man expect Negro leadership to go into a catatonic state just for his convenience. As for the division between the leaders on the matter of the moratorium, it reflected the logic of the unstable situation. It had seemed clear for a long time that the fate of the Negro Revolution is associated with the Democratic Party, and it seemed clear in July, 1964, that more riots, or disturbances of any kind, might give aid and comfort to Goldwater; therefore the position taken by King, Rustin, and Wilkins was logical. But the position taken by Farmer and Lewis had its own logic. Such a policy would keep the white man unsure of the price tag attached to the moratorium. Always the element of threat—ultimately the threat of violence, or at least of breakdown—is behind any effort at social change; if King and Wilkins held out the olive branch, Farmer and Lewis, slightly in the background, fingered the length of lead pipe. The tableau could have been arranged by Machiavelli; but in actuality it was, as we have said, inherent in the moment, and inevitable.

The proof of the pudding is in the eating, and the real point about the generalship of Farmer and Lewis is how, after they had reserved for themselves the assets of flexibility and threat, they actually did use that power. They kept control, for they, as much as King or Wilkins, knew what was at stake politically, and had as little inclination to throw out the baby with the bath.

* * *

Negro leaders have, we can be quite certain, a sense of power, and they are willing to apply it when and where it pinches. For power is the key. What the Negro hasn't the power to get he won't get. But power—as both Negroes and whites need to remember—may operate in more than one dimension.

A number of Negroes, feeling the new headiness of power and not bothering to reflect deeply on the dimensions in which it may operate, think of a physical showdown in the streets as their big threat. According to the survey in *The Negro Revolution in America* by William Brink and Louis Harris, some fifty-two per cent of all Negroes think that if things came to gut-fighting the Negro would win, and in the Northern slums the percentage is higher. "You give a Negro a good sharp knife," Brink and Harris quote one remark as typical, "and he can get him ten whites any day." But among the leaders the survey by Brink and Harris can discover only twenty-nine per cent who feel that in a showdown the Negroes would win; and I am certain that almost all of that twenty-nine per cent would be leaders in very low echelons. The leadership, aside from any theological or moral convictions about nonviolence, is realistic. As the Reverend Ralph Abernathy put it, "The white folks have more guns." And he might have added that they have more votes, more money, and more education.

Power in the absolute sense—as the showdown, even the showdown short of gun point—is not for the Negro. Negro leadership, including even Malcolm X, knows that it is concerned with *relative* power, and that the art it must practice is the art of picking the spot where a little pinch will hurt a lot. For instance, in 1948 the Negro vote was significant, and in 1960 actually elected a President. A Negro boycott might not do decisive damage to a Cadillac agency in Atlanta (and then, again, it might), but it would certainly bring howling to his knees a distributor of malt beverages in that city. The art is the art of locating the vulnerable point, and there are many kinds of vulnerability.

There is another aspect to the art of applying relative power. We may call it the art of application in context. A man may say that he is a hard-core segregationist. But how hard is that core? Is it as hard as his love for, or need of, money? As his desire to have his children educated? As his preference for social order? As his wish to be respectable? As his simple inclination to stay out of jail? The only real hard-core segregationist is one whose feeling about Negroes takes precedence over all other feelings mobilized in a given situation. For instance, the feeling for segregation among the parents of Prince Edward County, Virginia, took precedence over their desire for education for their children. But when parents in some other Southern communities, say Jackson, Mississippi, band together to keep the schools open despite integration, though it is probable that those same parents would prefer to have the schools segregated, their desire to have a school takes precedence over the desire for segregation. In other words, in all sorts of subtle and shifting combinations, Negro leadership is committed to playing a most complicated tune on the strings of white desires, and convictions.*

And the string the harpist touches most often, sometimes lightly, sometimes with an authoritative *whang*, is the white man's desire to be a just man, or his conviction that he is a just man. For few men are willing to say: *I am unjust.*

* See Howard Zinn, *The Southern Mystique,* Alfred A. Knopf, 1964; and Thomas F. Pettigrew, "Social Psychology and Desegregation Research," in *American Psychologist,* 1961.

To state it differently: By and large, the Negro leadership is con-cerned with relative power. But there is one kind of power Negro leaders feel they have which is not relative. It is moral power. For by the American white man's own professed standards the Negro is in the right, and enough white men know it to create a climate in which the Negro can proceed with his nonviolent Revolution. Imag-ine how well a Jewish sit-in would have worked in the climate of Berlin in 1940.

: 2 :

Let us return to that specter of the Negro leader as the gigantic glare-eyed robot. He does not exist. There is, instead, at all levels, an enormous variety of personality and talent among the individuals who are Negro leaders—plural. There is also an enormous variety of attitudes and policies. Here is a list of topics, drawn from my interviews, on which there is significant disagreement:

1. The nature of integration.
2. The probability and/or desirability of ethnic concentra-tion after the barriers are down: the relation to political power.
3. The Negro as "redeemer" of society.
4. The "specialness" of the Negro: the white man's incapac-ity to "understand" the Negro.
5. The "psychic split" of the Negro.
6. The nature and efficacy of nonviolence; its relation to "power."
7. The problems of "legitimate" and "illegitimate" demon-strations, with and without specific targets.
8. Techniques and methods of pressure beyond demonstra-tions.
9. The danger of "overreach."
10. The problem of unity and centralization.
11. Civil rights and legalism versus economic emphases.
12. The communal guilt of the white man.
13. The "debt" to the Negro: special privilege, preferential treatment, etc.

14. The problem of "Negro personality."
15. The "third phase": self-improvement.
16. The problem of Negro history and propaganda: delusion?
17. The obligation of the Negro to society.
18. The obligation of the white man to society.
19. The role of the white man in the Revolution.
20. The relation of the Negro problem and the poor-white problem.
21. The relation of the Negro problem and white labor.
22. Schools.
23. Christianity.
24. Historical "process" and "Freedom Now": historical "process" and moral evaluation.

This list is incomplete. The topics are not all on the same level, and some overlap others. They are not arranged in an order of importance. All are important, and some are of crucial importance.

They constitute, as it were, a seamless garment. It is clear, for instance, that a Negro's conception of integration would condition the techniques of action to be employed; or that his attitude toward the notion of the Negro as "redeemer" of society would condition his notion of integration; or that his theory of the relation of historical process to moral evaluations would, again, condition his choice of techniques for action.

If there is no consensus on such important questions, what are the consequences?

It is clear that mere drift would doom the Revolution to a dwindling failure or a blood bath. It is not at all certain that improvised tactics and ad hoc solutions of immediate difficulties would lead to a much happier conclusion. For one thing, the floundering consequent upon such a lack of philosophy would deflate one of the proudest boasts of the New Negro—that he, for once, can set the terms on which the question of his fate will be treated. Furthermore, the floundering of the Negro leadership would invite, in the white reaction, similar floundering, similarly disastrous. And, perhaps worst of all, the lack of a philosophy would invite the adventurer to try his hand with either a technique of overreach or a "cult of personality."

But what is to prevent drift or confusion?

We must recognize that the option does not lie between drift and confusion on one hand and an ironbound, brass-studded orthodoxy on the other. Fortunately, a number of Negroes in key, or influential, positions are men of intellectual power and depth of purpose, and these men have put their minds on these problems. Not all leaders have thought about all the problems,* but the thinking of one man supplements that of another; it all goes into a common pot into which anybody can dip a spoon. What is important in this *communal* effort is not the quick whipping up of an orthodoxy but the envisagement of a number of possibilities, options, relations, and consequences to be intellectually analyzed and imaginatively explored; for, as Whitney Young puts it in *To Be Equal*, there is no "monolithic approach to the problem of race relations."

There may be, and sometimes obviously are, violent disagreements on general policy or on particular programs of action. In fact, there is always the possibility of a fundamental split in leadership, with the consequent danger of violence as some fragment of the Movement spins out of control. But as long as even the characteristically uneasy cooperation prevails, centripetal forces will probably continue to outweigh the centrifugal, and the communal effort will continue to mean that choices of action do not have to be made blind.

The communal effort means that a more or less educated guess may be made about the figure on the face-down price tag attached to this or that decision. It means that shifts of policy do not have to be made in sheer desperation. It means that policy can develop flexibility through the process of exploration by action and envisagement by trained imagination. This is the kind of pragmatic and, it is to be hoped, constantly self-rectifying process appropriate to a democracy.

* For instance, Martin Luther King, involved by training and situation in developing his philosophy and technique of nonviolent action, seemed for a long time little interested in economic ramifications or in the school problem in big cities. In his last book, *Why We Can't Wait*, he comes out for a gigantic Bill of Rights for the Disadvantaged, which is another name for Whitney Young's Marshall Plan for Negroes. This is a shift of emphasis. But his remarks on school balancing, during his visit to New York after the July riots, did not indicate any deeper understanding of the complexities there; the remarks seemed, to the outsider, casual and, probably, prompted by tactical considerations.

This process, in which presumably the Negro leadership is becoming more and more expert, corresponds, we may say, to a life process. Some questions cannot be settled on *a priori* grounds. To take an obvious example, there seems to be a logical contradiction between the Negro's demand for color blindness in, say, public accommodations, and his demand for acute color consciousness in matters of, say, color-counting in employment, etc. For a time it was assumed by many that, in general, color blindness meant equality. But long experience has taught otherwise. It has taught that in any particular context, the question of color blindness may or may not be relevant to the underlying question of equality. Some questions—sometimes very fundamental questions—simply have to be lived into, and sometimes the "living into" divulges the fact that the question cannot be settled in any blanket and definite way; it may involve one of the basic tensions of life that elude programmatic treatment.

Integration itself is such a question. For some it is rhetoric, for some it is lines on a school map, for some it is a quota in a housing project, for some it is FEPC. It is, in one sense, all of these things, but at the same time, it is none. It is, ideally considered, the state of mind, the condition of the soul, in which human recognition and appreciation would be mutually possible for us all, black and white.

In speaking of a state of mind and a condition of the soul, I am not complacently repeating President Eisenhower's notion that "you cannot change people's hearts by law." To say that a certain condition of heart must generally and ideally prevail before a social change can occur is to say that no social change can ever come except in the Sweet Bye-and-Bye. For we know from history that you do not achieve an ideal spiritual condition and then set up a society to express it. Ideals grow out of the act of living, out of the logic of life; and in a long dialectic, even as they grow, they modify living. And so, for all practical purposes, we may think of integration as that process by which we exercise our will to realize and explore, individually and institutionally, in the contingencies of life, that ideal of mutual human recognition and appreciation. If we take this approach, we render irrelevant all the debate about race—whether it is "real" or merely a "superstition." And in doing so we even undercut the argument, so dear to so many liberals, that the Negro is only, as the historian Kenneth Stampp puts it, a white man with a black face. For we are assuming that *if* he is more than that—inherently or as the result of historical circumstances: who cares?—he may even be more interesting. For if there is a human community to be "recognized," there are also human differences to be "appreciated."

Negro leadership is inevitably concerned with trying to define the crucial points and predict and control institutional development in that process of integration. But since the process of integration is part of the process by which a free society evolves, it is very hard to predict particular arrangements; for by its very definition a free society is one in which there is a maximum range for all people in the expression of taste, preference, and choice, and it is very hard to predetermine what, under shifting circumstances, people will want. In fact, James Farmer defines integration itself simply as the "maximum opportunity for significant choices."

Let us take a simple instance. Let us assume a time when all desirable legal, economic, and social reforms have been accomplished and there is a reasonable sincerity in white acceptance of them. Now in that free society of civil rights, fair employment, welcoming suburbs, general prosperity and brotherly love, who has the slightest notion how many Negroes might perversely choose to live in their own communities—as James Farmer and Ruth Turner predict many would—and how many might want to bleed off into the prevailing white society. And who has the slightest notion what those Negroes who wanted to bleed off into the "prevailing white society" would do when they discovered that there was not one white society but many societies—Jews, WASPS (including Yankees, Southerners, Middle Westerners, and various other sub-classes), Italians, Irish, Greeks, Spanish, and God knows what—who, in varying degrees and from various motives, tended to keep their distance from each other and who regarded the right to do this as the very essence of their freedom in a free society?

There may be, of course, some doctrinaire bureaucrat skulking in the bushes who thinks he can plan it all out and, at benign gun point, make Negroes eat cake: i.e., move to Scarsdale.* But it is

---

* There are, in fact, some Negroes who feel that one of the aims of the Revolution is—or should be—to homogenize American society—that is, to create an abstract America. And there are, too, many whites who cherish the same "liberal" desire. In other words, the mystic fear of "difference" is not confined to the Ku Klux Klan.

doubtful that, in that happy time to come, he could swing it if the Negroes didn't really want that kind of cake.

Some Negro leaders do, no doubt, want to make Negroes eat cake, but it would seem that the great majority of them merely defend the right of a Negro to eat whatever he wants, or will, under new circumstances, want—even turnip greens and hog jowl. As Ruth Turner and others have pointed out, once the barriers are down, the human need to "prove" certain things tends to disappear: with freedom a man doesn't have to think he wants to live in a certain place merely because he is not permitted to live there. As Ralph Ellison puts it: "When the political structure changes and desegregation is achieved, it will be easily seen where Negroes were stopped by law and where they would have stopped anyway, because of income and their own preference—a matter of taste."

If Negroes can't predict as simple a thing as where they might want to live, think of the difficulty of imagining what integration in its deeper aspects might mean. Are we to think of a culture in a unitary or a pluralistic way? Some Negroes talk one way and some another, and some talk both ways and don't know it. How can ease and clarity be readily expected on this point, when, as Dr. William Stuart Nelson, of Howard University, says, the history of the Negro in America has been to live in a "dilemma—to want identification with the larger society but at the same time to be driven to unity along lines of race and common suffering."

The word *integration*, in fact, does not refer, clearly and distinctly, to one thing. It refers to a shifting, shadowy mass of interfusing possibilities. It refers, in short, to the future. Here, not only the unpredictability of the future is involved, but the fact that among Negroes—among Negro leaders—there is no commonly held vision of what they want the future to be. Think, for instance, of the difference between James Baldwin's Great Day and Whitney Young's more mundane vision.

Whatever integration may come to mean, it will mean a great change; and change, however deeply willed, is always shocking; old stances and accommodations, like the twinge of an old wound, are part of the self, and even as we desire new life and more life, we must realize that a part of us—of each individual person, black or white—has to *die* into that new life. As Harold Isaacs, in *The New World of Negro Americans*, puts it about the Negroes, the tensions of the old order and the shocks of the new will "jostle each other in a constant and bruising inward turmoil as each person seeks to discover the new terms of life—the older person fighting to hold on to and to throw off the older habits of mind and outlook; the younger person trying to find a new ground to stand on amid all the tangled fears and angers and despairs and exhilarations." Sometimes, for instance, when a Negro uses the word *compete* or the word *exposure*—and how often those words appear!—one can sense the stiffening and steeling of the self. And there is, of course, the unappeasable resentment that many Negroes must carry, and the suspicion of anything white—which are sometimes compounded because there is a chic of anger and an imperative of suspicion. I remember the pretty young woman who would not eat with her white guests and about whom the husband said to me later: "It's funny about my wife. The way she is. She just doesn't like to be around white people."

There is clearly not an agreement among Negro leaders, or among Negroes in general, about the vision of the future. But—and this is the important thing—there is a growing will to confront the risks of the future, whatever they may be. And there is a growing awareness that more than courage is required to face those risks. Many Negro leaders—more and more of them—are becoming aware of the fundamental need for an act of imagination to deal as systematically as possible with that fog of contingency which is the future. For many know that if you do not try to feel into, predict, and examine the possibilities of the future, you will become the victim of the future.

They know that only by this effort, in relation not only to integration, but to dozens of other crucial questions, can they avoid the ever-present temptations to substitute lingo for leadership, to take refuge in verbalism, slogan, rhetoric and, by consequence, self-delusion; and they know that only by this effort can they avoid a fundamental confusion between means and ends.*

As Judge Hastie points out, the leader of any movement must play a double game: "One of the great problems of leadership

* As an example of the confusion of means and ends created by a slogan, it is all too easy to imagine a situation where a number of inadequately prepared Negro pupils are dumped into an excellent all-white school and

is that, though ideas be oversimplified in the minds of people, the leadership with more sophisticated thinking attempts to adjust itself to the total need, viewed in a sophisticated way." In other words, the leader must be able to shout the slogan—but he must know its meaning at a level very different from that at which it starts the squirt of adrenalin in the blood stream of the good foot soldier.* Many Negroes are now deeply involved in the effort to penetrate, in Judge Hastie's "sophisticated" way, to the reality behind words. While moving through the hot dust or black mire of a back-country road in Mississippi, Robert Moses tries "to see ahead to what the shape of this country will look like in ten years." He gets lost he says, but he tries to see.

There is another question of means and ends that is acutely important for Negro leadership. A free society, one in which there is a range of choice for the individual, is the minimal aim of the Negro Revolution—or at least this is said by a number of people I have talked with or read. But it is clear that a certain amount of force is required to create the context for this freedom, that certain limitations of choice must be imposed to create the context for the range of choice.

The problem is to use present force and present limitation of choice on such terms and in such a way that the future freedom will not be prejudiced. It is all too easy to call for force; it is sometimes hard to know how to pick up the pieces afterwards. Some years ago,

---

left to sink or swim. For some people this would seem a triumph of integration. But the accentuation of a sense of inferiority by the day-to-day contrast with the better-prepared white children might compound the crippling already inflicted on the Negro children by bad training, etc. Or if some track system were in use, that system might well accentuate the evils of segregation, with the more immediate segregation of the Negro-populated low track in the white school. In either case, for these particular Negro children, except for some stray genius or two, there might be no surer way to disable them permanently for effective participation in a free and competitive society. *School integration is a mere device toward integration, not an end in itself.* In many cases, it is certainly a device which cannot, *when used in isolation from other devices,* be expected to be very effective. When used alone it may be a perfect example of the confusion of means and ends, of shibboleth-thinking, of panacea-thinking. Used in a proper context (and what is proper is bound to differ from case to case) of other devices, sometimes very complex and expensive devices, it may be made to serve reality.

* Judge Hastie adds: "Characterizations that analytically don't mean what they say are, I think, characteristic of all social struggle." This is not cynicism.

in the course of a conversation about the Supreme Court decision and the Deep South, Carl Rowan remarked to me that
"bayonets are very educational." They are. They have been used
with marked educational effect in Little Rock and Oxford, and I,
for one, cannot see that either Eisenhower or Kennedy had any
choice, for the duty of the government is to govern. But I should
doubt that Carl Rowan, after his prolonged sojourn in the shifting
lights and shadows of the political jungle, would now be as gaily
prompt to pick up that particular hickory stick to beat out the tune
for education—or for that matter to indulge in some of the rhetoric
we find in his book *Go South to Sorrow,* published in 1957.

In matters outside of education, it is easily understood why the
Negro, suspicious or contemptuous of local and state government,
turns to Washington for protection and redress; without federal
intervention he may not get the vote—or even live out the day; and
if it had not been for the FBI the three bodies would have lain forever under the dam near Philadelphia, Mississippi, and no arrests
would ever have been made. I hazard, in an unlawyerly way, that
the Negro Revolution will work some shift in the relation of Washington to state and local authorities, and that may be all to the good.
But the appeal to Washington may raise real problems, not merely
legalistic ones, about the centralization of power. The doctrine of
States' Rights has frequently been used, and is being used today, as
an alibi and a screen for some very unworthy proceedings—often
quite cynically used and only for some special ad hoc advantage, with
total contempt for the principle itself. But the doctrine of States'
Rights, as it now anachronistically appears, is a very different thing
from responsible localism, and we must ask ourselves if we are
prepared to inaugurate a system in which such localisms are encouraged to wither—or to have their roots cut. This is a question
which cannot be settled here, but one thing is certain: in the concentration of power there is no guarantee of the virtuous exercise
thereof. Those very persons who call loudest for the intervention of
the FBI, for instance, are the very ones who accuse the FBI of
corruption. Centralization of power gives no mystical solutions.

As for the use of power, there is, in general, a need for double
vision: force of any kind used for immediate tactical purposes, however worthy, has to be regarded in relation to the freedom being
striven for, and the human context in which that freedom is to be

exercised. What is now sauce for the goose might some day turn out to be sauce for any number of outraged ganders.

: 3 :

We have been glancing, all too cursorily, at some of the challenges and difficulties deriving from the fact that on many important questions there is no consensus among Negro leaders. But this lack of consensus, of an orthodoxy, should be of cold comfort to the hard-shelled segregationist, for there *are* matters on which Negro leaders *are* in agreement. And these are bedrock matters.

Negro leaders have the will and the strength to demand that they be recognized and respected. As Judge Hastie emphasizes, nothing that the white man can give the Negro is as important as the respect he withholds. And he goes on to say: "As the Negro wins the white man's respect, regardless of fondness or affection, it becomes easier for the two to deal with each other."* That respect can no longer be denied.

---

* The Reverend Kelly Smith, who was chairman of the Negotiations Committee for the sit-ins in Nashville, in 1960, gives a relevant account: "It's a tremendous thing to sit there with a group of people who come from two entirely different worlds. You don't even speak the same language, and they [the white negotiators] perhaps have never seen Negroes close up except as janitors and maids, never talked across a table at an equal level. You've got to overcome this kind of barrier. So then, once you overcome that, you must remember that they are part of an economic world about which you know nothing. To sit there and to try to get together on something is a rough experience . . . I certainly feel that there were people across the table who were sold on what we were trying to do, on our sincerity. Some of them had thought beforehand, I think, that we had horns and that we were all demons. But they found out we were real live human beings who wanted the same things out of life as they wanted, and had reasons, and had talked things out, and who were willing to suffer, sacrifice, in order to get this." Behind the Negro negotiators there was, of course, a bare fact of power: an effective boycott. But Charles Evers talks of the respect for courage. And Martin Luther King narrates how when marchers approached Bull Connor's men, ready with hoses and dogs, Connor ordered: "Dammit, turn on the hoses." Then: "What happened in the next thirty seconds was one of the most fantastic events of the Birmingham story. Bull Connor's men, their deadly hoses poised for action, stood facing the marchers. The marchers, many of them on their knees, stared back, unafraid and unmoving. Slowly the Negroes stood up and began to advance. Connor's men, as though hypnotized, fell back, their hoses sagging uselessly. . . ."

The Negro leaders are in agreement in their will to face the white man across the table, or across the gun muzzle or hose muzzle, eyeball to eyeball. Behind him the leader feels the weight of the mass of Negroes who may walk straighter because of what he does. As King has put it, in *Why We Can't Wait*: "The Revolution of the Negro not only attacked the external cause of his misery, but revealed him to himself. He was *somebody*. He had a sense of *somebodiness*." The leaders see themselves as "role models" for this *somebodiness*.

As a corollary of this the Negro leaders—and let it be clear that this applies to bi-racial organizations—agree on a will to independence of action. To quote Martin Luther King again: "The upsurge of power in the civil rights movement has given it greater maneuverability . . . to form alliances, to make commitments in exchange for pledges, and if the pledges are not redeemed, it remains powerful enough to walk out. . . ." The Negro leaders are determined that whatever change now comes in the status of the Negro will not come, as in the past, as merely a by-blow of the white man's history.

Some people say that the present success of the Negro's drive for recognition as a citizen of the United States is, again, only a by-blow of the white man's history—that as the war between the North and the South made emancipation possible, so the Cold War, in conjunction with the rise of Africa, makes success possible in the Negro's present endeavor. In one very broad sense this is, of course, true: nothing happens without context. But in another and more significant sense, it is false. History does provide the context in which the Negro's power—a relative power—may be used, but the will to use that power, the method of assembling it, and the strategy of its deployment are the work of the Negro himself. The evolution in this direction was clear even in 1941 when A. Philip Randolph's threat of a march on Washington forced Roosevelt's hand and gained Executive Order 88020. It is even clearer now that the Negro intends to be a maker, not a victim nor, as Howard Zinn has put it, a mere "hitchhiker," of history.

Even those leaders who recognize that the Negro cannot go it alone are agreed on this. They even feel independent of the white money which has, in considerable part, financed the Negro Revolution. And though, as is generally agreed, it would be healthier if there were more Negro money in the pot, it still seems highly improbable that the white hand that holds the purse strings can control policy.* For one thing, there are too many hands; the sources of white money are too numerous and too various; and in fact it would require a higher than usual quotient of paranoia to see in this a white plot to control Negro policy. For another thing, the number and variety of Negro organizations and leaders would scarcely permit white control of policy. Operation Overreach would take care of the situation. The logic of the moment prescribes Negro leadership. Negroes are stuck with themselves.

The most bedrock of all matters on which Negro leaders agree is simple: they mean business. They have been to jail, they have

---

* It is often said, even by Negroes, that a substantial part of the financing of the Negro Movement, even by some estimates a good deal more than half, comes from white sources. Some Negroes, for example, Malcolm X and Adam Clayton Powell, complain that this limits the freedom of action of the established civil rights groups. In reference to the pledges of $800,000 made at the breakfast organized by Mr. Currier of the Taconic Foundation, Mr. Powell told me that many Negroes smelled a sellout: "And I think to a certain extent they were justified, because one of the most able organizations in terms of demonstrations is Snick, and they didn't give Snick a penny." And he went on to say: "I don't care whether it's overt or not, subconsciously when you get that kind of money into organizations operating on a marginal basis, you're going to think twice before you do some things." On this point the Reverend Milton Galamison agrees with Powell. He says: "It's true of any institution, he who pays the piper will call the tune." Shortly before the Presidential election, Theodore White wrote, in *Life* magazine, that the White House, in attempting to stem the white backlash, had "acted discreetly but irresistibly both on civil rights leaders and their sources of financing among Northern whites"—implying that there is some control of Negro policy by the big white donors. But there seems, at first glance, to be something paradoxical in the situation. The NAACP, often said to be the least radical of the civil rights organizations in its program, received in 1963 around 90% of its income of $1,437,675 from Negro sources; and both Snick and CORE, which did not accept the moratorium on demonstrations in the summer of 1964 and which are advertised as the most radical groups, are reputed to receive a very high percentage of their income from the very "white liberals" who are so generously reviled by people like James Baldwin and Loren Miller. Some of the gears in the argument about funds and control do not seem to mesh. As for the suggestion from the White House that Negro leaders should cool it off, James Farmer, for one, says that he "was unaware that the President had made any such request," that he had seen no verification of the "claims made that Johnson had asked for a moratorium," and that he had "no evidence that there had been any pressure on donors."

been beaten, they have been shot, and they are still in business. And they are in business for the long pull. However loud in the schizophrenia of leadership they may shout "Freedom Now!" they know that the pull will be long. Months before the college students began to pour into Mississippi for the summer of 1964 to work in the voter-registration drive, Robert Moses told me that it would be ten years before the Negroes could elect a single legislator. And Ronnie Moore, in Louisiana, had counted each change of heart a victory, and such victories add up slowly. But for a really grim confrontation with reality go to the South Side in Chicago or drive through Harlem—and you don't have to go down the side streets where some taxi drivers, even in broad daylight, even before the riots, would not go.

The passage of the Civil Rights Bill merely defines some—not all —of the ground rules by which the real game is to be played, and it will take time and serious effort to interpret and enforce the rules. James Farmer says: "I think we'll have to struggle county by county, city by city, town by town, state by state." There is the danger that, as the limited, non-mystical significance of the Bill becomes apparent to the rank and file, disillusionment will set in, and that their apathy or anger will discourage the leadership from the sort of realistic and yet imaginative program which the Negro (not to mention the white) leadership must develop.

We can, in fact, ask if there is any historical precedent for such a program. Probably not—and, unaware of this fact, some leaders may turn to false parallels in history. But I am inclined to think that a good segment of the Negro leadership is indeed aware of the unique- ness of the situation and the uniqueness of the challenge. They know that it will be a long pull, and they are ready and willing to face the hard fact. Many of them are even willing to face the harder fact that the iniquity of the white man is not the only reason it will be a long pull.*

But they can face the long pull because they know they will win.

---

* "The scars resulting from generations of deprivation do exist in Negro citizens. . . . These are the facts of life that I think maturity on the part of the Negro and honesty on the part of the white person require be faced." To fail to recognize this is "stupid chauvinism." (Whitney Young, *To Be Equal.*) To take another kind of disability, Saunders Redding ends his re- markable autobiographical book *On Being Negro in America:* "I am not purged: I am not cured of my sickness."

They are riding the tide of history and they know it. And part of that tide is their own conviction of strength.

: 4 :

What reaction has the white man had to the Negro Revolution? And if there has been only a reaction, on what terms can mere reaction be converted into action?

We cannot discuss this question about the white man in a lump. For the white man is not a lump. To make the simplest relevant division there is the Southern white man, and the Northern (or non-Southern) white man. They are different from one another, and the difference is a little more than what James Baldwin suggests when he says that the South and the North merely have different ways of castrating you.

As a basis for indicating this difference, we may set up a little formula:

In the South the Negro is recognized, but his rights are not.

In the North, the rights of the Negro are recognized, but he is not.

But the formula needs a little footnote. If, in the South, as white Southerners like to claim, the Negro is recognized as human, this occurs only when the Negro is in certain roles. If, in the North, the Negro's rights are recognized, they are recognized only in the legal sense; the shadow of a "human right" rarely clouds the picture.

The white Southerner has had a shock. All at once, with little or no preparation, he has been confronted with the fact that what his cook or yard boy or tenant farmer had told him is not true. It is not true that the colored folks invariably just love the white folks. It is not true that the colored folks invariably like it the way it is. It is not true that just a few "bad niggers" are making all the trouble. It is not true that just some "Jew Communists" are making the trouble. A lot of things are not necessarily true. And maybe, even, never were.

Some more things aren't true, either. If the white Southerner is a book-reading man, he is in for another shock when he finds out that certain things he had been taught in school for gospel aren't true either. These things include some very important bits of anthropology, psychology and history—even Southern history, particularly of the Reconstruction.* It is a shock, too, to discover that a high percentage of the faculty of Southern colleges (including, even after a massive diaspora, a number at Oxford, Mississippi) don't believe in segregation, and that one professor of unimpeachably Southern origin, C. Vann Woodward, is the author of a book called *The Strange Career of Jim Crow;* and a professor of "Ole Miss," president of the Southern Historical Association, and incidentally, a friend of Dr. Aaron Henry, has written a book called *Mississippi, The Closed Society.* It is a shock to discover that eleven members of the faculty of the Divinity School of Vanderbilt University resigned when a Negro student organizing the Nashville sit-ins was expelled, or that Ralph (better known in the States' Rights Party and Citizens Council as "Rastus") McGill, of the Atlanta *Constitution,* got a Freedom Medal from the hands of Lyndon Johnson (another Southerner of dubious inclinations). It is a shock to realize that in Marietta, Georgia, the biggest single airplane factory in the world employs high-placed Negro engineers, mathematicians and technicians, and more horrendously, employs Negro foremen bossing white workers; that an Arkansas bank president is willing to

* I suppose there has never been a more obvious instance of history converted into mythology than the official story of the South. So I am inclined to worry a little when I hear some Negroes talk about Negro history. For example: "Negro history is quite different from the study of the Negro. Frankly, the former differs from the latter in that Negro history has a purpose which is built upon faith." That is exactly what official Southern history was. And the Negro's nature and needs are, no doubt, similar to those of the white Southerner. The quotation above is from Lawrence Reddick's "A New Interpretation of Negro History," in *Journal of Negro History,* July, 1937.

Kenneth B. Clark, in *Dark Ghetto,* remarks on the problem for the Negro scholar, generally considered: "He must deal with facts and ideas, and must articulate and interpret complex processes. If he is faithful to his craft, he must confront directly not only the dilemmas of his society, but the dilemmas within himself. The dilemma becomes even more focused when the Negro scholar is required to use his skill and insights and training in a critical and evaluative role, forced to look dispassionately at all aspects of his society and to describe as faithfully as he can the difficulties of both the white and the Negro worlds." In other words, the Negro scholar, like the Negro artist—or Negro anything else—is under the pressure of what Dr. Clark calls the "rules of the ghetto": to present "to the hostile white world a single voice of protest and rebellion," and to insist that "no issue can take precedence over the basic issue of race and, specifically, of racial oppression."

hire Negro tellers because, as he puts it, "it's coming." It is a shock to realize that the Memphis *Press-Scimitar* strongly supported the Civil Rights Bill. Or to read an editorial in the student paper of Vanderbilt University rebuking the administration for trying to ease out a coed who had allowed herself to be kissed good night by a Negro student (not a Vandy man) at the dormitory door:

> In dating the Negro, the coed was violating no rule of this University. Any rule forbidding such conduct would be incompatible with the tenets of the institution, which prides itself as being a center of tolerance for diverging behavior, so long as the behavior violates no valid, legal or moral rule. That is why we see ——'s behind-the-scenes enforcement of a regional social norm as placing the University in a somewhat hypocritical stance. If there are any man-made institutions that still can afford to respect integrity of principle, it seems that a university should make the greatest effort.*

Such items are even more shocking to many white Southerners than the discovery that Michael Schwerner, Andrew Goodman, and James E. Chaney had really been butchered and buried under the dam, and had not run off and hidden just to get publicity, as Neshoba County Sheriff L. A. Rainey had chosen to believe. The discovery of the corpses under the dam is not as shocking because, deep down and unacknowledged in his guts, the Southerner knows that that event, evil as it is, is implicit in the structure of the society in which he lives.

The other discoveries are not, he had thought, implicit in his society. Therefore, he is shocked. It is not evil that shocks, it is the unexpected.

This shock may make him feel—to use Izell Blair's words—that "you're rubbed out, as if you never existed." The white Southerner may feel rubbed out because a man's sense of personal reality, of identity, is intimately involved with his cultural identity. Long before these recent shocks, the white Southerner, in one dimension of his being, had harbored the scarcely specified memory of a gallantly defeated nationalism, and had felt himself part of a culture waning sadly before the dominant American ethos.† He had lived with

* *Vanderbilt Hustler,* February 14, 1964.

† There is some comedy in the fact that the attack made by those Negroes on integrating with the "burning house" of American values is the same attack made by some conservative Southerners on the values of "TV culture."

pieties and defensive impulses no less desperate for being unsaid or unsayable. Now when the world, which even in its decay had seemed stable, begins to crack, he is shaken to the core. He is then inclined to strike blindly back.

With the white Southerner the striking back has a special desperation, for in a way he strikes at the part of himself which has sold out, which is the household traitor, which lusts after the gauds and gewgaws of high-powered Yankeedom. When he strikes back, the act has in it something of an expiatory offering, an act of hara-kiri, the self-punishment of suicide. He is killing his bad self, and suddenly stands clean in the good self, guilt washed away—by somebody else's blood. The mystical, compulsive thing comes out over and over: I have had a dozen Southerners involved in the "resistance" say to me that they didn't expect to win, they "just somehow had to do it," they didn't know why.

So, if the Negro is experiencing a "crisis of identity," the white Southerner is, too. And now and then we get hints of some sort of mutual recognition of the fact. The jailer in Jackson, Mississippi, comes down to tell Stokely Carmichael goodbye, and clasps the steel bar and weeps and tries to explain what is happening to him. He wants to be understood. And in some sort of recognition springing from his own plight, he knows that the Negroes are "sincere," that they have to do what they have to do. The same thing appears with the sheriff of Canton, who, as Robert Moses reports, said to some of the Negro Snick workers: "Well, you all are fighting for what you believe is right, and you're going to fight. And we are fighting for what we believe is right, and we're going to fight also."

How can the white Southerner break out of his compulsion?

It is easy to say to the Southerner that he should give up his Southern-ness and just be a good American. It is easy to say to the Negro that he should give up his Negro-ness and just be a good American—who is got up in blackface. Negroes and white Southerners do, in fact, want to be Americans, but by and large they want to be themselves too; and the fact that both belong to minorities means that both may cling defensively to what they are, or what they take themselves to be. They may refuse to be totally devalued, gutted, and scraped before being flung into the melting pot. But that is one solution, and some Negroes and white Southerners, in self-hatred—

sometimes self-hatred disguised as liberalism—or in self-seeking, accept it; they "pass."

It is not the only solution. For the Southerner a much more significant and healthy solution is to inspect what his Southern-ness really means. If he chose to dip into the history of his South he would find that it is a very complicated thing; that the orthodoxy of slavery (for which, in later times, read "segregation" as the emotional equivalent) was a very late growth, and did not number among its adherents many a man who gallantly wore the sacred gray, among them Robert E. Lee; that Charleston, South Carolina—in fact, the whole Confederacy—between 1861 and 1865 was more tolerant of the dissident than is Mississippi today; that segregation was an even later growth than the orthodoxy of slavery—a growth forced, in fact, by artificial fertilizers, and one which many a Confederate veteran, in his self-certainty, would have found absurd, or perhaps an insult to his own personal liberties.

The modern white Southerner, if he looks a little deeper than the rhetoric of the UDC and the hustings, might decide that being against segregation would not necessarily mean that he is spitting on grandpa's grave, or is lacking in piety for those who held ranks up Cemetery Ridge on July 3, 1863, or for those who rode with Nathan Bedford Forrest. As Ralph Ellison says, "the heroes of Southern history would remain"; and the white Southerner could keep his heroes—for their heroism: not for whatever may have been their errors and frailties and the limitations of their historical moment, but for their virtues of fidelity, independence of spirit, courage, tenacity, kindness, and sometimes humility and wisdom which, in the tangled skein of human nature, they exhibited. For no virtue is so common that we can dispense with the pantheon of the past to exhibit the powerful exemplars. To look into the past to find the "group or racial" good is, as William Stuart Nelson puts it, what "every man has a right to do." But, he adds, it is necessary to see that good as "part of mankind," part of "human history."*

The white Southerner might realize, in fact, that human history

---

* See p. 298. But all Negroes do not accept Dr. Nelson's permissive view. The Joint Schools Committee for Academic Excellence Now, of Harlem, in attacking new textbooks as "insulting, insipid, and uninspiring," objects to one history for allegedly "playing up Robert E. Lee as a gentle, kind man." (*The New York Times*, December 23, 1964). It would seem that bigotry, like gold, knows no fatherland—or complexion.

is a story of the constant revision of values, and that the mastodon frozen in the glacier is not necessarily the creature most worthy of emulation. He might realize that a revision of values was implicit in the very past which commands his piety. The past was fluid—until it became the past; and then the fluidity of historical interpretation sets in. He might find many ancestors, spiritual or biological, who would not see eye-to-eye with Faubus, Wallace, Paul Johnson, Bull Connor, or Hoss Manucy—the prize "nigger-kicker" of St. Augustine, Florida. Yes, the white Southerner might find some ancestors who, were they alive, would not agree with the current heroes of Klan or Council, and would not be afraid to say so. That fact might even give the present-day Southerner the courage to say that he, too, disagrees.

Discovering his past, the Southerner might find himself, and the courage to be himself; he might free himself from a stereotype which does violence to some of his own most deeply cherished values and to the complexity of his history. He might realize that the obscene caricatures of humanity who have made Philadelphia, Mississippi, newsworthy are scarcely the finest flower of Southern chivalry or the most judicious arbiters of the Southern tradition. He might rediscover the strong and cantankerous brand of democratic temper which is part of his heritage—and then reapply it.* He might begin the reapplication by insisting on his right to reject the ready-made attitudes of the local press or the local politico or the local bully boys, even if the head local bully boy is a deputy sheriff, and to seek facts and make judgments for himself. He might find too, that Yankee Phariseeism affords him no alibi, for he is alone with the situation; he might find, even, a wry pleasure in undercutting Yankee Phariseeism by trying to make that philosophy to which the Yankee gives lip service, actually work.

Looking back into history, he might thoughtfully reread the statement by Faulkner:

> We accept insult and contumely and the risk of violence because we will not sit quietly by and see our native land, the South, not

* W. E. B. Du Bois, as early as 1903, observed in *The Souls of Black Folk*, that the "mass of the Southern whites" were "intensely democratic" and that, by consequence, they felt "acutely the false position in which the Negro problems place them." They did not, of course, feel it acutely enough.

just Mississippi but all the South, wreck and ruin itself twice in less than a hundred years, over the Negro question.

We speak now against the day when our Southern people who will resist to the last these inevitable changes in social relations, will, when they have been forced to accept what they at one time might have accepted with dignity and goodwill, will say, "Why didn't someone tell us this before? Tell us this in time?"*

I am not saying that a short course in history would automatically make the Southerner realize that to defend his identity he does not, to say the least, have to humiliate Negroes—nor have to condone such humiliation. But I am saying that the short course, prayerfully considered, might remove an impediment to such a realization— an impediment especially vicious in effect because it involves, in perverted form, some of his own finer instincts. And once that impediment is removed, he might be able to see facts as they are, and the Negro as he is. He might even be able to see himself as he is. He might find that he can be better than he thought he had to be.

The Yankee, like the white Southerner, has been in for a shock. He has lived in his dream world, too; I have heard many a Yankee say of Negroes, "Who do they think they are?" Or, "They've got every chance anybody has if they'd just get off relief." Or, "Look at the way they're acting, after all we've done for them up here." However little he likes the fact, the white man on the commuter train to Westchester has had to lift his eyes from the *Wall Street Journal,* to paraphrase Whitney Young, and look up the streets of Harlem. Or Harlem has come busting into his living room to dominate the TV screen. The white man (Yankee) at last has had to recognize the Negro as a human being, sometimes a rather appalling human being. And he has had to realize that the legal rights he had so complacently regarded all these years as his largess to the Negro hadn't, in themselves, amounted to a hill of beans.

If the Yankee is a liberal—even if he is what is called a "fighting liberal" and has signed statements and sponsored dinners and rung doorbells and made speeches and gone to bi-racial parties and has a life membership in the NAACP—he is apt to discover that no-

* *Three Views of the Segregation Decision,* Southern Regional Council, Atlanta, 1956.

body is very grateful to him. Nobody is going to be very grateful to him just because he gives a Freedom Dance (discreetly integrated) in Westchester or a Freedom Garden Party in Long Island, tickets $100 a couple, and sends the take to help liberate Mississippi. In fact, in regard to Mississippi, he might find it a penitential exercise to ponder a remark by James Farmer: "We find, incidentally, that many white liberals will give much more readily to support Mississippi than they will to support any activities in the North—because it's way down yonder and it's always easier to slay cobras in Borneo."

Not only may the Yankee liberal find that gratitude is in short supply; he may find that even the most charitable Negro is apt to regard him as a quaint figure of fun, a curious relic in the body politic like the spleen, without function. The only way he can be sure to regain function, and even then not in all circles, is to go to jail or get his head cracked by the "rosewood"—which is what the cop's stick is called in Harlem. Even then his function is to play third fiddle and take orders. He is declassed; and this is the worst shock of all.

No, the worst shock for the Yankee is to discover what he, himself, really feels. He has to find out if he really wants a Negro family next door. If he really wants to take orders from a Negro department head. If he really wants to be arrested by a Negro cop. If he really wants to have his children bused into a school in a Negro neighborhood. If he really wants a tax boost for a crash program for the "disadvantaged"—i.e., Negroes. If he really wants his daughter on mixed dates. If he really wants for himself this, that, and the other thing that he used to think was just fine for somebody else—usually some degrees of longitude down the social or geographic scale. He is, in fact, not only going to find out what he really wants. He is going to find out what he himself really is.

And if he is a book-reading man, he may find out, too, what his grandfather was. Even if his grandfather was a dyed-in-the-wool, card-carrying Abolitionist who regarded Abraham Lincoln as a minion of slaveocracy and, to quote Wendell Phillips, "the hell-hound of Illinois," he is apt to find out that the old boy—his grandfather—was also a dyed-in-the-wool racist. He is apt to find out that most Northern states then denied Negroes the franchise; and, even after the Civil War, Connecticut, Ohio, Michigan, Minnesota and Kansas voted down proposals for Negro suffrage; and that it wasn't until 1870 that the Fifteenth Amendment was adopted; and that in New York City a Negro couldn't ride the streetcar or attend an unsegregated ward school. He is apt to find out that after the Reconstruction, in 1890, Edwin Godkin, the one-time "radical" friend and staunch defender of the Negro, demanded, in an editorial in *The Nation,* why "we should put the interest of the 55,000,000 white people on this continent in peril for his [the Negro's] sake." If he does not find these things out for himself, some book-reading Negro will probably tell him.

He will find out that that noise he heard in his dream was somebody knocking the molasses jug off a very high shelf, and now he has to pick up the pieces, and they are sticky. He has to leave his dream and put reality back together again—the reality of America and himself. In other words, he, too, is suffering a crisis of identity.

Out of the two different kinds of shock that the Southerner and the Yankee have had, they may now be able to recognize the desperate gravity of the situation. Out of the shock, they both may have, too, a chance of self-discovery. Face to face with the Negro, and recognizing his human reality and the basic justice of his demands, they may now be able to substitute reasoned action for automatic reaction: to the Negro and to each other. But reasoned action is possible only if the white man can learn that he can't deal with the "Negro problem" until he has learned to deal with the white man's "white-man" problem. The white man's "white-man" problem is simple: it is to distinguish between whatever "de facto superiority" he may, in fact, have and whatever notion of inherent superiority he may cherish.

: 5 :

In recognizing the justice of the Negro's demands there are many temptations to sentimentality. One such temptation is to assume that it is all a matter of feeling—that we must consult our feelings in order to do justice. When Martin Luther King, standing on a platform, addressing an off-stage white society, says, "You don't have to love me to quit lynching me," he is disinfecting his doctrine of *agapē* from sentimentality—from the notion of easy solutions by easy love.

He is also making a grim and paradoxical joke, which Negroes greatly appreciate—to judge by the titter and applause. The joke frees them; it frees them from the need to be "lovable"—lovable by some set of white standards, i.e., servile—in order not to be lynched.

But the joke is one for the white man to ponder. For it frees him, too: from the need to "love" in order not to lynch. Translated, the joke frees him from the need to love in order to refrain from doing a whole lot of things—such as segregating buses, bombing churches, and conniving in racial covenants in housing developments.

In an ideal world, of course, our feelings would all be good—we would "love" all men—and the good feelings would express themselves immediately and effortlessly in good acts. There would be no moral problem—in fact, it might be said that there would be no moral consciousness, therefore no moral life. But in this world, the issue is not, so Dr. King is saying, one of achieving perfection; it is one of achieving a proper awareness of, and attitude toward, our imperfection. In this world, we may aspire to be pure in heart, but we can't wait for that far-off divine event before trying to be reasonably decent citizens who, with all their failings, may believe in justice. Since the odds are that, in this imperfect world, the old human heart remains rather impure, we can scarcely consult it to find out what to do. Rather than depend on our spontaneous and uncriticized feelings we had better consult our intelligence, fallible as it is, to see what is reasonable, decent, socially desirable—and even just—and then, as best we can, act on that.

When, in the South, a white woman says to me, as not a few have said, "I pray to God to change my feelings," she is recognizing the old human split—between her intellectual recognition that makes her pray for a change, and her feelings which she prays that God will change. But if the split exists—and the recognition of such splits is the ground fact of our moral life—there is no ultimately compelling reason why she should wait on the mystic change of feeling before she can take a practical step. To wait for the regeneration of feeling is sentimentality, a self-flattering indulgence and an alibi.

If we want to change feelings we can remember that the performing of an act does a good deal to change the feelings of the performer of the act. In fact, one of the surest ways for an intellectual recognition to change feelings is to put the recognition, in however minimal a way, into action. But it is sentimental, again, to expect immediate, easy, and absolute regeneration of feelings just because you have joined the NAACP or sent a contribution to CORE or marched in a demonstration. It is absurd to expect such cataclysmic, glorious, and easy purgation on the particular point of racial brotherhood, when you know that you have to live in a shifting complex of feelings about mother, father, sister, brother, wife, child, friend, the U.S.A., and God Almighty. Why should you think that feelings on the question of racial brotherhood are to be exempted from the ordinary complexities of life?

We do want to love our fellow men and live at peace with them, we do long for clarity of feeling, we do want as little lag as possible between feeling and action; and as human beings, we are certainly due for a good deal of healthy self-scrutiny and self-criticism. But is it healthy to go into a breast-beating routine of upside-down Pharisee-ism every time we—white people—discover some complication of feeling a little less than worthy according to the rule book? Or according to some self-appointed snooper with his portable couch? A deeply disturbing awareness of one's sins does not have to be the same thing as the masochistic self-indulgence not infrequently associated with the white man's (not the Negro's) sense of a communal white guilt—the thing described by Whitney Young as the guilt feeling that makes the white man abase himself before "Malcolm X or James Baldwin or Adam Clayton Powell," and cry out, "Beat me, Daddy, I feel guilty!"

It is not doing the Negro population much of a favor for a white man to indulge himself in a nice warm bubble bath of emotion, no matter how sweet he feels while in the suds. When a white man, fresh from his virgin experience on the picket line or in jail (with his bail money usually handy), begins to tell me how he feels clean for the first time in his life, I wonder if he has bemused himself into believing that the whole demonstration had been mounted exclusively for the purpose of giving him a spiritual cathartic.

Word filters out of Mississippi, in fact, that Negroes now and then express amusement or even resentment at some of the white helpers who seemed to feel that the Summer Project was a quick course in psychotherapy or a religious conversion without tears arranged for their personal convenience. And this reaction is to workers who, after all, had taken their risks. What about the white man who wants the nice feeling without taking the risks? As

Ruth Turner put it to me in Cleveland, "The Negro should not be a suffering servant for an American conscience." It is a strange and sad sort of sentimentality we have here—like all sentimentality it is ultimately self-centered, but here the self-centeredness is obscenely cloaked in selflessness, a professed concern for the rights and feelings of others.

Another form of sentimentality appears in the notion of the "debt" to the Negro—the idea that society owes "back wages" for slavery. There is, at first glance, a logic to this, and people as wise and good as Martin Luther King have accepted it.* He writes that his "Bill of Rights for the Disadvantaged" finds its "moral justification" in the idea of the "debt." But the logic is spurious and the notion is fraught with mischief.

The whole notion of untangling the "debts" of history smacks of fantasy. Would the descendants of an Athenian helot of the fifth century B.C., assuming that such a relationship could be established, have a claim today on the Greek government? And with or without accrued interest? Would the descendant of a mill girl in Lowell, Massachusetts, who died of lint-lungs in 1845, have a claim on Washington, D.C., in 1965? Or would it be Boston? And suppose the issue of the girl has been born, as was often the case in that class, out of wedlock—would that prejudice the claim? Or is debt never due to Caucasians who have been penalized by history?

If we assume that the U.S. Government does owe the Negro citizens back pay, how do we calculate it? Does a statute of limitations ever apply? And in equity what do we do about taxes collected for this purpose from citizens whose ancestors came over after Lincoln had signed the Emancipation Proclamation? Do they get a proportionate rebate? Or does the fact of whiteness make them automatically guilty, too?

And while we are on the subject, let us branch out and try to calculate how many explosion-prone trade guns, ankers of rum, and iron bars the Nigerian government owes what percentage of the twenty million American Negroes—those things being the common currency the ancestors of the said Nigerians demanded in payment for the ancestors of the said American Negroes whom the ancestors of the Nigerians had bagged in the bush and put up for

* In *Why We Can't Wait.*

sale. The whole thing is a grisly farce. Come to think of it, it smacks not of fantasy, but of Bedlam.

But before I proceed from the matter of logic to the matter of mischief, I shall say that I am totally in accord with Dr. King's notion of a "Bill of Rights for the Disadvantaged." We are facing a desperate crisis, and there must be a special crash program— or better, a series of intermeshed programs, governmental and private—involving Negroes *and* whites. To say, however, that this should be regarded as "back wages" for the Negroes denies the very basis on which such a program should be instituted. The basis for the Negro is his status as a citizen, just as it is for the white beneficiary.

Even after 1865, if the Federal Government, busy with the ·game of politics and business, had not tragically defaulted on its obligations, the justification for any program for the freedmen— even one involving a period of preparation for the franchise—would not have been in terms of back wages but would have been based on the status of citizenship potential in the situation. And now a hundred years later, the notion of the "debt" is not, as King would have it, a "moral justification"; it is an immoral justification. Immoral because it sets up a false relation between the Negro and society, distinguishing him from the white citizen who needs assistance. To regard the relation as based on a debt is a line of thought that, on one hand, would unman and demean the Negro, and on the other would lead straight to the happy inspiration in some hoodlum's head that the back wages are sitting there in the form of a new TV set and all he has to do is to kick in the show window and collect his pay.

What society may do to relieve the Negro's plight is not payment for work done; it is preparation for work to be done. Society does not owe the Negro, *qua* Negro, anything. But it does owe many individual citizens, who happen to be Negro and who happen to be disadvantaged, a chance to work—and to work at something that will fulfill them and will benefit society in general. The whole theory of a debt to the Negro is, as Stokely Carmichael puts it, "a drip from the Black Muslims."*

The point is not that the Negro citizen's rights are special. As a citizen he can expect nothing special. What is special is the fact

* Both Bayard Rustin and James Farmer explicitly repudiate the notion of the "debt."

that because of his situation he cannot fare equally with other citizens. He has the same claim as others, but because here race and class intersect in a long history of mutual aggravation, there is a special difficulty in fulfilling it; the program to meet his needs might require special tailoring to meet special difficulties.

Anything else would be racism—pure and simple. It would also be condescension. It would be to put the Negro on a reservation, like the Indian—even if a gilded reservation full of child psychologists, reading experts, electronic training laboratories, and computers to feed data into the office of the director.

Another form of sentimentality appears in the notion that the Negro—*qua* Negro—is intrinsically "better." This betterness is described in many forms, but, strangely enough, you never hear *the* Negro admired as a better philosopher, mathematician, nuclear physicist, banker, soldier, lawyer, or administrator. It would seem that the betterness is always something that can be attributed to the Noble Savage—if we give a rather generous interpretation to that term. This modern American Noble Savage is admired for athletic prowess, musicality, grace in the dance, heroic virtue, natural humor, tenderness with children, patience, sensitivity to nature, generosity of spirit, capacity to forgive, life awareness, and innocent sexuality. A white man may choose the particular version of the Noble Savage to suit his tastes. Here is Jack Kerouac, in a now well-advertised passage, making his choice:

> At lilac evening I walked with every muscle aching among the lights of 27th and Welton in the Denver colored section, wishing I were a Negro, feeling that the best the white world had afforded was not enough ecstasy for me, not enough life, joy, kicks, darkness, music, not enough night.*

It would, I imagine, be a very dull Negro who did not catch here the note of condescension. James Baldwin, who is definitely not dull, caught the tone, and remarked: "I would hate to be in Jack Kerouac's shoes if he should ever be mad enough to read this aloud from the stage of the Apollo Theater [in Harlem]."†

* *The Subterraneans.*
† Some of the most admired qualities of the Negro may be said to be compensatory, the result of deprivation, and may even be, in their origins, a mark not of freedom but of compulsion. Jazz, for instance, is not a product of

Over and over again, directly or as irony, we may encounter the Negro's resentment at such white man's praise. For instance, we may remember how Stokely Carmichael resented the praise and even the popularity he found at Bronx High. He read the condescension in it—and worse, the special condescension in the fact that he was being addressed as *the* Negro and not as himself. We may remember the classic example of unconscious condescension in the notion in the old sociology text book, by Park and Burgess, of the Negro as "the lady of the races."

The risk of condescension is always present in any romantic attachment to the simple—or to what, sometimes erroneously, may sometimes be taken as simple: Wordsworth's peasant, child, and idiot; Leatherstocking; the "worker" of the 1930's; folk song. Now that *the* Negro, from Ray Charles to Martin Luther King, is in for special attention, we find special versions of condescension. Even in the admiration, sometimes abject, for a man like King—who is far from peasant, child, idict, "worker," Indian scout, or box-beater— the paradox of inferiority-superiority, the sense of the complex person (white) recognizing simple worth (black), the psychology of the appeal of the pastoral poem, lurks in the very abjectness of the admiration granted.

Or to take another, a literary example, the now famous Kitten of *One Hundred Dollar Misunderstanding* is a special brand of Noble Savage, or a "naturally" wise and witty milkmaid in a pastoral of our time; and the author, in presenting her, has mobilized all the constellation of inferiority-superiority feelings. In writing his *One Hundred Dollar Misunderstanding*, Robert Gover is, in fact, very like the Southerner who makes the classic remark about his cook:

---

orgiastic joy but of deprivation—both an expression for, and a conquest of, deprivation. The same would hold for dancing, where the numbed and throttled emotional life would find a "safe" way to appear. Athletic prowess may be taken as a "safe" expression of the aggressive impulses. The point here is not that the achievements in themselves do not represent triumphs, but that the naïve and romantic admirer is apt to misinterpret the grounding as noble savagery. It is no wonder that Negroes sometimes regard the white who romantically tries to "go Negro" as an object of amusement or contempt: the white man wants something without knowing the price tag.

On the matter of art (and other things) as compensatory, the Negro, again, is not a special case. Many philosophers and psychologists have, for centuries, taken all art to be compensatory in one sense or another—a way of remedying the defects of nature or man's lot.

"Ole Sallie—now I tell you she is a better Christian than any of us. In Heaven, won't any of us be fit to tie her shoe." But that will be in Heaven. Just as Kitten is safely stowed away in a novel.

The admiration for the betterness of the Negro is often little more than a simple turning upside down of the white man's old conviction of the Negro's inferiority. The ineffable fear of what is mysteriously different becomes its inevitably linked opposite, an attraction; loathing becomes desire, strangely mixed. The Negro has been what is called a "contrast conception"*—that is, the thing on which the white man may project the opposite of all the fine qualities he attributes to himself. The Negro is the scapegoat, the inner enemy who must be ejected. He is, therefore, officially inferior. But the inner enemy, the secret sharer in darkness who has been ejected, leaves an ache of forbidden yearnings behind him. If the old-time Southern theologians, as Myrdal reminds us, attributed to the black man (as the old-time New England theologians did to the red) a disproportionate dose of Original Sin, unwittingly they encouraged the suspicion that the more Original Sin, the more fun.

This suspicion has not died. In fact, a thousand developments in our post-Protestant society tend to keep that piece of theology alive in various attractive disguises. In the hairy and breathless dark where such mumbo-jumbo takes place, the Negro's Original Sin— i.e., the notion of a superior and more free sexuality—may put on the disguise of superior moral force; which disinfects everything.

Civilization thwarts us, we are starved for instinctual and affective satisfactions—or at least have to locate them well down in a hierarchy of values and subject them to dreary postponements. So we turn to the Noble Savage. Or civilization tarnishes us, for we live in a texture of conflicting values and move in a maze of moral casuistries which block or distort what we regard as our purer and more generous impulses. So we turn to the Noble Savage. Or civilization gives us only false or derivative knowledge, and has cut us off from the well-springs of experience and truth, from nature and from our deeper selves. So we turn to the Noble Savage. He becomes the symbolic vessel of a number of things we yearn for, the image in which we find our vicarious satisfactions. And this modern American Noble Savage is obtruded upon the scene at a moment when

* Lewis C. Copeland, "The Negro as a Contrast Conception," in *Race Relations and the Race Problem,* ed. Edgar R. Thompson.

the tensions of civilization are unusually high. If we add to this the not uncommon impulse to romantic flight from some personal insufficiency, and the sense, not uncommon among the young today, that society offers no commanding values and that middle-class affluence is the death of the spirit, and the humbling effect of the spectacle of thousands of potent exemplars of courage and dedication among the young Negroes, then we have a heady brew. There is no wonder that to many the Noble Savage appears as a redeemer.

The only trouble with this negrophilism is that it doesn't recognize the Negro as a man. It recognizes him only as a Negro—if sometimes as a Negro Jesus Christ. And that is the worst condescension of all.*

At the same time that Negroes may recognize, and resent, this upside-down condescension, some may cling, paradoxically enough, to the very superiority which they, as good psychologists, have just condemned the white man for granting. Or is it cynicism to guess that sometimes it may not be the superiority granted that is resented, but the tone of voice of the granting? As various people have pointed out, the same Baldwin (or is it the same one?) who had taken Kerouac not gently to task for his negrophilism can write, in *The Fire Next Time,* a passage shot through with the black mystique, the glorification of the black life-awareness:

> I remember . . . rent and waistline parties where rage and sorrow sat in the darkness and did not stir, and we ate and drank and talked and laughed and danced and forgot all about the "man." We had the liquor, the chicken, the music, and each other, and had no need to pretend to be what we were not. This is the freedom that one hears in gospel songs, for example, and in jazz.

Some Negroes—even Whitney Young—may attribute special virtues to *the* Negro as a result of his slave experience: understand-

* Faulkner's treatment of Dilsey in *The Sound and the Fury* has sometimes been taken by Negroes as a condescending and offensive rendering, like Aunt Jemima. It is true that Dilsey, taken abstractly and schematically, is a cliché, the soothing Black Mammy, "better" than the white folks. But in the novel, she does not appear schematically and abstractly; she functions there before our eyes, psychologically three-dimensional—even if Faulkner has not given her the same full subjective rendering he gives his main white characters. She is capable of, for instance, resentments; and she is involved in a complicated set of relationships which imply meaning beyond that of the character taken in isolation. See Ralph Ellison's discussion of Faulkner's development of clichés of the Negro, in *Shadow and Act.*

ing, compassion, etc. And some, as we have noted, see the Negro as the redeemer of our society.

Now many Negroes, the sung and the unsung, people like Martin Luther King and Ruth Turner, and some nameless ones whom I could name, have exhibited great compassion. And I am confident that the effect of the Negro Revolution may be redemptive for our society—in the sense that Bayard Rustin suggests when he refers to the Negro Movement as a "catalytic." But at the same time, the white *homme moyen et sensuel* may be pardoned for seeing in the slaughter of a poor old woman for no other crime than that she was white and had a hole of a clothing store in Harlem, as something less than practical compassion, or the stomping of an old man on a subway platform as something less than redeemers at work. Negroes do have special reasons and special temptations to arrogate to themselves, as Negroes, special virtues, but no matter how clearly we understand this (and Southerners and Jews, as minorities, may have special reasons for understanding it), we had better stick to the old principle that if any man, black or white, isn't content to pass up a notion of group superiority, moral or any other kind, and to be regarded and judged as an individual man, with individual virtues and defects, there is something wrong with him. This is, of course, a principle which many Negroes are more than anxious to recognize. As Stokely Carmichael backhandedly puts it: "I am sure you know Negroes are bastards, too."

Power, success, and self-indulgence may degrade the human spirit. But it is well to remember that degradation degrades, too. The world is a world of risks.

Whether the Negro as redeemer is taken in the avatar of a Jesus Christ or a Noble Savage, or a combination of both, we have the question of why white society needs redemption. Clearly, redemption is in order, but the diagnosis of the case would seem to have some bearing on the kind of medicine to be prescribed.

The notion is current that history has failed us, specifically Western history, Western culture, the Judeo-Christian tradition. This notion has been with us a long time, and all our literature of this century, especially since World War I, has been shot through with it, with the sense of a crisis of culture. We have been living in the murky atmosphere of a Spenglerian Twilight of the Gods, waiting for the end. The notion was in Pound and Hemingway and Eliot and Auden and a hundred others; and I find it most recently in a college girl down South, of a most conventional upbringing and no intellectual distinction, who said to me: "I don't see what we, the white people, have got to defend or be proud of." For her, as for Pound, civilization—white civilization—is "an old bitch gone in the teeth."

White civilization: for despite whatever was absorbed by Europe of blood or culture from non-white sources, and despite whatever contributions have been made to America by non-whites, when a Negro attacks Western civilization he means *white* civilization. He sets himself apart from, and superior to, the "burning house."

The white man must grant, of course, that Western civilization, white culture, has "failed." We—the white race—have failed to respect the worth of the individual soul and person, to respect the rights of man, to achieve a common liberty, to realize justice, to practice Christian charity. But how do we know that we have failed? We know it only by applying to actuality those very standards which are the central fact of Western civilization. Those standards are, paradoxically enough, the major creation of that civilization which stands condemned by them.

Other civilizations have developed insights and values which demand our respect and admiration, and if we close our minds, our sensibilities, to them we do so at a grave risk to our own fulfillment. But to absorb such values means to absorb them into *something*— that is, into the progressive dialectic of all our values, into, in fact, ourselves. We have to remain ourselves in order to redeem ourselves. To think anything else is, again, sentimentality—a peculiarly destructive form of self-pitying sentimentality.

Only if we recognize the historical cost and significance of those standards by which we judge the failure of our civilization can that civilization have any chance of retrieving its failure. Meanwhile, whatever the values of other civilizations, we—American white men —may remember that, not only our history, but the whole of human history, has been brutal and nasty, as well as grave, noble, and tragic; and looking about us now—at India, China, Russia, Europe, South America, and Africa—we may see the grim failure, in terms of their own professions, of all other societies, too. If our failure seems grimmer it is only because our professions were grander, and better advertised. Looking about us, we find no clear and persuasive model for imitation. We must go it alone.

No, not alone, for there are the non-white Americans—specifically the Negro. But if he is to redeem America, he will do so as a creative inheritor of the Judeo-Christian and American tradition—that is, by applying the standards of that tradition—the standards of Western civilization developed and elaborated here. He will point out—as he is now pointing out with anger and irony, with intelligence, devotion, and distinguished courage—that the white man is to be indicted by his own self-professed, and self-created, standards. For the Negro is the Negro American, and is "more American than the Americans." He is, shall we say, the "existentialist" American. He is a fundamentalist of Western culture. His role is to dramatize the most inward revelation of that culture.

Even James Baldwin, for all the bitterness of his attacks on the white civilization, attacks that civilization merely because white men "do not live the way they say they do, or the way they say they should." If he preaches his gospel of redemptive sensuality, it sounds very like D. H. Lawrence, one of a long line of traditional "antibodies," we might say, of our culture. If he preaches his gospel of redemptive love, it sounds very like Christian charity. If he threatens us with "the fire next time," that fire is not so much a metaphor for mobs in the street or for political or military action as it is a "cosmic vengeance"—as we recognize who are old enough to have caught the stench of brimstone from many a pulpit of the old-time religion.

It is sentimental to think that the Negro will give us redemption in our spiritual bankruptcy. All he can bring to the question is the "catalytic" of his courage and clarity. If some of that rubs off on the rest of us, then we may redeem ourselves—by confronting honestly our own standards. For, in the end, everybody has to redeem himself.

Why have we dwelt on the various kinds of sentimentality which the well-intentioned white man may indulge in vis-à-vis the Negro? It would seem, in fact, that we should forget that whole business and accept the straight political view which holds that a vote is a vote no matter what motive prompts the casting. True enough: the most self-indulgent sentimentalist may cast a vote for justice—or give a million dollars to Snick, for Mississippi. But in the long haul, attitudes, like means, are important; they can fortify or poison a cause. Furthermore, since all sentimentality is, as we have said, self-referring, the sentimentalist is peculiarly open to disillusionment. For vanity—though sometimes vanity of the most subtly concealed order —is what sustains him, not principle, and vanity is like the wind-sock at a landing field: one end is firmly fixed (to the self, shall we say?), but the other may shift with every breeze.

Why had the host of friends of the Negro disappeared by 1876 and the Great Sell-Out? There are, no doubt, many reasons. But we may guess one.

: 6 :

There is one more kind of sentimentality that the white man cannot afford: a sentimentality about himself. He cannot afford to feel that he is going to redeem the Negro. For the age of philanthropy is over, and it would be a vicious illusion for the white man to think that he, by acting alone, can reach a solution and pass it down to gratefully lifted black hands.

It would be an even more vicious illusion to think that in trying to solve the problem he would be giving something away, would be "liberal," or would be performing an act of charity, Christian or any other kind. The safest, soberest, most humble, and perhaps not the most ignoble way for him to think of grounding his action is not on generosity, but on a proper awareness of self-interest.

It is self-interest to want to live in a society operating by the love of justice and the concept of law. We have not been living in such a society. It is self-interest to want all members of society to contribute as fully as possible to the enrichment of that society. The structure of our society has prevented that. It is self-interest to seek out friends and companions who are congenial in temperament and whose experience and capacities extend our own. Our society has restricted us in this natural quest. It is self-interest to want to escape from the pressure to conform to values which we feel immoral or antiquated. Our society has maintained such pressures. It is self-interest to want to escape from the burden of vanity into the hard and happy realization that in the diminishment of others there is a deep diminishment of the self. Our society has been organized for the diminishment of others.

More than a half-century ago, in *The Souls of Black Folk,* W. E. B. Du Bois called us "this happy-go-lucky nation which goes blundering along with its Reconstruction tragedies, its Spanish War interludes and Philippine matinees, just as though God were really dead." A lot has happened since he said that, but perhaps God is not dead yet.

It would be sentimentality to think that our society can be changed easily and without pain. It would be worse sentimentality to think that it can be changed without some pain to our particular selves—black and white. It would be realism to think that that pain would be a reasonable price to pay for what we all, selfishly, might get out of it.

✕ Index